Save Yourself the Time and Trouble of Manual File Entry . . . Order the *Turbo C* Programs on Disk

All the programs in this book are also available on disk (MS-DOS format), with full source code.

To order, return this postage-paid self-mailer with your payment of $25, plus sales tax if you are a California resident, to: M&T Publishing, 501 Galveston Drive, Redwood City, CA 94063. Or, call toll-free 800-533-4372 (In CA 800-356-2002). Ask for Item #46-1.

Yes! Please send me the **Turbo C** software on disk for $25 ______________

CA residents add applicable sales tax _____%_____

TOTAL ___________

☐ Check enclosed. Make payable to M&T Publishing.

Charge my ☐VISA ☐MasterCard ☐American Express

Card #______________________________________Exp.Date __________

Name ____

Address ____

City______________________________________State______Zip______

4029

NO POSTAGE
NECESSARY
IF MAILED
IN THE
UNITED STATES

BUSINESS REPLY MAIL
FIRST CLASS PERMIT 871 REDWOOD CITY, CA

POSTAGE WILL BE PAID BY ADDRESSEE

M&T Books

501 Galveston Dr.
Redwood City, CA 94063

Turbo C

M&T BOOKS

Turbo C

The Art of Advanced Program Design, Optimization, and Debugging

Stephen R. Davis

M&T BOOKS

M&T Publishing, Inc.
Redwood City, California

M&T Books
A Division of M&T Publishing, Inc.
501 Galveston Drive
Redwood City, CA 94063

M&T Books
General Manager, Ellen Ablow
Project Manager, Michelle Hudun
Assistant Editor, Sally J. Brenton
Cover Design, Michael Hollister
Production, Sahnta Pannutti

Printed in the United States of America
First Edition published 1987

Library of Congress Cataloging-in-Publication Data

Davis, Stephen R., 1956–
Turbo C.

Includes index.
1. Turbo C (Computer program) I. Title.
QA76.73.C15D38 1987 005.13'3 87-26159
ISBN 0-934375-38-0 (book)
ISBN 0-934375-46-1 (disk)
ISBN 0-934375-45-3 (book/disk)

91 90 89 88 87 4 3 2 1

Contents

Limits of Liability and Disclaimer of Warranty

The Author and Publisher of this book have used their best efforts in preparing the book and the programs contained in it. These efforts include the development, research, and testing of the theories and programs to determine their effectiveness.

The Author and Publisher make no warranty of any kind, expressed or implied, with regard to these programs or the documentation contained in this book. The Author and Publisher shall not be liable in any event for incidental or consequential damages in connection with, or arising out of, the furnishing, performance, or use of these programs.

How to Order the Accompanying Disk

All the software listings in this book are available on disk. The disk price is $25.00; California residents must add the appropriate sales tax. Order by sending a check, or credit card number and expiration date, to:

M&T BOOKS

Turbo C Disk
M&T Books
501 Galveston Drive
Redwood City, CA 94063

Or, you may order by calling our toll-free number between 8:00 A.M. and 5:00 P.M. PST: 800/533-4372 (800/356-2002 in California).

Acknowledgments

Without getting too carried away, there are a few people whom I would like to thank for their support in this project. There are my editors, who patiently accepted my pleas for extensions of other deadlines along with the excuse "I've been working on the book." But, of course, the largest deadline extensions had to be borne by my wife, Jenny, and young son, Kinsey. For their support, I am very grateful. Finally, I want to thank John Wilcoxson for his advice and comments concerning early versions of each chapter. Despite an illness during this period, he found time to slowly (some might say, excrutiatingly so) review each chapter with red pencil in hand.

Introduction

Turbo C: The Art of Advanced Program Design, Optimization, and Debugging is designed not only for the C programmer interested in investigating this new and exciting dialect of the language, but also for the Turbo Pascal programmer who has decided to investigate Turbo Pascal's more powerful cousin. *Turbo C* is also directed specifically to the IBM PC, XT, and AT computers and their clones, on which Turbo C is at home. While the principles of programming are applicable to all computers, the example programs in this book, as well as Turbo C itself, are specifically adapted to this host.

The History of Turbo

It all began with Phillippe Kahn and Borland International. This large man and his small company profoundly changed the personal computing world with a compiler for Pascal that he called Turbo Pascal. Turbo Pascal Version 1.0 for the IBM PC and CPM80 gathered a following around it in record time, partly because it was a quality compiler at a time when other compilers were either horribly expensive or mediocre in performance—or both. The real key, however, to Turbo Pascal's success was that it was more than just a compiler—it was a complete working environment.

Turbo Pascal included an integrated editor. After developing programs with the editor, the user was already in position to compile them from the same interface. If the compiler found an error, it would hop back to the editor, placing the cursor at the point of the infraction, in position to make the necessary correction. Since Turbo Pascal was a single pass compiler which could, optionally, compile directly to RAM (Random Access Memory), compiles occurred with lightning speed. Turbo Pascal could even successfully execute compiled programs without leaving the environment. The only facility that Turbo Pascal lacked was an integrated debugger, a short fall that third-party developers have since made up. The net result was that more working Pascal code could be generated in less time with Turbo Pascal than with any other compiler in existence, bar none.

At the time of its introduction, Pascal was not the number one language for personal computers. BASIC was still king of the micros, with C and a subset known as Small-C just beginning to challenge. But Borland only offered one compiler, and to enjoy the advantages of the Turbo interface you simply had to learn to speak Pascal. The rush was on to learn this picky little Swiss language. In very short order, Turbo Pascal was king of the PC languages.

Not everyone was happy with this situation, of course. My case was not that uncommon. I was just beginning to appreciate the power of C, having come from more of an assembler background, when Turbo Pascal arrived. At first I resisted, but in the end I just couldn't ignore all the enjoyment my fellow programmers were having with their instantaneous turnaround times. My 3 and 4 pass C compilers with their five-minute plus compile times drove me into the arms of another language.

I kept my old C compilers around, of course, and would often bring them out for a spin from time to time, even though I had adopted Turbo Pascal. Others like me did the same. Some programmers could not forgo the power of C, and so they stayed with these lumbering monstrosities. As C compilers got better and better, together we longingly wondered when a souped up, Turboed version of our favorite language would arrive.

Finally, in late 1986 Turbo versions of other languages began to appear. First came Turbo Prolog, then Turbo Basic and then, at last, Turbo C in the summer of 1987. Those of us who had reluctantly adopted Turbo Pascal were ready to rejoin the C holdouts in adopting Turbo C as our native tongue, and we were bringing more than a few Pascal diehards with us. This book is primarily directed to these two groups: the Turbo Pascalers, who are curious to learn this C language of which they have heard so much, and experienced Cers, finally able to make the transition to the Turbo version of their favorite language.

This Book

The C language was first invented by Dennis M. Ritchie at AT&T's Bell Labs in 1972. C was an evolution of the older BCPL language. It is interesting to note that the first descendant of BCPL was also developed at Bell Labs by Ken Thompson and called B. B was named after the first letter in BCPL and C after the second. The next language to evolve from C should logically be named P, if the pattern holds.

The definition of C was originally contained in a book, *The C Programming Language*, written by Brian W. Kernighan and Dennis M. Ritchie. Today, standard C implementations are referred to as simply K&R C compilers, implying that they adhere to the specifications laid out in that book. Over the years, K&R has begun to show a little wear, and, as a result, the superset ANSI standard and slightly deviant C++ languages were formulated. Turbo C implements most of the ANSI standard for C.

In addition to the power of the language itself, the initial success of C can be traced back to the success of the UNIX operating system. So closely tied in people's minds were the fortunes of C and UNIX that some felt that they were interdependent. While it is true that the majority of the UNIX operating system is written in C, it is not true that C is somehow dependent on UNIX. C is such a simple language that it finds use on applications that have no operating system at all, or at least a very simple one. In any case, C has no problem existing under the roof of the IBM PC's PC-DOS operating system.

C uses a terse syntax, for example preferring a simple *{* over Pascal's *BEGIN* and a *}* over *END*. This is probably due to the fact that C was developed on machines equipped only with teletypes as terminals. The natural tendency with such loud and slow devices is to keep output as short as possible. Many feel that this terseness makes C cryptic. It is true that, to the uninitiated, C code looks like just so much gibberish. Once you master the language, however, C is no more or less cryptic than any other language. Is Pascal any more understandable just because it uses primitives with more letters? If this was so, then why are we not all programming in a really verbose language like COBOL?

There are many C books on the market, some of which I take exception to. Some attempt to make C look as much like other languages as possible. Some restrict themselves to a subset of the language, preferring to only use constructs that look more like Pascal or BASIC, the so-called *safe* constructs. Some even go so far as to redefine C primitives, using *BEGIN* to mean *{*, etc. It's like the old joke, "Real programmers can program FORTRAN in any language."

Bunk! This is akin to climbing into an expensive sports car and deciding not to shift it out of third gear so that it performs more like the family station wagon. C is a powerful, low-level language capable of "hanging" its programmers in many ways. Forgoing the power and elegance of C will not make it any safer. If you are going to be forced to accept the treacheries of C, you should at least enjoy the heady power of it also.

In their zeal for high-level language structuredness and portability, some texts completely ignore the underlying machine. This is especially true of authors of Pascal, but is not completely unknown in C books. A high-level language is a metaphor for the machine code below it. No matter what you do, it is the machine code generated from your program that will be executed and not the C program itself. Ignoring that fact is not going to change it. As long as performance is any consideration at all, you cannot completely ignore the underlying hardware.

Programmers are encouraged, for example, to avoid *x >> 3* (shift x right by three bits) as being too cryptic, preferring instead the equivalent *x / 8*, even though the divide instruction is hundreds of clock cycles slower than the shift instruction on the 8088 microprocessor, the heart of the IBM PC. To them, I might suggest instead the equivalent *antilog (log x - log 8)* as being even more preferrable because of its generality, never mind the fact that it might be time for breakfast before it finishes executing.

Like it or not, programmers must consider the machine code that their programs generate, since that is what the eventual user is going to see. As the saying goes, "If your software ignores the hardware, your hardware will ignore the software." I have never once heard a user, when confronted with a slow application, remark, "Sure its slow, but I use it because its source code follows all the modern coding styles!". While this book attempts to present a structured programming style, you will be considering how small changes to your source code may affect the speed and size of the resulting executable program.

There have long been several fine general books on the C language. Even when these books could be directed specifically to the IBM PC and its clones, there was, until now, no dominant C dialect. In anticipation of the rush to market the introduction of Turbo C, many publishers have repackaged existing books to be *Turbo C* books, rather than simply *C* books. Unlike these retreads, this book has been designed from the ground up to specifically address Turbo C on the IBM PC and its clones. While this may lock out some potential readers, it will allow me to delve into topics of special interest to Turbo C and the PC in greater detail.

Organization

Turbo C: The Art of Advanced Program Design, Optimization, and Debugging is organized into several distinct sections. In my conversation of Turbo C I do not differentiate between the compiler when invoked from the command line or from the Interactive Development Environment (IDE), since they are the same language. (There is one exception to this in Chapter 8.)

The first two chapters are intended to give you an overview of Turbo C. Chapter 1 runs quickly through the primitives of the language, while Chapter 2 centers on differences between Turbo C and the K&R standard. Readers already familiar with C will probably want to start with Chapter 2. The discussion of pointers in Chapters 3 and 4 attempts to give you a fundamental understanding of this most basic of all concepts to the C language. Chapters 5 through 7 look at some of the system tools available to the DOS programmer. Chapter 8 delves into methods to optimize existing applications, while Chapter 9 concludes with the subject of terminate and stay resident applications and interrupt handlers.

Often, I will examine the same problem several times, each program representing a refinement of its predecessor. This may seem unusual, but remember that it is not my intent to anticipate every problem you may have and provide C solutions. Rather, the goal is to help you create your own better solutions to problems. By developing and comparing different solutions to the same problem, you can better understand the relative advantages of each.

The commenting of example programs in a book is always a touchy subject. Since the programs are described within the text of the book, I debated not commenting them at all to leave the structure more visible. I dropped this idea, however, as I did not want to encourage the practice among readers of not commenting programs. Still, comments have been kept slightly sparce with the knowledge that small points can be addressed within explanatory chapters.

When addressing the less easily offended programs within the text I have adopted the standard of referring to variables in all upper case. This allows sentences such as *the value of VALUE* to have meaning. Function names are always followed by *()*. Experienced C programmers will instantly recognize this as the symbol for functions. Using this convention, even sentences such as *the value of the VALUE passed to value()* have meaning (don't worry, this example is purely hypothetical).

Finally, note that portability is not our goal. There are already many good books on the C language that include machine-independent programs. I have not specifically chosen the example programs to be machine specific, but neither have I avoided it. By allowing ourselves to concentrate on one dialect of C—Turbo C—and on one machine—the IBM PC and its clones—we will be able to do more with our programs than we would be able to do with other works, and cover what I think are more interesting topics. Although *Turbo C* moves quickly in places, perseverance will be repaid. We have a long way to go in mastering this language, and the sooner we get started the better!

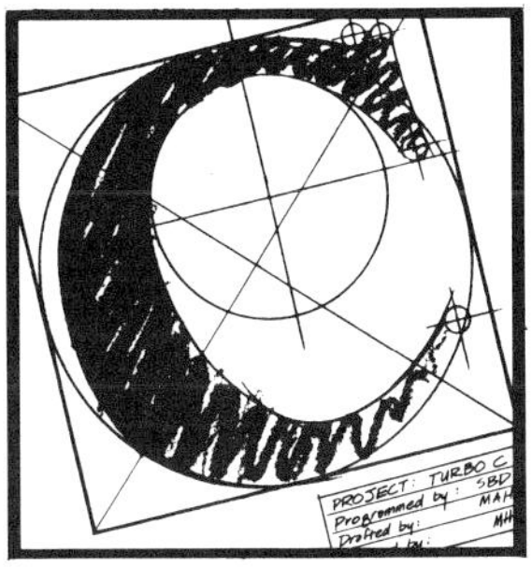

1 Overview of C

As an advanced text on the Turbo C language, *Turbo C: The Art of Advanced Program Design, Optimization, and Debugging* is designed to start where your manual leaves off, continuing into some of the more technical applications of Turbo C on the IBM PC and its clones. In the interest of completeness, however, it is difficult not to start with a quick overview of the C language. This is not intended as an introduction for the beginner previously unfamiliar with the concepts of programming on a personal computer. Rather, it is designed to serve as both a jog to the memory of the reader already familiar with C and as a quick introduction to the Turbo Pascal or other programmer making the transition. It may seem odd that in this chapter I might delve into every nuance of a particular language construct, such as the declaration of variables, before ever mentioning how to use it. This will be appreciated later on, however, when you are able to use this chapter as a reference for the rest of the book.

There is a changing of the guard in the C world. The language currently in vogue is that described in Kernighan and Ritchie's *The C Programming Language*. So far, no standard for C has existed other than that represented by this book. To formalize the definition of C a bit, the American National Standards Institute formed the X3J11 committee in the mid-1980s to formulate an ANSI standard for the language. Realizing that the K&R standard contained several weaknesses, X3J11 adopted a few enhancements. At the time of this writing (summer 1987) the ANSI standard is only a proposal, X3.159. Its adoption, however, is all but assured. In any case, the X3 enhancements have already been included in the Turbo C language and are presented in this book. In general, ANSI extensions beyond K&R are noted as such for those only familiar with the older "standard."

Program Structure

A C program consists of optional global variable declarations followed by any number of functions, at least one of which must have the name *main()*. The simplest C program in the world appears on the next page. The principle parts of a C function are clearly marked in the listing.

```
/*This is a simple program*/          <--comment
main()                                <--function name
{                                     <--beginning
}                                     <--end
```

Comments in C are any text contained within an opening /* and a closing */. Comments may contain any text desired and may extend over multiple lines. Following the ANSI standard, Turbo C allows comments to optionally be nested; that is, the same number of */s as /*s must appear to close a comment. This allows large sections of code to be commented out with one set of open and close comments, even if that code segment contains comments itself. (K&R does not allow nested comments.) C treats a comment the same as spaces and tabs, referring to them all as white space.

Simple functions begin with a name followed by *()*. Arguments to the function can, optionally, be contained within the parentheses as you will see later. The body of a function starts with a *{* and ends with a *}*. It is the function *main()* which is first given control when the program is executed. Unlike Pascal, nesting of functions is not allowed, but on the other hand functions can be called before they are defined.

The body of a function consists of any local variable declarations followed by executable statements, each ending with a *;*. It should be stressed that C uses the semicolon as a statement *terminator* and not as a *separator* as in Pascal, saving the programmer the confusion over semicolons that is so common in the Pascal world. Spaces, tabs, and comments can be included anywhere within a program (except within variable names and keywords) to improve readability. They are ignored by the compiler.

C functions are called by including the function name followed by a parenthesis containing any arguments. The second simplest C program appears in the figure below. Since every C expression has a value, all C functions correspond to Pascal functions. C has no construct that corresponds to Pascal procedures.

```
/*the second simplest C program*/
main()
{
   proc();                            <--invoke function
}
proc()                                <--define function
{
}
```

Declaring Variables

C requires all variables to be declared. Some example variable declarations appear below.

```
int a;                    /*declaring a signed integer variable 'a'*/
int b,c;                  /*declaring two more, 'b' and 'c'*/
char d;                   /*here we declare a character...*/
float e;                  /*...a floating point...*/
double f;                 /*...and a double precision, floating point*/

unsigned int g;           /*the unsigned subtype of integer*/
unsigned h;               /*the 'integer' can be ommitted*/
```

The type *INT* has three subtypes, short integer, long integer and unsigned integer. The *INT* is assumed if missing from any of these subtype declarations. The variable types, their sizes and legal range of values appear in Table 1.1.

Table 1.1
Variable Types in Turbo C

Name	Type	Size[bytes]	Range
char	character	1	
signed			-128..127
unsigned			0..255
int	integer		
signed		2	-32768..32767
short		1	0..255
unsigned		2	0..65535
long		4	-2.13*10**9..2.1*10**9
float	single prec real	4	3.4*10**-38..3.4*10**38
double	double prec real	8	1.7*10**-308..1.7*10**308

Actually, C considers *unsigned* to be a modifier and allows it to be applied along with long and short, so that one could have an *unsigned short int*, for example. In like fashion, C defines the opposite modifier *signed*. Both modifiers can also be applied to type character as well as integer.

Two additional modifiers that Turbo C defines are *const* and *volatile*. Declaring a variable to be *const* implies that it cannot be changed; that is, it cannot be the object of an assignment operator. *Volatile* is exactly the opposite. To improve the performance of the machine code that it generates, Turbo C assumes that variables are not changing in memory unless it is changing them. *Volatile* overrides that assumption, telling Turbo C to reload a variable every time it appears in a statement as its value may be changed by other programs working in the background.

Arrays are declared by adding a size enclosed in brackets *([])* to a simple variable declaration. The number appearing within the brackets is the number of elements to allocate. Since all arrays in C are assumed to start with subscript 0, the largest legal subscript of an array is one less than the number appearing in the declaration. For example, *int a[5]* declares an integer array with five elements ranging from *a[0]* through *a[4]*.

Just like Pascal, C views a matrix as an array of arrays. Unlike Pascal, C does not allow a special, FORTRAN-like declaration with both indices within the same brackets and separated by a comma. The code sample below shows some example array and matrix declarations. Additional dimensions can be added, ad infinitum, by viewing an Nth order matrix as an array of N-1th order matrices.

```
int array[5];           /*declare a 5 element array*/
int matrix[5][3];       /*and a 5 x 3 matrix*/
```

In addition to defining simple variables, as in the examples above, it is also possible to declare pointer variables. Rather than containing *integers*, *floats*, or *chars*, these variables contain the addresses of these simple types (or these variables "point to" these simple types). The following pointer declaration:

```
int *ptr;
```

declares a pointer, *PTR*, to an integer. That is, the variable *PTR* points to, or contains the address of, an integer. I will study pointers in detail in Chapters 3 and 4. Suffice to say at this point that *pointer to an integer* is every bit as valid a variable type as *integer* itself.

C allows the user to assign names to particular data types by using the *TYPEDEF* command. Consider the following program excerpt:

```
TYPEDEF int array[10];

array simple, matrix[5];
```

The *TYPEDEF* statement appears identical to a normal declaration of a variable, except what is actually being declared is not a variable but a user-defined type. In this case, the user has defined a type *ARRAY* that is actually a ten-element array of integers. A sample variable declaration appears on the next line. The variables *SIMPLE* and *MATRIX* are declared as a simple *ARRAY* and a five-element array of *ARRAYs*, respectively. The equivalent declaration is arrived at by inserting the complete *SIMPLE* and *MATRIX* declarations into the *TYPEDEF* in place of *ARRAY* as such:

```
int (simple)[10], (matrix[5])[10];
```

*TYPEDEF*s do not add any new capability. These are not user-defined data types in the sense that the term is used in Pascal. *TYPEDEF* defines a new type to the human reader only. C still reduces the *TYPEDEF* to a type that it is already familiar with. They can be used, however, to make code more readable by assigning meaningful names to intermediate data types.

In addition to data type, variables have a property called storage class. There are four storage classes: *auto*(matic), *extern*(al), *static* and *register*. Any one of these storage class designators may be placed in front of the data type in a declaration with the exception that register variables can only be *char*, *int*, or two-byte pointers.

Auto variables are stored on the stack. Auto variables can only be declared within a function, being created when the function is invoked, lost when the function is exited, and generally known only to the function. Auto variables do not retain their value from one invocation of a function to another. However, auto variables are *reentrant*. That is, a function that uses only auto variables can call itself recursively. Variables declared within a function default to the auto storage class.

Extern variables are stored in their own separate data area. Extern variables must be declared outside of any functions and are known to all functions. Extern variables are even known outside of the module in which they are declared. They are initialized when the program is first executed and retain their value as functions are entered and exited. Functions that access extern variables must be careful not to call themselves and must be especially careful with other functions that might access and modify the same variables. Extern is the default storage class for variables declared outside of functions and for functions themselves.

Static variables are much like extern except for their scope. The word *static* does not imply that a static variable cannot be modified. A static variable declared outside of any function is known to all functions within the module. It is not known outside of the module. Static variables declared within a function are only known within that function. ASCII strings default to type static.

Register variables are assigned to individual registers within the microprocessor. In microprocessors that have a large number of registers, most notably the

Motorola 68000 family, it is advantageous to reserve several of these registers for variables that are heavily used. Since access to a register is so much quicker than to memory, performance can be greatly enhanced by carefully selecting certain variables to be of type register. When it is not possible for C to grant a register request, either because the base machine does not have a sufficient number of registers to allow any register variables or because too many register variables have been defined already, register variables revert to storage class auto. Turbo C recognizes up to two register variables per function.

Register variables have some restrictions—most notably they have no address in memory (since they aren't stored in memory!). Applying the *address of* operator, &, on register variables is illegal. Furthermore, register variables must be of simple types, such as *char*, *int*, or *near pointer*, since that's all that will fit in a single 8086 register. Despite these restrictions, judicious use of the register storage class can significantly decrease execution time, as you will see in Chapter 8.

One final property that can be imparted on pointer variables is that of nearness and farness. I will discuss this property of pointer variables in the 8086 family of microprocessors in Chapter 3, but suffice it to say that the reserved words *far* or *near* (as well as the segment names *_cs*, *_ds*, *_es*, and *_ss*) may appear before a pointer variable name, as in:

```
char far *char1;          /*declare a 4 byte pointer...*/
int near *int2;           /*...and a 2 byte pointer*/
```

Extern and static variables are guaranteed to initially have the value 0. The value of auto and register variables is initially undefined. However, extern and static variables may be initialized to some other value at declaration by including an = sign followed by the appropriate number of values. Lists of values, such as required for array declarations, must be enclosed in braces. (In fact, simple auto variables can also be initialized at declaration, but doing so does not save any time or code and merely serves to obscure the resulting program.) An example declaration might be:

```
int a = 5;
int array1[5] = {1, 2, 3, 4, 5};
int array2[] = {1, 2, 3, 4, 5};
int matrix1 [2][3] = {1, 2, 3, 4, 5, 6};
int matrix2 [2][3] = {{1, 2, 3},
                      {4, 5, 6}};

main()
{  .
.
.
```

The first declaration declares a variable *A*, initially with the value 5. The second declaration assigns *ARRAY1[0]* to the initial value of 1, *ARRAY1[1]* to 2, etc. Notice the third declaration, however. *ARRAY2* has been declared identically with *ARRAY1*—when a list of entries is provided, it is not necessary to include the index as it is calculated by merely counting the number of entries in the initialization list.

MATRIX1 declares a matrix and initializes it to the integers 1 through 6. *MATRIX2* represents the same declaration, made in a more readable fashion. Notice how a matrix can be considered to be an array of arrays, even in the initialization lists. Incomplete initializing lists can also be provided. Consider the following examples taken directly from the ANSI draft standard:

```
float y1 [4][3] = {{1, 3, 5},
                   {2, 4, 6},
                   {3, 5, 7}};
float y2 [4][3] = {1, 3, 5, 2, 4, 6, 3, 5, 7};

float y3 [4][3] = {{1},
                   {2},
                   {3},
                   {4}};

struct {
        int a [3];
        int b;
       } w = {{1, 2, 3},
              4};
```

The initializing list for *Y1* above is incomplete. The first three rows of three entries are set to the values given in the list. The last row receives no initial value and is left to 0. *Y2* has the exact same effect, but in a much less clear fashion. Initialization lists may also be column-wise incomplete. *Y3* contains values for all four rows; however, only the first location in each row receives any value. The remaining two columns in each row is left 0. There is no equivalent form without multiple braces. Lastly, notice that structures other than simple arrays and matrices can be initialized at declaration time. The structure *W* is initialized in a perfectly readable fashion.

Finally, pointers may also be initialized at declaration time. Ignore for a moment the cast appearing in front of the following declaration:

```
int *ptr = {(int *)100};
```

This declares the pointer variable *PTR* and sets it to the value 100. The cast converts the integer 100 into a *pointer to an integer*, the type of *PTR*, as you will see later in this chapter.

Initializing an extern variable or array in the declaration can conserve both time and machine code. Such a declaration does not generate object code to perform the initialization. Space for extern and static variables is included in the *.EXE* executable files along with the space for machine code. Normally this space is filled with *0*s. Including an initialization statement merely causes values to be stored into these locations. Since these initialization values are evaluated at compile time, they must be constants and cannot contain function calls.

Variables used as arguments to functions must also be declared. For example, consider the following function:

```
extern double log (n, base)
                double n;
                int base;
{
        double temporary;
                .
                .
                .
```

Declarations of arguments are identical in appearance to the declaration of variables within the procedure itself except that they appear before the opening brace. An argument variable must be assigned a type but may not be assigned a storage class. Alternatively, arguments may be declared *in place*. For example, an equivalent declaration to that above is:

```
extern double log (double n, int base)
{
         double temporary;
                .
                .
```

Declaring Functions

Functions should also be declared. (ANSI C leaves this optional since the original K&R C did not require such declarations. In this book, I will consider it a requirement.) A function is declared much as a variable, by listing its name with the type of value returned and followed by parentheses. It is the parentheses that tell C that this is a function name.

Declaring a function tells C the type of the value returned from that function. Functions left undeclared are assumed to return a value of type integer. Normally, functions are declared both when defined and within other functions which call them or at the beginning of the module. For example, consider the following code segment:

```
int main()
{
   double a, add1();
          .
          .
          .
    a = add1();
          .
          .
          .
}

double add1()
{       .
        .
        .
```

OR

```
double add1();
int main()
{
    double a;
        .
        .
        .
```

Some functions do not return any meaningful value. Leaving such a function undeclared will cause C to assign it type *INT*. To indicate to other programmers and to the compiler that this function really does not return any useful information, the ANSI standard defines a type *VOID*, meaning *returns or contains nothing*. Declaring a function of type *VOID* indicates that it returns no meaningful data.

Arguments to functions should also be declared at the same time as the returned type. Not doing so deprives C of the information it needs to check for argument errors. The so-called prototype declarations appear much as they do in Pascal or other typed languages, except that variable names are optional. Consider the following declarations:

```
/*prototype declarations*/
  void func1 (int, char);                 void func1 (int i, char c);
  char func2 (double);         OR         char func2 (double x);

  /*func1 - performs some useful function*/
  void func1 (i, c)
       int i;
       char c;
  {
          ==body of program==
  }

  /*func2 - performs an even more useful function*/
```

```
char func2 (x)
     double x;
{
        ==body of program==
}
```

Wherever *func1()* and *func2()* might be used within the module, C can check the arguments supplied against the prototype declaration for proper type. The prototype declarations are separate from the "normal" declarations for two reasons. First, the actual routines might be defined in a separate module to be linked in during the link step. Second, in the interest of speed, Turbo C is but a single pass compiler. To be of use, C must know the type of function before it is used. Therefore, it is convenient to place all of the prototype declarations at the top of the module, either explicitly or in an include file.

Notice that I showed the prototype declarations above in two formats: one with variable names and one without. Both forms are allowed. If variable names are present in the prototype declaration, they are ignored.

What if a third function, *func3()*, has no arguments? Leaving the field blank within the prototype declaration would confuse Turbo C into thinking that this is an older program which follows the less restrictive K&R standard and does not declare its arguments. In these cases, C allows use of the *VOID* type as follows:

```
char func3 (void);
```

Here *func3()* takes no arguments (although it returns a character). Attempting to pass it an argument will be flagged as an error by C.

One other problem occasionally arises: What if the number or type of arguments in a function call after a certain point is indeterminate, such as the case with *printf()*? C allows this to be specified by concluding the prototyping declaration with ellipsis:

```
char func4 (int, char, ...);
```

C insures that the first two arguments passed to *func4()* are of type integer and character, respectively. Subsequent arguments are not checked for size or number.

The *in place* form of declaration more resembles that of the prototype declaration. Your *func1()* and *func2()* above could have been declared as follows:

```
/*initial prototype declarations*/
void func1 (int i, char c);
char func2 (double x);
```

```
/*func1 - performs some useful function*/
void func1 (int i, char c)
{
        ==body of program==
}

/*func2 - performs an even more useful function*/
char func2 (double x)
{
        ==body of program==
 }
```

The distinguishing characteristic between the program and prototype declaration is the presence or absence of the semicolon at the end. If it appears, then the declaration is merely a prototype declaration and no code actually follows. If not, then a program body must follow. Notice that this form of procedure declaration does not add any capability that you did not already have with the older K&R format—it is merely more consistent in appearance with prototype declarations.

Remember, of course, that prototype declarations are optional since they were not part of the original K&R definition of C. In this text, I will consider them a requirement. I will continue to use the standard K&R procedure definition format, however, since the newer format provides no new capability. In addition, I will not provide dummy argument names in prototype declarations.

Functions may also be declared either *extern* or *static*. Remember, variables that were declared outside of any functions defaulted to type *EXTERN*. By analogy, all functions default to *EXTERN* since functions cannot be declared inside other functions. Here, as with variables, the *EXTERN* implies that the function is known outside of the module.

Turbo Pascal programmers may not understand what is meant by the phrase "known outside of the module." A module is a separately compilable source code file. In Turbo Pascal programmers may define as many functions as desired to properly structure their programs, but, no matter how many are needed, every function invoked within a Turbo Pascal module must also be defined within that module. Thus, Turbo Pascal is a one module language. This is a severe limitation made bearable only by Turbo's allowance of *INCLUDE* files and by its incredibly high compile speed.

C compilers, including Turbo C, allow programs to call functions that are actually defined in other modules. In this way a program can be physically broken up into several parts, each one devoted to a particular aspect of the problem at hand. Rather than generating an executable file directly, the output of the C compiler is called an object file and carries the extension *.OBJ*. After all the modules of a program have been separately compiled, the resulting *.OBJ* files are combined into an executable *.EXE* program in what is known as the link step. It is the link process that matches calls in one module with external procedures defined in other modules. If one of the modules makes a call to a procedure that is not defined anywhere, the linker will generate an error message complaining of an "unresolved external," and the resulting *.EXE* file will not run.

Declaring a function *STATIC* causes it to be known only to functions within the current module. Therefore, *STATIC* functions cannot be called from other modules. Functions might be declared *STATIC* if it desirable to hide the internal structure of a series of routines from the outside world. For example, in defining two routines, *sin()* and *cos()*, it might be desirable for both to call a separate routine *taylor()* to perform the Taylor series expansion. Since the potential for abuse of *taylor()* is high, it might be declared *STATIC* while the other two routines are left *EXTERN*.

Declaring User-Defined Types

There are two user-defined types in C: structures and enumerated data types. Structures are used when it is desirable to combine related data of different types in such a way that they might be dealt with as a single entity. For example, a street address consists of several parts: the street number, name of the street, city, state, and zip code. While it is sometimes necessary to handle the individual fields separately, it is often desirable to consider the address as an entity. This could be achieved via a structure definition such as:

```
struct address {
        int streetnum;
        char streetname [20];
        char city [20], state[2];
        long int zip;
                } myadd, youradd;
struct address hisadd, theiradd[10];
struct address heradd = {1234,
                        {"Mystreet"},
                        {"Anytown"},
                        {"Tx"},
                        78400};
```

This defines a structure named *ADDRESS* consisting of the five fields that commonly make up an address. Four simple variables and an array of type *ADDRESS* are declared. Notice how variables may be declared at the same time as the structure is defined (as in *MYADD* and *YOURADD*) or in a separate statement (as in *HISADD*). A structure definition need not carry a name.

In general, variables of any type can be defined within a structure, even another structure. Such declarations appear identical to normal declarations, except that they may not have storage class and they may not have an initialization value. Structures may be initialized at declaration by attaching a list of values to the structure name, much as with an array initialization, as in the example above. To access a particular element of a structure variable, the variable name is followed by a '.' and the element name. For example:

```
youradd.zip = 20231;
theiradd[4].streetnum = 1001;
```

Besides the normal types, variables within structures may be defined as bit fields. These are variables that are not a multiple of eight bits in size. Such declarations appear followed with a ":" and a number. This number indicates the number of bits assigned to this variable. For example, consider the following definition field for the keyboard status:

```
struct word {
            unsigned capslock    : 1;
            unsigned control     : 1;
            unsigned alternate   : 1;
            unsigned left_shift  : 1;
            unsigned right_shift: 1;
           } kbrdstatus;
```

The main reason for using bit field declarations is the savings in data space they can provide. For example, even though the above structure contains five flags, it occupies only one byte. It should be kept in mind that bit field variables cannot extend over word boundaries. This can adversely affect the amount of space saved. For example, the following declaration does not actually save any space:

```
struct mistake {
               unsigned field1 : 10;
               unsigned field2 : 10;
               unsigned field3 : 12;
              };
```

Adding up the sizes of all three fields, you might think that all three variables could be stored within two single sixteen-bit words. However, after *FIELD1* is defined, *FIELD2* can no longer fit completely within the same word, so it must be placed in its own word. Similarly, *FIELD3* must also be stored in its own word. The end result is that the above declaration consumes three bytes, exactly the amount as three *INT* variables.

Despite the bit fields potential space savings, Turbo C programmers should show extreme discretion in their use, as they can add considerably to the execution time and size of the resulting program. This is especially true since the 8086 family of microprocessors does not have bit instructions for efficiently setting clearing and testing individual bits out of a field. Often, programmers are better off using their own bit access routines and performing the packing and unpacking themselves.

Unions are similar to structures except that all of the individual fields occupy the same memory space. This is useful when it is necessary to treat the same variable as two (or more) different data types (such as signed and unsigned integer) at different times.

Turbo Pascal programmers should note that C structures are not as powerful as Pascal structures. None of the C operators are defined for an entire structure except for the *address of* operator, *&*. I will discuss structures and their uses in greater detail in Chapter 4.

Finally, C allows programmers to define their own enumerated data types, much like in Pascal. In C the effect is less dramatic than in Pascal. Consider the following declarations:

```
enum birds {canary, finch, cardinal, dove, duck, goose};
enum birds fowl;

enum hunters {duck = 1, goose = 1, deer, bear = 4};
```

The first defines an enumerated type, *BIRDS*, and declares one variable of that type, *FOWL*. Unlike Pascal, however, C treats FOWL as if it was of type *UNSIGNED INT*, and treats each of the bird types as respective values (for example, canary is equivalent to 0, finch to 1, cardinal to 2, etc.). The programmer can influence the order of assignment as in the declaration of type *HUNTERS* above. The value 0 has been skipped, assigning *DUCK* to value 1. Notice also that values can overlap (since *GOOSE* has also been given the value 1) or skipped (there is no equivalence for 3 above).

There is no type, other than integer, assigned to enumerated types. Therefore, no special operators are required. No *ord()* function is defined and, since the order of enumerated types is not fixed, no *succ()* or *pred()* functional equivalents exist (is *DUCK* or *GOOSE* the predecessor to *DEER*?). C does not provide strong type checking of enumerated types. C's enumerated type is little more than a convenient way to define meaningful integer constants to increase program readability.

Expressions

An expression is a constant, a variable, a function call, or a combination of constants, variables, and function calls connected with operators. Every expression has a value. Assignments store the value of an expression into a variable by placing the variable name to the left of an equals sign. Assignments do not change the value of the expression. For example, *a = b + 5;* takes the contents of variable B, adds 5 and stores the result into A.

There are six types of operators: math, relational, logical, bit-wise logical, the ternary operator, and assignment. The operators and their meanings are defined in Table 1.2. There is one other operator, the *&*, which returns the address of whatever variable to which it is applied. It is not a true operator, however, since it can only be applied to data variables. *&* will be discussed in detail, along with other addressing concepts, in Chapter 3.

All of the mathematical operators are analogous to similar operators in other languages. C does not have two different types of division as Pascal does.

C does not have a separate Boolean variable type. Instead C treats integer 0 as *FALSE* and nonzero as *TRUE*. The logical operators are used to perform Boolean type operations on zero and nonzero values, returning either a 0 or a 1. For example:

```
5 && 2          <-- returns a 1
5 && 0          <--   "     " 0
0 && 0          <--   "     " 0

5 || 2          <--   "     " 1
5 || 0          <--   "     " 1
0 || 0          <--   "     " 0

!5              <--   "     " 0
!0              <--   "     " 1
```

Remember that these are integer expressions, and their results are of type integer. It would be perfectly legal to multiply any of the above logical expressions by an integer constant.

Turbo C performs a certain amount of optimization here. If the left side of a logical expression determines the result, the other side will not be evaluated.

Table 1.2
Operators

<table>
<tr><td>Assignment</td><td></td></tr>
<tr><td>=</td><td>assignment</td></tr>
<tr><td>Mathematical</td><td></td></tr>
<tr><td>+</td><td>add</td></tr>
<tr><td>-</td><td>subtract</td></tr>
<tr><td>*</td><td>multiply</td></tr>
<tr><td>/</td><td>divide</td></tr>
<tr><td>%</td><td>modulus</td></tr>
<tr><td>-</td><td>change sign (unary)</td></tr>
<tr><td>Relational</td><td></td></tr>
<tr><td>==</td><td>equality</td></tr>
<tr><td>!=</td><td>inequality</td></tr>
<tr><td><</td><td>less than</td></tr>
<tr><td><=</td><td>less than or equal to</td></tr>
<tr><td>></td><td>greater than</td></tr>
<tr><td>>=</td><td>greater than or equal to</td></tr>
<tr><td>Logical</td><td></td></tr>
<tr><td>&&</td><td>and</td></tr>
<tr><td>||</td><td>or</td></tr>
<tr><td>!</td><td>logical complement (unary)</td></tr>
<tr><td>Bit-Wise</td><td></td></tr>
<tr><td>&</td><td>bitwise and</td></tr>
<tr><td>|</td><td>" or</td></tr>
<tr><td>^</td><td>" exclusive or</td></tr>
<tr><td><<</td><td>left shift</td></tr>
<tr><td>>></td><td>right shift</td></tr>
<tr><td>~</td><td>one's complement (unary)</td></tr>
<tr><td>Ternary</td><td></td></tr>
<tr><td>?:</td><td>ternary operator</td></tr>
</table>

For example, if the left-hand expression in a logical *AND* results in a 0, then the right hand expression is not evaluated since the result is 0 no matter what the value of the right side.

The relational operators are similar to relational operators in other languages except that the results of these operators are integer also. Each returns a 0 if the relationship is *FALSE* and a 1 if *TRUE*.

```
5 > 2          <-- returns a 1
5 < 2          <--    "    " 0

5 != 2         <--    "    " 1
5 == 2         <--    "    " 0
```

The bit-wise operators perform the normal bit operations. For example:

```
5 & 2              <--returns a 0   (5 = 0101b, 2 = 0010b)
5 | 2              <--   "     " 7
5 << 2             <--   "     " 20
5 >> 2             <--   "     " 1
```

The last operator, the ternary operator, is unique to C. It is the only C operator that accepts three arguments. They have the following significance:

```
expr1 ? expr2 : expr3;  <--returns expr2 if expr1 != 0 and
                                   expr3 if expr1 == 0

1 ? 5 : 2              <-- returns a 5;
0 ? 5 : 2              <--    "     " 2;
```

Despite appearances, the ternary qualifies as a true operator. Ternary can be used any place that any other expression is allowed. As with other operators, mixed mode expressions are allowed. For example, if *EXPR2* is an integer and *EXPR3* is a double the result of the expression will be a double, irrespective of which is "selected."

As in other common languages, C allows a variable to appear on both sides of the equal sign, as in:

```
value = value + 1;
```

This takes the contents of *VALUE*, adds to it a one and stores the result back into *VALUE*. Since this is such a common operation, C allows a shortened form:

```
value += 1
```

In this shorthand, the operator is placed in front of the equals sign. This can be read *add the value 1 to VALUE*. The expression to the right of the equals can be as complicated as desired. All of the math and bit-wise logical operators can be combined with the equals sign in this form of construct. The value of this expression is the same as that stored into the operand on the left of the equal sign.

If you were to determine which operator was used most often in this type of construct, you would find that addition and subtraction would lead the list by a large margin. Furthermore, if you were to determine what constant was added or subtracted most often, *1* would lead the list. Therefore, C defines an even *shorter hand* for *add 1 to a variable* or *subtract 1 from a variable* called the autoincrement and autodecrement:

```
value++;          <--postincrement: returns value
value--;          <--postdecrement:    "    value
++value;          <--preincrement:     "    value+1
--value;          <--predecrement:     "    value-1
```

In the autoincrement the operator ++ is simply attached to the variable name. The effect is to add 1 to the variable. Notice that there are two forms. When the ++ follows the variable name, the value of the expression is the value of the variable *BEFORE* incrementing. When it precedes the variable name, the value is that of the variable *AFTER* incrementing. Decrement (--) works in an exactly analogous fashion.

C allows mixed mode expressions. That is, the two operands on both sides of an operator do not have to agree in type. For example, an integer may be added to a float, a char may be added to an integer, etc. Conversion proceeds pretty much as you would expect: the "lower" type is promoted to the "higher" type, the operation proceeds, and the result is converted to the type of the target variable.

There are two aspects of implicit conversion that are completely unexpected, however. *CHAR* is always promoted to *INT* and *FLOAT* to *DOUBLE* before beginning an operation. This is somewhat surprising since it implies in the following equation:

```
float a, b, c;

a = b + c;
```

no fewer than three type conversions take place! First *B* and *C* are converted to type *DOUBLE*, then the addition is performed resulting in an answer of type *DOUBLE*, which is rounded down to type *FLOAT* before being stored into variable A. Similarly, since the arguments to functions are considered expressions, they, too, are converted to the proper type. These automatic conversions can be very time-consuming tasks, especially converting *FLOAT* to

DOUBLE on a machine not equipped with a numerical processor, so these conversion rules should be kept in mind. The following table shows how different type variables are handled in expressions:

```
char    -->    int           |   mixed modes
short   -->    int           |     promote
int     -->    int           |     in this
long    -->    long          |    direction
float   -->    double       \ /
double  -->    double        v
```

Flow Control

There are 10 flow-control statements in C. The first is simply the open and closed brace pair *{}*. Just as with Pascal's *BEGIN* and *END* statements, any number of C statements, when surrounded by open and closed braces, are viewed as one statement. Even though *{}* is considered a statement, a semicolon is not necessary after the close brace

C's *IF* statement looks much like that of other languages:

```
if (expr1)
        STATEMENT1;
else
        STATEMENT2;
```

EXPR1 is evaluated. If its value is nonzero, *STATEMENT1* is executed, otherwise, *STATEMENT2* is executed. Once *STATEMENT1* or *STATEMENT2* are complete, execution continues with the next statement after the *IF* statement. As always, either *STATEMENT1* or *STATEMENT2* may be either a simple statement or any number of C statements surrounded by braces. The *ELSE* clause in a C *IF* statement is optional.

The simplest looping structure in C is the *WHILE* loop:

```
while (expr)
        STATEMENT1;
```

First *EXPR* is evaluated. If the result is nonzero, *STATEMENT1* is executed. Once complete, control returns to the *WHILE*. In the absence of any other control statements, program execution will not pass to the statement after the *WHILE* loop until *EXPR* evaluates to 0.

Sometimes it is convenient to execute the body of the loop before testing the conditional. For these cases, C has the *DO...WHILE* loop. In this case,

STATEMENT is executed and then *EXPR1*. If *EXPR1* evaluates to nonzero control returns to the beginning of the loop. As with the *WHILE* loop, control will not pass to the next statement until *EXPR1* evaluates to 0.

```
do
    STATEMENT1;
while (expr);
```

A third form of loop is the *FOR* loop. The syntax of the *FOR* loop corresponds roughly to that of the *FOR* loop in Pascal or BASIC but is much more flexible. In fact, the C *FOR* loop is flexible almost to the point of being arbitrary:

```
for (expr1; expr2; expr3)
   STATEMENT1;

    is equivalent to

expr1;
while (expr2) {
     STATEMENT1
     expr3;
}
```

EXPR1 is evaluated first. This normally initializes any loop counters. If *EXPR2* evaluates to 0 control is passed to the statement after the *FOR* loop, otherwise *STATEMENT1* is evaluated. Finally, *EXPR3*, which normally increments any *FOR* loop index, is executed and control returns to the conditional. Any of the four statements and expressions may be left out. If *EXPR2* is ommitted, it is assumed to be nonzero so that *"FOR (;;)"* represents an infinite loop. An example *FOR* loop is shown below:

```
for (i = 0; i < 10; i++)      /*loop from i = 0 thru 9*/
     sum += value [i];
```

It is sometimes desirable to be able to change the flow of a program from within the body of a loop. For this, C defines two control structures, *BREAK* and *CONTINUE*. When C executes a *BREAK*, control is immediately passed to the statement following the inner most loop or *SWITCH*. *CONTINUE* passes control to the last statement of the loop, which has the effect of starting the loop over.

The *SWITCH* statement is a multi-way version of the *IF* statement. It has the following format:

```
switch (expr1) {
    case const1: STATEMENT1;
    case const2: STATEMENT2;
```

```
            .
            .
        default:  STATEMENTN;
    }
```

Here *EXPR1* is evaluated. It is then compared to each of the constants following thc *CASE* statements. If it is found to be equal to any of the *CASE*s, control is passed to the corresponding statement. If not, control is passed to the *DEFAULT* case. Notice that this is *NOT* like a Pascal *CASE* statement in that, if *EXPR* is equal to *CONST2*, *STATEMENT2* alone is not evaluated, but rather control is passed to *STATEMENT2*. Unless some other control statement intervenes, *STATEMENT3*, *STATEMENT4* and so on will then be executed in turn down to and includng *STATEMENTN*. This may seem extremely odd, but in fact it gives the programmer more control. If *STATEMENT2* is to be executed alone, it need only be followed by a *BREAK* statement. Encountering a *BREAK* causes execution to continue at the statement following the closing brace of the *SWITCH* statement.

The comma operator almost only arises in the context of flow control:

```
expr1, expr2;
```

With the comma operator, *EXPR1* is evaluated first and then *EXPR2*. The value and type of this expression is that of *EXPR2*. This peculiar operator can be used almost anywhere, but in fact is primarily intended for the initialization and incrementing clauses of the *FOR* loop. Consider, for example, the following segment of code intended to reverse the order of an array.

```
for (indx1 = 0, indx2 = SIZE; indx1 <= SIZE/2; indx1++, indx2--){
    temp = array[indx1];
    array[indx1] = array[indx2];
    array[indx2] = temp;
}
```

By using the comma operator, you have effectively "squeezed" two expressions in place of one in the *FOR* loop. Other than such cases, the comma operator should be avoided as unnecessary obfuscation.

Finally, as with all languages, C defines both a *GOTO* command and statement labels. The *GOTO* is written as one word, followed by a label. Label names use the same syntax as variable names except that they are followed by a colon. A *GOTO* can reference any label, either forward or backward, within the same function.

Invoking Functions

A somewhat implicit flow control is achieved by invoking and returning from functions. Just as in Pascal, a function is invoked by simply naming it, followed by any arguments enclosed in parentheses and separated by commas. Unlike Pascal, the parentheses are not optional. If there are no arguments, the parentheses appear alone. The type of a function is declared or, if not declared, defaults to *INT*. The value of a function is whatever it happens to return.

The *RETURN* statement may appear anywhere within a function and effects an immediate return to the caller. It may optionally be followed by an expression, in which case the expression is evaluated and the result is returned to the caller as the value of the function. If no *RETURN* statement is present, an implicit return is assumed at the closing brace of the function. Consider the following simplistic example. (In the following chapters I will have many examples of invoking and returning from functions.)

```
int add2 (arg)
    int arg;
{
    return arg+2;
}

main ()
{
        int a, add2();

        a = add2(a);
}
```

In the above example, the routine *add2()* returns the integer 2 plus whatever integer value it receives.

It should be pointed out that unlike Fortran and some other languages, C always passes by value (as opposed to "by reference"). In the above example, when *ADD2* is called, it is the value of A which gets passed and not the address of A. Therefore, changing the value of an argument within a function does not change its value within the caller. As you will see in Chapter 3 with the introduction of pointer variables this becomes no restriction at all.

Casts

Even though Turbo C is not a strongly typed language, it is not totally oblivious to them either. In the interest of attempting to catch programming errors, Turbo C will flag assignments that do not look correct. In any case, it is simply bad form to rely on the compiler to make type conversions. If you make the conversions yourself, then future readers will have no doubt of your intentions. Type conversions are made using what is called a *cast*. A cast consists of a type declaration enclosed in parentheses in front of an expression or constant. For example, in the following expression:

```
int a;
double b;

b += (double) a;
```

the variable A would be converted to a *DOUBLE* before being added to B in any case. By casting A into a *DOUBLE*, you are telling Turbo C that you know what you are doing and that this type mismatch was not the result of some programming error. Casts can appear in front of any expression. We will use them a great deal in our later discussion of pointer types.

C Preprocessor

The definition of C includes a C preprocessor which runs in advance of the compiler. While not strictly part of the C language itself, the preprocessor is nonetheless an important tool to the C programmer. The preprocessor is a prepass of the C compiler—preprocessor commands are found and converted to C statements which are subsequently compiled. Preprocessor statements always begin with a #. They are not terminated with a semicolon. Preprocessor statements may be continued over multiple lines by ending each line with a \. The syntax of preprocessor commands is different because they are a language of their own, independent of C.

The most important preprocessor command is *#INCLUDE*. *#INCLUDE* followed by a file name inserts the contents of that file at the point of the include statement. The *#INCLUDE* statement has two forms:

```
#include <stdio.h>
#include "myfile.h"
```

Files enclosed in quotes are first searched for in the directory of the search file (usually the current default directory) and then the compiler directory. Those in < > are only searched for in the compiler directory. The compiler directory is the directory that contains the Turbo C's *TC.EXE* or those specified in the option menu under *include file directory*. Include files can have any name, but it is something of a C standard that they end in *.H*. Every C program should include

STDIO.H. This include file allows the C environment to make whatever definitions it desires.

Constants can be defined via the *#DEFINE*. This follows the format:

```
#define identifier token-string
```

For the remainder of the program, any appearance of *IDENTIFIER* will be replaced with *TOKEN-STRING*. This is usually used to define certain constant values which have particular meaning, such as defining *FALSE* to be 0 and *TRUE* to be 1.

Notice that *#DEFINE* is not like a Pascal constant. The token-string is compiled *AFTER* it has been inserted. Because of this, it need not be a constant. In fact, *#DEFINE*s can even be used to rename C key words. For example, defining *BEGIN* to be *{* and *END* to be *}* would allow the programmer to code *BEGIN* and *END* instead of braces making the resulting C program more similar to Pascal. In general, this renaming of keywords is a very bad idea—I only mention it because you will see it done from time to time.

In addition to simple definitions, it is also possible to define preprocessor macros. A macro has the appearance of a function call. For example, consider the following common definition of *min*:

```
 #define min(a,b)  (a>b)?b:a

in use:

 min(var1,2*var2);   -- expands to -->   (var1>2*var2)?2*var2:var1;
```

Everywhere in the program that *min* is used it is expanded as in the example given above. Although similar in appearance, *min* is not a function. It does not have a type, nor do its arguments. *DEFINE*s are a means of making a C program, especially a very large one, more readable.

Programmers should be very careful about comments placed after preprocessor definitions as they get expanded also. For example, consider the following:

```
 #define min(a,b)  (a>b)?b:a     /*definition of min*/

in use:

 min(var1,var2) + 1;  -- expands to -->
           (var1>var2)?var1,var2  /*definition of min*/ + 1;
```

In this particular example, the comment causes Turbo C no confusion in evaluating the expression and everything works out fine—if I were doing the evaluating, I might not have been so understanding. Not so fortunate are the following common macro mistakes:

```
#define min(a,b)  (a>b)?b:a          /*this is an incorrect
                                       macro definition*/
#define max(a,b)  (a>b)?a:b;
```

In the first case, the comment becomes part of the macro definition as before. In this case, however, the comment is not complete. Only part of the opening /* gets copied. Fortunately the dangling second line of the comment appears by itself after the preprocessor removes the *#define* line to be caught by the compiler and flagged as an error.

The problem represented by the definition of *max()* is much more subtle. *Max()* has incorrectly been *terminated* with a semicolon. In use, this semicolon will get expanded along with the reset of the macro definition. Often the presence of this extra *;* causes no problem. In cases such as the following, however, the error message generated is very unclear.

```
if (a)
     b = max (a,b);
else
     b = 0;

gets expanded to

if (a)
     b = (a>b)?a:b;;
else
     b = 0;
```

Notice the presence of the double semicolons after the ternary. The macro definition contributed one, and the line into which the macro was insert contained the other. Null statements are acceptable in C, but the extra statement after the *IF* statement effectively closes off the possibility of an *ELSE* clause. Subsequently, the *ELSE* statement generates a very cryptic message about *no IF corresponding statement.* In general, users should be very careful in their macro definitions. If, despite great care, a problem is suspected with a macro, use the Turbo CPP utility to expand the .C source file preprocessor definitions into a separate listing file. This allows the user to see exactly what the compiler sees after the preprocessor has done its work.

A third group of preprocessor commands are the conditional compile commands. The conditional preprocessor commands are listed in Table 1.3. These allow the preprocessor to cause certain sections of code to be compiled or not, depending upon the environment. This is often used with programs designed to be compiled on different machines. Certain variable definitions which are machine dependent can be conditionally compiled. As you are only addressing the PC, you will probably not be using this aspect. One other area where conditional compilations are very useful is that of debug. You will use this trick in some of the later programs.

Table 1.3

#IF	--> compile clause if value following is non-zero
#IFDEF	--> " " " variable defined
#IFNDEF	--> " " " variable not defined
#ELSE	--> same as with C if statement
#ENDIF	--> terminates #IF or #ELSE clause

For example, suppose while debugging your program, you would like a test message to be printed on the screen whenever a certain function is called. When the program is to be delivered, however, that test message is undesirable. You might do something like the following:

```
#define DEBUG 1          /*define to 0 to turn off msg.s*/
        .
        .
        .
int proc ()
{
#IF DEBUG
        printf ("we just entered proc\n");
#ENDIF
        .
        .
        .
```

As long as the statement at the beginning of your program defines *DEBUG* to be non-zero, the *#IF* statement below will cause the call to *printf()* to be compiled. By changing the value of *DEBUG* to 0, the various *#IF* clauses will not be compiled and the test messages will no longer appear. *DEBUG* did not have to be defined with a *#DEFINE*; it could just as easily been defined using the *Options/Compiler/Defines* menu of the Interactive Development Environment (IDE). It is important to remember that these precompiler decisions are made at compile time and not at run time—once the program has been compiled, the *printf()* calls are either there or not. There is nothing you can do to the executable *.EXE* file to change that.

Turbo C defines, but barely uses, a preprocessor directive made popular by the Ada programming language, *#PRAGMA*. A pragma is a directive from the source code to the compiler itself. *#PRAGMA* serves two purposes in Turbo C, one is to control which warnings get displayed by the compiler. The other is used to indicate that inline code is being generated using the *ASM* directive in this source file. Both of the these functions can be handled by command-line arguments and/or IDE switches.

One last command which acts like a preprocessor macro automatically defined by the system is *SIZEOF()*. *SIZEOF()* accepts one argument and returns the size of that argument in bytes. This can best be demonstrated with the following examples:

```
char a, b[10];
int c;
double d;

sizeof(a)         --> returns 1
sizeof(b)         --> returns 10
sizeof(b[0])      --> returns 1
sizeof(c)         --> returns 2
sizeof(d)         --> returns 8
sizeof(int)       --> returns 2
sizeof(int *)     --> returns either 2 or 4
```

Any data element can be an argument to *SIZEOF*, including user defined structures. Unlike ANSI C, Turbo C allows *SIZEOF* to be used in other *#DEFINE* statements. This macro is primarily used to remove machine dependency from a C program. Even though you are mostly interested in the PC, you will use it in later programs in connection with structures, since they can be of any size. *SIZEOF* should always be used in connection with pointer variables—the size of a pointer variable or a structure or union containing a pointer variable is determined by the memory model selected at compile time.

C Philosophy

You, should appreciate, if you don't already, that there is a fundamental difference in philosophy between C and other languages, particularly Pascal. Pascal is a very high-level language. Its strong typing and strict syntax try very hard to protect programmers from themselves. C, by contrast, is more of a low-level language. Some have even called C a machine-independent macroassembly language. C tries to view each keyword as an operator separate from those around it. This allows C commands to be strung up in myriad of different ways.

In addition, every expression in C has a value. You may have noticed that some of the phraseology used above to describe = seemed a bit strained. What, for example, is all this talk of equals sign not changing the value of the expression to the right? In fact, this is the case. Consider this very simple series of expressions:

```
1)      a = 1;
2)      b = (a = 1);
3)      a = fn();
4)      fn();
5)      2 * a;
```

In the first equation C begins by finding the rightmost expression, in this case *1*. The equal sign then takes the current value (1) and stores it into the variable A. The value after making the assignment is still 1. This may not seem important until you look at equation 2). Given what I just said above, you see that the value 1 also gets saved into B. Since the parentheses are not really necessary in this case, you see that C handles naturally what other languages must make a special case for, that of simultaneously assigning multiple variables.

Now consider statement 3). Here, function *fn()* is invoked and the value returned is stored into A. But what about equation 4)? Here the function *fn()* is invoked and the value returned is simply thrown away. You might protest, *fn()* didn't return a value. But remember that all C functions return a value, and it's left up to the programmer to decide whether that value has any meaning. Then it may not be too surprising that most C compilers accept statements like 5) without protest. Here you have instructed C to generate the machine code to take the contents of A and multiply them by 2, doing nothing with the result!

Now consider the following C statements:

```
1)      if ((a = b / c) == 1)
2)      a = (b > c);
        if (a) printf ("Hi\n");
3)      a = 5 * (b > c);
```

To understand the first statement you begin with the innermost parenthesis. First, take the value of B and divide it by the value of C and store that value into A. Then compare that same value, unchanged by the assignment, with 1. If equal, you return a 1 and if not a 0. The *IF* statement branches accordingly. What about equation 2)? Here you compare the value of B with the value of C. If B is greater than C you return a 1, otherwise a 0. This value is then stored into the variable A. You subsequently retrieve the value of A and if nonzero, you perform the *printf()*; if zero, you don't. This is not too far fetched for those familiar with Boolean variables, but what about equation 3)? Here, you take the result of the comparison and use it in a calculation, leaving A with the value 5 if B is greater than C and 0 if not.

As you can see, this philosophy represents somewhat of a departure from that of other languages. It is this perspective that both attracts and repels programmers. This freedom allows programmers to build some very powerful constructs. On the other hand, programmers are given all the rope they could possibly need to hang themselves.

Some languages, most notably FORTRAN, have compilers with very strong optimizers. This allows the compiler to take whatever source statements and rearrange and compact them to generate the minimum amount of code. C puts the onous on programmers to optimize for themselves. For example, *IF ((A = B/C) == 1)* probably generates less code than first calculating A and then testing A against 1 in a separate *IF* statement, as would be required in other languages. Furthermore, it was not only for your convenience that C provides the shorthands *A+=1* and *A++* for *A=A+1*. On most machines, *A+=1* generates less object code and *A++* even less than its wordier sibling, even though the final effect is the same in each case.

C has very few primitives. Just compare the overview above with a list of the BASIC keywords. C is heavily dependent on its library of functions for much of its interface to the base machine and, therefore, much of its power. You are not left completely at the whim of Borland and the library they supply with Turbo C. You can build your own libraries, adding functions of your design to those already present. For example, there are no primitives for setting, testing and clearing a bit in C. After you have gained more experience with C, you might write functions to perform these functions like those in listing Prg1_1a.

```
/*Prg1_1a - Simple bit manipulation functions
   by Stephen R. Davis, '87

  Simple C lacks "bit picking" primitives.  The following routines
  provide some simple bit manipulation capabilities.
```

```
*/

#include <stdio.h>
#include "mylib.h"

/*define an array of bits which we use for the following routines*/

static char bitarray[] = {0x80,0x40,0x20,0x10,0x08,0x04,0x02,0x01};

/*SetBit - set the 'bitnum'th bit offset from 'ptr'*/
void setbit (ptr, bitnum)
    char *ptr;
    unsigned bitnum;
{
    unsigned bitpos, bytepos;

    bytepos = bitnum >> 3;
    bitpos = bitnum & 0x07;
    *(ptr+bytepos) |= bitarray[bitpos];
}

/*ClrBit - clear the 'bitnum'th bit offset from 'ptr'*/
void clrbit (ptr, bitnum)
    char *ptr;
    unsigned bitnum;
{
    unsigned bitpos, bytepos;

    bytepos = bitnum >> 3;
    bitpos = bitnum & 0x07;
    *(ptr+bytepos) &= ~(bitarray[bitpos]);
}

/*TestBit - test the 'bitnum'th bit offset from 'ptr'.
            Return a 0 if the bit is cleared, and a 1 if set.*/
char testbit (ptr, bitnum)
    char *ptr;
    unsigned bitnum;
{
    unsigned bitpos, bytepos;

    bytepos = bitnum >> 3;
    bitpos = bitnum & 0x07;
    if (*(ptr+bytepos) & bitarray[bitpos])
        return(1);
    return(0);
}

/*HexDump - display in 1's and 0's from 'nobytes' number of bytes
            starting from 'ptr'*/
void hexdump (ptr, nobytes)
    char *ptr;
    unsigned nobytes;
{
    int nobits;

    for (; nobytes;) {
        for (nobits = 0; nobits < 8; nobits++) {
            if (testbit (ptr,nobits))
                printf ("1");
            else
                printf ("0");
        }
        printf (" ");
```

```
 70[ 2]:          if (!(--nobytes % 8))
 71[ 2]:              printf ("\n");
 72[ 2]:          ptr++;
 73[ 1]:     }
 74[ 0]: }
 75[ 0]:
 76[ 0]: /*Main - test the above routines*/
 77[ 0]: main ()
 78[ 0]: {
 79[ 1]:     char buffer[16];
 80[ 1]:     int i,bit;
 81[ 1]:
 82[ 1]:     for (i = 0; i < 16; i++)       /*test SetBit*/
 83[ 1]:          buffer[i] = 0;
 84[ 1]:     for (;;) {
 85[ 2]:          hexdump (buffer,16);
 86[ 2]:          printf ("\nenter the number of bit to set (>=128 quits):");
 87[ 2]:          scanf ("%d",&bit);
 88[ 2]:          printf ("\n");
 89[ 2]:          if (bit >= 128)
 90[ 2]:              break;
 91[ 2]:          setbit (buffer,bit);
 92[ 1]:     }
 93[ 1]:
 94[ 1]:     printf ("\n\n");
 95[ 1]:
 96[ 1]:     for (i = 0; i < 16; i++)       /*now test ClrBit*/
 97[ 1]:          buffer[i] = -1;
 98[ 1]:     for (;;) {
 99[ 2]:          hexdump (buffer,16);
100[ 2]:          printf ("\nenter the number of bit to clear (>=128 quits):");
101[ 2]:          scanf ("%d",&bit);
102[ 2]:          printf ("\n");
103[ 2]:          if (bit >= 128)
104[ 2]:              break;
105[ 2]:          clrbit (buffer,bit);
106[ 1]:     }
107[ 1]:     printf ("\n\nThat's all folks!");
108[ 0]: }
```

Without going into too much detail of pointer manipulation, the functions *setbit()*, *clrbit()* and *testbit()* perform the desired function. The *main()* and *hexdump()* routines that appear below are used to test these functions. Compile this program and convince yourself that these functions perform as advertised. Once convinced, *main()* and, perhaps, *hexdump()* (lines 54–108) would be removed and the bit routines compiled by themselves. The resulting object file could then be converted into a new library or added to an existing library. For all subsequent programs you will be able to use these functions. Your personalized Turbo C environment now has bit primitives!

This example demonstrates the bottom-up approach to programming incorporated into the C language. After outlining the problem, the programmer decides which simple utilities will be needed and implements these first (including testing them completely!). Working with already tested simple routines, he or she then builds

higher level routines. Because of this design philosophy, most C functions are purposefully kept pretty short.

Routines with only specific application can be kept with the particular program. Generally useful, low level routines can be added to the programmers library for future use. Reinventing the wheel is frowned upon by C programmers. For this to work, of course, the programmer must keep a good log book describing each routine. Not only should it state what the routine does but what the number, type and meaning of arguments for each routine are, and the type and meaning of the value returned. The page from my log book which describes the bit routines just defined appears below.

Additionally, users should build their own *include* files containing the prototyping declarations for their routines. This is included in programs that use any of these library routines, or just included routinely for the chance that one of the routines gets used. The prototyping *include* file containing only the bit routines appears below.

Bit Routines

```
Setbit -
        given an address and a bit offset, sets the
        corresponding bit.  Bit 0 is assumed to be
        the most significant bit.  Offsets must be
        in the range [0,7].

        prototype: void setbit (char *address,
                                unsigned offset)

        usage: setbit (address, offset);

        include file: MYLIB.H

        contained in: MYLIB.LIB

Clrbit -
        given an address and a bit offset, clears the
        corresponding bit.  See Setbit().

Testbit -
        given an address and a bit offset, return a
        0 if that bit is cleared and a 1 if that bit
        is set.  See Setbit().

        prototype: char testbit (char *address,
                                 unsigned offset)

        usage: if (testbit (address, offset))
                    printf ("Bit set!");

        include file: MYLIB.H

        contained in: MYLIB.LIB
```

```
HexDump -

          given an address and a number of bytes, dump
          memory in hexadecimal fashion to STDOUT.

          prototype: void hexdump (char *address,
                                   unsigned numbytes);

          usage: hexdump (array, sizeof(array));

          include file: MYLIB.H

          contained in: MYLIB.LIB
```

```
-- MYLIB.H INCLUDE FILE
/*Prototype definitions for my personal libarary routines -- */

void setbit (char *, unsigned);
        /*set a the nth bit from a pointer*/
void clrbit (char *, unsigned);
        /*clear the nth bit from a pointer*/
char testbit (char *, unsigned);
        /*return a 0 if the nth bit from a pointer is not set;
          else return a 1*/
void hexdump (char *, unsigned);
        /*display a hex dump of memory starting at first arg for
          second arg number of bytes*/
```

Programmer's libraries can be added to, both from commercial packages you might purchase as well as computer magazines. Don't be afraid to adopt other's work if it saves your own.

Good C programmers spend at least half of their programming time just thinking about the problem. Of course, this is true in any language, but with so much riding on the programmer and his decisions, this becomes even more important in C. For example, let us say that as part of a larger program you required a function that converts a binary number into its ASCII equivalent and places the result into a buffer for printing. The non-C programmer might code the solution as it appears in Prg1_2a. *convnum()* fulfills the requirements.

```
/* Prgl_2a -- Convert a number into a numeric ASCII string
     by Stephen R. Davis, 1987

     This is the 'first shot' crude attempt which the non-thinking
     programmer is likely to settle for.  It's problems are that it
     is limited to base 10 and that it must have special logic to
     take care of leading zeroes, etc.
*/

#include <stdio.h>

/*prototype definitions --*/
int main (void);
void convnum (int, char *);

/*ConvNum - given a number and a buffer, place the ASCII
               presentation of the number into the buffer*/
void convnum (number, buffer)
     int number;
     char *buffer;
{
     int basenum,nextpower,digit;

     if (number < 0) {                    /*if neg, attach leading '-'*/
          number = -number;
          *buffer++ = '-';
     }
     basenum = 1;                         /*find power of 10 to start*/
     while ((nextpower = basenum * 10) <= number)
          basenum = nextpower;

     for (;basenum; basenum /= 10) {     /*divide repeatedly by 10...*/
          digit = number / basenum;
          number -= digit * basenum;      /*...saving the residue*/
          *buffer++ = (char)(digit + '0');
     }
     *buffer = '\0';
}


/*Main - test the above conversion routine*/
int test[] = {1, 10, 100, 1000, -1, -15, -25, -35, 0};
main ()
{
     int i;
     char buffer[25];

     i = 0;
     do {
          convnum (test [i], buffer);
          printf ("%s\n", buffer);
         } while (test[i++]);
     printf ("\nfinished\n");
}
```

The "real" C programmer would be more inclined to come up with a more general solution. This one would make a more valuable addition to his library, and be more like Prog1_2b. Although slightly less obvious in its execution, this *convnum()* is not limited to base 10 numbers, which is obvious from the test output shown. In fact, it is not even limited to Arabic numerals. This *convnum()*, once included in the programmers' library, might find applications completely unforeseen in future programs.

```
/* Prg 1_2b -- Convert a number into a numeric ASCII string
    by Stephen R. Davis, 1987

    This second attempt is much more flexible and more of a 'C'
    approach.  The differences may not seem all that significant,
    but notice that this routine can handle octal and hexidecimal
    as well as decimal output, it has no leading zero problem, and
    it can even output a limited form of Roman numerals!
*/

#include <stdio.h>

/*prototype definitions --*/
int main (void);
void convnum (int, char *, int, char **);

/*ConvNum - given a number, a buffer, a base and the names of the
            digits, convert the signed number using the base into
            the buffer (for unsigned conversion, use 'unsigned'
            declaration*/
void convnum (number, buffer, base, names)
    int number;                 /*either signed or...     */
    /*unsigned number;*/        /*...unsigned conversions*/
    int base;
    char *buffer, *names[];
{
    int basenum,nextpower,digit;
    char *c;

    if (number < 0) {
        number = -number;
        *buffer++ = '-';
    }
    basenum = 1;
    while ((nextpower = basenum * base) <= number)
        basenum = nextpower;

    for (;basenum; basenum /= base) {
        digit = number / basenum;
        number -= digit * basenum;
        for (c = names [digit]; *c; c++)
            *buffer++ = *c;
    }
    *buffer = '\0';
}


/*Main - use a slightly more elaborate test*/
int test[] = {1, 10, 100, 1000, 15, 25, -1, 0};

char *decsys[] = {"0", "1", "2", "3", "4",
                  "5", "6", "7", "8", "9"},
     *octsys[] = {"0", "1", "2", "3",
                  "4", "5", "6", "7"},
     *binsys[] = {"0", "1"},
     *hexsys[] = {"0", "1", "2", "3", "4", "5", "6", "7",
                  "8", "9", "A", "B", "C", "D", "E", "F"};
main ()
{
```

```
    int i;
    char buffer[25];

    printf ("\ndecimal:\n");
    i = 0;
    do {
        convnum (test[i], buffer, 10, decsys);
        printf ("%s   ", buffer);
      } while (test[i++]);

    printf ("\noctal:\n");
    i = 0;
    do {
        convnum (test[i], buffer, 8, octsys);
        printf ("%s   ", buffer);
      } while (test[i++]);

    printf ("\nbinary:\n");
    i = 0;
    do {
        convnum (test[i], buffer, 2, binsys);
        printf ("%s   ", buffer);
      } while (test[i++]);

    printf ("\nhexidecimal:\n");

    i = 0;
    do {
        convnum (test[i], buffer, 16, hexsys);
        printf ("%s   ", buffer);
      } while (test[i++]);

    printf ("\nfinished\n");
}
```

If you do not understand the finer points of these example programs, don't worry. Consider the point being made, that good C programmers write their programs as general as possible, and write them to last. Later, after I have discussed some of the details of pointer manipulation in Chapter 3, you can return to these programs and you will have a much easier time reading them. By the way, feel free to add these routines to your own C library.

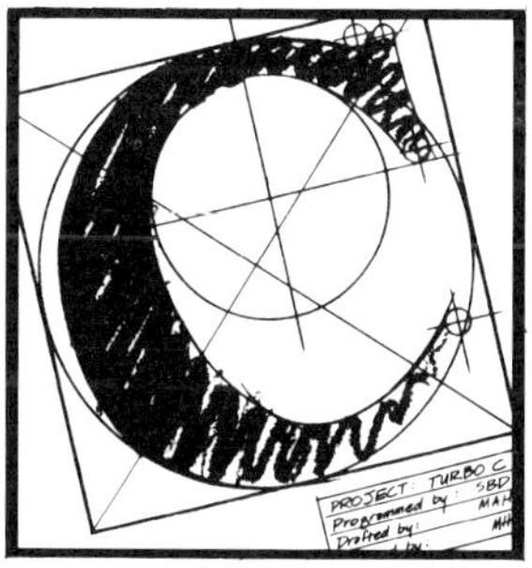

2 Turbo C vs. K&R C

As with any compiler, there is more to using Turbo C than just the language. To be effective, the programmer must also understand and appreciate the entire Turbo C package. This is especially true of Borland languages, as these present the user with an environment, within which the programmer must work. It is just this powerful environment, however, which accounts for their high popularity in the user community.

This chapter attempts to highlight some of the differences between Turbo C and other C compilers, including those found under operating systems other than PC-DOS. Readers already familiar with other such C implementations can use this chapter to help them get up to speed more rapidly. This chapter also touches, at least briefly, on those facets of Turbo C important to generating working code in a short time. It can also be of use to prospective customers attempting to evaluate Turbo C for their application.

Chapter 2 is not a complete description of every aspect of the Turbo C environment. Little purpose is served in generating page after page of such long-winded explanations. Not only are most of the options fairly self-explanatory in use, but the *User's Guide*, which Borland includes with the Turbo C compiler, already does a quite competent job of explaining them. In this chapter I will touch briefly on features of Turbo C that are of special interest to the C programmer. I will leave a detailed analysis of many of these features to later chapters.

The Integrated Development Environment

No other C compiler uses the Borland Integrated Development Environment (IDE) user interface. Its look and feel is not even similar to that of older versions of Turbo Pascal (Versions 3.X and earlier), although it is common with the newer Borland languages, such as Turbo Prolog and Turbo Basic. Users who are new to the IDE should have little trouble familiarizing themselves with its pull-down menus and appreciating its lightning quick compilations.

The first menu option, both physically and in order of use, is the File menu. It is from this menu that the programmer selects the source file to be edited and compiled. Additionally, this menu provides simple DOS functions, such as listing directory contents, etc. It is also from this menu that the user quits back to PC-DOS when finished. One other menu selection, Shell to DOS, is particularly advantageous, since it allows the user to drop down to DOS without disturbing the program being worked on. This is extremely useful when more access to DOS is necessary than the simple *File* menu can provide. It can also be used to execute a separate debugger on a Turbo C generated executable file.

Having selected a source file, the editor is automatically entered. The Turbo C editor is very similar to the Turbo Pascal editor, in that it uses the WordStar command set unless otherwise installed via the TCINST utility. Fortunately, the tab key in Turbo C really generates a tab rather than the Turbo Pascal interpretation. Returning to the menu is via the *^K^D* (Control-K, Control-D) or *F10* command.

Once edited, a C program is compiled by selecting the *Compile* menu. (Selecting the *Run* menu option will also compile and link the C program, but let's take one step at a time.) Turbo C offers two possibilities: *Compile to Object* and *Compile to .EXE*. The ability to generate an object file and go through a subsequent link step was a capability sorely missing with Turbo Pascal. Its presence here opens up the possibility of combining Turbo C modules with those written in assembler and other programming languages.

Compiling a simple program to an *.EXE* file results in an automatic link step being performed. The necessary Turbo C routines are automatically included from the proper *.LIB* files. If the current file being edited is a *.H* file included within some other C source program, Turbo C can be informed as to which program to compile by filling in the *Primary C File* option. If the program consists of more than one C source file, then a project file must be created and selected in the Project menu. This will be demonstrated later with an example.

The *Options* menu is perhaps the most exciting aspect of the IDE. Other compilers allow some user control of the way they go about compiling, but usually through such complicated switch options that few venture to use them. The *Options* menu allows the operator to select which memory model Turbo C should generate code for, what types of optimizations Turbo C should make, which instruction set to use, etc. I will discuss those concepts most pertinent to the advanced Turbo C programmer in the appropriate chapter.

A few of the options available from this menu do not affect the actual code generation of the Turbo C compiler. The first are the warning selections. These messages advise the user of such potential problems as type mismatches in assignments or an "=" in an if statement where an "==" was probably meant. As ANSI C is more restrictive in its type checking than K&R, older C programs from other sources can generate a large number of warnings when compiled under Turbo C. It may be desirable to suppress these warning messages by deselecting them in this menu (or, indeed, just deselecting warnings from appearing at all).

In general, a heavy handed approach to warning messages is not a good idea. The absence of type checking under K&R C was felt so acutely that a separate syntax checker for C, called *lint*, was written. Programmers could run lint against their source code to warn them of potential problems, even when the program appeared to be working correctly. The type checking rules of ANSI C, coupled with Turbo C's warning messages, go a long way toward making lint unnecessary. To simply ignore this capability is a big mistake.

The second noncode generating option area is the directory selections. Especially as hard disk sizes grow, getting efficient use out of them means organizing directories carefully along functional divisions. Mixing C source files, object files, and include files all in one directory, not to mention the Turbo C package itself, is not only a very bad idea, but it also limits the number of files you can have on your disk. Smart C programmers will organize their directories—for example, devoting one to source files, another to objects, and a third to include files, with perhaps all under the umbrella of a master directory.

Although this has always been a good idea, C compilers were not always too helpful. Fortunately, Turbo C allows the user to place each of these program elements in a different directory by specifying their names in the *Options* menu. All of the preferences selected from the *Options* menu can then be saved to disk for automatic recall by the IDE at the beginning of the next Turbo C work session.

Linker and Library Support

In my earlier programming example, I built several routines for setting, clearing, and testing bits, capabilities otherwise lacking in the Turbo C library. At that time I said that it was characteristic of C programmers to write such routines and keep them for inclusion in future programs, but I was pretty vague as to the mechanism involved. Exactly how does the Turbo C programmer go about that?

Experienced Turbo Pascal types might pipe up at this point and suggest creating *include* files for inclusion in future C source programs much like Turbo Pascal. Certainly Turbo C has an *#include* facility and its compilation speed is probably up to the task, but this approach has some serious draw backs. First of all, you must compile *include* files every time you compile the file that includes them. This is probably not much of a problem with simple bit routines, but, at least theoretically, you are going to grow as programmers and collect many more such useful routines over your C career to be included in your personal library.

Second, you might not want your C source routines held up to the world for ridicule. You might be happier letting others enjoy the fruits of your labor, without having the entertainment of laughing at your foibles. Worse yet, when compiling such a program, the entire include file gets included in the object code, even if only one of the routines contained in it is called. Again, this problem grows as your library grows. For these and other reasons, C projects are almost never organized this way.

The first alternative is to break off the include file as a separate C source file, called a module, but specify to Turbo C that these modules somehow "belong together." You do this by building what is known as a *project*. First, you create a *.PRJ* file that contains the names of both source modules. You must then specify in the *project* menu the name of the project upon which you are working.

Turbo C is very helpful in this respect. When you instruct it to build an *.EXE* file for your project by selecting that option from the *compile* menu, Turbo C checks the creation date of each of the source modules, comparing them against the date of the corresponding *.OBJ* file. (The creation date of a file reflects the last time it was edited.) Whenever a source module is found with a later creation date than the *.OBJ* file, Turbo C concludes that it must have been edited recently and recompiles it before generating the executable! This insures that all changes in the C source programs are accurately reflected in the executable file.

You can verify this even with one file by selecting any C source module and compiling it to an object file. Without editing it, recompile it. Notice that Turbo C refuses. This is because Turbo C concludes that the object file is "fresh" and there is no need to recompile it. Now enter the editor and change something, no matter how trivial. You can even change something and then put it back the way it was; Turbo C doesn't know the difference. This updates the source file's "last changed" time. Select *compile to object* and it compiles as expected.

What if a source module includes another file, such as a *.H* file? If the *include* file changes, even though it has a different name, it will be necessary to recompile the source module to a fresh object file. Such, so called, dependencies must be specified in the project file explicitly by including their names enclosed in parentheses after the source file name.

This has been done with the example bit routines in the listing below. Notice first the two source files, *Prg1_1b* and *Prg1_1c*, look identical to how they previously appeared. The module *Prg1_1c*, which contains *main()*, includes the *.H* file, which you defined earlier with the prototype definitions describing the bit routines. This allows Turbo C to check for calling sequence errors in the calling module.

```
/*Prg1_1b - Simple bit manipulation functions
    by Stephen R. Davis, '87

  This is the same source code as is Prg1_1a, only now broken
  up into separate source modules similar to real projects.
*/

#include <stdio.h>
#include "mylib.h"

/*define an array of bits which we use for the following routines*/

static char bitarray[] = {0x80,0x40,0x20,0x10,0x08,0x04,0x02,0x01};

/*SetBit - set the 'bitnum'th bit offset from 'ptr'*/
void setbit (ptr, bitnum)
    char *ptr;
    unsigned bitnum;
{
    unsigned bitpos, bytepos;

    bytepos = bitnum >> 3;
    bitpos = bitnum & 0x07;
    *(ptr+bytepos) |= bitarray[bitpos];
}

/*ClrBit - clear the 'bitnum'th bit offset from 'ptr'*/
void clrbit (ptr, bitnum)
    char *ptr;
    unsigned bitnum;
{
```

```
     unsigned bitpos, bytepos;

     bytepos = bitnum >> 3;
     bitpos = bitnum & 0x07;
     *(ptr+bytepos) &= ~(bitarray[bitpos]);
}

/*TestBit - test the 'bitnum'th bit offset from 'ptr'.
              Return a 0 if the bit is cleared, and a 1 if set.*/
char testbit (ptr, bitnum)
     char *ptr;
     unsigned bitnum;
{
     unsigned bitpos, bytepos;

     bytepos = bitnum >> 3;
     bitpos = bitnum & 0x07;
     if (*(ptr+bytepos) & bitarray[bitpos])
          return(1);
     return(0);
}

/*HexDump - display in 1's and 0's form 'nobytes' number of bytes
              starting from 'ptr'*/
void hexdump (ptr, nobytes)
     char *ptr;
     unsigned nobytes;
{
     int nobits;

     for (; nobytes;) {
          for (nobits = 0; nobits < 8; nobits++) {
               if (testbit (ptr,nobits))
                    printf ("1");
               else
                    printf ("0");
          }
          printf (" ");
          if (!(--nobytes % 8))
               printf ("\n");
          ptr++;
     }
}
```

```
/*Prg1_1c - Simple bit manipulation functions
     by Stephen R. Davis, '87

  This is simply the test code for the bit routines
  defined in Program 1_1b.  This is identical to main()
  defined in Program 1_1a.
*/

#include <stdio.h>
#include "mylib.h"

/*Main - test the above routines*/
main ()
{
     char buffer[16];
     int i,bit;

     for (i = 0; i < 16; i++)          /*test SetBit*/
```

```
        buffer[i] = 0;
    for (;;) {
        hexdump (buffer,16);
        printf ("\nenter the number of bit to set (>=128 quits):");
        scanf ("%d",&bit);
        printf ("\n");
        if (bit >= 128)
            break;
        setbit (buffer,bit);
    }

    printf ("\n\n");

    for (i = 0; i < 16; i++)        /*now test ClrBit*/
        buffer[i] = -1;
    for (;;) {
        hexdump (buffer,16);
        printf ("\nenter the number of bit to clear (>=128 quits):");
        scanf ("%d",&bit);
        printf ("\n");
        if (bit >= 128)
            break;
        clrbit (buffer,bit);
    }
    printf ("\n\nThat's all folks!");
}
```

This solution is somewhat better than the first attempt. Needless recompilations are avoided: the bit routines can be compiled once and more or less forgotten after that. This technique has the further advantage of allowing problems to be logically divided up into separate parts. A large program may consist of many modules, each containing routines that are in some way similar to each other and different from other routines in the system. Not only is such a program easier to understand, but it is more easily divided among different programmers.

This technique still does not address the other two concerns of privacy and the inclusion of routines that are really not necessary. Nevertheless, this is the way modules that are being debugged (therefore, in a state of flux) are organized. This is particularly true if the routines being written are specific to the particular problem and not of general interest.

In the discussion above, I skirted the issue of exactly how Turbo C combined the various source modules into a single, complete executable *.EXE* file? All modern compilers support this process known as *linking*. The source module is compiled into a special binary file, called an object file and carrying the extension *.OBJ*. These object files contain not only the machine instructions for that source code, but also the name and location of all the external functions and variables declared within the module. They can also carry similar information on other variables and even the address of each line of C code.

Before they can be executed as a complete program, the object files for the various modules that make up a program must be combined in what is known as the link step. It is the LINK utility provided with PC-DOS and MS-DOS or the TLINK facility with Turbo C that performs this step. Linking can also be performed from the IDE by selecting the Make option under the Compile menu or by simply selecting the *Run* menu. Not only does the linker physically concatenate the object files, but it also resolves cross references. For example, if a routine defined in Module A is called from Module B, it is the linker that supplies the proper routine address.

If you have invoked a function in one of your routines without defining it, usually by misspelling it or by mixing upper and lower case letters in the name, it is the linker that flags the error with the message *<proc name> is unresolved in module <module name>*. We have been using the linker in every program you have executed so far, but since Turbo C handles routine matters for us, it may not have been obvious. The two-module problem above was the first time that you were forced to explicitly build a project file, and the first time the linking function became obvious was when it recombined into one executable the two C modules that you had manually split apart.

In addition to the source files specified in the project description, you can include object files by including their names with the extension *.OBJ*. (It is not legal in Turbo C to have a C source file with the extensions *.OBJ* or *.EXE*.) Similar to its handling of C source files, the link facility in the *IDE* compares the creation date of the *.EXE* file with those of any *.OBJ* files specified. If the *.EXE* file is not newer than all of the others, the *IDE* relinks to generate a new *.EXE*.

Object files still require accompanying *.H include* files containing prototype declarations for inclusion in those modules which intend to use them. It is also a good idea to maintain a log book containing a description of the functions contained within the various *.OBJ* files, although these descriptions may be kept as comments in the *.H* files, if desired. Such descriptions, while always a good idea, become critical when there is no source code to reference.

Your bit-test project description, rewritten to provide for a directly specified *.OBJ* file containing the actual bit functions appears below:

```
prg1_1b.obj
prg1_1c (mylib.h)
```

This solution is slightly better than the one proposed previously. Not only does it address both the problem of unnecessary compilations and that of source code privacy, but it even allows you to combine your Turbo C source code with objects generated by other computer languages. You will use this to optimize your programs by linking them with assembly routines in Chapter 8. This approach does nothing to address the final concern, however. Again the entire object file gets included in the final executable, regardless of whether or not any of its routines are invoked.

All three of the above solutions share a common management headache. In order to keep the executable files reasonable size, you are compelled to break up your collection of routines into small files. Whenever you desire to use one of these routines, you must be concerned with including the correct file, either in the compile or link step. If you include too many, your executable file swells needlessly. If you leave some out, you are confronted with unresolved linker errors.

How much nicer it would be if you could just present the linker with a menu of routines. Let it compare this against the requirements of the program being linked and select what is needed. This you can do with a utility known as an *object code librarian.* (Unfortunately, not part of the Turbo C 1.0 package, a librarian was added to the first update.)

A librarian combines object files into a library file with the extension *.LIB*. Library files are included in a project description by entering their name, and including the *.LIB* extension, just as with object files. Library files are in such a format that the linker can extract only those routines that it needs. As you create more and more routines of general interest, these new routines can be added to the existing library using the librarian utility. Careful programmers will also want to keep an include file containing prototype definitions for all of the routines in the library.

The project file for a corresponding solution using my personal library, *MYLIB.LIB*, appears below:

```
prg1_1b (mylib.h)
mylib.lib
```

Notice that it is necessary that the *.LIB* name appear last in a project description. Otherwise, not all of the files which must be extracted for linkage will be known when the library is searched.

This final solution answers all of the objections. It avoids needless recompilations, the source code is protected, and only those routines necessary get included in the final executable. All this occurs while avoiding the headaches of managing multiple source or object files.

The linker has one other beneficial side effect. The Turbo C linker is capable of generating a Microsoft compatible load map (a complete load map is gotten by selecting the *detailed map file* from the *linker* option under the *Options* menu). A load map is a detailed description of every external function and variable location within your program.

While the load map may be simply interesting just to see where things are getting placed in memory, it serves a vital function when it comes to debugging. Turbo C's one failing is a lack of debug support (at least, in Version 1.0). This being the case, it will often be necessary for Turbo C programmers to Shell into DOS (from the *File* menu), where they can run their programs under a debugger such as *DEBUG*. (Turn line numbers on in the *compile* options of the *Option*s menu to include the address of each line of C source code for easier debugging.) Once the error has been found, the programmer exits the debugger and uses the *DOS EXIT* command to pop right back into Turbo C, where the program is waiting to be corrected and recompiled. To do this successfully, requires the information contained within the load map.

Even better, many source-code debuggers for C gain their location information from the load map. In particular, Periscope and PFix can read Microsoft format load maps (there are many others also). A source-code debugger allows the programmer to set break points on and single step C source code statements rather than individual machine instructions. (Line numbers must be on for this to work.) Such source code debuggers are very powerful tools, and one that serious programmers should not do without.

Turbo C from the Command Line

Turbo C comes in two forms: the Integrated Development Environment and a more traditional command line set of utilities. Throughout this book, I will be using the IDE, since it provides the same capabilities with greater ease of use. For those who feel more comfortable with the other environment, however, it is available.

The compiler is essentially the same, carrying the name TCC rather than TC. All of the example programs in this book will compile properly under TCC. Like other command line compilers, user preferences are selected by including a series of switches along with the source file names (a list of these switches with descriptions appears in Table 2.1). Since the number of switches can become quite large, almost no one types them all in more than once. Generally, a programmer will create a DOS batch file which invokes TCC with the proper switches set.

A sample batch file appears as:

```
tcc -G -f87 -ml -n%2 %1
```

If this batch file was given a mnemonic name, such as *COMP.BAT*, then entering *COMP SIEVE D:* would expand to:

```
tcc -G -f87 -ml -nD:\ SIEVE
```

therefore compiling *SIEVE.C* under the large memory model while optimizing it for speed and while using the 8087 floating-point library, consequently sending the output file to *D:*.

There is one capability that TCC has but TC is lacking: that of generating assembly language output via the –S and –B switches. This assembly file can subsequently be assembled to create the same object that TCC would have generated normally (Borland recommends Microsoft MASM assembler Version 3.0 or later).

The –B allows assembly statements to be included within the C source code program, a practice known as INLINE assembly. Version 1.0 of Turbo C does not automatically assemble these instructions, but instead copies them into the assembly language output generated from compiling the C statements. Even without INLINE instructions, TCC generates an assembly output file when the –S switch is present. This file can be very useful to programmers familiar with 8086 machine language, especially when debugging a Turbo C program without a symbolic debugger. It is also interesting to those wishing to take a closer look at the kinds of assembly code different C instructions generate. You will make use of these features in your study of performance in Chapter 8.

Command-line linking can either be performed directly by invoking *TLINK*, or indirectly by using the powerful *MAKE* utility. *MAKE* functions are similar to the IDE in its handling of source and object file updates, except that *MAKE* has a more powerful command set. The *TLINK* and *MAKE* command-line switches are listed in Tables 2.2 and 2.3, respectively. Both are described in the *Turbo C Reference Guide*.

Table 2.1
Switches for Command-Line Turbo C

Switch	Description
-A	ANSI keywords only
-a	word alignment (default = byte)
-B	#asm inline assembler in source file
-C	nested comments on
-c	compile to object
-Dname	defines the symbol <name>
-Dname=value	(alternative form)
-d	merge duplicate strings (default)
-efilename	define filename as project file
-f	floating point emulation library (default)
-f878087	library
-f-	no floating point
-G	optimize for speed
-g#	stop after # warnings
-Idirname	include files contained in directory dirname
-i#	set identifier length to #
-j#	stop after # errors
-K	default chars to unsigned (default = signed)
-Ldirname	library files contained in directory dirname
-M	generate map file
-m<c,h,l,m,s,t>	set memory model to compact, huge, large, medium, small or tiny (default = small)
-N	include test stack overflow code
-ndirname	set output directory to dirname
-O	optimize for size
-ofilename	output object to filename.obj
-p	default to Pascal calling conventions
-r-	disable register variables (default = on)
-S	generate MASM compatible .ASM output
-Uname	undefine symbol name
-w-	display warnings off (default = on)
-wxxx	enable specific warnings
-w-xxx	disable specific warnings
-Y	use standard stack frame
-y	enable line numbers
-Z	enable register optimization
-zAname	name code class
-zBname	name data class
-zCname	name code segment
-zDname	name BSS segment
-zGname	name data group
-zPname	name code group
-zRname	name data segment
-zSname	name BSS group
-zTname	name BSS class
-1	generate 186/286 code (default = 8086)

Table 2.2
TLINK Switches

/m	generate a complete map file with all publics
/x	generate no map file at all
/i	output segments to executable even if they are empty
/l	include line numbers in load map
/s	generate detailed segment map
/n	no default libraries
/d	warn of duplicate symbols in libraries
/c	perform cas sensitive link

Table 2.3
MAKE Switches

-Dname	define label name
-Dname=string	(alternate form)
-Idirectory	specify directory for include files
-Uname	undefine any previously defined label
-s	do not print commands before execution
-n	print commands but do not execute them
-ffilename	use filename as the make file
-h	print make help
-?	(alternate form)

The Turbo C Language

As I have stated several times, the Turbo C compiler implements the proposed American National Standards Institute (ANSI) standard for the C language. At the current time, most C compilers in common use implement the lesser K&R standard. Below is a short list of some of the more important features which the ANSI standard adds to K&R:

- ANSI C is case sensitive (most Cs ignore the case of letters used in identifiers). This allows such conveniences as giving a structure definition and its invocation the same name. For example:

  ```
  struct DATA {
   int a, b, c;
  } data;
  ```

  Case sensitivity can be removed during the link step by forcing all labels to upper case. This is usually necessary when linking with object code of other languages, since most languages generate only upper case labels. Case sensitivity is always removed when using Pascal rule functions.

- Typing rules are more strongly enforced in ANSI C. Through the prototype declaration, the compiler knows the number and type of each argument. Function calls which violate these definitions are immediately flagged. As part of this type expansion, ANSI C fully implements the VOID type. This, by and large, obviates the need for a separate *lint* facility.

- ANSI C defines enumerated data types. Although not nearly as powerful as the user defined data types of Pascal, enumerated data types can enhance the readability of the resulting program.

Turbo C also adds a few enhancements of its own. These should be avoided if portability is a concern:

- "x""y" is treated the same as "xy". This is primarily used for continuation lines on character strings which run off the right margin. K&R C proposes a \ before the carriage return in such cases.

- Turbo C provides a Pascal-like call interface in addition to the normal C function interface. To support this, Turbo C defines the function declaration descriptors, PASCAL and CDECL. In addition, the default type can be selected from the Options menu. These two models differ primarily in the order that arguments are pushed onto the stack. This can be useful when linking object modules from other languages together with Turbo C. A third INTERRUPT type is useful in the generation of interrupt routines such as those discussed in Chapter 9.

- The *#asm* directive for the inclusion of inline assembler code in C source modules. Although this can be a very powerful tool, it is not nearly as necessary as it is in Turbo Pascal due to Turbo C's improved low-level support. I will cover the entire topic more thoroughly in Chapter 8.

- Finally, the Turbo C library differs from the standard UNIX library. Many of these stem from the differences between UNIX and the DOS operating systems. I will concentrate on these routines in Chapters 5 and 6. Other differences are related to Turbo C's excellent low-level support of the underlying PC hardware, which I cover in Chapter 7.

Intel Processors and the IBM PC

The 8086 family of microprocessors and the IBM PC and AT hardware impose their own features on Turbo C. Far from avoiding these topics, we will be investigating them fully in later chapters. Let us quickly review them here.

The 8086 microprocessor uses a segmented memory model. In this model an address consists of two parts: a segment and an offset. These two 16-bit values are combined to generate a single 20-bit address, corresponding to the 8086's 1 Megabyte address space (the 80286 has a 24-bit, 16-Megabyte address space, but can only access the first 1 Megabyte in Real Mode, the only mode which DOS and Turbo C currently support).

There are two types of pointer variables in Turbo C. *NEAR* pointers contain just an offset into a default segment, whereas *FAR* pointers contain both segment and offset. Turbo C includes the descriptors *NEAR* and *FAR* that can be applied to pointers and functions. In addition, the default pointer type is chosen by selecting the memory model from the *Options* menu. A detailed discussion of *NEAR* vs. *FAR* pointers follows at the end of Chapter 3, after you have had more time to familiarize yourself with C pointers in general.

The 8086 microprocessor can only perform simple arithmetic and then only on simple integers. To aid it in more complex operations and in the support of floating point numbers, the 8086 architecture includes a separate Numerical Processor (*NP*). The *NP* designed to work with the 8086, 8088 and 80186 processors is the 8087. The 80287 is essentially the identical *NP* redesigned to work with the 80286 and 80386. The 80387 is an improved *NP* compatible with the 80386.

Turbo C generates programs designed to utilize the *NP*, if present. The first time a floating point instruction is attempted, the library will look for the presence of a numerical processor. If one is found, it will be used for all subsequent floating point work. If an *NP* is not found, its function will be simulated by the Turbo C library using software routines. This represents an ideal, "smoke if you have 'em" solution.

Even though subsequent operations will use the *NP*, the initial test takes some small amount of time. If you know that the target machine has an *NP*, you may select the strictly 8087 library in the *Options* menu to generate slightly faster and smaller programs; however, a program generated in this manner will crash when executed on a machine without an *NP*.

In addition, the standard floating point library can be affected by making environment entry *87* equal to *Y* or *N* before execution, using the command:

```
SET 87=Y
```

or

```
SET 87=N
```

If set to *Y*, the library will use the *NP* without checking for its presence; if set to *N*, it will not be used, even if present.

The Turbo C compiler provides a high level of machine support, including such features as pseudo-variables, which refer directly to microprocessor registers, and to library routines devoted to special features of the 8086 architecture. The pseudo-variable *_AX* refers directly to the *AX* register, *_BX* to the *BX* register, etc. These features reduce the number of times that *INLINE* code must be resorted to.

Unlike the majority of C compilers for the IBM PC, Turbo C supports up to two register variables, which it houses in the SI and DI registers. Declaring register variables can result in significant improvement in execution performance. Register variables will be discussed as part of our optimization efforts in Chapter 8.

Conclusion

Turbo C is a very capable compiler. The Integrated Developement Environment offers a highly polished combination of power and ease of use. While implementing the ANSI standard for C, Turbo C also adds several features designed specifically to support the 8086 microprocessor and the IBM Personal Computer. I will investigate the most important of these features in the remainder of this book.

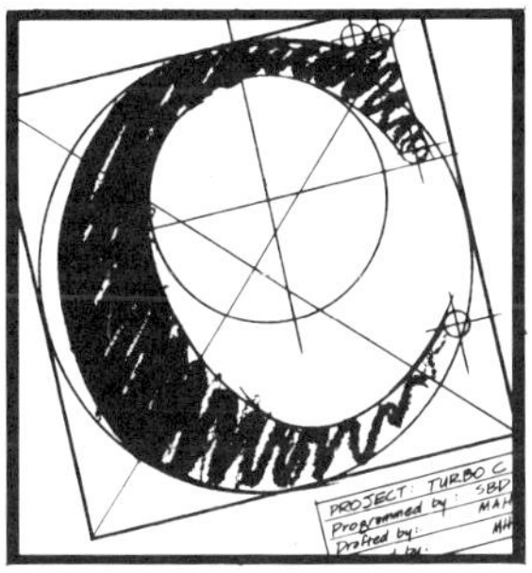

3 Pointer Variables

It is important for programmers in any language to have some feel for the way a computer accesses its random access memory (RAM), but nowhere is it more important than in C. No computer language, short of assembly code itself, makes more use of variable addresses. This, as much as anything, contributes to the power of C and to its large following in the programming community. To use Turbo C effectively, programmers must have a thorough understanding of microcomputer addressing.

A *bit* is the smallest piece of computer memory. A bit is capable of being in either of two states that we variously label as *1* and *0*, *YES* and *NO*, or *UP* and *DOWN*. Groups of eight bits are called *bytes*. A byte is the smallest piece of memory that most microprocessors can access at one time; it is the only size that the 8088 microprocessor in the IBM PC can access. Each byte of memory in the PC has a unique address. Much like houses along a crowded street, the address of each byte is one greater than its neighbor on one side and one less than its neighbor on the other.

Unlike any neighborhood in my home town, however, the decimal (base 10) numbers are inconvenient for numbering RAM locations. Although some use the octal (base 8) system, most programmers prefer hexidecimal (base 16) numbers. The hexidecimal numbering system uses the digits 0 through 9 and then continues with the digits *A* through *F* before restarting at 10. Either way, remember that the choice of numbering scheme is not a property of the computer itself, as all modern computers use simple binary (base 2) numbering.

Variables declared by the programmer within his program must all be assigned addresses in memory. Machine language programming requires the programmer to make these assignments himself. For example, the index to a *FOR* loop might be at location 0100, the variable used to hold user input might be called location 0101, etc. As you might imagine, such machine level programming puts a heavy burden on the programmer. Not only is it not at all obvious upon rereading the program that location 0100 is to be used as the index to the *FOR* loop and not location 0101, but it becomes quite a chore to remember which locations have already been allocated and which have not.

Fortunately, assemblers and compilers relieve the programmer of the task of assigning locations in memory. Modern programmers might define a byte variable, *INDEX,* which is to be used as the index to a *FOR* loop and another variable, *USER_INPUT,* to hold user input. It is now easy to keep memory locations separated. (It would be silly indeed to use a variable with the name *USER_INPUT* as the index to a *FOR* loop.) Of course nothing is fundamentally different. The index is still being stored at location 0100 and user input at 0101. It's only that the programmer no longer has to worry with such details.

Programmers who code only in BASIC or Pascal sometimes forget the correspondence between variables and the memory they occupy. Somehow they get the idea that *INDEX* is where the *FOR* loop index is stored, as if the variable *INDEX* had a significance in and of itself and not merely as a temporary pseudonym for a memory location. The good Turbo C programmer cannot ignore the fundamental addressing of the underlying machine. In this chapter we will examine all the ways that C allows the user access to the addressing of the underlying machine.

Simple Pointers

C allows the declaration of *pointer type* variables. A pointer variable is intended to hold the location of other variables. (I touched upon simple pointer declaration in Chapter 1, but I did not discuss it in any depth.) Pointers are declared much like any other variable. For example, in the listing below I have declared two character variables *INDEX* and *USER_INPUT*. Similarly, I have declared a pointer to a character, *POINTER*. It is the * in front of the variable name that indicates that the variable contains the address of a character rather than the character itself. Instead of repeatedly saying that *POINTER* is a pointer to a character, as a form of short hand, we often say that *POINTER* is of type *CHAR* * (which is read, *character pointer*).

```
char index, user_input;
char *pointer;
```

Let us go back to our example and take a closer look at what this means. If free data memory starts at location 0100, C would assign *INDEX* to address 0100 and *USER_INPUT* to address 0101. Pointer variables in Turbo C normally require two bytes, so POINTER is assigned locations 0102 and 0103. The next variable to be declared would be assigned memory starting at location 0104.

Figure 3.1

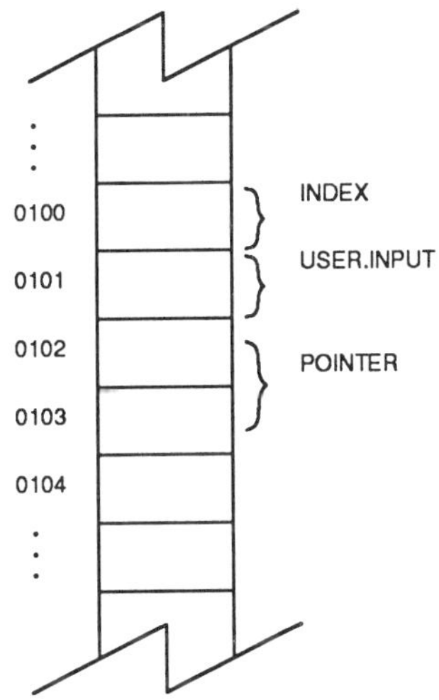

Remember, two things have happened so far: 1) Turbo C has set aside locations 0100 through 0103 for your three variables and agreed not to use that memory for something else, and 2) Turbo C has agreed that whenever you use the word *INDEX*, you are referring to the byte at location 0100, *USER_INPUT*, the byte at location 0102, etc. Assigning values to the simple variables presents no problem. You execute the C statements:

```
index = 'A';
user_input = 'B';
```

and everything is fine. But you cannot assign simple values to *POINTER* since such values are not of type *CHAR* *. The only thing you can assign it is the address of a character. This we can get with the &, the *take the address of,* operator. So we make the following assignments:

```
pointer = &user_input;
*pointer = 'Z';
```

The first expression sets *POINTER* equal to the address of the variable *USER_INPUT*, that is the value 0101. The second expression uses the * in a slightly different meaning than we used it in the declaration of *POINTER*. There we read * as *is a pointer to*, but in an assignment we read * as *at the location* *contained in*. Thus the second assignment stores the character *Z* at the location contained in *POINTER*, 0101. The net effect of these two instructions is the same as storing a *Z* into *USER_INPUT* directly.

Figure 3.2

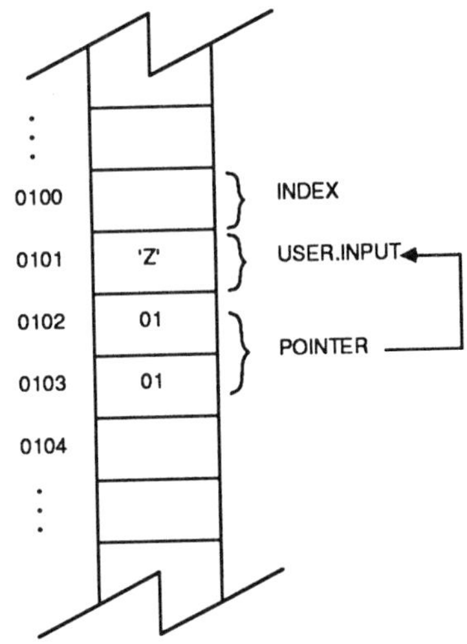

For the second assignment to be legal the types must match. Do they? Look back at the declaration of *POINTER*. Forgetting what we know about * and that it means *pointer to* and all, let's assume for a second that it were just part of the name. What type, then, would **POINTER* be? Type *CHAR*, which is exactly the type of 'Z'. In fact, **POINTER* can be used in any expression where a variable of type *CHAR* is allowed, because that's exactly what **POINTER* is.

We should not confuse pointers with integers. In general, they have nothing to do with each other. Simple integers are always two bytes in length. Pointers in Turbo C may be either two bytes or four bytes, depending on memory model, and have a format all of their own. Integers cannot be assigned directly to pointers and neither is the reverse allowed. This confusion is more common on machines in which pointers and integers have the same format, but even there they should not be interchanged.

Few of the operators which are defined for integers and characters are defined for pointers. There is one arithmetic operator, however, which is defined for pointer variables. What could possibly be the result of:

```
pointer + 1;
```

Logically, if we took the contents of POINTER (location 101) and add 1 we should get location 102. This is just exactly what happens here. If we wanted to access what was stored there, we would use the * to find the character pointed at:

```
*(pointer + 1);
```

This returns the character pointed at by the contents of (*POINTER* plus 1). In the equation, the parentheses are necessary since + is of lower precedence than *—leaving the parentheses off would cause Turbo C to return the result of 1 added to the character pointed at by *POINTER*. Adding the parentheses forces the * to operate on the results of the addition. If addition is defined then subtraction must also be defined, as should such short hand versions of addition as += and ++ and so they are. In our example, incrementing or decrementing *POINTER* has no particular significance but what if we had made the following declarations instead:

```
char index, user_input[5];
char *pointer;

pointer = &user_input[0];
*(pointer + 1);
pointer++;
```

Memory would then have the appearance:

Figure 3.3

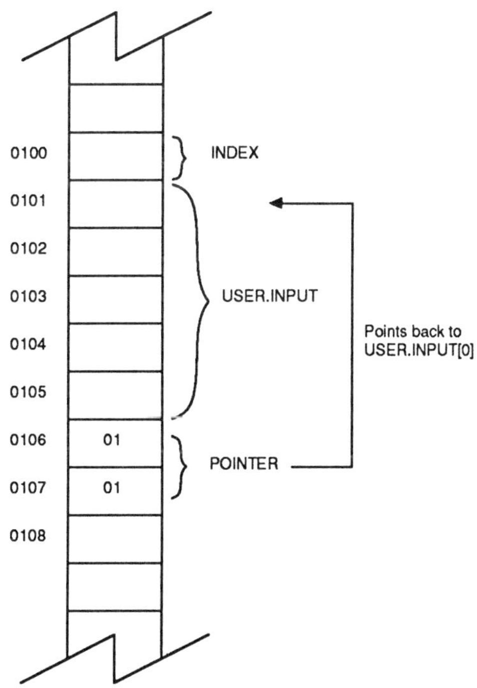

Now adding 1 to *POINTER* does have some meaning. The first assignment caused *POINTER* to point at the first member of the array *USER_INPUT*. Adding 1 results in the address of the next entry in *USER_INPUT*. Incrementing *POINTER* has the same significance, causing POINTER to "move over" from *USER_INPUT[0]* to *USER_INPUT[1]*. By repeatedly incrementing *POINTER*, we can cause it to scan the entire array.

Of course, there are two increment operators, the preincrement and postincrement, both of which are allowed on pointer variables. Since the result of incrementing a pointer variable is also of type pointer, the * operator may be applied to the result as in the following:

```
*++POINTER = 'A';
*POINTER++ = 'B';
```

Since ++ is defined for both pointers and the characters pointed at by pointers, the order of precedence above is not obvious. To maximize its usefulness, however, we say that the increment operator applies to the pointer in such as structure. The above equations are not equivalent, however. The first assignment increments *POINTER* over one entry and then stores the character *A* at that location. The second assignment first stores a *B* into the location pointed at by POINTER and then increments *POINTER* over to the next entry. The decrement operators are defined in a similar way.

This is a very powerful combination, allowing C programs to scan arrays, either assigning or examining the individual entries as they go. Not only is this construct conservative of source statements, but tends to generate very compact machine code.

We were very lucky in that **POINTER* and *USER_INPUT* were both of type *CHAR*, which happens to be one byte in length. What if they had been declared *INT* instead, allocating two bytes to each element of *USER_INPUT*. Simply adding a 1 to POINTER would not cause it to move properly from one element to the next. We would have to add two each time since integers occupy two bytes. This would require the programmer to keep track of the size of each variable type.

To avoid this, C wisely defines addition to pointers in terms of the size of the type of datum pointed at. That is, if POINTER were of type *INT **, then *POINTER++* would actually increment the contents of *POINTER* by 2. If it were of type *DOUBLE **, then by 8. We were not lucky at all—our analogy above would have worked no matter how **POINTER* and *USER_INPUT* were declared. Incrementing *POINTER* moves it correctly from one entry in the array to the next, no matter how large an entry in the array happens to be, as long as the type of the array and of **POINTER* match. This greatly increases the usefulness of the + and – operators on pointer types by relieving the programmer of the burden of worrying about word sizes.

Assuming that *INDEX* is an index into *USER_INPUT*, it may seem odd that the following two statements point to the same location and are of the same type (given that POINTER still contains the address of *USER_INPUT[0]*):

`*(pointer + index)` is equivalent to `user_input[index]`

If you consider for a minute what the effect of indexing into an array is, you can convince yourself easily that this is, in fact, the case. The correspondence is so strong that it is actually an equivalence! C makes the following substitution during compilation:

`user_input[index]` is replaced with `*(user_input + index)`

This is interesting. In my example, I had previously declared *POINTER* to be of type *CHAR ** and set it to the address of *USER_INPUT[0]*. The substitution on the right implies that *USER_INPUT* without the *[]* is of type CHAR * also. In fact, this is true. If you declare an array *CHAR USER_INPUT[]* you automatically declare a constant of type *CHAR ** with the name *USER_INPUT* (without brackets).

This is a very strong statement about C's perspective on life and represents a significant divergence from the outlook of other languages. Think for a minute at how Pascal and C both treat a common problem, that of passing arrays to functions. I said earlier that both Pascal and C pass by value, that is by passing the contents of the variable, and not by reference, passing the address of the variable (let's ignore *VAR* variables in Pascal for now). But Pascal runs into a problem when passing an array: should it pass each value of the array separately? What if the array is of considerable length?

C does not have this problem. If we make the following call:

```
char user_input[5], function ();

function (user_input);
```

C passes the value of *USER_INPUT*, which just happens to be the address of the array. C handles naturally what Pascal must make an exception for.

So, what then is the difference between an array of type *CHAR* and a pointer of type *CHAR* *? First, the array name is a constant and cannot be changed, whereas the pointer is a variable. But even more important, the array declaration allocates space for all of the elements of the array. The pointer declaration only allocates enough space to hold an address.

For example, consider the following two declarations and the equate:

```
char *a, b[10];

a = b;
```

The two variables *A* and *B* must be of the same type or Turbo C would complain about the equate. In fact, since both *A* and *B* are of type *CHAR* *, both can be indexed, that is, *A[I]* and *B[I]* are both legal statements. However, not only is *B* a constant and not subject to change (it would be illegal to place *B* on the left hand of the equals sign), but the declaration of *B* allocates some 10 bytes, space for 10 characters. The declaration of *A* only allocates space for the pointer.

To see an example use of pointers, let us examine our first pointer program. Prg3_1 is a useful programming aide. It inputs C source programs, adds line numbers and a "nesting level," truncates the result to fit on one line and outputs the result. The level of nesting is calculated by starting with 0, adding a 1 whenever a { is encountered and subtracting a one whenever } is seen. This can be used as a simple indicator of what blocks go where, logically, to aid in the interpretation of the program.

```
 1[ 0]: /* Prg 3_1 -- Pretty print for the remaining listings
 2[ 0]:     by Stephen R. Davis, '87
 3[ 0]:
 4[ 0]:   Prints standard input to standard output after adding line numbers,
 5[ 0]:   truncating to 80 chars, etc.  Used to generate listings in this
 6[ 0]:   book.
 7[ 0]: */
 8[ 0]:
 9[ 0]: #include <stdio.h>
10[ 0]: #define min(x,y) (x<y) ? x:y
11[ 0]:
12[ 0]: /*prototype definitions*/
13[ 0]: int main ();
14[ 0]: void nesting (unsigned *, char *);
15[ 0]:
16[ 0]: /*Main - read from STDIN one line at a time.  Reprint each
17[ 0]:           line to STDOUT after adding line numbers and nesting
18[ 0]:           levels*/
19[ 0]: main ()
20[ 0]: {
21[ 1]:     char string[256];
```

```
22[ 1]:     unsigned linenum,level,newlevel;
23[ 1]:
24[ 1]:     linenum = 0;
25[ 1]:     newlevel = 0;
26[ 1]:     while (gets(string)) {
27[ 2]:          level = newlevel;
28[ 2]:          nesting(&newlevel,string);
29[ 2]:          string[70] = '\0';
30[ 2]:          printf ("%3u[%2u]: ",++linenum,min(level,newlevel));
31[ 2]:          puts (string);
32[ 1]:     };
33[ 1]:
34[ 1]:     while (linenum++ % 66)  /*<-- if printer has no form feed*/
35[ 1]:          printf ("\n");
36[ 1]:     /*printf ("\f\n");*/    /*<-- if printer does have ff*/
37[ 0]: }
38[ 0]:
39[ 0]: /*Nesting - search the given string for "{" and "}".  Increment
40[ 0]:              nesting level on "{" and decrement on"}".*/
41[ 0]: void nesting (levelptr,stringptr)
42[ 0]:     unsigned *levelptr;
43[ 0]:     char *stringptr;
44[ 0]: {
45[ 1]:     do {
46[ 2]:          if (*stringptr == '{')
47[ 3]:               *levelptr += 1;
48[ 2]:          if (*stringptr == '}')
49[ 2]:               *levelptr -= 1;
50[ 1]:     } while (*stringptr++);
51[ 0]: }
```

Prg3_1 uses a common trick in Turbo C to simplify disk I/O. The Turbo C library routines require that files be opened before they can be accessed and closed when finished. At the same time, one of the fundamental concepts of UNIX is to treat hardware devices like files. Like UNIX, DOS considers the keyboard as a read-only file for input and the screen as a write-only file for output. It would be a terrible nuisance to have to "open" the keyboard and screen at the beginning of every program. Besides, if an error was reported upon opening the screen, how would the program tell the operator?

To avoid both problems, there are three files that are automatically opened at the beginning of every program. These are *STDIN*, the standard input device, *STDOUT*, the standard output device, and *STDERR*, the standard error device. *STDIN* defaults to the keyboard while *STDOUT* and *STDERR* default to the screen. While it is legal to use Turbo C's normal file routines to access these three files, it is not usually necessary. Most of the file access routines have a corresponding simpler sibling which automatically accesses *STDIN* or *STDOUT*. For example, while the routine *fprintf()* performs formatted output to any file. *printf()* automatically performs the identical function on *STDOUT*.

Rather than worrying with opening and closing files, Prg3_1 takes its input from *STDIN* using the function *gets()* and sends it to *STDOUT* via *printf()*. At first glance, this seems to make the program just slightly useless: nobody wants to retype an entire Turbo C program. Remember, however, that the default input and output can be redirected to any desired file at execution time using the < and > redirection operators. For example, to run this program on its own source and direct the result to the printer you would enter the DOS command:

```
prg3_1 <prg3_1.c |more
```

To direct the result to the terminal, simply leave off the *>lpt1* and *STDOUT* remains the monitor screen (you could also use the argument *>con,* which redirects screen output to itself).

These common tricks will allow us to avoid the complexities of DOS file handling until Chapter 5, where we specifically discuss DOS file access. Even after reading about DOS file handling, you may want to continue to use the < and > to get simple programs up and running in shorter time and with less bother.

Prg3_1 is not too complicated. Input is via the function *gets()* (line 26), which takes a line from *STDIN* and places it at the address in the single argument (*STRING*). If you examine the documentation for *gets(),* you will notice that it returns a 0 when it reaches the end of file, thus terminating the loop. You might also notice, however, that the input to *gets()* is described as a pointer to a character and yet we are passing it the name of a character array. This is an example of what we said above: an array name without the subscript represents the address of the array.

Notice also the call to *nesting()* (line 28). Rather than passing *NEWLEVEL* directly, *main()* passes the address of *NEWLEVEL. Nesting()* declares the corresponding argument as a pointer to an integer. This is necessary so that *nesting()* can change the value of *NEWLEVEL* in the parent routine. Since C passes by value, were we to pass just NEWLEVEL itself, its value in the calling program would not be changed no matter how it was modified in the function. By passing the address, *nesting()* can refer back to the copy of *NEWVALUE* stored in *main()* and change that one.

The other point to notice is how *nesting()* examines each character of the input array by assigning *STRINGPTR* to the beginning (in the call) and incrementing it through each character (line 50). As you shall see, this is a very common operation in C and is the normal way to scan an array or a string. Be sure that you completely understand this, and subsequent, programs. You will use these concepts again as each program builds upon its predecessors.

Prg3_1 is intended primarily for output to printers. Printers are page oriented devices, so it is desirable for programs which access them to leave the page at top of form when complete. This allows several files to be queued up for output without the need for the user to manually depress the "top of form" button in between listings. For those printers which support it, outputting a "form feed" at the end of the listing is all that is required. For those which don't, the alternative *WHILE* loop (lines 34–35) continues outputing line feeds until a multiple of 66 lines in all has been sent. You will need to change this number if your printer prints a different number of lines on one sheet of paper.

NOTE: In actuality, I had an ulterior motive in presenting Prg3_1. This program was used to generate all of the program listings in this book, including the listing of Prg3_1.c itself.

Strings in C

As we saw in Chapter 1, a character string in C is a sequence of ASCII characters enclosed in double-quotes. Every string is implicitly terminated with a 0. C handles a string just like the declaraction of arrays of characters. For example:

```
char *c;

c = "This is a string";
```

The appearance of the string causes C to allocate space for and store the 17 characters: the characters *T* through *g* and the terminating 0 The value of the string is the location where C stored it. What about the type of the string? If a string is like an array of characters, then a string must be of type *char []*, which, as we have seen, is equivalent to saying that a string is a pointer constant to a char, or is of type *CHAR **.

Assigning the string to the variable C has the effect of storing the address of the string into the variable. It is interesting to compare this with Turbo Pascal. Assigning one string to another causes Turbo Pascal to copy the entire string. C only copies the address of the string. This gives C the advantage of speed. It is obviously much faster to transfer one address than it is to move an entire string of characters. On the other hand, C does not define the powerful string operations of Pascal, such as + for concatenate, since C is not doing anything with the string at all.

There is one other comparison worth making. Both Turbo Pascal and C allow strings to be of (almost) any length, so both languages have the problem of knowing exactly how long a given string is. Turbo Pascal wants to make this as invisible as possible to the user, so it keeps the string length in the first byte of the string. The user is not allowed access to this character count. C does not keep any counts, but instead makes the rule that the character 0 (also called NULL) terminates all strings. It is the responsibility of the programmer to check for this null character in his programs to determine when the end of string has been reached.

If the value of "*This is a string*" is an address, then how do I get a single character when I want one? The single quote is reserved for this purpose, so that *A* returns the value of the ASCII character capital-A. This is referred to as a character constant and can be used anywhere that a *CHAR* is allowed. Never confuse *A* with "A" as they are not alike. ("A" is a pointer to a character string of 2 bytes; *A* is the value of a single character of 1 byte length.) C also defines some special characters to ease in the generation of strings. These are defined in Table 3.1.

There is one single exception to this rule and that concerns initializing static variables at declaration time. A character array should logically be initialized according to the following declaration:

```
char string [] = {'T', 'h', 'i', 's', ' ', 'i', 's',
' ', 'a', ' ', 's', 't', 'r', 'i',
'n', 'g', '\0'};
```

Table 3.1
Special ASCII Characters

\n	newline (carriage return - line feed)
\t	tab
\b	backspace
\f	form feed
\\	back slash (\)
\'	single quote (')
<CR>	ignored (used to extend strings over multiple lines)
\nnn	the ASCII char represented by the octal value nnn
\0xnnn	" " " " " " hex " "

These special characters are all treated by C as one ASCII character.
A backslash followed by any other character is ignored.

As you can see, for long strings this could get quite laborious so C makes one exeception and allows the following construct:

```
char string [] = {"This is a string"};
```

Some might argue that this is no exception at all since a string is, in fact, an array of characters. This point is not critical as you seldom see the first construct anyway.

Since strings are of type *CHAR* *, just like arrays, you might argue that strings can be indexed just like arrays, for example:

```
int i;
char c;

c = "0123456789" [i];
```

Oddly enough, you would be correct. Perhaps this is not so confusing if you keep in mind the substitution C makes whenever it encounters []. This statement takes the address of the the string, moves over *I* characters from the beginning of the string and fetches the character at that address, storing it into the variable C.

Pointer Constants

Indexing the above string and, in fact, any array, points up the fact that pointers can be constants as well as variables. The address of a string such as "0123456789" is viewed by C as a constant just like the integer 10 or the float 15.5. This, however, is a constant whose value has been assigned by the Turbo C compiler. C also allows the programmer to define pointer constants. For example, the following statements are more or less legal C:

```
char c, *ptr;

ptr = 100;                 /*almost legal*/
c = *ptr;

c = *100                   /*ditto*/
```

I said "more or less" because the above statements have a problem. The constant 100 defaults to type *INT* and cannot, therefore, point to anything. We must tell the compiler to convert 100 from its default type to the pointer type we desire. This is done via casts.

```
char c, *ptr;

ptr = (char *)100;              /*now legal*/
c = *ptr;

c = *((char *)100);             /*ditto*/
```

Although the nomenclature might seem a bit tortured, let us work it out for the second example. The cast (*CHAR* *) casts the constant at its right into type *pointer to character*. This leaves us with a pointer to a character whose value is 100. The outer * then resolves to the character pointed at by that pointer, i.e., the character pointed to by the character pointer 100 or, more simply stated, the character at location 100. The outer parenthesis insure that the order of evaluation is what we expect.

Seemingly we are going backward here. We started in the old days by assigning the addresses of variables ourselves. As technology improved, we allowed compilers to make these assignments for us. Now here we are accessing memory locations directly again! Pointer constants should only be used to access locations fixed in memory either by the PC's BIOS (Basic Input/Output System) ROM or by the hardware. The most notable example of the latter is the screen memory located at physical addresses *0xA0000, 0xB0000, or 0xB8000,* depending on adapter type and mode.

Array Indexing

You may have noticed that in C arrays are indexed starting with 0 rather than 1 as in most languages. Rather than a design criteria, this is the natural result of the equivalence that C makes between array indexes and pointer addition. You may have been dissappointed that the initial array index was not selectable by the programmer, as with Pascal. In fact, it is!

Consider the following code segment:

```
int space [11], *array;

array = &space [5];

array [-5] = 0;          /*<-- refers to space[ 0]*/
array [ 5] = 0;          /*                    [10]*/
```

First, you allocate space for an eleven-element array by allocating *SPACE [11]*. Rather than index off of the name *SPACE* as you might otherwise do, you declare a pointer *ARRAY* and set it equal to the address of the 5th element in *SPACE*. If you subsequently index off of *ARRAY*, then clearly the 0th element of *ARRAY* corresponds to the 5th element in *SPACE*. This implies, however, that the 0th element of *SPACE* corresponds to the –5th element of *ARRAY*. The diagram below describes the situation pictorially:

```
          -------------------------------------------------
space:  | 0  | 1  | 2  | 3  | 4  | 5  | 6  | 7  | 8  | 9  | 10|
          -------------------------------------------------
array:  |-5  |-4  |-3  | -2| -1| 0  | 1  | 2  | 3  | 4  | 5  |
          -------------------------------------------------
```

By carefully selecting which element to assign to the pointer *ARRAY*, we can design it so that we can index over any range desired. Notice that although this is not quite as clean as with Pascal, the resulting code might actually be just a tad more efficient since the index is not subtracted to acheive the index offset.

Complex Pointers

In the discussion so far we should have come away with the feeling that a pointer to a character is just as valid a variable type as any other. Just as surely, we can use the *&* to get the address of a pointer variable. Then you must be able to declare a pointer to a pointer to a character, type *CHAR* **. Additionally, we should be able to define pointers to user defined structures, unions, and enumerated types. In fact, the C programmer can declare a pointer to almost anything in C. I say "almost" not because I know of a case, but only because I feel sure there must be something you can't point to. Let's look at some of the more involved pointer structures.

It is not always easy, to make sense out of complex variable declarations. For example, consider the following:

```
int *ptr[10];
```

Does this declare a pointer to an array of integers or is this, instead, an array of pointers to integers? Contemplating these two possibilities for a second should convince you that the difference is considerable. (In fact, building such mental images of these types of hypothetical declarations is an excellent way to accustom yourself to the concept of complex pointers.) You use what is called the *right-left rule* for determining which it is to be.

The right-left rule can best be illustrated with an example. Consider the following declaration:

```
int (*var[5])[2];
```

To understand this declaration, you first find the variable name, *VAR*. You then look immediately to the right of the variable to find brackets, which indicate this is an "array of. . .". You next look immediately to the left of the variable name to find *, ". . .pointers to. . ." At this point you look back to the right of the parenthesis to see ". . .array of" and then finally to the *INT*, indicating ". . .integers". Therefore, in this example *VAR* is an "array of pointers to an array of integers".

Figure 3.4

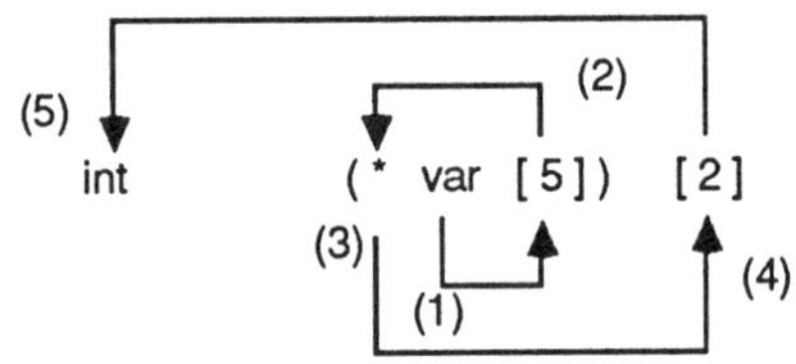

VAR (1) is an array (2) of pointers to (3) arrays (4) of integers (5)

Admittedly the above declaration is somewhat arbitrary, but complex pointer definitions can arise as elegant solutions to some fairly common problems. For example, suppose we desire to write a program that accepts a number between 1 and 12 and prints out the name of the corresponding month. A more or less classic solution appears as Prg3_2a.

```
/*Prg 3_2a - Print the names of the month
    by Stephen R. Davis, 1987

  The following program inputs a number between 1 and 12 and outputs
  the name of the corresponding month.  This program uses the
  "straightforward" approach.
*/

#include <stdio.h>

/*prototyping definitions --*/
int main (void);
unsigned putmonths (unsigned);

/*Main - input a number and output the corresponding name of the
         month*/
main()
{
    unsigned innum;

```

```
21[ 1]:     do {
22[ 2]:          printf ("Enter another month: ");
23[ 2]:          scanf ("%d",&innum);
24[ 1]:        } while (putmonths(innum));
25[ 0]: }
26[ 0]:
27[ 0]: /*Putmonths - given a number, print the name of the corresponding
28[ 0]:               month.  Return that number, unless it is out of range,
29[ 0]:               in which case, return a 0.*/
30[ 0]: unsigned putmonths(month)
31[ 0]:     unsigned month;
32[ 0]: {
33[ 1]:     switch (month) {
34[ 2]:     case 1:   printf ("January\n\n");
35[ 2]:               break;
36[ 2]:     case 2:   printf ("February\n\n");
37[ 2]:               break;
38[ 2]:     case 3:   printf ("March\n\n");
39[ 2]:               break;
40[ 2]:     case 4:   printf ("April\n\n");
41[ 2]:               break;
42[ 2]:     case 5:   printf ("May\n\n");
43[ 2]:               break;
44[ 2]:     case 6:   printf ("June\n\n");
45[ 2]:               break;
46[ 2]:     case 7:   printf ("July\n\n");
47[ 2]:               break;
48[ 2]:     case 8:   printf ("August\n\n");
49[ 2]:               break;
50[ 2]:     case 9:   printf ("September\n\n");
51[ 2]:               break;
52[ 2]:     case 10:  printf ("October\n\n");
53[ 2]:               break;
54[ 2]:     case 11:  printf ("November\n\n");
55[ 2]:               break;
56[ 2]:     case 12:  printf ("December\n\n");
57[ 2]:               break;
58[ 2]:     default:  printf ("Bye bye\n\n");
59[ 2]:               month = 0;
60[ 1]:     }
61[ 1]:     return(month);
62[ 0]: }
```

In this program, we output a prompt and accept input via the *scanf()* function call (lines 22–23). The function *putmonths()* is called to print the name of the corresponding month, which it does using a *SWITCH* statement. *Putmonths()* returns the number it receives unless the number is greater than 12, in which case it returns a 0. This 0 terminates the loop, causing the program to terminate.

This is deemed a classic solution since this program could be directly translated into almost any programming language. A less obvious, but much more elegant solution appears as listing Prg3_2b.

```
/*Prg 3_2b - Print the names of the month
    by Stephen R. Davis, 1987

  The following program demonstrates in a simplistic fashion
  the concept of arrays of pointers.  Almost unknown in other
```

```
 6[ 0]:   languages, this concept can save much code both in terms of size
 7[ 0]:   and speed.  Compare this program to the "Pascal-like" Program 3_2a
 8[ 0]:   which does the same thing. */
 9[ 0]:
10[ 0]: #include <stdio.h>
11[ 0]:
12[ 0]: /*prototype definitions --*/
13[ 0]: int main (void);
14[ 0]: unsigned putmonths (unsigned);
15[ 0]:
16[ 0]: /*an array of pointers to the names of the months*/
17[ 0]: char *months[] = {"Bye bye\n\n",
18[ 1]:                   "January\n\n",
19[ 1]:                   "February\n\n",
20[ 1]:                   "March\n\n",
21[ 1]:                   "April\n\n",
22[ 1]:                   "May\n\n",
23[ 1]:                   "June\n\n",
24[ 1]:                   "July\n\n",
25[ 1]:                   "August\n\n",
26[ 1]:                   "September\n\n",
27[ 1]:                   "October\n\n",
28[ 1]:                   "November\n\n",
29[ 0]:                   "December\n\n"};
30[ 0]:
31[ 0]: /*Main - input a number and output the corresponding name of
32[ 0]:          the month*/
33[ 0]: main()
34[ 0]: {
35[ 1]:     unsigned putmonths();
36[ 1]:     unsigned innum;
37[ 1]:
38[ 1]:     do {
39[ 2]:          printf ("Enter another month: ");
40[ 2]:          scanf ("%d",&innum);
41[ 1]:        } while (putmonths(innum));
42[ 0]: }
43[ 0]:
44[ 0]: /*Putmonths - given a number, print the corresponding month.  Return
45[ 0]:               the number, unless it is out of range, in which case,
46[ 0]:               return a 0*/
47[ 0]: unsigned putmonths(month)
48[ 0]:     unsigned month;
49[ 0]: {
50[ 1]:     if (month > 12)
51[ 1]:          month = 0;
52[ 1]:     printf(months[month]);
53[ 1]:     return(month);
54[ 0]: }
```

The beginning of this program (lines 17–29) is devoted to defining an array of pointers to characters called *MONTHS*. The zeroth location is occupied by a sign off message, but could just as easily have been a null string. The remaining positions are occupied by strings containing the names of the months. The main program is identical to the solution above, but the function *putmonths()* is reduced to some 4 lines. First the function makes sure that the value entered is within the range 0 to 12. Then *putmonths()* simply references the proper name of the month from the array and returns the value of the month.

This program brings up a couple of points. First, if *MONTHS* is an array of pointers to characters, then what is the type of *MONTHS[]*? This can best be answered by reexamining the declaration while pretending that the variable name is *MONTHS[]*. You see that *MONTHS[]* is a pointer to characters, which is what the function *printf()* wants to see.

The second point is that this solution to the problem is more elegant than the first. Admittedly, elegance is a subjective term, but for our purposes we shall agree that an elegant solution is one that executes faster and/or generates less code. The second solution generates less code and executes faster.

The observant reader might note at this point that there was no need to resort to such shennanigans; we could have declared *MONTHS* to be a character matrix with the number of the month in one direction and the letters of the months in the other. Any language would have allowed such a construct. Such a matrix solution would have worked reasonably well for the example of the names of the months since they are all of approximately the same length, but such matrix solutions are horribly wasteful when the lengths of the various entries differ greatly. Let's compare how computer memory appears under the two solutions (Figure 3.5).

Such matrix solutions are not even possible when the maximum length of the strings is not known in advance, since you don't know how large to make the second index.

Pointers to Structures

Much as we declared pointers to simple variable types above, we can just as easily declare pointers to more complex types such as structures. Consider the following structure definition:

```
struct address {
                int number;
                char name[15];
               } my, *ptr1;

struct address *ptr2;
```

Here we have defined a structure, *ADDRESS*. Simultaneously, we have declared one and called it *MY* (presumably, "*my address*"). Next to it we have declared a pointer to such a structure *ADDRESS* and called it *PTR1*. Notice that *PTR2* is an equivalent definition.

Figure 3.5

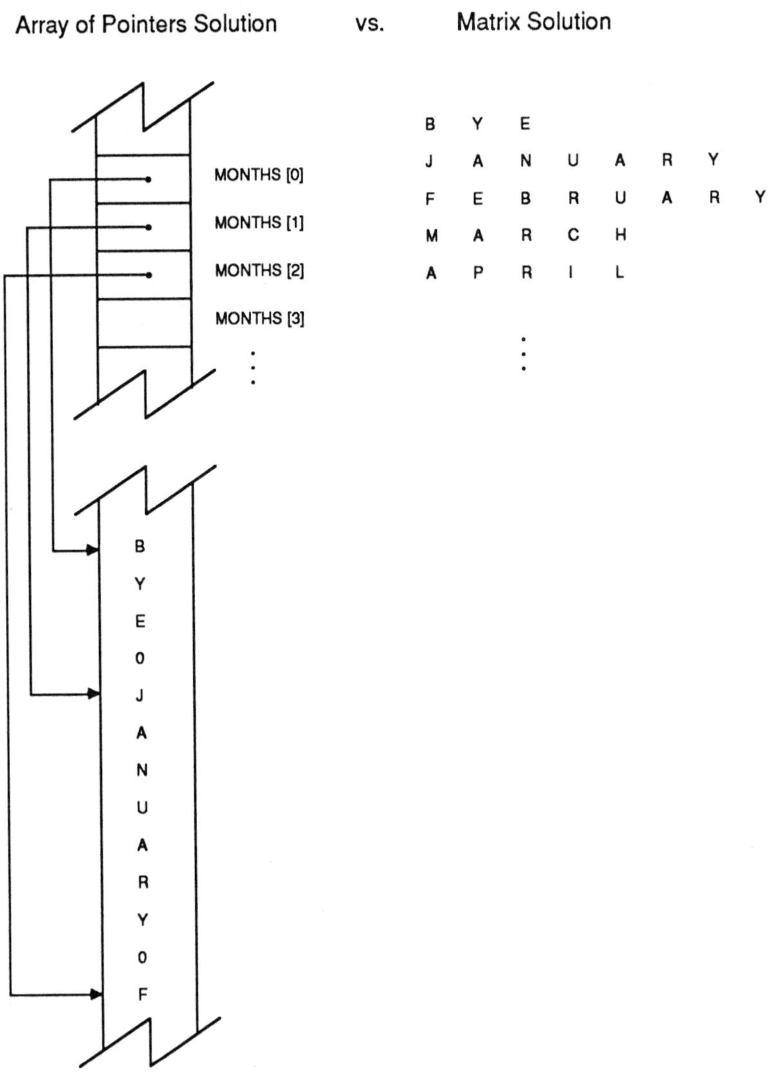
Array of Pointers Solution
vs.
Matrix Solution
MONTHS [0]
MONTHS [1]
MONTHS [2]
MONTHS [3]
B Y E 0 J A N U A R Y 0 F
B Y E
J A N U A R Y
F E B R U A R Y
M A R C H
A P R I L

Given that *PTR1* contains the address of a valid structure of type *ADDRESS*, how do we gain access to its elements, *NUMBER* and *NAME*? When we want to access the elements of the structure *MY*, we use the same syntax as in Turbo Pascal, namely *MY.NUMBER* and *MY.NAME*. Likewise, you may be able to replace *MY* with anything of the same type. *MY* is of type *STRUCT ADDRESS* and so is **PTR1*. Therefore, the elements of the structure pointed at by *PTR1* are *(*PTR1).NUMBER* and *(*PTR1).NAME*. The parentheses are necessary to force C to evaluate the asterisk before evaluating the period.

Although this is true and some programmers code things this way, this is a somewhat clumsy syntax. Just as with the indexing of arrays above, C makes an equivalence here to allow programmers to adopt a more readable syntax:

`PTR1 -> name;` is equivalent to `(*PTR1).name;`

Wherever C finds the syntax on the left, it replaces it with that on the right. Programmers are free to use whichever form they prefer. This book uses the syntax on the left.

So what about *PTR1++*? Just as we claimed above, addition to pointers is always defined in terms of the size of the thing pointed at. Adding 1 to *PTR1* has the effect of moving it down in memory some 17 bytes (the size of *STRUCT ADDRESS*). Since we can declare arrays of *STRUCT ADDRESS*, everything I said about arrays and pointers to *CHAR*s and *INT*s applies equally well to structures.

Pointers to Functions

Not only can the programmer manipulate the address of data, but also the address of functions. The following declarations declare a function that returns an integer and a pointer to a function which returns an integer:

```
int func();
int (*funcptr)();
```

All of the parenthesis are required. The parenthesis following *FUNC* indicate that *FUNC* is a function. The remainder of the declaration indicates that function *FUNC* returns an integer result. Remember that in declarations we read *()* as *a function which returns a*.

Now use the right-left rule to evaluate the second term. The parenthesis around *FUNCPTR* force the * to be evaluated before the *()*, so *FUNCPTR* is a *pointer to* *a function which returns an integer*. (Without the inner parenthesis to influence the order of evaluation, *FUNCPTR* would be a *function which returns a pointer to an integer*.) We have actually declared a pointer variable which is to hold the address of a function.

I noted above that when an array appeared without the brackets it referred to the address of the array. By analogy you could argue that a function name appearing without the paretheses refers to the address of the function. In fact, this is the case so that the following assignment is perfectly valid:

```
int func(), (*funcptr)();

funcptr = func;
```

This assigns to *FUNCPTR* the address of the function *func()*. Of course, this declaration says nothing about type and number of arguments that *FUNC()* takes. As you already know, ANSI C allows this to be specified also:

```
int func (int), (*funcptr)(int);
```

Since we now know that *FUNC()* requires one integer argument, we could call it with the statement:

```
(*funcptr)(10);
```

So why have such a thing? Not everything that can be done is worth doing. One of the most common uses for pointers to functions is to pass one function to another one. In saying this, I do not mean passing the results of one function to another, but actually passing one function to another. To see how this might be useful, let us consider several examples.

First, Prg3_3a is a function that calculates the numerical (also called definite) integral of a function. One of the earliest concepts taught in calculus is that of integration. At least initially, integration is explained in terms of *the area under the curve*. That is, assume you have a function *F(x)* and you plot it. That plot might look something like Figure 3.6. The integral of *F(x)* from *a* to *b* is given by the area bounded by *a, b, F(x)* and the x-axis, which appears shaded in the figure.

Figure 3.6

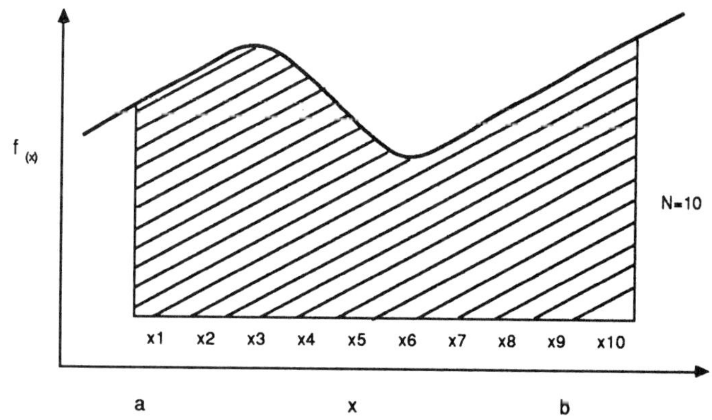

Of course, from that point students go on to learn techniques of integration that do not rely on pictorial models. Later on, when asked to build a program to take the numerical integral of a function, they think in terms of these mathematical manipulations and tend to conclude that it cannot be done. They forget about those simple pictures presented to them when the concept of integration was first being learned. In fact, writing a program to approximate the numerical integral by directly measuring the area under the curve is quite straightforward.

Let's go back to our picture and decide how we might approximate an integral by hand. We would probably divide the range *[a,b]* into *N* equal intervals. You could then draw rectangles with sides at these intervals whose heights are the value of the function at the midpoint. The area of a rectangle is simply the product of the width and the height. By calculating the areas of all these little rectangles separately and adding them up, we arrive at the area under the curve (Figure 3.7).

To turn this into a computer program, let us call the left boundary x_0, the first interval x_1, the second x_2 and so on until we have x_N at the right boundary. Rather than calculate the value of the function at the middle of each rectangle, we approximate it by averaging the value of *F(x)* at the left and right sides. The area of any given rectangle is then given by the equation:

```
AREAi = (xi+1 - xi) * [F(xi) + F(xi+1)]/2
```

Figure 3.7

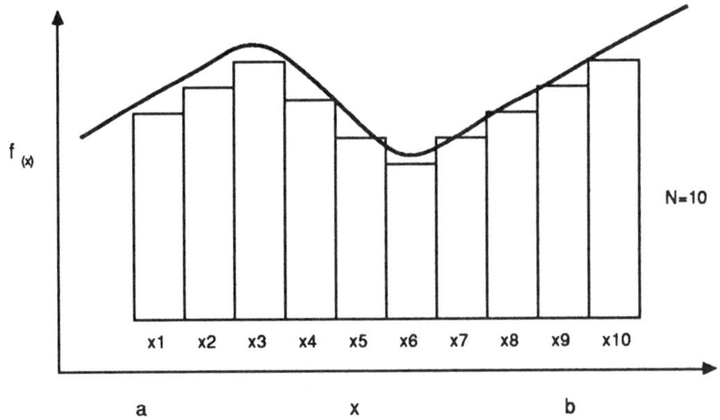

Of course, the first term is merely the width of each subinterval. Since we have divided the interval *[a,b]* equally, this value is the same for all subintervals. Also, notice that each interior *F(xi)* appears twice: once paired with *F(xi+1)* and once with *F(xi-1)*. Only *F(a)* and *F(b)* are not paired with any other entry. Therefore, if you add up the equations for all the rectangles and reduce the resulting equation you get:

```
AREA = spacing * [F(b)/2 + F(a)/2 +   Sigma     F(xi)]
                                    i=1 to N-1

where spacing = (b - a) / N
```

Assuming that *F(x)* can be evaluated at each of the subintervals, it should be easy to write a program to implement the above equation. Prg3_3a is such a program as it might be written by a programmer new to C. The function *main()* in this case requests the range of *x* and the value of *N* to use to calculate the integral. If the range is 0, execution stops (lines 66–67). The function *integrate()* is called to actually perform the calculation and the results are printed (line 68). For comparison, the actual value of the integral is printed on the next line (line 70).

Integrate() is a more or less direct implementation of the equation given above. First the spacing and the value of *F(x)* at the left and right end points (lines 28–29) is calculated, then the value of *F(x)* at each *xi* is accumulated (lines 30–32). Finally, the two are multiplied together to get the final result (line 34). To test the program, a sample *F(x)* and its integral, *answer()*, are provided (lines 41–50). The reader is free to provide his own sample *F(x)*.

```
/*Prg3_3a -- Integration of a user function 'func'
   by Stephen R. Davis, 1987

  This function integrates a user function 'func' using the trapezoid
  rule to evaluate a definite integral over the range 'a' to 'b' by
  dividing it into 'steps' number of discrete intervals.
*/

#include <stdio.h>

/*prototype definitions --*/
double integrate (double, double, unsigned);
double func (double);
double answer (double);
int main (void);

/*Integrate - evaluate the definite integral of a user function
              'func' over the interval 'a' to 'b' by using the
              trapazoid rule on 'steps' number of subintervals*/
double integrate (a, b, steps)
    double a,b;
    unsigned steps;
{
    double func ();
    unsigned i;
    double integral, spacing, x;

    spacing = (b - a) / steps;          /*divide the interval evenly*/
    integral = (func(b) + func(a)) / 2.;
    for (i = 1,x = a; i < steps; i++) { /*accumulate value over...*/
         x += spacing;                  /*...the interval*/
         integral += func(x);
    }
    return (integral * spacing);
}

/*Func - a test function to integrate and its value.
         (the integral of x**2 is equal to (x**3)/3).  Replace
         func() and answer() with any desired function/integral
         pair and recompile.*/
double func (x)
    double x;
{
    return (x*x);
}
double answer (x)
    double x;
{
    return x*x*x/3.;
}

/*Main - test routine integrate() w/ 'func'at various starting
         value, stoping value and step size.  Compare with 'value'
         for accuracy.*/
main ()
{
    float a,b;
    unsigned steps;

    printf ("Enter starting x, ending x and number of steps\n");
    printf ("   (exit by entering starting x equal ending x)\n");
    for (;;) {
```

```
            printf (">");
            scanf ("%f %f %d", &a, &b, &steps);
            printf ("a = %f, b = %f, steps = %d\n", a, b, steps);
            if (a == b)
                 break;
            printf ("Integral is %f\n", integrate((double)a,
                                              (double)b, steps));
            printf ("(actual value is %f)\n", answer(b) - answer(a));
      }
}
```

The problem with this implementation is that in order for *integrate()* to invoke the function *F(x)*, it must call it something, in this case *func()*. If you later wanted to include this *integrate()* into some larger program, you would have to remember to call the function to be integrated *func()*. What if more than one function is to be integrated? Would you need several versions of *integrate()*, each calling a different name? And why should we be restricted in what we call our function? Why can't *integrate()* be more adaptable? Prg3_3b represents a more elegant, C-ish solution, which does not have these problems.

```
/*Prg 3_3b -- Integration of a user function using Trapezoid Rule
  by Stephen R. Davis

  This program demostrates how by allowing a function to be passed
  to another function, C allows some very general purpose routines
  to be designed.  This is a more general routine than that of 3_3a
  since it makes no restrictions on the name of the user function.
  This is the type of function which could be included in a C library
  for later use.
*/

#include <stdio.h>

/*prototype definitions --*/
double integrate (double (*)(double), double, double, unsigned);
double func (double), answer (double);
int main (void);

/*Integrate - evaluate the definite integral of the function pointed a
              by 'fn' by applying the trapezoid rule to the function
              over the range 'a' to 'b' by dividing it into 'steps'
              number of intervals.*/
double integrate (fn, a, b, steps)
    double (*fn)(),a,b;
    unsigned steps;
{
    unsigned i;
    double integral,spacing,x;

    spacing = (b - a) / steps;
    integral = ((*fn)(b) + (*fn)(a)) / 2;
    for (i = 1,x = a; i < steps; i++) {
         x += spacing;
         integral += (*fn)(x);
    }
    return (integral * spacing);
}

/*Experiment - a sample user program to integrate.  (It has renamed
```

```
40[ 0]:                    from 'func' to avoid any confusion with the pointer
41[ 0]:                    to a function 'fn' in 'Integrate')*/
42[ 0]: double experiment (x)
43[ 0]:      double x;
44[ 0]: {
45[ 1]:      return (x*x);
46[ 0]: }
47[ 0]: double answer (x)
48[ 0]:      double x;
49[ 0]: {
50[ 1]:      return x*x*x/3.;
51[ 0]: }
52[ 0]:
53[ 0]: /*Main - same as before*/
54[ 0]: main ()
55[ 0]: {
56[ 1]:      float a,b;
57[ 1]:      unsigned steps;
58[ 1]:
59[ 1]:      printf ("Enter starting x, ending x and number of steps\n");
60[ 1]:      printf ("     (exit by entering starting x equal ending x)\n");
61[ 1]:      for (;;) {
62[ 2]:           printf (">");
63[ 2]:           scanf ("%f %f %d", &a, &b, &steps);
64[ 2]:           printf ("a = %f, b = %f, steps = %d\n", a, b, steps);
65[ 2]:           if (a == b)
66[ 2]:                break;
67[ 2]:           printf ("Integral is %f\n", integrate(experiment,
68[ 2]:                                         (double)a, (double)b, steps));
69[ 2]:           printf ("(actual value is %f)\n", answer (b) - answer (a));
70[ 1]:      }
71[ 0]: }
```

The program seems identical except for one important point. This *integrate()* accepts the function to be integrated as one of its arguments. When invoked, *main()* passes the address of the test function *experiment()* to *integrate()*. *Integrate()* calls this pointer to a function by the name FN and declares it on line 24. Notice that **FN* must be surrounded by parentheses when called to force the order of evaluation just as with the declaration (lines 31 and 34).

This version of *integrate()* is much more suitable. Not only does *integrate()* put no restrictions on the name of the function to be integrated, but multiple functions can be integrated using the same routine. Once this program has been tested with various different *F(x)* functions, it can be included in our own personal library for future use with any user supplied function.

By the way, try Prg3_3b on several different functions for several different values of *N*. As *N* grows larger the answer becomes more and more accurate, but the compute time grows. If *N* becomes too large, an overflow occurs calculating the sigma (line 34). Repeat the test with functions that fluctuate more wildly than *x*-squared. Notice that a larger *N* is necessary to achieve accurate results.

A second, more classic, example of the use of pointers to functions is that of the perfectly general bubble sort. A version of this routine first appeared in Kernighan and Ritchie's *The C Programming Language*. K&R relied on the fact that the bubble sort accesses the data being sorted in only two ways: once to compare two entries, and again, when necessary, to exchange two neighboring locations. However, K&R assumed that neighboring entries were actually physically adjacent in memory. Our even more general version allows the user the further flexibility of defining what "next" means. If the user can provide routines to perform these functions, then the generalized bubble sort can sort any data type. This is a powerful statement and one not easily appreciated, but none the less true.

```
/* Prg 3_4 - the classic Bubble Sort using user-supplied routines
     by Stephen R. Davis, 1987

   The bubble sort routine first appeared in Kernighan and Ritchie as
   an example of the passing of one routine to another.  This is a
   further generalization of that routine.  This version is as
   completely general as is possible.

   SORT () can sort ANY data type, including any user defined
     structure, if provided with three routines: one to compare two
     entries, another to swap two entries and a third to sequence from
     one entry to the next.  The details of these routines are given
     below.  Sort returns a 0 if the sort is successful and a -1
     otherwise.

   COMPARE(ptr1, ptr2)
     receives two pointers to the structures to be compared.
     Returns a -1 if *ptr1 < *ptr2, a 0 if *ptr1 == *ptr2, and 1 if
     *ptr1 > *ptr2 for ascending order and the opposite for
     descending.

   SWAP (ptr1, ptr2)
     receives two pointers to structures.  Upon returning *ptr2 is
     in the location of *ptr1 and visca versa.  If ptr1 == ptr2 then
     swap() has no effect.  Swap() returns a 0 if the exchange is
     successful and a non-zero otherwise.

   SEQUENCE (ptr1)
     receives a pointer to an entry.  Returns a pointer to the
     next entry.  Notice that the definition of "next" is left to
     the user.  If ptr1 == 0, sequence() returns the first entry.
     If sequence () == 0 then the end of sequence has been reached.
*/

#include <stdio.h>

/*prototype definitions --*/
int sort (int (*)(void *, void *), int (*)(void *, void *),
          void *(*)(void *));

/*Sort - implement bubble sort*/
int sort (compare, swap, sequence)
     int (*compare)(void *, void *), (*swap)(void *, void *);
     void *(*sequence)(void *);
{
     int flag;
```

```
    void *p1, *p2;

    do {
         flag =  0;
         p2 = (*sequence)(0);                /*starting w/ first entry...*/
         while (p1 = p2, p2 = (*sequence) (p2)) /*...sequence thru*/
         {
              if ((*compare)(p1, p2) > 0) {       /*if p1 > p2...*/
                   if ((*swap)(p1, p2)) return -1;/*...swap p1 & p2*/
                   flag = 1;
              }
         }
      } while (flag);                        /*stop when all are in order*/
    return 0;
}


/*simple example of using SORT() --
  let's simply sort an array of integers called "data" declared
  globally with N entries.  Convince yourself that the 3 routines
  below actually operate according to the description above.  Then
  prove that it works at all by executing the program.
*/

#define N 10
int data [N];


int compare (i1, i2)
     int *i1, *i2;
{
     if (*i1 != *i2) return (*i1 > *i2) ? 1: -1;
     return 0;
}

int swap (i1, i2)
     int *i1, *i2;
{
     int temp;

     temp = *i1;
     *i1 = *i2;
     *i2 = temp;
     return 0;
}

void *sequence (i)
     int *i;
{
     if (i)
          if (i == &data[N - 1])         /*if last entry...*/
               return 0;                 /*...return a 0; else...*/
          else
               return ++i;               /*...return the next entry*/
     else
          return data;                   /*return first entry*/
}

main ()
{
     int i;

     printf ("Enter a sequence of %d integers\n", N);
     for (i = 0; i < N; i++)
```

```
111[ 1]:          scanf ("%d", &data[i]);
112[ 1]:      if (sort (compare, swap, sequence))
113[ 1]:          printf ("Error during sort!\n");
114[ 1]:      printf ("\n\nHere is the sorted sequence\n");
115[ 1]:      for (i = 0; i < N; i++)
116[ 1]:          printf ("%d  ", data[i]);
117[ 0]: }
```

The bubble sort algorithm (lines 49–60) makes multiple passes through the data. On each pass it compares each entry with its neighbor. If the next entry is smaller than the current, it swaps the two and continues. Once it reaches the end of the list it starts over again. If the program ever makes it all the way through the list without having swapped any entries, then the list is sorted and it terminates.

Sort() accepts three arguments, all of which are pointers to functions, two of which return integers and one of which (**SEQUENCE()*) returns a pointer to a void. **COMPARE()* decides if the first entry is less than, greater than or equal to the second entry. If the answer is *greater than*, **SWAP()* replaces the first entry with the second and visa versa. *Sort()* traverses the list by using the routine **SEQUENCE()*, which when passed a pointer to the current entry, returns a pointer to the next. **SEQUENCE()* returns a pointer to the first entry when given a 0 and returns a 0 when passed the last entry in the list. The variable *FLAG* is used to indicate when the list is completely sorted. The program terminates when *sort()* can traverse the entire list with *FLAG* remaining 0.

A particularly simple example of *compare()*, *swap()*, and *sequence()* are provided, which sorts a string of integers. Although this may seem much ado about nothing (why so much fuss over sorting integers?), consider how general this actually is. Imagine some user defined type and build these three routines for it. For example, *sort()* could sort user defined enumerated types, structures, street addresses, full names, etc. It could even sort cities by geographical location, if you can define a suitable *compare()* function to decide when one city is *less than* another and a *sequence()* function to move you from one city to the next. In fact, we will use this routine to sort *IRS* data in Chapter 4.

Notice how *sort()* defines **COMPARE()*, **SWAP()*, and **SEQUENCE()* to be pointers to *VOID*. Remember in our earlier discussion that we may declare a function of type *VOID* to indicate that it returned nothing or its arguments to be of type *VOID* to indicate that it had none, but what is a pointer to type *VOID*? A pointer to nothing? Not quite.

It is more like declaring a pointer to an unknown type. Any pointer value can be assigned to a VOID * variable type and visa versa. Since the type of the target is unknown, however, VOID pointers cannot be resolved with the * operator nor can they be operated on by the ++, --, or any other form of addition normally defined for pointers. This is particularly useful in defining general library routines, which will be receiving and returning pointers to unspecified data types. Although not necessary, it is good practice to cast these pointers into the proper type in the calling routine. We will follow this practice.

One last area where pointers to functions find particular use is in arrays of functions. Let's apply the right-left rule to the following declaration:

```
int prog0(int), prog1(int), prog2(int), prog3(int),prog4(int);
int (*funcs[5])(int) = {prog0, prog1, prog2, prog3, prog4};
int argument, index, answer;

        .
        .
        .
answer = (*funcs[index])(argument);
        .
        .
        .
```

If we follow the declaration we see that *FUNCS* is *an array of pointers to functions*. The five elements of *FUNCS* have been set equal to the address of *prog0()*, *prog1()*, etc. In the example call, the *INDEX*th function is being called with the integer *ARGUMENT*. In order for this technique to work, all of the functions pointed to must accept the same type and number of arguments and return the same type of result; however, when this is the case, such program structures can result in both smaller and faster code.

One common application of this technique is that of user shells. Such shells present a menu of possible actions to the user and await his selection. Depending on the number entered, the shell performs one of several, usually dissimilar, functions. The example program below demonstrates such an application, that of calling a sequence of functions rapidly. User input, either from the keyboard or from a file via the < pipe operator is printed out in 5 different formats by invoking the five different functions indirectly from an array. Although we could just as easily have invoked each function explicitly, the point here is to demonstrate the technique.

```
/* Prg 3_5 -- Reformat the input stream in one of 5 ways
     by Stephen R. Davis, 1987

   The input stream is output to stdout using one of 5 programs
   to perform the task.  This is primarily meant as an example
   of using arrays of functions.  Notice that this is really a
   form of self modifying code.
*/

```

```
#include <stdio.h>

/*prototype definitions --*/
int main (void);
void putlower (char *);
void putupper (char *);
void puthex (char *);
void putoctal (char *);
void putdecimal (char *);


/*an array of pointers to functions returning nothing (void)*/
char *fnames[5] = {"lower case    ",
                   "upper case    ",
                   "hex output    ",
                   "octal output  ",
                   "decimal output"};
void (*func[5])() = {putlower,
                     putupper,
                     puthex,
                     putoctal,
                     putdecimal};

/*Main - input a string a output it in 5 different ways*/
main ()
{
    char string[256];
    int choice;

    printf ("Input a character string (up to 15 characters)"
            "followed by return\n\n");
    while (gets(string)) {
         string [15] = '\0';
         for (choice = 0; choice < 5; choice++) {
              printf ("%s:  ", fnames[choice]);
              (*func[choice])(string);
              printf ("\n");
         }
    }
}

/*example output routines*/
void putlower (ptr)
    char *ptr;
{
    for (; *ptr; ptr++)
         printf ("  %c,", tolower(*ptr));
}
void putupper (ptr)
    char *ptr;
{
    for (; *ptr; ptr++)
         printf ("  %c,", toupper(*ptr));
}
void puthex (ptr)
    char *ptr;
{
    for (; *ptr; ptr++)
         printf ("%3x,", (unsigned) *ptr);
}
void putoctal (ptr)
    char *ptr;
{
    for (; *ptr; ptr++)
```

```
74[ 1]:          printf ("%3o,", (unsigned) *ptr);
75[ 0]: }
76[ 0]: void putdecimal (ptr)
77[ 0]:     char *ptr;
78[ 0]: {
79[ 1]:     for (; *ptr; ptr++)
80[ 1]:          printf ("%3u,", (unsigned) *ptr);
81[ 0]: }
```

The five different display functions are defined at the bottom of the listing (lines 51–80). The array is initialized at declaration (lines 27–31). Input is made from *STDIN* until end-of-file (line 41) and passed to the output functions indirectly (line 45).

One pitfall with invoking functions indirectly from arrays: the program must make absolutely sure that the index being used is within the legal range of the array. If the index is allowed to exceed this range, the program will surely crash.

Argv and Argc

In our programs so far we have always written *main()* with no arguments. In fact, *main()* is allowed two optional arguments: *ARGC* and *ARGV[]*. The standard declaration is:

```
int main (argc, argv)
    int argc;
    char *argv[];
```

When a program is invoked, these two arguments are set up before *main()* is given control. *ARGC* is the count of the number of arguments in the command line (not counting redirection specifiers) and *ARGV* is an array of pointers to these arguments. This mechanism provides the user program access to any arguments entered on the command line with the program name. (There is, in fact, a third argument, *CHAR *ENVPTR[]*, which is an array of pointers to the strings defined in the environment. I will describe this argument further in chapter 8, after discussing the environment.)

There are a few points of secondary interest here. The above declaration is sometimes written:

```
int main (argc, argv)
    int argc;
    char **argv;
```

As pointed out above, the principle difference between an array declaration and a pointer is that the array declaration allocates space for the array and the pointer declaration does not. However, when an array is being passed to a routine, the space has already been allocated by the caller. This is why nothing appears between the brackets in the first example. Whatever value you might have put there, C will ignore it. In an argument definition, therefore, there is no difference at all between declaring a variable to be a pointer and an array. In general, it is best to declare the variable the same way as it is to be used within the program.

The *ARGC/ARGV* convention was first invented on UNIX versions of C. Under UNIX and DOS 3.x the name of the program itself is known and, therefore, is included in both *ARGC* and *ARGV*. *ARGV[0]* points to a string containing the full path of the calling program. Unfortunately, this information is not immediately accessible from DOS 2.x. In the interests of portability, Turbo C goes ahead and counts the program itself but places a pointer to a null string in *ARGV[0]* when under DOS 2.x. While this is not a completely satisfactory solution, it maximizes compatibility with UNIX C and later versions of DOS.

Like UNIX, DOS interprets redirection specifiers itself. When a program is called with a *<file1*, the default input device is automatically redirected to *file1* before the program ever receives control. The *<file1* does not appear as any of the *ARGV*'s and is not counted in *ARGC*. The applications program does not see the redirection specifier and cannot tell that input has been redirected. This is exactly as with UNIX C.

When executing programs from the Interactive Development Environment (IDE), the arguments to a program are specified by opening the *Options* window and selecting *Args*. For reasons not completely clear to me, pipes are not interrupted properly when entered from within the IDE, however.

Let us simply take a look at the input arguments using the following example program:

```
/*Prg 3_6 - Print out the Arguments to the Program
    by Stephen R. Davis, 1987

  More or less trivial example of accessing the arguments to
  a C program; however, this does allow the user a simple means
  of testing what various things look like to the program.  Note
  that argv[0], normally the program name, is empty under DOS 2.x.
*/

#include <stdio.h>

main (argc, argv)
    int argc;
    char *argv[];
```

```
15[ 0]: {
16[ 1]:     unsigned i;
17[ 1]:
18[ 1]:     i = 0;
19[ 1]:     for (; argc; argc--) {
20[ 2]:          printf ("argument #%u: %s\n", i, argv[i]);
21[ 2]:          i++;
22[ 1]:     }
23[ 0]: }
```

This program is quite simple, merely accepting any number of arguments (lines 12–14) and spitting them on the display, numbered for easy identification (line 20). Notice how cavalierly the program manipulates *ARGC*, decrementing it in line 19. Since C always passes by value, a function is always free to do whatever it desires with its copy of arguments. Look carefully at the call to *printf()*. Notice that if *ARGV* is of type *char *[]*, then *ARGV[]* is of type *char **. This matches the string inclusion *%s* within the call to *printf()*.

As simple as this program is, it is not totally without its uses. It is interesting to enter various arguments to see exactly what Turbo C programs receive from DOS. This is readily done from the IDE by repeatedly changing the arguments via the Options window. Notice in particular that entering a space automatically ends one argument and starts another. To create a single argument with embedded spaces, enclose the argument in double-quotes. Try this with Prg3_6. In fact, it is useful to keep this program around as a sort of programmers' utility.

Less trivial is the next example. This program accepts one arguement which is assumed to be an ASCII string. It then searches *STDIN* for the appearance of that string. The program prints whatever is input onto *STDOUT* with line numbers added. In addition, those lines which contain the string are marked at the beginning with an asterisk. In the interest of simplicity, the program does not worry about key words which might be wrapped across two lines.

```
/* Prg3_7a - Search STDIN for a given string
   by Stephen R. Davis, 1987

  Search the input stream (STDIN) for a given character string.
  Ouput on the output stream (STDOUT) everything input with those
  lines containing the string marked.  Print totals at the bottom
  of number of lines with string and number of lines total.
*/

#include <stdio.h>

/*prototype definitions - */
int main (int, char **);
int find (char *, char *);

/*Main - after making sure one argument is present, search for
         that argument in the input stream STDIN.  Mark and count
         the occurrences*/
main (argc, argv)
```

```
20[ 0]:     int argc;
21[ 0]:     char *argv[];
22[ 0]: {
23[ 1]:     unsigned linenum, flagged;
24[ 1]:     char flagc, string [256];
25[ 1]:
26[ 1]:     if (argc != 2) {
27[ 2]:          printf ("Illegal input\n"
28[ 2]:                  "      try : prog12a <file string\n");
29[ 2]:          exit (-1);
30[ 2]:     } else {
31[ 2]:          linenum = flagged = 0;
32[ 2]:          while (gets (string)) {
33[ 3]:               flagc = ' ';
34[ 3]:               if (find (argv[1], string)) {
35[ 4]:                    flagc = '*';
36[ 4]:                    flagged++;
37[ 3]:               }
38[ 3]:               printf ("%c %3u: %s\n", flagc, ++linenum, string);
39[ 2]:          }
40[ 2]:          printf ("\nTotals:\n  all lines %3u\n  matched   %3u\n",
41[ 2]:               linenum, flagged);
42[ 1]:     }
43[ 0]: }
44[ 0]:
45[ 0]: /*find - find string1 in string2; if found return 1, else 0 */
46[ 0]: int find (ptr1, ptr2)
47[ 0]:     char *ptr1, *ptr2;
48[ 0]: {
49[ 1]:     char *tptr1, *tptr2;
50[ 1]:
51[ 1]:     for (; *ptr2; ptr2++) {
52[ 2]:          tptr1 = ptr1;
53[ 2]:          tptr2 = ptr2;
54[ 2]:          while  (*tptr1++ == *tptr2++)
55[ 2]:               if (!*tptr1)
56[ 2]:                    return 1;
57[ 1]:     }
58[ 1]:     return 0;
59[ 0]: }
```

Before starting, the program checks the number of arguments. If more than 1 argument is provided, the program assumes the user has made a mistake and halts with an error (lines 26–29). It is a common practice to make at least some test of whether the user has made proper input. Often, if the count does not check, the program outputs some help to prompt the user as to what the program expects in the way of input.

If *ARGC* checks out, the program continues to read in lines from *STDIN* until an end-of-file is encounted (lines 32–39). Each string is passed to *find()* which returns a 1 if the argument is found and a 0 if not. The flag character is set to either a ' ' or a '*', depending upon what *find()* returns. *Main()* then prints the string, with the line number and flag character attached. Once *STDIN* has been exhausted, totals are printed (line 40).

The function *find()* is interesting. It starts by scanning through the input string (line 51). For every character, it compares each character of the input string, starting from that point, with the argument until a discrepancy is found (lines 54–56). If no discrepancy is found before exhausting the argument, it returns a 1 indicating success (line 56). If the input string is exhausted without success, a 0 is returned indicating failure (line 58). While this may not be the fastest possible algorithmn, it is certainly simple enough. (Notice that we could have used the routine *index()* provided in the Turbo C library to perform the same function, but without the instructional effect.)

Once again, this program does not expect the user to type in input from the keyboard. Instead, a file is expected to be redirected to using the *<filename* operator on the DOS command line. This shows how a program can mix arguments from the command line with redirected input.

Often, however, we like to add so-called "switches". These are usually one letter arguments preceded immediately with a / that somehow modify the way a program works (UNIX uses the – character instead of /). In the interest of flexibility, most programs allow switches to appear separated (*/a /b*) or concatenated (*/ab* or */a/b*), but they generally must precede any other arguments (*/a arg1* is legal, but *arg1 /a* is not). Programs differ on whether the case of switches is important or not. Unlike pipes, DOS does not interpret these switches for us, leaving the job instead to the applications program.

As an example of interpreting switches, let us add three possible switches to the program above. Let's say that if the user adds a */i*, he desires the program to ignore case in performing its search (i.e., *a* = *A*). We will use a */l* to indicate that the program should not print those lines which do not have a match in them. Finally, a /t will instruct the program to not print the input string at all, but only the totals. This version of the program appears below:

```
/* Prg3_7b - Search STDIN for a given string
     by Stephen R. Davis, 1987

   search the input stream (STDIN) for a given character string.
   Output whatever is input with lines containing the string
   marked.  Accept optional arguments controlling details of the
   search:
      /i - ignore case (this has the side effect of outputting
                         everything in lower case also)
      /t - only print totals
      /l - print the matching lines only
*/
#include <stdio.h>
#include <ctype.h>
#include <process.h>
#define FALSE 0
#define TRUE 1
```

```

/*prototype definitions -*/
int main (int, char **);
int find (char *, char *);
void forcelow (char *);

/*Main - scan the input stream for the appearance of the first
         argument considering the switches noted above*/
main (argc, argv)
    int argc;
    char *argv[];
{
    unsigned linenum, flagged;
    char flagc, string [256], *ptr;
    int ignore, alllines, body;

    ignore = FALSE;                     /*assume no switches*/
    alllines = TRUE;
    body = TRUE;

    while (*argv[1] == '/') {           /*now, look for switches*/
         for (ptr = argv[1]; *ptr; ptr++)
              switch (tolower (*ptr)) {
                   case '/': break;     /*ignore imbedded /'s*/
                   case 'i': ignore = TRUE;
                             break;
                   case 'c': body = FALSE;
                             break;
                   case 't': alllines = FALSE;
                             break;
                   default : printf ("Illegal switch: /%c\n",
                                          *ptr);
                             exit (-2);
              }
         argc--;                        /*remove switch from args*/
         argv++;
    }

    if (argc != 2) {
         printf ("Illegal input\n"
                  "    try : prg3_7b <file [/ilt] string\n");
         exit (-1);
    } else {
         linenum = flagged = 0;
         if (ignore)
              forcelow (argv[1]);

         while (gets (string)) {
              if (ignore)
                   forcelow (string);
              linenum++;
              flagc = ' ';
              if (find (argv[1], string)) {
                   flagc = '*';
                   flagged++;
              }
              if (body)
                   if (flagc == '*' || alllines)
                        printf ("%c %3u: %s\n", flagc,
                                        linenum, string);
         }
         printf ("\nTotals:\n  all lines %3u\n  matched   %3u\n",
              linenum, flagged);
    }
```

```
 82[ 0]: }
 83[ 0]:
 84[ 0]: /*Find - find string1 in string2; if found return 1, else 0 */
 85[ 0]: int find (ptr1, ptr2)
 86[ 0]:     char *ptr1, *ptr2;
 87[ 0]: {
 88[ 1]:     char *tptr1, *tptr2;
 89[ 1]:
 90[ 1]:     for (; *ptr2; ptr2++) {
 91[ 2]:          tptr1 = ptr1;
 92[ 2]:          tptr2 = ptr2;
 93[ 2]:          while  (*tptr1++ == *tptr2++)
 94[ 2]:               if (!*tptr1)
 95[ 2]:                    return 1;
 96[ 1]:     }
 97[ 1]:     return 0;
 98[ 0]: }
 99[ 0]:
100[ 0]: /*Forcelow - force all characters to lower case*/
101[ 0]: void forcelow (ptr)
102[ 0]:     char *ptr;
103[ 0]: {
104[ 1]:     for (; *ptr; ptr++)
105[ 1]:          if (isalpha (*ptr))
106[ 1]:               *ptr = tolower (*ptr);
107[ 0]: }
```

Compare the two programs as they are not that dissimilar. The first thing you notice is that version b has defined three flags, *IGNORE*, *ALLLINES*, and *BODY*, which indicate to the main program whether the corresponding switch was present or not. Initially these switches are set to their "switch not present" state (lines 34–36). The program then examines the input arguments to determine if, in fact, any of the switches are present (lines 38–54).

The first argument (after the program name) is examined to determine if the first character is a / . If it is, then each character after it is examined for the presence of an *i*, *c*, or *t*. If a character which is not one of these is found or another /, an error message is printed and the program stops. The call to *tolower()* makes the examination of switches case insensitive. Once a non-switch is found, the program continues on as before.

In the program body, case is ignored by forcing the argument and input string to lower case if the flag *IGNORE* is true. Output of the text is suppressed by making the call to *printf()* conditional on the flag *BODY* (line 74). The flag *ALLLINES* forces all lines to be output; otherwise only those lines which have a flag character of '*' are output (line 75). If *BODY* is false, the flag *ALLLINES* has no effect, since the conditional is never reached. The totals are always output. Compare this behavior with the stated goals of our switches. Other than including *IF* statements for the various flags, the rest of version b of the program is identical to version 1.

It may have seemed odd that after a switch is found, the program increments *ARGV* and decrements *ARGC* (lines 52–53)! This bizarre behavior has the effect of removing the switch from the command line for the remainder of the program. Think about this carefully for a second and convince yourself that incrementing a variable of type *char *[]* left shifts each argument one position, dropping the leftmost argument into the "bit bucket".

This technique has the extreme advantage of removing the switches from the command line at the beginning of the program. (The line *ARGV[1] = ARGV[0]* before incrementing retains the pointer to the program in *ARGV[0]* for the remainder of the program. Since this pointer is not used, this line has been dropped.) The remainder of the program can ignore the presence of these switches, since the first part of the program has "parsed them away" and set flags accordingly. This is the normal C way of handling input switches to programs. Invoke the program a few times and try entering various combinations of legal, illegal and no switches to convince yourself that this is, in fact, a resilient approach to handling input switches and arguments.

Pointers and the 8086

The 8086 family of microprocessors puts some interesting demands on Turbo C and, occasionally, on the Turbo C programmer. The 8086 uses a segmented model of computer memory. In this model, a physical address is arrived at by combining a 16 bit offset with another 16-bit value, called the segment address, according to the formula:

```
physical address = segment address * 16 + offset
```

This equation results in a 20-bit address capable of accessing 1 Megabyte of memory, the maximum address space of the 8086. Notice that since the offset is 16 bits, any given segment, specified by the segment address, is limited to 64 kbytes in length.

In the 80286 and 80386 microprocessors it's a bit more complicated than this (actually, its a lot more complicated than this), but both chips can emulate the operation of the simpler 8086 and 8088 microprocessors in what is known as Real Mode. Since DOS can only operate in this Real Mode, we do not need to worry too much with the alternative Protected Mode of these chips. (OS/2, the next-generation replacement for DOS, operates in this Protected Mode. Borland has already announced its intent that Turbo C eventually support Protected Mode.

Addresses for Turbo C variables come in two types: *NEAR* and *FAR*. A *NEAR* address consists only of the offset part into a default segment. A *FAR* address contains both the offset and its segment.

Turbo C allows the programmer to default function and data addresses in a program to either *NEAR* or *FAR* by selecting one of the memory models in the *Options* menu of the IDE or by a switch on the command line to TCC, the command line version of Turbo C. Turbo C supports four "normal" memory models and the special Tiny and Huge models outlined in the Table 3.2. Selecting a *NEAR* default for either function or data addresses limits that area to a maximum of 64k bytes in length.

Table 3.2

model	program addresses	data addresses	program size	data size	max array
tiny	near	near	64k	64k	64k
small	near	near	64k	64k	64k
medium	far	near	1M	64k	64k
compact	near	far	64k	1M	64k
large	far	far	1M	1M	64k
huge	far	far	1M	1M	1M

Selecting a model also defaults pointer variables to either 16 bit (offset only) or 32 bit (segment and offset) in length to accommodate the corresponding address size. No matter what the default pointer size is, however, we can always specifically declare any given pointer to whichever size we desire by using the *NEAR* or *FAR* attribute as shown below:

```
int far *farptr;
int near *nearptr;
```

As a small exercise it is interesting to compile and execute Prg3_8 under each of the six memory models. The output from each model is shown below.

```
/*Prg3_8 - Output addresses and Size of a few variables
   by Stephen R. Davis

  Just as a demonstration of the different memory models, output
  a few addresses and pointer sizes.
*/

#include <stdio.h>

/*Main - output some sample variable sizes*/
```

```
main ()
{
        printf ("The sizes are as follows:\n"
                "  character    - %u bytes\n"
                "  integer      - %u bytes\n"
                "  float        - %u bytes\n"
                "  double       - %u bytes\n"
                "\n"
                "  pointer      - %u bytes\n"
                "  far pointer - %u bytes\n"
                "  near pointer- %u bytes\n"
                "  proc         - %u bytes\n",
                sizeof (char),
                sizeof (int),
                sizeof (float),
                sizeof (double),
                sizeof (int *),
                sizeof (int far *),
                sizeof (int near *),
                sizeof (main));
}
```

Notice that the size of the simple variables does not change with the different memory models, nor does the size of the explicitly declared *NEAR* and *FAR* pointers. However, the size of the "default" pointer and the function address change to either *NEAR* or the *FAR* size with changing model.

How do we use *FAR* pointers? Suppose we wanted to declare a pointer to screen memory on the Color/Graphics Adapter (CGA), which is located at address 0xB8000. If we plug this physical address into *physical address = segment address * 16 + offset*, you will notice that we are presented with a single equation in two variables: segment and offset. It doesn't take a mathematics whiz to figure out that such an equation can not be solved uniquely for both variables. In fact, there are some 4096 combinations of segment and offset which together point to any given physical address. It is convention to use the segment: offset combination of 0xB800:0000 when accessing CGA memory. The following declaration makes this assignment:

```
int far *screen;

screen = (int far *)0xB8000000;
```

Forget for a moment the *int* portion of the above declaration. We will discuss the reasons for that when we discuss display memory later. The *far* in the declaration insures that *SCREEN* is a far pointer, irrespective of the memory model under which we might be compiling.

As for the assignment, the first sixteen bits (four hexidecimal digits) of the long integer (0xB800) are assigned to the segment and the remaining sixteen bits to the offset portion of the address. The cast converts what would otherwise be a

LONG INT into a *INT FAR* * to agree with the type of *SCREEN*. This is the same nomenclature which Microsoft first used in its C compilers.

To aide in dealing with *FAR* pointers, Turbo C defines 3 macros: *FP_SEG()*, *FP_OFF()* and *MK_FP()*. The first two return the segment and offset parts, respectively, of an address while the third builds an address from two integer values. For example

```
int far *screen;

screen = MK_FP (0xB800, 0x0000);
         .
         .
         .
```

has the same effect as the previous assignment. Having constructed such a pointer, we can then "pull it apart":

```
         .
         .
         .
segment = FP_SEG (screen);        /* == 0xB800*/
offset = FP_OFF (screen);         /* == 0x0000*/
```

The same routines can be used on the address of a variable (as opposed to the contents of a pointer), via the following:

```
unsigned variable;

printf ("our variable is at segment %x, offset %x\n",
                     FP_SEG (&variable), FP_OFF (&variable));
```

We said above that a pointer of type *NEAR* represents an offset into a default segment. Since there are four different segment registers in the 8086, Turbo C defines four different sub-types of *NEAR* named after the segment registers:

```
char _cs ptr1, _ds ptr2, _es ptr3, _ss ptr4;
```

The default segment register for globally defined data, such as external variables and string constants, is *DS*, the default for functions is *CS*, and the one for stack variables is *SS*. With these special *NEAR* declarations, it becomes possible to declare a near data pointer off of the *CS*, for example. Such a pointer would have direct access to the program's machine code (the mind boggles at what a C program might do with such access). These special forms of *NEAR* declaration are most useful when mixing *NEAR* and *FAR* pointers in the same program. It is not normally necessary to worry with these special types, however.

Turbo C maintains a different support library for each memory model. These libraries are identical except for the size of the addresses they accept as arguments. Selecting the compilation memory model also selects the proper library included during the link step. Generally it is best to compile and link under the smallest memory model practical and declare any *FAR* pointers, specifically, to avoid the overhead of manipulating the larger 32-bit addresses unnecessarily.

From time to time we will want to pass *FAR* pointers to library routines, such as *write()* or *read()*. We select the size of addresses passed to Turbo C library routines by selecting compilation memory models. This might mean that a particular program only works properly if compiled under a specific memory model. Fortunately, we can enforce such a requirement specifically by examining the size of default pointers via the *sizeof()* preprocessor command. This technique, as well as the entire topic of *NEAR* and *FAR* pointers, will become clear as we actually use them in real programs.

Review

In this chapter we have examined the properties of pointers in Turbo C. We have discovered that not only does C allow the programmer to declare pointers to integers and characters, but also to arrays, structures and even functions. This capability allows the C programmer to solve some common problems in very efficient ways.

Turbo C's strings are heavily tied with its concepts of pointers. Pascal allows a string to be assigned to a string variable (for example, 'data := "string";') because Pascal is a high level language with built-in support for string manipulation. Besides just assignments, Pascal defines other string handling primitives, such as concatenation. C also allows a string to be assigned to a pointer variable, but only because the value of a string is nothing more than the address of the string of characters in memory. C has no primitives for manipulating ASCII strings.

We saw that an array name appearing without brackets refers to the address of the array. In like fashion, unresolved function and structure names also refer to their addresses. Since C defines addition to pointers, indexing an array becomes equivalent to adding an index to a pointer:

```
array[i]    <=>    *(array + i)
```

The syntax *ARRAY[I]* is merely a shorthand for the other, more imposing looking, syntax. Similarly, a short hand was developed for using pointers to structures:

```
given:
    struct {
            int a,b;
            } *ptr;
```

then:

`(*ptr).a;`	is equivalent to	`ptr -> a;`
	and	
`(*ptr).b;`	is equivalent to	`ptr -> b;`

Both of these equivalencies are meant to enhance the readibility of C. Even though the shorthand is preferrable, the reader should not forget the "crude" way as this is what C actually "sees" (no pun intended).

By using the right-left rule you can manufacture some truly tortured variable declarations. Arrays of pointers to arrays of functions, ad nauseum, are possible. No matter how complicated the declaration, you always begin at the immediate right of the variable name, proceed to the immediate left, and continue on the right. Any variable that you can declare you can resolve, since the resolution always looks the same as the declaration.

Finally, we looked at using and defining pointers to functions. Even programmers accustomed to thinking in terms of the addresses of data structures may be uncomfortable dealing with the addresses of code, but they shouldn't be. The idea of treating programs like data is fundamental to the von Neumann concept of computer architecture upon which our PCs are based. It is interesting to note that Pascal allows the definition of pointers to functions—Turbo Pascal simply did not implement this feature!

This business of viewing array function and structure names as nothing more than typed addresses is consistent with our view of C as an "intermediate" level language. Remember how we claimed that you can think of = as an operator which takes the current value of the expression and assigns it to the variable on the left? Similary, you can think of *[]* and *()* as operators. Brackets index off of the address that appears to their left, and parentheses call the value to their immediate left. In fact, Small-C will call any expression which appears to the left of parentheses—even the result of a numerical calculation.

Having examined the topic of C pointers closely, we are now in position to look at some practical applications. You might want to start by going back and reexamining your *Bit* and *convnum()* routines of Chapter 1. You now have the fundamentals necessary to allow you to research the power of Turbo C.

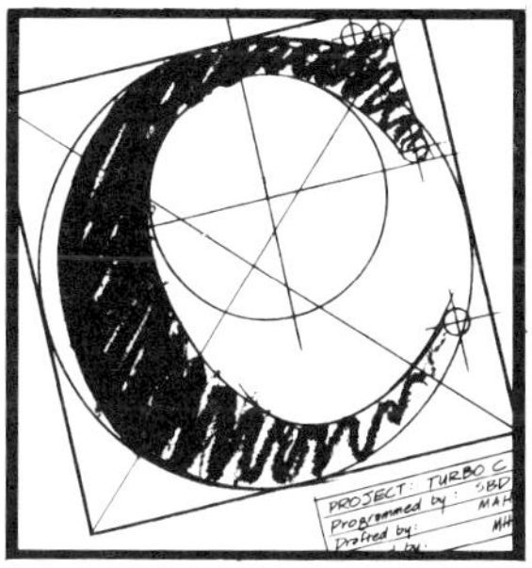

4 Linked Lists

Now that we have a firm handle on the topic of pointers in C, let's apply that knowledge to one of their most important applications, that of linked lists. Actually, linked lists are not unique to C at all. Turbo Pascal supports linked lists every bit as well as Turbo C. That does not mean, however, that every Turbo Pascal programmer has yet mastered the topic. Those that have can view this chapter as a quick review—a good understanding of the topic is too important to leave to chance.

The Problem

Before we begin explaining what a linked list is, let us examine why one is needed. Linked lists solve a problem that used to plague me as a young programmer out of college struggling with FORTRAN IV (a language that, by the way, does not support linked lists). Suppose we are charged with writing a program to manipulate some type of data that consists of several parts. Say, for example, sorting IRS personnel data.

The IRS keeps lots of data on different people (more on some than others), but just to keep things simple, let's limit ourselves to the typical name, rank, and serial number. Suppose in our problem, we are to take the name, sex, address, social security number, and tax bracket of various people and sort them.

Of course, such data should be grouped together. Mr. Jones' address and his social security number should stay together with his name, just as should Mrs. Smith's. (We certainly wouldn't want to sort all of the names separately from the social security numbers, for example!) When confronted with data fields that logically belong together, our immediate reaction should be to create a structure to handle them. A structure allows us to group dissimilar but related data into a single entity; one to which we can give a name and type, if needed.

In our example problem, the various fields we need for each entry are pretty much defined for us. A corresponding structure definition appears as:

```
struct IRSdata {
        char lastname [11];
        char firstname [11];
        char sex;
        struct {
                char street [16];
                char city [11];
                char state [3];
               } address;
        char ssnum [10];
        int taxrate;
       };
```

This definition does not allocate any space but merely defines a structure *IRSdata* that has entries for each of the kinds of data needed. We will actually declare entries of type *STRUCT IRSDATA* later, thereby allocating them memory.

Let's examine the individual fields more closely. For simplicity, name has been broken into two fields: *LASTNAME* and *FIRSTNAME*. If we were going to include middle name or initial we would have added a third field for it. In general, we should always divide such data into the smallest groupings possible. Dividing aggregate entries into their constituent parts simplifies the resulting software.

Notice that a decision was made as to how large a name we can handle. There is a trade off here that must be considered. Allocating a tremendously large array might handle every name we can think of but will surely waste space on all of the Smiths and Jones of the world. On the other hand, making the array too small saves space but might cut names so short that they are no longer unique, throwing all the Thomases in with the Thompsons, lumping the Davises together with the Davidsons. For the above structure I selected a last name and first name size of 10 characters. I declared each field to be 11 *CHAR*s long to allow a *NULL* to be appended to each name. This allows these character arrays to conform to the rules of normal strings.

The very observant reader might have noticed that, in fact, I did not need to pick a size for each name at compile time. Instead, I could have declared *LASTNAME* and *FIRSTNAME* to be of type *CHAR* * as so:

```
struct IRSdata {
                 char *lastname;
                 char *firstname;
                   .
                   .
                   .
```

Such a structure definition could handle names of any size easily. Harkening back to our discussion of pointers vs. arrays however, we will remember that the above declaration does not actually allocate any space for the names, relying instead on the space to be allocated by some other mechanism. We will see as we continue in our discussion that this is unacceptable. For what follows, we will want not only the names of the various data entries kept together, but also the space these entries occupy. This requires the space to be allocated within the structure itself.

If a name is shorter than 10 characters we do not want to be forced to print the entire 10 character field including a terminating string of blanks to pad the length out. By appending a *NULL* to the end of our name, wherever that might be within the allocated space, we can use the normal string handling routines to only print the actual name; however, we must still assume (and enforce) some maximum size. (It is, in general, a very good idea to allocate one more character than necessary to arrays of characters for a terminating *NULL*. All of the C library routines assume the existence of such *NULL*s at the end of ASCII strings.)

Notice how the address field within the structure definition is also a structure with the street name, city name and state all split apart. As we mentioned above, data that has substructure should always be split into the smallest reasonable subdivisions in the structure definition. Perhaps making the address a structure was unnecessary but, logically speaking, it makes good sense to bundle up such fields into like groups. Doing so makes the resulting program more understandable. (I would not disagree with those that might argue that *NAME* itself should have been a structure with two entries: *FIRST* and *LAST*.)

Bringing up the rear are *SSNUM* and *TAXRATE*. Since social security number consists only of digits, *SSNUM* could also have been declared as a long integer (a short integer cannot hold a 9 digit field). Even though printing a long integer in the common social security format of *XXX-XX-XXXX* is not terribly easy. *TAXRATE* is assumed to be a number between 0 and 99 indicating the percentage tax bracket.

How do we allocate the space we will need to sort our structure? The obvious way is to just declare an array. This has several fundamental problems, however. First of all, how many should we declare? Typically, at compile time we do not know how many entries we will need to deal with. We could just calculate the amount of available memory and allocate that many elements to our array, but that only works if we plan to run the program on only one machine and even then only if that machine's memory does not change. What if we decide that there is space for 1,000 entries only to have our program be executed on a machine with less memory where there is not room for quite that many? That would really be a shame if it turned out we only needed to sort ten entries! We would much rather make such memory decisions at run time, when the program is actually executed.

A second, more subtle, problem arises from the architecture of the 8086 microprocessor in the PC. In actual fact we cannot allocate all available memory to our array of structures. A single memory segment in the 8086 and 80286 cannot exceed 64k bytes in length. This means that an array can also not exceed 64k in length, no matter how big each array entry is. Most of the memory in a 640k machine could not be used by such an array solution. (Individual arrays may exceed 64k bytes in length under the huge memory model, but at considerable penalty in speed.)

Finally, as we get to be more adept at handling structures we will find that it is often convenient to mix structures of different types. In our simple example, only the one type was necessary, but what if we had made the problem a little more complicated? Suppose we also wanted to include names of dependents, maiden name, years retired, etc. Not all of such data makes sense for all types of people. Of course, we could just define one very large structure containing every possible field, most of which are blank for any given individual, but each of which is filled in for at least one person. This is a very inefficient use of memory, however. It would be much better to define different types of structures for the single and married, home owners and renters, short form and long form taxpayers, etc. Each structure would only contain the data relevant to its particular type of taxpayer. It is not possible to mix different structures in a single array declaration.

There must be a better way. There must be some method that can address the difficulties inherent in arrays of structures. The answer is the linked list.

The Linked List

An analogous problem exists with files stored on the PC's disk drive. What method should be used to tell the operating system which sectors belong to a certain file and in what order? At first glance you might answer, "Simple, just place the address of each sector of the file in the directory entry for that file." In fact, this system is sometimes used. Such files are called random access files because each sector can be accessed at any time in any order.

This is not, however, the method that DOS uses since it suffers from problems very similar to those of our array above. (For example, how much directory space do we allocate when the file is created?) Instead, the directory entry for each file points to one sector, the first sector of the file. That sector contains the address of the second sector of the file, and so on until the end of the file. All of the sectors of the file are linked together in what is called a linked list. Such files are called sequential access files, since each sector must be accessed in order. (Actually, DOS increases access speed by maintaining a File Allocation Table that links the sectors together sequentially, but the principle is unchanged.)

Similarly, we could use the sequential access approach to solve our IRS problem and link our structures together into a sequential list. Somewhere we would store the address of the first structure. Each structure would then contain a pointer to the next in line.

Consider the following declaration:

```
struct main {
                int data;
                struct main *link;
               } *ptr;
```

It may seem that we have created an infinite loop by declaring a pointer to *STRUCT MAIN* within the definition of *STRUCT MAIN* itself, but this is not so. Although it is important to distinguish pointers by what they point to, the size of a pointer variable is fixed and independent of the thing pointed at. Therefore, the above declaration is perfectly legal.

If the variable *PTR* contained the address of a structure element of type *MAIN* then *(*PTR).DATA* would contain the integer data of that element. We will avail ourselves of the equivalent shorthand introduced in Chapter 3:

`PTR -> DATA` <=is equivalent to=> `(*PTR).DATA`

PTR -> LINK is also of type *STRUCT MAIN* *, thus, if *LINK* pointed to the "next" element in the list, the assignment:

```
PTR = PTR -> LINK;
```

would cause *PTR* to point to that next element. Repeating the function moves *PTR down the list* of structure elements. Figure 4.1 shows pictorially what is happening here.

Figure 4.1

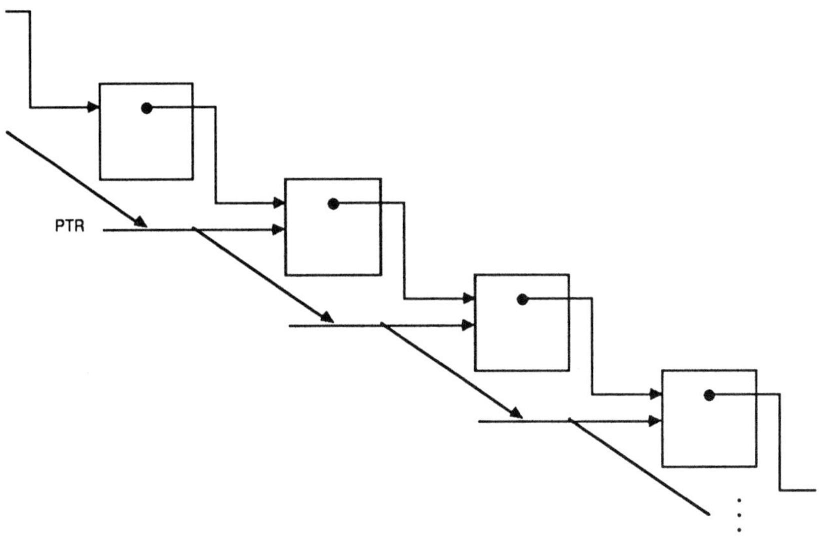

Traversing a singly linked list

By traversing the list of linked structure elements we can eventually gain access to all of the *DATA*'s they contain. Of course, we have neglected two problems represented by the two ends of the chain: how do we get started and how do we know when to stop? Getting started is easy. Somewhere we reserve a variable containing the address of the first element of our linked list, analogous to the directory entry of our DOS sequential file.

C comes to our aid in solving the latter problem by reserving the pointer value 0. C will not assign any variable or structure the address 0. Therefore, we can set the value of *LINK* in the last element of the linked list to 0. As we move through the list we must be ever watchful for this value, for when we encounter it, we know that the list has been exhausted. C aids us further in this by interpreting the value 0 as *FALSE* if it appears in an *IF* statement or in a *FOR*, *DO WHILE* or *WHILE* loop.

The Heap

This is all very nice given that such a linked list of structures exists, but how did it come to be in the first place? Where did the elements come from? In both C and Pascal there exists a block of memory collectively known as the *heap*. The heap consists of all the memory available to the program that has not already been used for some other purpose. That is, the heap is simply the rest of memory.

This may seem a bit strange to the uninitiated, but consider for a moment what the PC's memory must look like when you execute a program you have just written. At the bottom is PC-DOS and assorted fixed addresses. Above this are stacked DOS buffers plus any device drivers you included in your *CONFIG.SYS* file. Sitting atop that are SideKick or any other Terminate and Stay Resident (TSR) programs you may have loaded before executing your program. Next comes your program.

The first section of your program to be loaded is the machine code. Its size and organization are strictly a function of your source code. The second section, which is the data, consists of all the static and extern declared variables. Third, and last, is the stack space. Turbo C examines the number of functions you have, how they are called, and how many auto variables each has to arrive at a reasonable amount of stack space for your program. The space above your program and its stack up to 640k does not belong to anyone (one gets into video RAM above 640k). This space is the heap, as shown in Figure 4.2.

Variables contained in either the data or stack areas are statically allocated variables. Their space is either marked out and reserved ahead of time, as with externs, or is at least reserved, as with auto variables. That is because decisions affecting these variables must be made at compile time and are, therefore, not subject to change without recompiling. Any data that we might place in the heap must be dynamically allocated. Their space is not reserved at compile time but, instead, at run time when the program is actually executed.

Figure 4.2

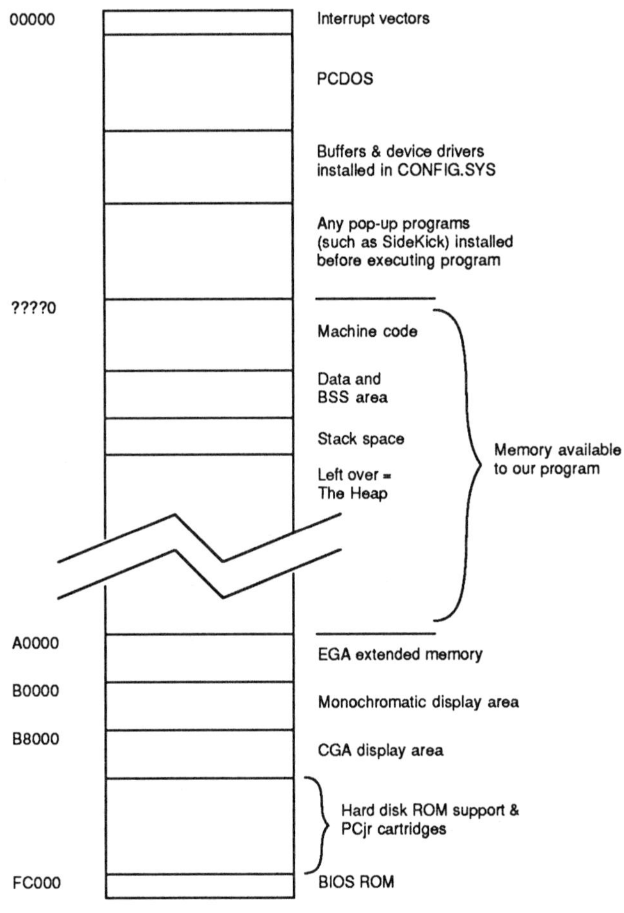

Memory on the PC

C provides two principle routines for accessing the heap: *malloc()* and *free()*. (The library routine *calloc()* can be used in place of *malloc()* if desired.) These functions have the following prototype declarations:

```
void *malloc (unsigned numofbytes);
void free (void *ptr);
```

To allocate space the user program calls *malloc()*, passing to it the number of bytes to allocate off of the heap. *Malloc()* returns either a 0, indicating that the requested amount of space is not available, or a pointer to the requested space. Eventually, when the program has finished with that block of memory, it can return it to the heap (to be used again by some other routine) by passing its address to the function *free()*. Any memory allocated to a program when it exits is automatically returned to the heap.

With power comes responsibility. Dynamic memory allows the user program access to all of the free memory in the host machine, but the user program must be careful in using it. Once a block of memory has been passed to the user program by *malloc()* it is the responsibility of the program to keep track of it. If it looses a pointer, the data in that space is also lost. Once returned to the heap via *free()* that space belongs to the system again and the user program must not attempt to access it further.

Singly Linked Lists

The mechanism that we described above for sequential files is called a singly linked list since there is one pointer or link attaching each structure to the next succeeding structure. Singly linked lists are ideal for maintaining queues, both of the Last-In-First-Out (LIFO) and First-In-First-Out (FIFO) variety.

A FIFO queue can be used to store off incoming data that might arrive faster than it can be worked. The FIFO expands and contracts, with entries being attached to one end as they arrive, and pulled off the other end for processing. Averaged over a long period of time entries must be processed as fast as they arrive, but a FIFO can store off data *bursts* for later processing. This gives the resulting system a certain *springiness*.

As an example of a singly link list implementation, let us use the slightly simpler LIFO. Expanding the code to implement a LIFO queue into that of a FIFO queue is straightforward. Prg4_1 implements a very simple Reverse Polish Notation (RPN—Hewlett Packard style) calculator. An RPN calculator maintains a data stack of entries. Values are pushed onto the top of the stack—operators take their arguments from the top of the stack. For example, to add 1 and 3 on an RPN calcualtor one first enters *1 [ENTER]* then *3 [ENTER]* followed by +. The result appears on the display and is also placed on the top of the stack. Our simplistic calculator uses the *RETURN* as its *ENTER* key and implements the simple arithmetic functions.

```
/*Prg 4_1 -- Simple Integer RPN Calculator using Singly Linked LIFO
   by Stephen R. Davis, 1987

  Singly linked lists are most commonly used to implement FIFO
  (first in, first out) queues and LIFO (last in, first out) queues.
  In this case, we will use a LIFO to simulate a reverse Polish notati
  (HP-style) calculator.  This calculator is quite simplistic, but
  the principle could be expanded to encompass much larger projects.
*/

#include <stdio.h>

/*prototype definitions --*/
int pop (void);
void push (int);
void clear (void);
void view (void);
int main (void);

/*stack structure definition*/
struct stack {
              int number;
              struct stack *link;
             };
struct stack *HEAD = NULL;

/*Pop - pop an integer value off of the stack*/
int pop ()
{
    struct stack *old;
    int value;

    if (HEAD) {
         value = HEAD -> number;
         old = HEAD;
         HEAD = HEAD -> link;
         free (old);
    } else
         value = 0;                      /*queue empty*/
    return value;
}

/*Push - push an integer value onto the stack*/
void push (value)
    int value;
{
    struct stack *new;

    if (new = (struct stack *)malloc (sizeof (struct stack))) {
         new -> number = value;
         new -> link = HEAD;
         HEAD = new;
    }
}

/*Clear - clear the LIFO of all entries*/
void clear ()
{
    while (HEAD)
         pop();
}

/*View - view the elements on the stack*/
void view ()
```

```
 65[ 0]: {
 66[ 1]:     struct stack *ptr;
 67[ 1]:
 68[ 1]:     ptr = HEAD;
 69[ 1]:     printf ("   stack = ");
 70[ 1]:     while (ptr) {
 71[ 2]:          printf ("  %i", ptr -> number);
 72[ 2]:          ptr = ptr -> link;
 73[ 1]:     }
 74[ 1]:     printf ("\n");
 75[ 0]: }
 76[ 0]:
 77[ 0]: /*Main - accept input commands and execute them using the
 78[ 0]:          stack commands*/
 79[ 0]: main()
 80[ 0]: {
 81[ 1]:     char string[80];
 82[ 1]:     int value;
 83[ 1]:
 84[ 1]:     printf ("Enter any integer plus the symbols:\n");
 85[ 1]:     printf ("+  add\n-  subtract\n*  multiply\n/  divide\n"),
 86[ 1]:     printf ("C  clear stack\n=  pop value\n?  view stack\n\n");
 87[ 1]:     for (;;) {
 88[ 2]:          while (!gets (string));
 89[ 2]:          switch (string[0]) {
 90[ 3]:               case '*': value = pop() * pop();
 91[ 3]:                         break;
 92[ 3]:               case '+': value = pop() + pop();
 93[ 3]:                         break;
 94[ 3]:               case '/': value = pop() / pop();
 95[ 3]:                         break;
 96[ 3]:               case '-': value = pop() - pop();
 97[ 3]:                         break;
 98[ 3]:               case '=': pop();
 99[ 3]:                         value = pop();
100[ 3]:                         break;
101[ 3]:               case 'C': clear();
102[ 3]:                         value = 0;
103[ 3]:                         break;
104[ 3]:               case '?': view();
105[ 3]:                         value = pop();
106[ 3]:               default : sscanf (string, "%i", &value);
107[ 2]:               }
108[ 2]:          push(value);
109[ 2]:          printf ("    %i\n", value);
110[ 1]:     }
111[ 0]: }
```

The heart of an RPN calculator is its push-down stack, which is by its very nature a LIFO. To implement this push-down stack we have defined a structure *STACK* that contains a single value and a pointer to the next entry in the stack called *LINK*. In addition, we define *HEAD*, a pointer to the first entry in the linked list. Notice that *HEAD* is initialized to 0, indicating that at the beginning of the program the list is empty.

Two key functions manipulate the stack, *pop()* (lines 28–41) and *push()* (lines 44–54). *Pop()* removes the newest entry from the top of the stack and returns its value. *Push()* accepts an integer value, builds a structure and links it onto the top of the stack. These routines provide an example of the use of *malloc()* and *free()*.

Pop() begins by first checking if there are any entries on the stack to pop. If the contents of *HEAD* are 0 then the list must be empty and *pop()* returns a 0. Notice lines 35 through 37 especially, where *pop()* unlinks an entry. Line 36 causes *HEAD* to point to the next entry in the list, but why is the variable *OLD* necessary? Why not instead use the simpler code section below?

```
free (HEAD);                    /*this will not work*/
HEAD = HEAD -> link;
```

You should be on your guard for this trap as it is a very common mistake with linked list novices. We *cannot* free the first entry in the list and *then* attempt to fetch its link entry. Once we have returned a structure to the heap we no longer have permission to access it—no *if*s, *and*s, or *but*s!

Push() requests a block of memory of the proper size from the heap in line 49. It is good programming practice to use *SIZEOF* as the argument to *malloc()* rather than merely entering 4. For one thing, we may decide to add more fields to our structure at some future date. *SIZEOF* automatically inserts the proper size of our structure, removing one more source of error. Besides, how do we know the size of our structure is 4 bytes? In fact, depending on memory model, it might be 6 bytes in length. *SIZEOF* sidesteps the problem by automatically calculating the proper size.

Remember that the pointer returned from *malloc()* is of type *VOID* * and should ideally be recast into the type of the pointer variable into which the value is being stored. Secondly, we should always be watchful of running out of heap. If no more memory is left on the heap, a 0 is returned, the *IF* statement is not satisfied and *push()* has no effect. Once *push()* receives a structure, it stores the data value passed into it and then links it onto the top of the list.

The main body of this program is contained in *main()* (lines 84–111). After printing an initial explanatory banner, *main()* enters an infinite loop. Keyboard input is requested on line 88 using *gets()*. Notice the *WHILE* loop is here to discard inadvertent null lines. The subsequent *SWITCH* statement (lines 89–107) compares the first character entered against each of the legal commands. If the first character entered cannot be matched with any of the possible commands, it is assumed to be a number (line 106). The C routine *sscanf()* is used to convert the input number into the variable *VALUE*. *Sscanf()* is similar to *scanf()*, the normal input routine, except that it accepts input from memory rather than from the input stream.

Figure 4.3

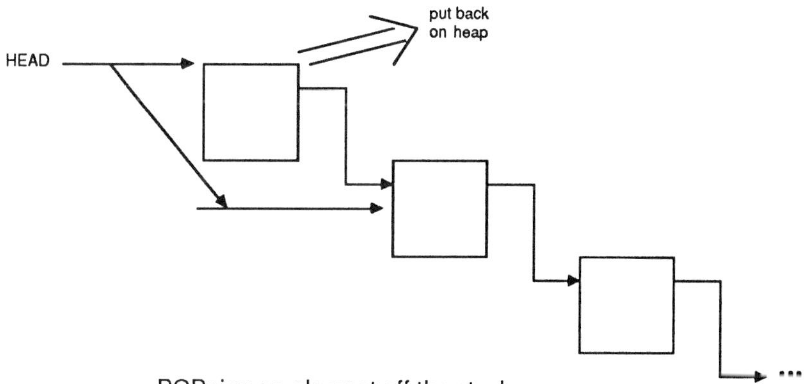

POPping an element off the stack

Figure 4.4

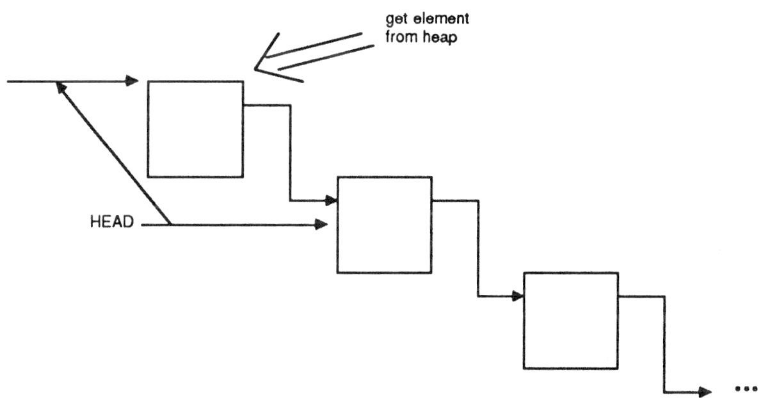

PUSHing an element onto the stack

Actually, implementing a particular calculator function is very simple. For example, addition is interpreted on line 92. Here we simply pop the top two values off of the stack and add them, placing the result in *VALUE*. Those functions such as *?* (examine) that do not perform an arithmetic function, go ahead and pop the topmost value into *VALUE* so that it might be printed as in a normal command.

No matter where *VALUE* gets set, it subsequently gets pushed back onto the top of the stack and displayed in lines 108 and 109. The routine *clear()* clears the stack by popping values until *HEAD* equals 0, indicating the stack is empty. *View()* displays the stack contents. This is an example of a routine that traverses the stack without modifying it.

The Doubly Linked List

Let us return to our IRS problem. The singly linked list was ideal for our RPN calculator since we were always adding and removing entries to/from the top of the queue. Singly link lists work just as well when we are always adding to the beginning and removing from the end of the queue. In our IRS problem, it is clear that in order to sort the entries we will be manipulating entries in the middle of the queue as well as at both ends.

In order to remove an entry from the middle of a linked list one merely links the entry's predecessor to its successor, "routing around" the current entry. The link pointer in the entry points to the successor, so that's easy, but finding the predecessor is a problem. If we could somehow link the list in the other direction, we might know the predecessor but then we lose the address of the successor (let's forget about the semantic details of predecessor and successor given that the links point in the opposite direction). So what if we link the list in both directions at the same time? This is the doubly linked list.

Figure 4.5

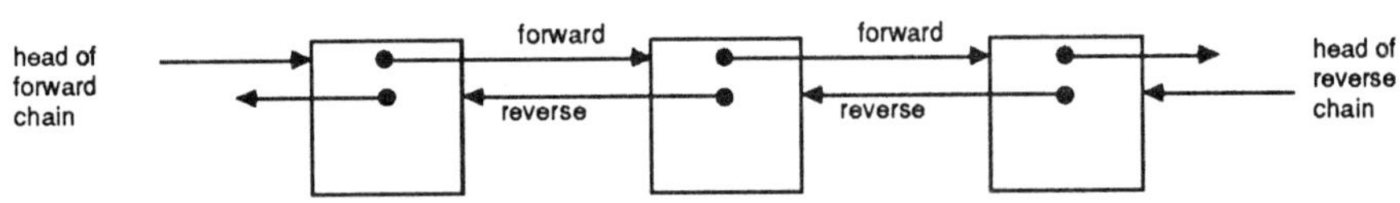

A doubly linked list

Each entry of a doubly linked list has not one but two link pointers. One of the link pointers links all of the entries in the list from the beginning to the end. This is called the forward pointer. The other link pointer links the same entries in the opposite direction, starting with the last entry and ending with the first. This is the backward pointer. Often times there is no obvious ordering in a doubly linked list, in which case, it is somewhat arbitrary which entry is called the forward and which entry is called the reverse pointer. A simple doubly linked structure declaration appears as:

```
struct main {
            int data;
             struct main *previous, *next;
           } *HEAD, *TAIL;
```

Notice that besides the two link words, *PREVIOUS* and *NEXT*, we must define two *head* pointers, one for each end of the list.

Doubly linked lists carry more overhead. Not only must they carry the extra pointer variable that must be allocated for each structure, but also the code to manipulate these pointers. In return, doubly linked lists are more easily manipulated. Now, each entry contains the address of both its neighbors. We are no longer limited to pulling entries off of one end or the other. We can manipulate interior entries just as easily.

How does a doubly linked list compare with our array of structures? Not only do they address all of the problems mentioned in that connection, but they have one other advantage: doubly linked lists can be sorted very rapidly. Unlike arrays, the order of a doubly linked list is not derived from the location of its entries but instead from its order in the list. To order an array one must move the actual array entries to their proper place in the list. Ordering a linked list merely involves changing the values of pointer variables. This can be an extreme advantage when each of the list entries is very large as can happen with IRS data.

The IRS Problem

OK, so the doubly linked list is the apparent data structure for our IRS data sorting problem. Since this is not a trivial problem, however, we will need to break it up and solve it in pieces. Not only is this worthwhile from an instructional point of view, but this is actually the way a large C program gets built.

We already devised a perfectly good data structure to be used when we first introduced the problem. The first thing we will need then are routines to both create and output these entries. Normally, we would also need a destroy function that does nothing more than return a structure to the heap by calling *free()*. This problem does not require it. A program to define and test *create()* and *output()* appears as Prg4_2a.

```
/*Prg4_2a - Sort IRS data
   by Stephen R. Davis, 1987

  Accept several different types of data on individuals in random
  order and sort it.  This initial version defines the structure
  we will use to store the data and provides a 'create()' to generate
  the entries and an 'output()' function to output them again.
*/

#include <stdio.h>
#include <ctype.h>
#include <alloc.h>

/*prototype declarations --*/
struct IRSdata *create (void);
void getfield (char *, char *, unsigned);
void output (struct IRSdata *);
int main (void);

/*structure declaration for IRS data*/
struct IRSdata{
               char lastname [11];
               char firstname [11];
               char sex;
               struct {
                       char street [16];
                       char city [11];
                       char state [3];
                      } address;
               char ssnum [10];
               int taxrate;
              };
char buffer [256];

/*Create - allocate an IRSdata entry and fill in the data from 'stdin'
struct IRSdata * create ()
{
    char answer [2];
    struct IRSdata *ptr;

    getfield ("Another entry? ", answer, 1);
    if (tolower (answer [0]) == 'n')
         return NULL;

    if (ptr = (struct IRSdata *)malloc (sizeof(struct IRSdata))) {
         getfield ("Enter last name:    ", ptr -> lastname, 10);
         getfield ("      first name:   ", ptr -> firstname, 10);
         getfield ("      street addr:  ", ptr -> address.street, 15);
         getfield ("      city address: ", ptr -> address.city, 10);
         getfield ("      state (2 ltr):", ptr -> address.state, 2);
         getfield ("      soc sec #:    ", ptr -> ssnum, 9);
         printf   ("      tax bracket:  ");

         gets (buffer);
         sscanf (buffer, "%d", &(ptr -> taxrate));
         printf ("\n");
    } else {
         printf ("Sorry.  No more room for data.\n");
    }

    return (ptr);
}

/*GetField - pose a question, then get an answer.  Save up to
```

```
                        'size' characters*/
void getfield (question, answer, size)
       char *question,*answer;
       unsigned size;
{
       unsigned i;

       printf (question);
       while (!gets (buffer));
       for (i = 0; size; size--)
            *answer++ = buffer [i++];
       *answer = '\0';
}

/*Output - output a subset of IRSdata structure to 'stdout'*/
void output (ptr)
       struct IRSdata *ptr;
{
       if (ptr)
            printf ("%s %s, %s\n", ptr -> firstname,
                           ptr -> lastname, ptr -> ssnum);
}

/*Main - invoke create() and output() to test them.*/
main ()
{
       output (create ());
}
```

The function *output()* does nothing more than receive the pointer to a structure and print out certain key fields. *Create()* is equally straightforward, asking the user whether he desires to create another entry, requesting a structure from the heap, using *getfield()* to fill in the various entries from the keyboard and then returning the address of the structure. It is assumed that *create()* will be called repeatedly until it returns a 0, either because the user entered *N* or because the heap emptied. Either way, that is all the entries we will process.

Create() uses the routine *getfield()* to handle the tedious job of actually stuffing data into the structure entries. *Getfield()* prompts the user for input and then accepts the ASCII response using the library routine *gets()*. Since *gets()* has no checks for size, input cannot be read directly into the user defined field. Instead *gets()* reads into an appropriately large buffer that is subsequently transferred to the user defined space. *Gets()* will add a 0 to the end of the entered string, that will get copied into the user field. A *NULL* is tacked onto the end of the string in case more than the specified number of characters were entered without a *NULL* encountered.

The above program could just as easily have been written without defining a routine *getfield()*. It should be so ingrained in the C programmer's mind that it should almost be a reflex, however, to recognize repetitive functions and define routines to handle them. Under normal circumstances, this is through the mechanism of functions, but if speed is of the absolute maximum importance, macro definitions can be used.

The next functions we need are an *insert()* routine to add an entry to a doubly linked list and *remove()* to remove an entry. Of course, the structure we declared at the beginning of the chapter did not yet have any link pointers. In order to insert and remove entries we will have to add a *PREVIOUS* and *NEXT* pointer to our structure definition. A simplistic *insert()* and *remove()* appear as listing Prg4_2b.

```
/*Prg4_2b - Sort IRS data
   by Stephen R. Davis, 1987

  Define the first stab at the insert() and remove() functions.
*/

#include <stdio.h>

/*prototype declarations --*/
int insert (struct IRSdata *, struct IRSdata *, struct IRSdata *);
int remove (struct IRSdata *);

/*structure to contain IRS data w/ pointers added*/
struct IRSdata {
               struct IRSdata *previous,*next;
               char lastname [11];
               char firstname [11];
               char sex;
               struct {
                       char street [16];
                       char city [11];
                       char state [3];
                      } address;
               char ssnum [10];
               int taxrate;
              };


/*Insert - insert a structure in between two doubly linked entries.
           Return a 0 if successful, and a nonzero if not*/
int insert (before, after, current)
    struct IRSdata *before, *after, *current;
{
    if (before -> next != after) return -1;
    if (before != after -> previous) return -1;

    before -> next = current;
    current -> previous = before;

    after -> previous = current;
    current -> next = after;
    return 0;
}

/*Remove - remove an entry from a doubly linked list*/
int remove (entry)
    struct IRSdata *entry;
{
    struct IRSdata *before, *after;
```

```

    before = entry -> previous;
    after = entry -> next;

    before -> next = after;
    after -> previous = before;

    entry -> previous = entry -> next = (struct IRSdata *)NULL;
}
```

Both *insert()* and *remove()* can potentially return values. Zero implies success and nonzero implies something went wrong. (This convention is often used even though it might seem backwards, since the nonzero value can be used to indicate the problem.) *Insert()* accepts 3 arguments: the element to be inserted, *CURRENT*, and the two elements around the point of insertion, *BEFORE* and *AFTER* (Figure 4.6). Insert begins by making sure that *BEFORE* and *AFTER* actually point to each other. If the forward pointer of *BEFORE* does not point to *AFTER* and the reverse pointer of *AFTER* does not point to *BEFORE*, then the two entries are not neighbors. Continuing with *insert()* would corrupt the linked list.

Figure 4.6

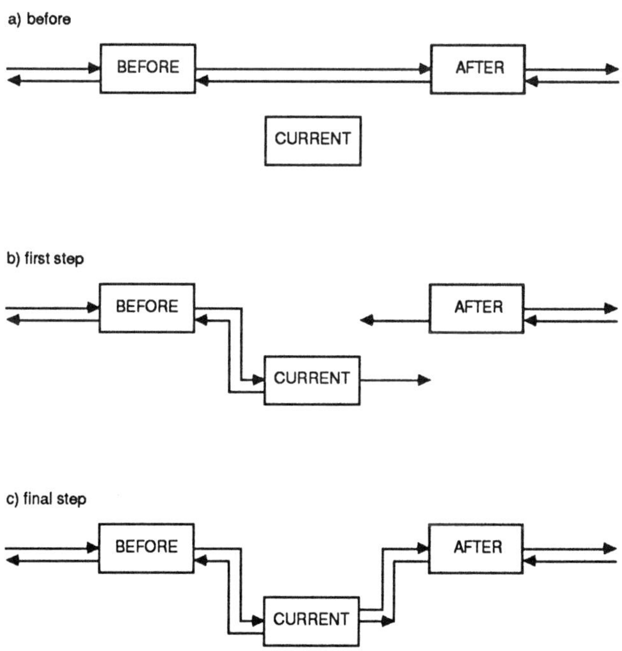

Inserting an element in a doubly linked list

Given that the two entries are neighbors, the problem then becomes to insert the current entry *CURRENT* between them. Lines 37 and 38 connect *BEFORE* and *CURRENT* together. Lines 40 and 41 connect *CURRENT* and *AFTER* (Figure 4.6). Having completed the interconnection, *insert()* returns a success indicator.

Remove() reverses the process, removing an entry from inbetween its two neighbors. Notice that it is not necessary to specify more than just the one argument to *remove();* the ability to infer an entry's neighbors in both directions is the advantage of the doubly linked list. The pointers *BEFORE* and *AFTER* are assigned on lines 51 and 52. *BEFORE* and *AFTER* are linked together, thus excluding *ENTRY,* on lines 54 and 55. Although not absolutely necessary, the link pointers of *ENTRY* are zeroed (line 57), indicating that it is not connected to anything (Figure 4.7).

Figure 4.7

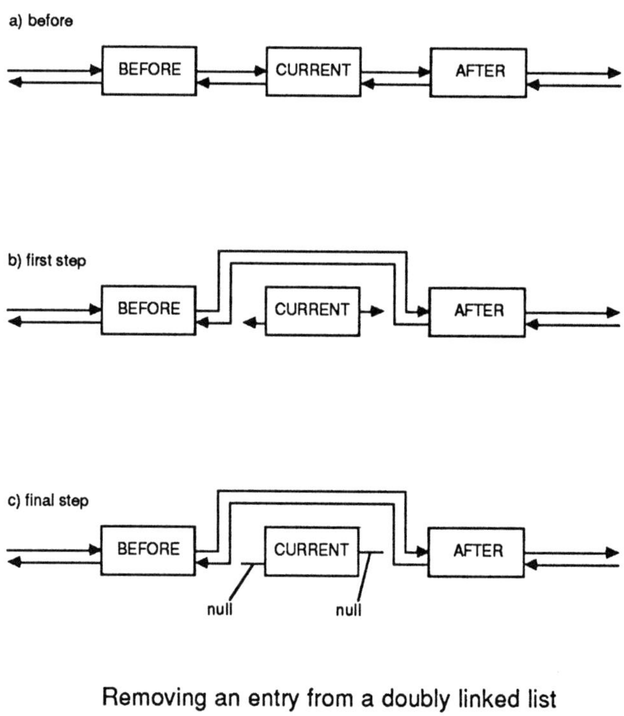

Removing an entry from a doubly linked list

While this demonstrates the principle of linking and unlinking entries nicely, this version of *insert()* and *remove()* has problems. Linked lists are not infinitely long and, therefore, have a beginning and an end. Most books handle this with beginning and end pointers, which we have already called *HEAD* and *TAIL*. So, what if an entry is being added to or removed from either end of the list? In such a case the variables *BEFORE* or *AFTER* would be 0, which is not the address of a structure. Not only must *insert()* and *remove()* realize that *BEFORE* or *AFTER* are not structures in this case, but they must also update *HEAD* and *TAIL* appropriately. These boundary problems are normally taken care of explicitly. Listing Prg4_2c shows *insert()* and *remove()* with these this added.

```
/*Prg4_2c - Sort IRS data
   by Stephen R. Davis, 1987

  Define an insert() and remove() functions which account for the
  boundary conditions inherent in a HEAD/TAIL implementation
*/

#include <stdio.h>
#define NULL (struct IRSdata *)0

struct IRSdata{
               struct IRSdata *previous,*next;
               char lastname [11];
               char firstname [11];
               char sex;
               struct {
                       char street [16];
                       char city [11];
                       char state [3];
                      } address;
               char ssnum [10];
               int taxrate;
              };
struct IRSdata *HEAD, *TAIL;


/*Insert - insert a structure in between two doubly linked entries.
           Return a 0 if successful, and a nonzero if not*/
insert (before, after, current)
    struct IRSdata *before, *after, *current;
{
    if (before -> next != after) return -1;
    if (before != after -> previous) return -1;

    if (before != NULL) {
         before -> next = current;
         current -> previous = before;
    } else {
         HEAD = current;
         current -> previous = NULL;
    }

    if (after != NULL) {
         after -> previous = current;
         current -> next = after;
    } else {
         TAIL = current;
```

```
48[ 2]:          current -> next = NULL;
49[ 1]:     }
50[ 1]:
51[ 1]:     return 0;
52[ 0]: }
53[ 0]:
54[ 0]: /*Remove - remove an entry from a doubly linked list*/
55[ 0]: remove (entry)
56[ 0]:     struct IRSdata *entry;
57[ 0]: {
58[ 1]:     struct IRSdata *before, *after;
59[ 1]:
60[ 1]:     before = entry -> previous;
61[ 1]:     after = entry -> next;
62[ 1]:
63[ 1]:     if (before != NULL)
64[ 1]:          if (after != NULL) {
65[ 2]:               before -> next = after;
66[ 2]:               after -> previous = before;
67[ 2]:          } else {
68[ 2]:               before -> next = NULL;
69[ 2]:               TAIL = before;
70[ 1]:          }
71[ 1]:     else
72[ 1]:          if (after != NULL) {
73[ 2]:               HEAD = after;
74[ 2]:               after -> previous = NULL;
75[ 1]:          } else
76[ 1]:               HEAD = TAIL = NULL;
77[ 1]:
78[ 1]:     entry -> previous = entry -> next = NULL;
79[ 0]: }
```

In each case, an explicit check is made of *BEFORE* and *AFTER* for a 0. If so, *HEAD* and/or *TAIL* are updated instead of a structure. Remember that both *HEAD* and *TAIL* could be 0 (implying the linked list was empty). For example, Line 76 of *remove()* represents the case where the last element of a list is being removed.

Such an implementation, although the normal method, is somewhat clumsy and spoils much of the elegance of linked lists. Elegance is a very desirable trait in software. The simpler and more straightforward a function is, the more assured the programmer can be of its correctness. Could we perhaps regain some of the simplicity of our "boundariless" solution?

HEAD and *TAIL* are pointers to structures. Above we treated them differently, but they are of exactly the same type as *PREVIOUS* and *NEXT* within any structure. In fact, rather than having two independent pointer variables, we could just allocate a dummy structure that we will call *MARKER*. *MARKER*'s data have no meaning, but we can let its *NEXT* pointer correspond to *HEAD* by making it point to the beginning of the list and its *PREVIOUS* pointer to *TAIL* by pointing to the end of the list. We do this to make *HEAD* and *TAIL* less unlike "normal" link pointers.

A doubly linked list with *MARKER* pointing at the beginning and end of the list resembles somewhat a circle. *MARKER* plays a keystone role, holding the circle together. To complete the illusion, we make the *PREVIOUS* pointer of the first entry point back to *MARKER* as well as the *NEXT* pointer of the last entry in the list (Figure 4.8, page 140). This may seem to be making the problem unnecessarily complicated. In fact, this solution is considerably simpler. By replacing *HEAD* and *TAIL* with the forward and backward pointers of a special structure, the boundary problem has been completely removed.

Examined from a slightly different angle, we could argue that we have removed the boundary conditions represented by the end points of the list by removing the end points. Apart from the data, the structure *MARKER* is not different from any other structure in the list. A circle has no beginning or end and, therefore, no end points for which to check.

If we adopt the common convention of assigning *MARKER.PREVIOUS* and *MARKER.NEXT* to 0 when the list is empty, however, the circle analogy is lost. We would have to include special conditionals to check for an empty list whenever an entry is removed or added. To avoid this, we start by initializing both *MARKER.PREVIOUS* and *MARKER.NEXT* to the value *MARKER*. That is, we make the *MARKER* structure point to itself! In both directions!!! By doing so we have removed another singularity for which we must ordinarily check, that of an empty list. At least one structure always exists, *MARKER* itself, and the linked list is always circular even if it contains *MARKER* alone.

While this may all seem a bit strange, examine the new, circular doubly linked list functions. Compare them to both our boundaried and boundariless routines before. The circular implementation restores the elegance of our original solution. Look again at Figure 4.8 and consider for a moment the concept of a circular implementation. (If you are still unsure, remember that the binary number system as implemented on digital computers is circular for exactly the same reason, to remove the boundary considerations of negative and positive numbers.)

```
/*Prg4_2d - Sort IRS data
   by Stephen R. Davis, 1987

  Define an insert() and remove() functions using a circular
  implementation to minimize the boundary conditions
*/

#include <stdio.h>
#include <alloc.h>

#define NULL (struct IRSdata *)0
```

```

/*prototype definitions*/
int insert (struct IRSdata *, struct IRSdata *, struct IRSdata *);
int remove (struct IRSdata *);
void init (void);
void printit (void);
struct IRSdata *findit (unsigned);

/*structure definition of IRS data*/
struct IRSdata{
               struct IRSdata *previous,*next;
               char lastname [11];
               char firstname [11];
               char sex;
               struct {
                       char street [16];
                       char city [11];
                       char state [3];
                      } address;
               char ssnum [10];
               int taxrate;
              };
struct IRSdata *MARKER;


/*Insert - insert a structure in between two doubly linked entries.
           Return a 0 if successful, and a nonzero if not*/
int insert (before, after, current)
    struct IRSdata *before, *after, *current;
{
    if (before -> next != after) return -1;
    if (before != after -> previous) return -1;

    before -> next = current;
    current -> previous = before;

    after -> previous = current;
    current -> next = after;
    return 0;
}

/*Remove - remove an entry from a doubly linked list*/
int remove (entry)
    struct IRSdata *entry;
{
    struct IRSdata *before, *after;

    before = entry -> previous;
    after = entry -> next;

    before -> next = after;
    after -> previous = before;

    entry -> previous = entry -> next = NULL;
    return 0;
}

/*Init - initialize the linked list to empty*/
void init (void)
{
    MARKER = (struct IRSdata *)malloc (sizeof (struct IRSdata));
    MARKER -> previous = MARKER -> next = MARKER;
}

```

```
/*test the above routines*/

void printit (void)
{
     struct IRSdata *ptr;

     printf ("\n\n");
     for (ptr = MARKER -> next; ptr != MARKER; ptr = ptr -> next)
          printf ("%u  ", ptr -> taxrate);
     printf ("\n");
}

struct IRSdata *findit (count)
     unsigned count;
{
     struct IRSdata *ptr;

     for (ptr = MARKER -> next; count; count--)
          ptr = ptr -> next;
     return ptr;
}

main()
{
     unsigned i;
     struct IRSdata *to, *from;

     init ();

     for (i = 0; i < 10; i++) {
          to = (struct IRSdata *)malloc (sizeof (struct IRSdata));
          to -> taxrate = i;
          insert (MARKER -> previous, MARKER, to);
     }

     printf ("Enter entry to remove followed by"
              "where to insert it\n"
              "(Control-C to terminate");
     for (;;) {
          printit ();
          printf ("Input entry to remove:");
          scanf ("%u", &i);
          from = findit (i);
          remove (from);

          printit ();
          printf ("Now where should I put it:");
          scanf ("%u", &i);
          to = findit (i);
          insert (to, to -> next, from);
     }
}
```

Insert() and *remove()* are identical to the boundariless versions; however, the routine *init()* has been added, that must be invoked before either of the other two routines. *Init()* allocates a dummy structure, stores the address into the extern variable *MARKER* and initializes its forward and backward pointers to itself. Also added are a few lines of test code at the bottom to allow thorough testing of these routines (the previous versions of *insert()* and *remove()* did not have test code since we did not intend to use them).

Figure 4.8

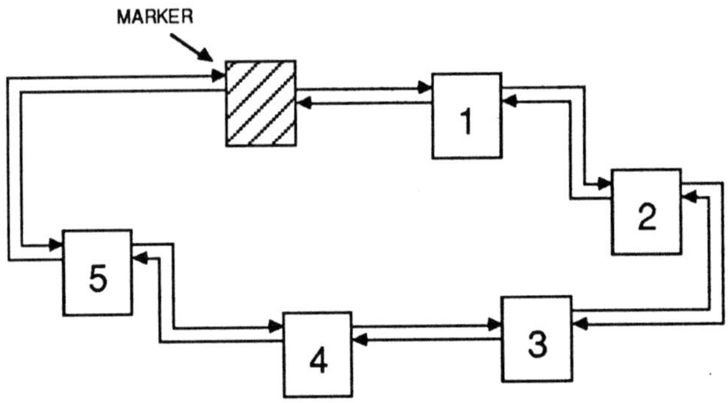

Doubly linked list formed into a circle

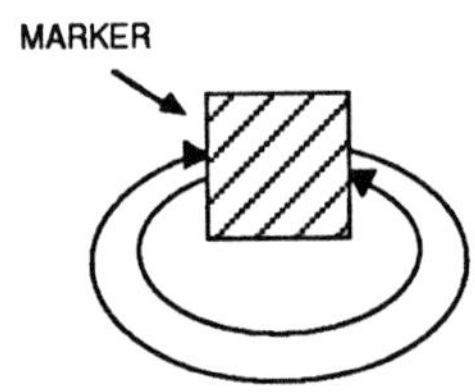

Empty circular list consists of the marker element pointing to itself

The Home Stretch

So we now have the routines we need to create, output, insert, remove and initialize our doubly linked list to handle *IRSdata*. We are very close to the complete solution, but before we mount the final assault, there is one further consideration when dealing with linked lists: pointer integrity. Corrupted pointers are very difficult to trace and *always* fatal.

In discussing pointer integrity, we are not concerned with pointers of questionable morals, but rather pointer variables that do not point to anything. Of course, in a perfectly working program, this cannot happen. In the real world, it is all too easy to forget some critical path through which a pointer variable is not initialized or set to some wrong value and then used as if it pointed to a structure.

In our IRS problem it may not be worth worrying about. We have been careful to keep our functions short and to thoroughly test each before integrating them together. Real world programs can reach up into the many thousands of lines of source code. Even though we might still keep each routine short, pointer problems are definitely going to arise.

We all realize that variables can get illegal values in them. Why are such errors so much worse with linked list pointers? As we vector through linked lists we are like a train. Everything is great as long as we stay on the tracks. As soon as a pointer variable gets corrupted, its akin to a derailment. Once our train leaves its program track it is only through the most incredible luck that the train would ever accidentally make it back onto the track. Much more likely is that the train will run along until it falls into an infinite loop (a chain of "structures" in random memory that point to each other in a loop) or until it crashes into some critical piece of code, the overwriting of which brings the whole thing to an ignominious end. Either way the result is a crash necessitating a complete reset. Its bad enough that such errors are fatal. Worse is that the crash generally occurs many miles from the derailment itself, making it very difficult to track back to its source. Besides, if the system is in an infinite loop, there is generally no way to get it back to even find out what happened. In this case, a pound of prevention is worth many truck loads of cure.

Other than following careful programming practices there is nothing we can do to keep pointer variables from occassionally getting corrupted. What we can do, however, is arrange things so that a derailment is detected almost immediately and very close to the source of the problem. We can then stop the program with the problem detected before we crash the host PC. We do this by adding an identification field to our structure. The new structure definition appears as:

```
struct IRSdata {
                struct IRSdata *previous, *next;
                unsigned fingerprint;
                char lastname [11];
                char firstname [11];
                char sex;
                struct {
                        char street [16];
                        char city [11];
                        char state [3];
                       } address;
                char ssnum [10];
                int taxrate;
               }
```

By setting *FINGERPRINT* to a particular, hopefully unusual, value at creation time, each routine that manipulates pointers to *IRSdata* can easily check that what is being pointed at is indeed a structure. As soon as a routine gets passed an errant pointer, the fact will be noted and the program halted in place. Prg4_2e shows the new routine *check()* whose job it is to perform this test. A new constant, *IRSsignature*, has been defined to the value *0x1234*. The routines *insert()* and *remove()* have been updated to call *check()* before using any pointer data. *Create()* initializes this value.

```
/*Prg4_2e - Sort IRS data
   by Stephen R. Davis, 1987

  Define insert() and remove() functions.  Include an integrity
  check to catch errant pointers without allowing the system
  to crash.  If we had more than one type of structure, each would
  have its own signature.  This is a very worthwhile but all too
  uncommon a practice on large systems under development.  Get into
  the habit early.
*/

#include <stdio.h>
#include <alloc.h>
#include <process.h>

#define NULL (struct IRSdata *)0
#define IRSsignature 0x1234

/*prototype declarations*/
int insert (struct IRSdata *, struct IRSdata *, struct IRSdata *);
int remove (struct IRSdata *);
int check (struct IRSdata *, char *);
void init (void);
struct IRSdata *alloc (void);

/*structure declaration for IRS data*/
struct IRSdata{
               struct IRSdata *previous,*next;
               unsigned fingerprint;
               char lastname [11];
               char firstname [11];
               char sex;
               struct {
                       char street [16];
                       char city [11];
                       char state [3];
                      } address;
               char ssnum [10];
               int taxrate;
              };
struct IRSdata *MARKER;


```

```
/*Insert - insert a structure in between two doubly linked entries.
           Return a 0 if successful, and a nonzero if not*/
int insert (before, after, current)
    struct IRSdata *before, *after, *current;
{
    if (before -> next != after) return -1;
    if (before != after -> previous) return -1;

    if (check (before,  "arg 'before' to insert()")) return -1;
    if (check (after,   "arg 'after' to insert()")) return -1;
    if (check (current, "arg 'current' to insert()")) return -1;

    before -> next = current;
    current -> previous = before;

    after -> previous = current;
    current -> next = after;
    return 0;
}

/*Remove - remove an entry from a doubly linked list*/
int remove (entry)
    struct IRSdata *entry;
{
    struct IRSdata *before, *after;

    if (check (entry, "arg 'entry' to remove()")) return -1;

    before = entry -> previous;
    after = entry -> next;

    before -> next = after;
    after -> previous = before;

    entry -> previous = entry -> next = NULL;
    return 0;
}

/*Init - initialize the linked list to empty*/
void init (void)
{
    struct IRSdata *alloc ();

    MARKER = alloc ();
    MARKER -> previous = MARKER -> next = MARKER;
}

/*Check - check the integrity of an IRS pointer.  If OK, return a
          0, else print message and return a -1.*/
int check (ptr, msg)
    struct IRSdata *ptr;
    char *msg;
{
    if (ptr -> fingerprint == IRSsignature)
        return 0;
    printf ("Error:\n  Pointer failure on %s\n", msg);
    return -1;
}
```

```

/*Alloc - allocate a structure and "sign it" with the IRS
          signature*/
struct IRSdata *alloc()
{
    struct IRSdata *ptr;

    ptr = (struct IRSdata *)malloc (sizeof (struct IRSdata));
    ptr -> fingerprint = IRSsignature;
    return ptr;
}
```

Once again, this may seem like overkill, but believe me, it's not. When your program has reached a few thousand lines and you have multitudes of different linked lists, some of them singly linked, some doubly, it is all too easy to get them mixed up and all too difficult to straighten them back out. Get into the habit of including such signature fields early.

The Finish Line

So we have discussed doubly linked lists and how making them circular solves lots of boundary problems and how adding markers to our structures saves debugging headaches. We still haven't said anything directly about solving our IRS sort problem! Actually, we had the heart of the solution from the beginning. Sorting IRS data is, after all, at its core a sort problem, a complicated sort problem perhaps, but a sort problem nonetheless. Back in Chapter 3 we defined a *sort()* function that we said could sort "anything." Surely, then, it can sort our IRS data structures, and, in fact, it can. (Had it not been able to, you can be assured I would have tempered my claims back in Chapter 3!)

To use *sort()* we must define three routines: *compare()*, *swap()* and *sequence()*. *Compare()* is no problem. We simply compare the sorting field (whichever field that might be) from two different entries and return a 1, 0 or -1 indicating their relationship. What about *swap()*? Implementing *swap()* directly might be difficult, but there is no need. It is more straightforward to *remove()* an entry from the list and re-*insert()* it in its new home. We already have both routines. Finally, *sequence()* is simple now that we understand linked lists, being merely a matter of chaining through the doubly linked list starting with *MARKER* and ending with the same. All three routines are shown in listing Prg4_2f.

```
/*Prg4_2f - Sort IRS data
   by Stephen R. Davis, 1987

  Define the 'swap()', 'compare()' and 'sequence()' routines
  required by our previously defined "perfectly general
  bubble sort".  These routines will allow us to use our bubble
```

```
    sort to sort the IRS data by social security number.
    Use the previously defined 'insert()' and 'remove()' to
    implement the new 'swap()'.
*/

#include <stdio.h>

#define NULL (struct IRSdata *)0
#define signature 0x1234

/*prototype definitions*/
int swap (struct IRSdata *, struct IRSdata *);
int compare (struct IRSdata *, struct IRSdata *);
struct IRSdata *sequence (struct IRSdata *);

/*structure declaration for IRS data*/
struct IRSdata{
               struct IRSdata *previous,*next;
               unsigned fingerprint;
               char lastname [11];
               char firstname [11];
               char sex;
               struct {
                       char street [16];
                       char city [11];
                       char state [3];
                      } address;
               char ssnum [10];
               int taxrate;
              };
struct IRSdata *MARKER;


/*Swap - swap the position of the two entries passed.  Return
        a 0 if successful and a -1 if not.*/
int swap (first, second)
    struct IRSdata *first, *second;
{

    if (remove (second))
         return -1;
    return (insert (first -> previous, first, second));
}

/*Compare - compare two IRS data structures.  Return as follows:
            1 -> a.taxrate > b.taxrate
            0 -> a.taxrate = b.taxrate
           -1 -> a.taxrate < b.taxrate*/
int compare (a, b)
    struct IRSdata *a, *b;
{
    if (a -> taxrate > b -> taxrate)
         return  1;
    if (a -> taxrate < b -> taxrate)
         return -1;
    return 0;
}

/*Sequence - given an entry, return the address of the next
             entry*/
struct IRSdata *sequence (entry)
    struct IRSdata *entry;
{
    struct IRSdata *value;
```

```

    if (entry == 0)                          /*given a 0...*/
        entry = MARKER;                      /*...start at beginning*/

    if (check (entry, "arg 'entry' to sequence()"))
        return NULL;

    if ((value = entry -> next) == MARKER) /*if end of chain...*/
        return NULL;                         /*...return a NULL*/
    else
        return value;
}
```

When we sort a list of structures, we are taking for granted that one is *greater than* another. With all of the varying data types within a structure, it may not be clear that any such a relationship exists. *Compare()* implicitly defines what the term *greater than* means when applied to our structure. In our case, we decided to sort our taxpayer data by taxrate. If we later decide instead to sort it by the taxpayer's last name, it would only be necessary to modify *compare()* to effect the change.

Even if *sort()* did not require a routine *compare()*, we probably would have written one anyway. It is always preferable to have such concepts embodied in a single routine rather than strewn throughout the program. Not only does this fit well with our modular approach to programming, but it results in programs that a easier to maintain and modify.

(It is even possible to doubly link the same entries in different lists in differ orders, by having more than one pair of forward and backward pointe Databases do this to sort the same entries by different criteria. The principles exactly the same.)

The final solution appears as Prg4_2g below. Test code has been added in *mc* to allow test data to be entered. A test run with sample data and output app as Figure 4.9, page 151.

```
/*Prg4_2g -- The Final Solution to the IRS Sort
   by Stephen R. Davis, 1987

  This is merely a combination of the various parts of the solution
  already developed.  This program would normally be linked together
  the General Sort function -- we have included directly into the
  same source here for clarity.
*/

#include <stdio.h>
#include <ctype.h>
#include <alloc.h>
#include <process.h>

#define NULL (struct IRSdata *)0
#define IRSsignature 0x1234
```

```

/*prototype declarations --*/
                                                  /*structure creation*/
struct IRSdata *create (void);
void getfield (char *, char *, unsigned);
void output (struct IRSdata *);
                                                  /*linked list routines*/
int insert (struct IRSdata *, struct IRSdata *, struct IRSdata *);
int remove (struct IRSdata *);
int check (struct IRSdata *, char *);
struct IRSdata *alloc (void);
void init (void);
                                                  /*swap routines*/
int swap (struct IRSdata *, struct IRSdata *);
int compare (struct IRSdata *, struct IRSdata *);
struct IRSdata *sequence (struct IRSdata *);
int sort (int (*)(void *, void *), int (*)(void *, void *),
          void *(*)(void *));

/*structure declaration for IRS data*/
struct IRSdata{
               struct IRSdata *previous,*next;
               unsigned fingerprint;
               char lastname [11];
               char firstname [11];
               char sex;
               struct {
                       char street [16];
                       char city [11];
                       char state [3];
                      } address;
               char ssnum [10];
               int taxrate;
              };
struct IRSdata *MARKER;
char buffer [256];

/*Create - allocate an IRSdata entry and fill in the data from 'stdin'
struct IRSdata * create ()
{
    char answer [2];
    struct IRSdata *ptr;

    getfield ("Another entry? ", answer, 1);
    if (tolower (answer [0]) == 'n')
        return NULL;

    if (ptr = alloc ()) {
        getfield ("Enter last name:     ", ptr -> lastname, 10);
        getfield ("      first name:    ", ptr -> firstname, 10);
        getfield ("      street addr:   ", ptr -> address.street, 15);
        getfield ("      city address:  ", ptr -> address.city, 10);
        getfield ("      state (2 ltr): ", ptr -> address.state, 2);
        getfield ("      soc sec #:     ", ptr -> ssnum, 9);
        printf   ("      tax bracket:   ");

        gets (buffer);
        sscanf (buffer, "%d", &(ptr -> taxrate));
    } else {
        printf ("Sorry.  No more room for data.\n");
    }

    return (ptr);
}
```

```

/*GetField - pose a question, then get an answer.  Save up to
                'size' characters*/
void getfield (question, answer, size)
     char *question,*answer;
     unsigned size;
{
     unsigned i;

     printf (question);
     while (!gets (buffer));
     for (i = 0; size; size--)
          *answer++ = buffer [i++];
     *answer = '\0';
}

/*Output - output a subset of IRSdata structure to 'stdout'*/
void output (ptr)
     struct IRSdata *ptr;
{
     if (ptr)
          printf ("%s %s, %s, taxrate = %u\n", ptr -> firstname,
                       ptr -> lastname, ptr -> ssnum, ptr -> taxrate);
}

/*Insert - insert a structure in between two doubly linked entries.
             Return a 0 if successful, and a nonzero if not*/
int insert (before, after, current)
     struct IRSdata *before, *after, *current;
{
     if (before -> next != after) return -1;
     if (before != after -> previous) return -1;

     if (check (before,  "arg 'before' to insert()")) return -1;
     if (check (after,   "arg 'after' to insert()")) return -1;
     if (check (current, "arg 'current' to insert()")) return -1;

     before -> next = current;
     current -> previous = before;

     after -> previous = current;
     current -> next = after;
     return 0;
}

/*Remove - remove an entry from a doubly linked list*/
int remove (entry)
     struct IRSdata *entry;
{
     struct IRSdata *before, *after;

     if (check (entry, "arg 'entry' to remove()")) return -1;

     before = entry -> previous;
     after = entry -> next;

     before -> next = after;
     after -> previous = before;

     entry -> previous = entry -> next = NULL;
     return 0;
}

/*Init - initialize the linked list to empty*/
```

```
void init (void)
{
    struct IRSdata *alloc ();

    MARKER = alloc ();
    MARKER -> previous = MARKER -> next = MARKER;
}

/*Check - check the integrity of an IRS pointer.  If OK, return a
          0, else print message and return a -1.*/
int check (ptr, msg)
    struct IRSdata *ptr;
    char *msg;
{
    if (ptr -> fingerprint == IRSsignature)
         return 0;
    printf ("Error:\n  Pointer failure on %s\n", msg);
    return -1;
}

/*Alloc - allocate a structure and "sign it" with the IRS
           signature*/
struct IRSdata *alloc(void)
{
    struct IRSdata *ptr;

    if (ptr = (struct IRSdata *)malloc (sizeof (struct IRSdata)))
         ptr -> fingerprint = IRSsignature;
    return ptr;
}

/*Sort - implement bubble sort*/
int sort (compare, swap, sequence)
     int (*compare)(void *, void *), (*swap)(void *, void *);
     void *(*sequence)(void *);
{
    int flag;
    void *p1, *p2;

    do {
         flag =  0;
         p2 = (*sequence)(0);            /*starting w/ first entry...*/
         while (p1 = p2, p2 = (*sequence) (p2)) /*...sequence thru*/
         {
              if ((*compare)(p1, p2) > 0) {      /*if p1 > p2...*/
                   if ((*swap)(p1, p2)) return -1;/*...swap p1 & p2*/
                   flag = 1;
              }
         }
       } while (flag);                   /*stop when all are in order*/
    return 0;
}

/*Swap - swap the position of the two entries passed.  Return
         a 0 if successful and a -1 if not.*/
int swap (first, second)
    struct IRSdata *first, *second;
{

    if (remove (second))
         return -1;
    return (insert (first -> previous, first, second));
```

```
}

/*Compare - compare two IRS data structures.  Return as follows:
             1 -> a.taxrate > b.taxrate
             0 -> a.taxrate = b.taxrate
            -1 -> a.taxrate < b.taxrate*/
int compare (a, b)
    struct IRSdata *a, *b;
{
    if (a -> taxrate > b -> taxrate)
         return  1;
    if (a -> taxrate < b -> taxrate)
         return -1;
    return 0;
}

/*Sequence - given an entry, return the address of the next
              entry.  Return a 0 on end of list.*/
struct IRSdata *sequence (entry)
    struct IRSdata *entry;
{
    struct IRSdata *value;

    if (entry == 0)                    /*given 0...*/
         entry = MARKER;               /*...start with beginning*/

    if (check (entry, "arg 'entry' to sequence()"))
         return NULL;

    if ((value = entry -> next) == MARKER) /*if end of chain...*/
         return NULL;                  /*...return a NULL*/
    else
         return value;
}

/*Main - now invoke the above routines*/
main ()
{
    struct IRSdata *ptr, *ptrold;

    /*initialize linked list to empty*/
    init ();

    /*now read in entries and add them to the chain*/
    ptrold = MARKER;
    while (ptr = create ()) {
         if (insert (ptrold, MARKER, ptr))
              abort ();
         ptrold = ptr;
    }

    /*display the entries in input order*/
    printf ("\n\n\nHere are the entries as entered:\n\n");
    ptr = MARKER;
    while (ptr = sequence (ptr))
         output (ptr);

    /*now sort the list*/
    if (sort (compare, swap, sequence))
         printf ("failure during sort!\n");
```

```

    /*and reoutput the list*/
    printf ("\n\n\nHere are the entries sorted by taxrate:\n\n");
    ptr = MARKER;
    while (ptr = sequence (ptr))
         output (ptr);

    printf ("\nCompleted successfully\n");
}
```

Figure 4.9

```
Output of Prg4_2g with sample data

Here are the entries as entered:

Stephen Davis, 123456789, taxrate = 30
Mary Smith, 234567890, taxrate = 20
Tom  Jones, 987654321, taxrate = 25
Heimmi Smeckawitz, 876543210, taxrate = 15


Here are the entries sorted by taxrate:

Heimmi Smeckawitz, 876543210, taxrate = 15
Mary Smith, 234567890, taxrate = 20
Tom  Jones, 987654321, taxrate = 25
Stephen Davis, 123456789, taxrate = 30

Completed successfully
```

Review of the Solution

Let's step back from the IRS problem and review our solution before we continue. We began by defining a structure that was well adapted to our problem. After deciding that a doubly linked list was the proper method for organizing our structures, we built two basic utilities for manipulating such lists: *insert()* and *remove()*. Any subsequent routine we might invent to affect the order of the structure entries will use these two primitives rather than manipulating the pointers themselves.

Such a modular approach to programming results in routines that are easier to test and have more general appeal. Although *create()* and *output()* are specific to this particular problem, the remaining routines could be added to our own personal program libraries. These routines do not depend on the details of the data defined in the structure. In particular, *insert()*, *remove()*, and *sequence()* will make valuable additions. These three routines will work for *any* future doubly linked structures we might create, so long as we are careful to define the *NEXT*, *PREVIOUS* and *SIGNATURE* fields in the same place within the structure (at the beginning).

Finally, we avoided needless work by selecting the already written and tested *sort()* routine from our program library to perform the actual sort. To aid in the debug process, we added a special error checking signature to each structure to detect errant pointers and we tested each function by itself before integrating it into the final program.

Notice that our program could just as easily have handled structures of different sizes. Different structures for married and single, employed and retired people would cause our routines no trouble at all. Only the routines *create()* and *output()* would have to be modified to make them smart enough to generate and print the data in the different structure types. As was mentioned earlier, this ability to handle differing sized data is a strength of the linked list.

Note that I was heavy handed above with the rejection of defining *LASTNAME* and *FIRSTNAME* as character pointers. If it is important to allow names of any length, our routines would be perfectly happy with such declarations. Only *create()* must be modified. *Create()* would allocate space for the people's names out of the heap in separate calls to *malloc()*, passing it the length of the names input. The resulting addresses would then be stored into the *LASTNAME* and *FIRSTNAME* pointers. Although slightly more complicated, this technique has the advantage that it places no limitations at all on the lengths of the name fields, that tend to be indeterminate in size.

Thoughts on Optimizing Linked Lists

Although we will leave a complete discussion of optimization techniques to Chapter 8, let's take a look at a few of those techniques most relevant to linked lists while the subject is fresh on our minds.

Manipulating linked lists is a very fast proposition. Though it might take us humans a few minutes to make the jump from one linked list entry to the next, a microprocessor can do it in just a few instructions. Linked lists can generally be traversed even faster than arrays. If we cannot increase program speed, what about decreasing its size?

It may seem obvious to say, but the size of a program consists of two parts: the code space, where the program itself resides, and the data space, where the structure elements are stored. There is an insidious relationship between these two parts. While we can often reduce our data requirement by shrinking the size of a structure element through careful packing of the constituent fields, for example, using only a single bit to indicate sex, we must usually increase the size of the program that handles these elements, since it must pack and unpack these various fields for use. This is true whether the programmer generates the code, by explicitly coding bit test and set routines, or if Turbo C generates the code, as is the case with bit field variables in structure definition. However, if the number of elements is very large, then the savings in the data area can more than offset the increases in the code area.

Since the structure definition for different problems varies so greatly, it is difficult to advise any particular method for packing data economically. There are a few tricks we can use to pack the fields common to all doubly linked lists.

As we make our way along from one entry to another of a doubly linked list, no matter in which direction, we generally only use one or the other of the pointers. The other pointer provides redundant information since it points back in the direction from which we are coming. For example, if we are moving from the front of the list to the back, we only need to know the next entry since we already know the previous. Therefore, we really only need one *pointer's worth* of information, rather than the two we have allocated. Is there some way we can pack the two pointers into one word, using the value of the pointer we know to get the value we don't know during execution?

Mathematicians spend a large part of their careers studying operations on numbers. All operators that map a range of input into an output range, uniquely, have an inverse function over that range. For example, if there is a function *F()*, that for every *X* renders a unique *Y = F(X)*, then there must be a function *G()* that given *Y* returns *X*. A few of these operators are of special interest because they form their own inverse. The *exclusive or*, commonly written *XOR*, is one of those functions.

If we *XOR* a value *X* with another value *Y*, we get some result *Z*. If we then *XOR Z* with *X*, the result is *Y*, and if we *XOR Z* with *Y*, we are rewarded with *X* for our efforts. Realizing that it doesn't prove anything mathematically, it might give us a better feeling if we just try it once to make sure:

```
0x1234    XOR    0x789A    ->    0x6AAE
```

now

```
0x6AAE    XOR    0x1234    ->    0x789A
0x6AAE    XOR    0x789A    ->    0x1234
```

Therefore, rather than storing the address of both the previous and next entry we can simply *XOR* their addresses together and save that in the structure. Once we get to where we need either address, we will always have the other. We can use this to extract the desired address. This is the way the small model version looks in practice:

```
struct X {
          unsigned cp;            /*combined pointer*/
          unsigned otherdata;     /*some data*/
          };

/*Traverse - given an entry and the address of the previous (next)
             entry, returns the address of the next (previous)
             entry.*/
struct X *traverse (prev, curr)
     struct X *prev, *curr;
{
     return (struct X *)(curr -> cp ^ (unsigned)prev);
}
```

Pictorially it looks like Figure 4.10.

So traversing such a list is pretty simple, but what about insertion and removal? After all, it was this problem that drove us out of the arms of the singly linked list and into those of the doubly linked list in the first place. This, as it turns out, is no more difficult from a programming standpoint, although it might be a little more challenging from a conceptual perspective.

Figure 4.10

Traversing a merged doubly linked list

Given a doubly linked list with combined pointer CP consisting of the XOR of its previous and next neighbors

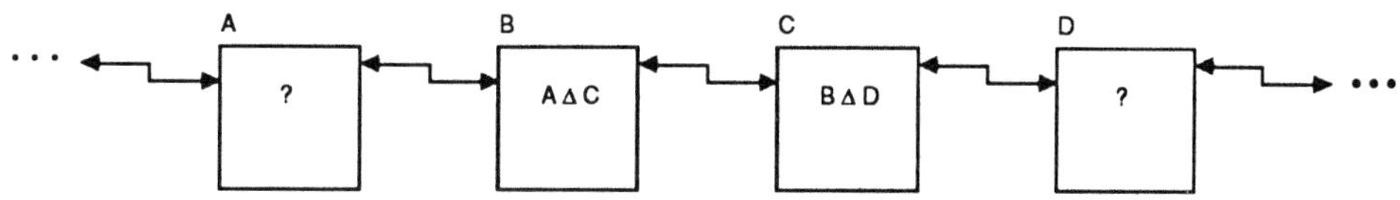

If we are currently at element C, having come from element B, how do we get to element D?

$$
\begin{aligned}
D &= ? \\
&= D \Delta (B \Delta B) \\
&= (B \Delta D) \Delta B \\
&= C.CP \Delta B
\end{aligned}
$$

therefore

$PTR = PTR \text{->} CP \Delta B$

Let's consider a pictorial representation on the next page. Here we have four entries, labeled conveniently *A* through *D*, and we want to insert a new structure, *E*, between *B* and *C*. Creating the combined pointer *CP* for element *E* is no problem, being just the *XOR* of address *B* and *C*. Before we can insert *E* between *B* and *C*, however, we must remove each from the other. This we do by *XOR*ing *C* into *B.CP*, thus removing *C*, and *XOR*ing *B* into *C.CP*. The insertion is completed by *XOR*ing both *B.CP* and *C.CP* with *E*. Removing an entry from the list is very similar, as is depicted.

While this technique saves one pointer from the structure definition, it has some pitfalls that should be considered. We were able to combine the two pointers into one, because, under normal circumstances, the two pointers represented redundant information. If this information is, in fact, not redundant, then we must retain both pointers. Further, this redundant information allows opportunities for error checking—removing this redundancy, removes those opportunities. This makes the inclusion of signature fields in the structure definition even more critical to the overall implementation.

Figure 4.11

Inserting and removing elements in merged doubly linked lists

Inserting

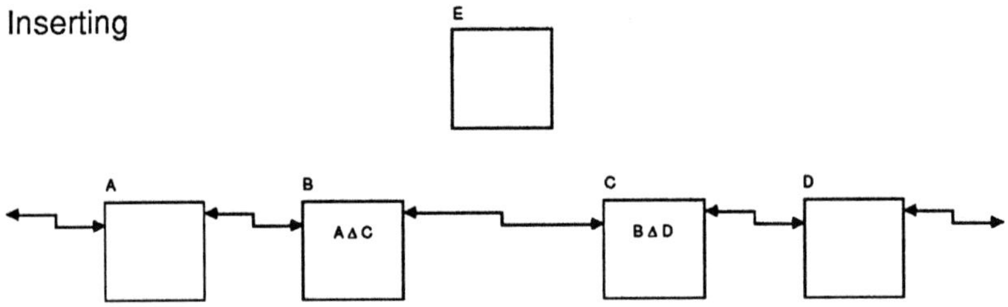

First we must remove B and C from each other:

B.CP ∆ C -> A store this back into B.CP
C.CP ∆ B -> D store this back into C.CP

Now we insert E by XORing back into B and C:

B.CP ∆ E -> A ∆ E store this back into B.CP
C.CP ∆ E -> E ∆ D store this back into C.CP
B ∆ C store this back into E.CP

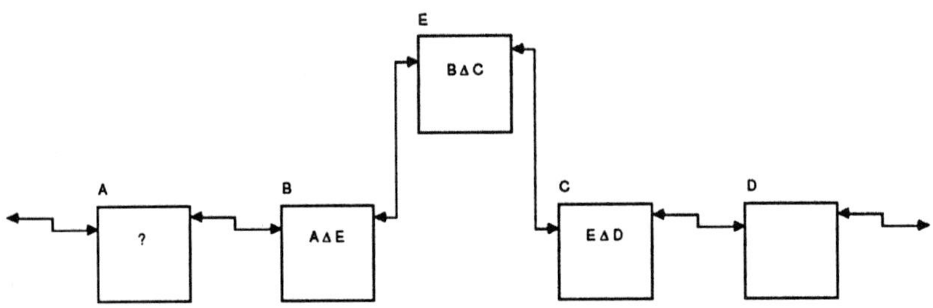

Figure 4.11 (*cont.*)

Removing

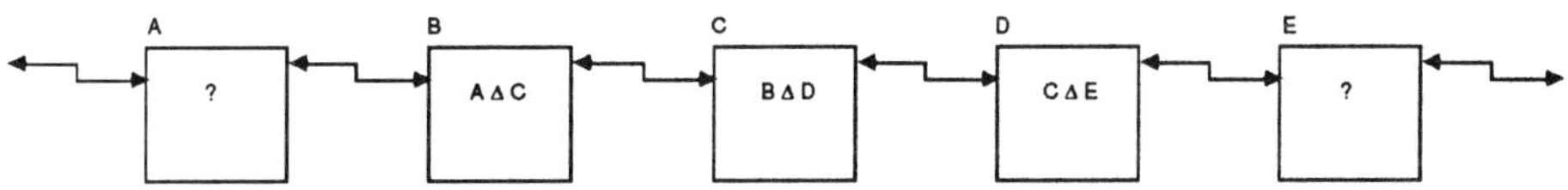

To remove C from the list, we first remove its effects from its neighbors B and D:

B.CP Δ C -> A   store this into B.CP
D.CP Δ C -> E   store this into D.CP

Now we link the two elements together:

B.CP Δ D -> A Δ D   store this into B.CP
D.CP Δ B -> B Δ E   store this into D.CP
0   store this into C.CP

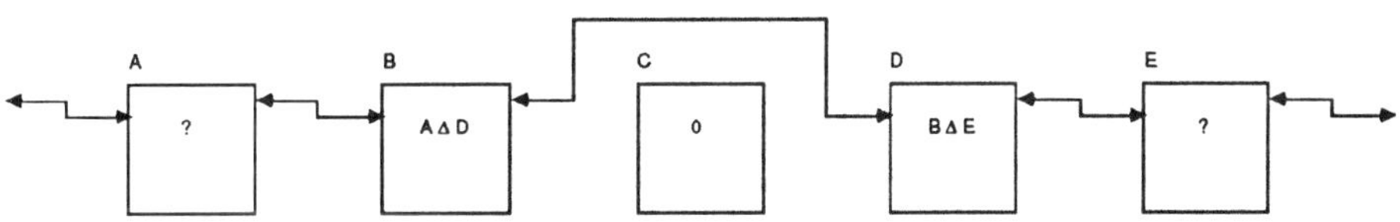

The signature field is another place for space savings. Since the signature field is intended as a debug tool, it may seem that once debugging is complete this space can be removed from the final application, saving the space entirely. In a smaller program, this is probably acceptable, but in a large project it is not at all obvious when debug is complete. Errors are routinely found in such large systems years after they have been deployed into the field.

Another complication arises from the fact that people are loathe to change things in a system that is working. Technically, removing debug code from a working system should have no adverse effect on the functioning of the system, but programmers are a superstitious lot. (After experiencing some of the mysterious things that computers can do, there is little wonder.) The very idea of changing the basic structure definition in a working system, even if it is just to remove the signature field, is a total anethema.

If totally removing this field is not an option, shrinking its size is certainly feasible. Allocating a full 16 bits to such a field is probably overkill. A program with even a one bit signature field has a 90 percent chance of finding an errant pointer within 4 chainings, statistically speaking. This may be a bit extreme, but a signature field as small as 4 bits is probably sufficient.

A variation of this is possible if the data structure can be forced to a size that is a power of two. In such cases, the least significant bits of the structure address are all the same for all structures allocated. For example, assume a structure definition that is 16 bytes in length and that the first structure is allocated at an address of *0x1234*. As shown in the diagram below, subsequent structures will always be allocated at addresses who's least significant digit is a *4*. We can test for this fact within our program, in effect, turning part of the address into our signature field.

This is probably not a very good technique, even though you will see it used in practice frequently. First, if you must add bytes to the structure definition to force it's size to a power of two, then it defeats the whole purpose. Why not just add a byte of signature and forget the hocus pocus? Secondly, it is very nonportable. Nothing in the definition of *malloc()* guarantees that Turbo C does not add some overhead, say a word or two, to the structures itself to provide for the orderly disposal of memory back to the heap. Besides the size of a structure that contains pointer variables is a function of the memory model used—changing memory models completely corrupts the plan.

Other Types of Linked Lists

Beyond simple singly and doubly linked lists, more complicated linked structures find their way into almost every aspect of programming. The difficulty in describing these myriad forms lies exactly in their flexibility. There is just no limit to the number of variations they can assume. The techniques employed with each, however, are identical to those we have already studied. If the reader understands the approach above, he can apply it to his own problem.

One form of particular note, however, is the state table. A state table describes the state of a system, much as our IRS structure described the state of individuals. State tables are most often used in applications such as communications, hardware control and game playing. Structurally, these tables resemble our linked lists of structures except that where our linked lists were always dynamic in nature, state tables can just as often be static.

Figure 4.12

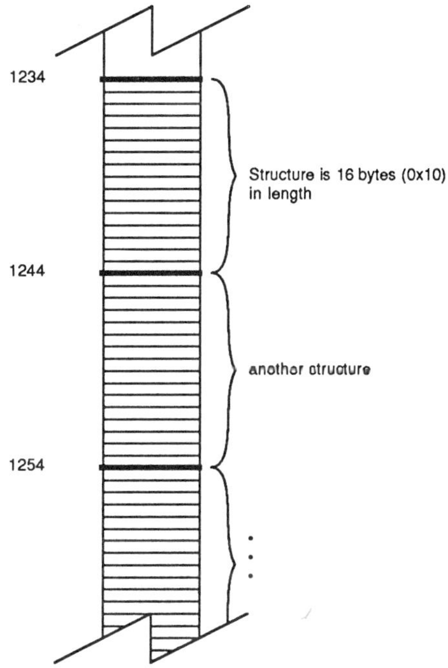

Structures of 16 (0x10) bytes
in length in memory

Static state tables are defined by the programmer as part of writing the program and do not change as the program executes. Static tables are most often used to define a set of rules to the system. That is, in any given condition, the state table defines how the system will respond to different stimuli. As with most things, this is best explained with an example.

Suppose we are tasked with writing a punctuation checker. Our program should take free text and analyze the spacing with respect to commas, periods, etc. Errors should be marked for correction. To keep the problem manageable, let's limit ourselves to capitals at the beginning of sentences and names, commas, periods, question marks and spaces. Specifically we are ignoring semicolons, colons, quotations, and contractions as well as spacing of paragraphs. The state table solution to this problem appears as Prg4_3.

```
/*Prg4_3 - Simple gramatical parser using state tables
   by Stephen Davis, 1987

  Implement a simple sentence parser using a state table approach.
  Program recognizes uppercase, lowercase, comma, space, period
  and newline.
*/

#include <stdio.h>
#include <ctype.h>
#define maxcases 5
enum chartype {invalid = 1,  period,
               space,     comma,    newline,
               lowercase, uppercase};
#define marker 0x5678

/*prototype definitions --*/
enum chartype evaluate (char);
int parse (struct state **, char);
void fixup (void);
int main (void);

/*grammatical state table*/
struct state {
               unsigned signature;
               char currvalue;
               struct {
                       enum chartype value;
                       struct state *next;
                      } choice [maxcases];
               struct state *error;
              } *current;

struct state start = {marker, 0,         {{uppercase, NULL /*&normal*/
                                           {0,         NULL},
                                           {0,         NULL},
                                           {0,         NULL},
                                           {0,         NULL}},
                                          NULL /*&normal*/},
             normal= {marker, lowercase, {{lowercase, &normal},
                                           {space,     NULL /*&break1*/
                                           {comma,     NULL /*&break2*/
                                           {period,    NULL /*&end1*/},
                                           {newline,   NULL /*&begline*
                                          &normal},
             break1= {marker, space,     {{lowercase, &normal},
                                           {uppercase, &normal},
                                           {0,         NULL},
                                           {0,         NULL},
                                           {0,         NULL}},
                                          &normal},
             break2= {marker, comma,     {{space,     &break1},
                                           {newline,   NULL /*&begline*
                                           {0,         NULL},
                                           {0,         NULL},
                                           {0,         NULL}},
                                          &normal},
             end1 =  {marker, period,    {{space,     NULL /*&end2*/},
                                           {newline,   &start},
                                           {0,         NULL},
                                           {0,         NULL},
                                           {0,         NULL}},
                                          &start},
             end2 =  {marker, space,     {{space,     &start},
```

```
                                                    {0,          NULL},
                                                    {0,          NULL},
                                                    {0,          NULL},
                                                    {0,          NULL}},
                                                    &start},
                  begline={marker, newline,        {{uppercase, &normal},
                                                    {lowercase, &normal},
                                                    {0,          NULL},
                                                    {0,          NULL},
                                                    {0,          NULL}},
                                                    &normal};



/*Evaluate - evaluate the current character. Return corresponding
             chartype*/
enum chartype evaluate (c)
    char c;
{
    switch (c) {
                case '.':
                case '?': return period;
                case ',': return comma;
                case ' ': return space;
                case '\n':return newline;
                default:
                          if (islower (c))
                               return lowercase;
                          else
                               if (isupper (c))
                                    return uppercase;
                               else
                                    return invalid;
               }
}

/*Parse - given the current state, compare the current character
          against the legal choices to select the next state.
          Return a 1 on no error and a 0 on error.*/
int parse (stateptr, c)
    struct state **stateptr;
    char c;
{
    unsigned i;
    enum chartype val;
    struct state *localptr;

    localptr = *stateptr;
    if (localptr -> signature != marker) {
         printf ("pointer error!\n");
         *stateptr = &start;
    } else {
         val = evaluate (c);
         for (i = 0; i < maxcases; i++)
              if (localptr -> choice [i].value == val) {
                   *stateptr = localptr -> choice [i].next;
                   return 1;
              }
    }
    *stateptr = localptr -> error;
    return 0;
}

/*Fixup - forward references are not allowed in data initializations.
          Fixup initializes those values which would generate error
```

```
129[ 0]:           messages in a data initialization.*/
130[ 0]: void fixup ()
131[ 0]: {
132[ 1]:     start.choice[0].next = &normal;
133[ 1]:     start.error = &normal;
134[ 1]:
135[ 1]:     normal.choice[1].next = &break1;
136[ 1]:     normal.choice[2].next = &break2;
137[ 1]:     normal.choice[3].next = &end1;
138[ 1]:     normal.choice[4].next = &begline;
139[ 1]:
140[ 1]:     break2.choice[1].next = &begline;
141[ 1]:
142[ 1]:     end1.choice[0].next = &end2;
143[ 0]: }
144[ 0]:
145[ 0]: /*Main - read in strings from STDIN.  Parse them against our state
146[ 0]:          table grammar rules.  Point out any errors detected.*/
147[ 0]: main ()
148[ 0]: {
149[ 1]:     char buffer [256], *ptr, mark;
150[ 1]:
151[ 1]:     fixup ();                            /*complete pointer init*/
152[ 1]:
153[ 1]:     current = &start;
154[ 1]:     while (gets (buffer)) {
155[ 2]:          printf ("%s\n", buffer);
156[ 2]:          for (ptr = buffer; *ptr; ptr++) {
157[ 3]:               if (parse (&current, *ptr))
158[ 3]:                    mark = ' ';
159[ 3]:               else
160[ 3]:                    mark = '^';
161[ 3]:               printf ("%c", mark);
162[ 2]:          }
163[ 2]:          parse (&current, '\n');        /*tack on a carriage return*/
164[ 2]:          printf ("\n");
165[ 1]:     }
166[ 0]: }
```

To understand the approach this program takes, we should examine a typical sentence. Suppose we had just read the 'l' in the 'typical' of the last sentence. From that point, we could reasonably expect another lower-case letter, a space, a comma or a period. We could not accept an upper-case letter, since uppercase letters do not appear immediately after lowercase letters in English. This is our state. Once we proceed to the space following 'typical' our options are limited to either a lower or upper-case letter. The comma and period are no longer legal after a space, but the upper-case now is. We have now moved to a new state.

In such a problem we should always begin by defining the different *types* of characters we will accept. This we do in our enumerated type *CHARTYPE* in line 12. (We equate the question and exclamation mark with the period, considering them the same for grammatical purposes.) *INVALID* is reserved for characters that do not fall into any the other categories, such as numbers.

Now examine the state table structure we have defined for this solution. After the standard *SIGNATURE* to be used for pointer integrity checking, is the *CURRVALUE* field. This field defines, more or less, the character that got us into this state. Not only is this field not necessarily unique, it isn't even required—it does not appear anywhere in the program itself. This field is included to help the programmer in creating the field definitions and in the debug process. Appearing next are the different types of input we understand in that state coupled with the state we assume when receiving that stimulus. Up to *MAX* = 5 different state/stimulus pairs can be differentiated. Finally, we add the state to go to next if we receive some input that we just don't understand--we can never anticipate all possibilities.

To follow these tables, start with an easily identifiable state, such as the beginning of a sentence, *START*. Sentences must begin with capital letters, so *UPPERCASE* is the only type stimulus we accept. Anything else generates an error. If an *UPPERCASE* is encountered we move into the "normal" interior state. From here we will accept anything *EXCEPT UPPERCASE*. As long as only lower-case letters are found, notice how we stay in the same state. (This corresponds to the interior of words.) A state may point to itself. Other characters cause us to vector into different states. A pictorial representation of our state tables appears in Figure 4.13.

Earlier I noted that *CURRVALUE* is not unique. This is not intuitive, but consider just as an example, that not all spaces are created equal. A space following a letter must be followed by either a lowercase or uppercase letter. By contrast, a space following a period *must* be followed by another space which in turn must be followed by an uppercase letter (we assume here that periods are always followed by two spaces). This *trichotomy of spaces* is expressed in three different space states appearing in our state tables. Once you understand the state tables, writing the actual code is simple. Keeping with our modular approach, we start by defining a function *evaluate()* that categorizes input characters into their proper type. *Parse()* takes the output of this routine and compares it against the legal types for the current state. If a match is found, the state pointer is moved to the new state and a 1 (success) is returned; otherwise, the error state is assumed and a 0 (failure) is returned.

After starting with state *START*, *main()* accepts ASCII input from *STDIN* using our old standby *gets()*. Errors are marked by first printing the string and then following along below, printing a space every time *parse()* returns a 1 and a caret whenever it returns a 0. This causes grammatical errors to be clearly marked from underneath. Since *gets()* filters out newlines, we must print and parse the *\n* explicitly.

Figure 4.13

Pictorially representative grammer parser state tables

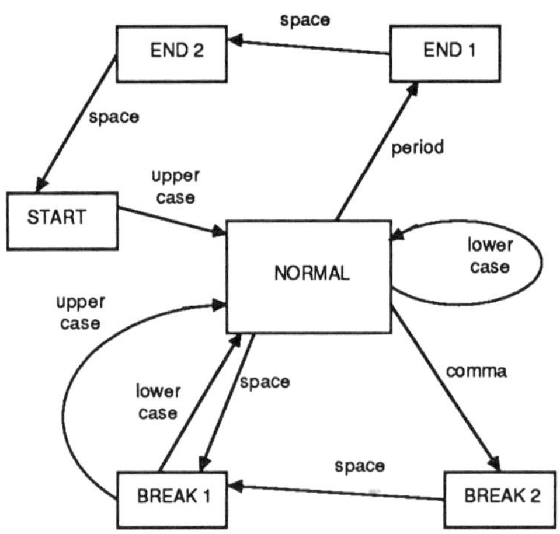

The above diagram does not include Newline for simplicity's sake. From each state, the arrows leading outward represent valid input from that state. For example, a period is legal when in state NORMAL. This transitions the parser to state END 1, from which only a space followed by another space is considered legal. This is a state table representation of the rulethat a period must be followed by two spaces.

Even though the grammatical rules used here have been purposely kept simple, the results are fairly impressive. A sample run is shown in Listing 4.13. Although the program gets confused fairly easily (especially by numbers and by tabs and spaces at paragraphs breaks), real grammatical errors were detected. Even when confused, the error case gets us back in sync fairly quickly. Try the program out on some sample text of your own. Considering the output, the actual program is surprisingly small. Interestingly, if we were to make our grammatical rules more complex by considering more different cases, our source code would not change (except, perhaps, for adding the new types to *evaluate()*). Instead we would add new grammatical rules merely by adding different states to our state tables. It is characteristic of state table solutions to problems that, once written, the code tends not to grow with increasing complexity of the problem, as is normal with most programs. Instead the state tables grow. This valuable property adds considerably to the maintainability of state table programs.

(If you don't believe this, try the following problem. Add numbers using the following grammatical rules: numbers may appear at the beginning of any word; numbers may only be followed by numbers or a space, comma or period. Numbers and letters may not follow each other immediately. Try this new program out on some text that contains imbedded numbers. Even these rules get confused with numbers containing embedded commas.)

Further, state table implementations of programs are somewhat unintuitive to set up and a little hard to read initially. To those familiar with the technique, however, state table implementations are very easy to follow. (Again, try rewriting the above program using standard *IF..THEN..ELSE* logic.)

Dynamic state tables are most often used in areas where decisions must be made. These so-called decision trees are built to investigate the possibilities open to a program. The classic example here are programs that play chess. A chess program starts from the current board position and calculates all of the legal moves open to it. A state table entry is built to describe the state of the board after each move. To each of the board states, all of the legal responses are considered and an entry built for each. These second level tables are attached to the first level state table from which it came. This process is repeated for deeper and deeper levels to some arbitrary depth. This results in what is known as a decision tree. Once all of the board states have been constructed, they are evaluated for position. A number is calculated reflecting how advantageous that board position is to the program. The most advantageous board is selected and the tree limbs traced back up through the nodes to the first move that led to that position. The program then makes its move.

Of course, real chess programs are not quite this simple. Sophisticated tree pruning algorithms are used to minimize the search time by prematurely terminating search paths that cannot be advantageous. Unfortunately, an example chess program is beyond the scope of this book.

Conclusion

In this chapter we have briefly covered the topic of linked structure solutions to common problems. In doing so we have stressed some of the good programming techniques that should come natural to experienced C programmers, the most important of which is modularity both in code, through proper function definition, and in data, through proper structure definition. Finally, we have seen some time saving coding techniques, such as pointer integrity checking, that can drastically reduce debug and test time.

Although linked list solutions to problems are not always the most obvious, one should seek them out. Not only are they more flexible and much more easily maintained, they are easily read by programmers familiar with the technique. Linked structures represent a powerful tool that every programmer should have in his or her repertoire.

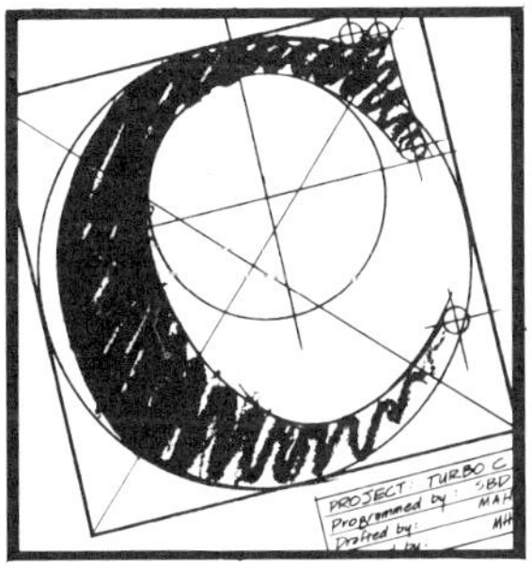

5
Accessing DOS and the Turbo Library

The topic of the Disk Operating System (DOS), by which term I'm referring to either PC-DOS or the equivalent MS-DOS, is a very large one. There are a million stories in the big city and we can't possibly tell them all. In fact, some of them we don't even want to tell. Once again, not everything that can be done is worth doing.

Although not advisable, it is certainly possible to back up on a crowded freeway. (It may not be possible to do it more than once.) Similarly, it might be possible to edit the *File Allocation Table* (FAT) with a debugger. It would be crazy for me to present a chapter on doing so, however. One wrong move and you start wiping out files from here to the New Jersey turnpike. Crashed disk, angry reader, book in the trash can. It's not a pretty sight.

Other, more mundane, topics are probably not worth dwelling on either. Everyone gets the hang of *printf()*ing to the screen pretty quickly. Once you get tired of the straight ASCII characters, you can start printing the special characters above 0x7f. These are the characters normally used in foreign languages or in blocking out windows on non-graphics screens. Finding these characters for yourself is part of the joy of hacking, however. Delving into every nuance of the *printf()* in this book probably serves little purpose.

There are, however, plenty of topics of interest to the new DOS programmer or even the old DOS programmer who has never examined the DOS operating system from the vantage point of a *low level programmer*. In this chapter I will try to give a broad overview of the DOS system calls, while at the same time examining in a little more detail some of the more difficult or interesting of these functions. I will not describe each of the arguments to the different calls—these are explained adequately in the *Turbo C Reference Guide*. Instead I will present sample programs using these functions while, at the same time, discussing some of the concepts behind them. As DOS is so varied, this may at times give the chapter the appearance of a collection of disconnected concepts.

It should be pointed out that the programs in this chapter require PC-DOS 2.1 (MS-DOS 2.11) or later. This should be no problem as Turbo C itself requires at least DOS 2.0. PC users who are still using DOS 1.1 will want to run, not walk, to the phone to order one of the newer versions of DOS. In fact, users of DOS 2.x will probably want to update to one of the 3.x series. A few of the programs presented here require its enhancements.

What is DOS?

DOS is the operating system which is most often purchased for or supplied with IBM PCs, ATs and compatibles. Like all operating systems, DOS provides a shell over the underlying hardware, for example, relieving the programmer from worrying about the details of UART control when executing that *printf()* mentioned in the introduction. Were it not for this software support, explaining even the simple string output provided by *printf()* may have taken up this entire chapter.

DOS began as a copy of CPM80 (tm Digital Research), a popular operating system for 8080 and Z80 based microcomputers. In its first version, its commands were similar to CPM80 and its capabilities similarly limited. Fairly quickly, DOS left its precursor behind. As DOS aged, its system calls became simpler and its user interface began adopting some of the popular aspects of UNIX: the same subdirectory structure, piping, redirection, etc. Support was added for larger and differently formatted floppy drives and hard disks.

Bound by its humble beginnings, however, it has not been able to truly shake off the shackles of it ancestry. DOS has always remained a non-multitasking, non-virtual memory, single threaded executive. It is simply not possible to retrofit these concepts into an existing system. It is for this reason that users have been searching for a replacement for DOS in such systems as UNIX, Xenix and OS/2.

When we think of DOS, the first thing to come to mind is the ubiquitous *A>* prompt. (In actuality, with the prompt customization provided in the later versions of DOS, most of us have not seen a simple *A>* prompt in years, but the idea is the same.) In fact, the *A>* prompt has little to do with the DOS your application program sees. User commands are handled by a program called *COMMAND.COM*. While this program has some special previledges, it runs under DOS much like programs written in Turbo C. *COMMAND.COM* makes the same DOS calls that other programs do.

The DOS actually consists of two files that the user seldom if ever sees. These files are variously described as *IBMBIO.SYS* and *IBMDOS.SYS* or *IO.SYS* and *MSDOS.SYS* depending on version. The names of these files are not important as you cannot (or, at least, should not) access them directly anyway. These two files are loaded into low memory by the boot loader at power-on and not accessed again. It is these two files and not COMMAND.COM which contain the code defining the DOS calls which we will see in this chapter.

There is actually a level of software between the user's Turbo C program and the operating system. Much as DOS forms a shell around the hardware, the Turbo C library forms a shell around DOS, protecting the programmer from some of its harshities. For every DOS function of any importance there is a Turbo C library function to access it. The Turbo C library equivalent is more user friendly, either providing capabilities not available in the simple DOS call or simply defining easier, more mnemonic arguments.

Figure 5.1

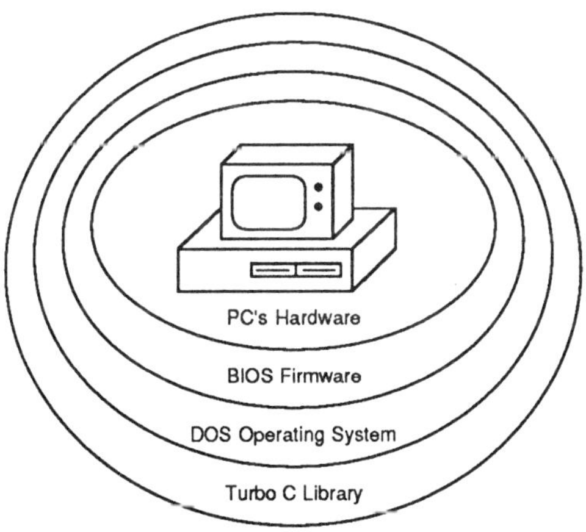

The Turbo C programmer is protected from the harshities of the PC's hardware by layers of software, each of which relies upon the layers below it.

In general, it is good programming practice to use the highest level routine which does the job (in the required amount of time). In the interest of legibility, it is probably preferable if a program calls the Turbo C function *findfirst(),* for example, and avoids invoking the equivalent system call *0x4e,* even if that's all that *findfirst()* does. Not only are the arguments easier to set up, but the casual reader is much more likely to understand *findfirst()*.

Even among Turbo C functions, some are more portable than others. The Reference Guide is careful to point out those functions which are unique to DOS and those which are shared with UNIX. A certain amount of effort has been expended maintaining as much portability as possible. For example, arguments are defined to the *open()* call which have little or no meaning under DOS, merely to enhance its similarity with the *open()* under UNIX systems. A far greater number of Turbo C library calls are common to other C environments for the PC, most notably the Microsoft C compilers.

DOS is far from optimum in many respects. From Chapter 6 almost until the end of this book we will study ways and reasons to avoid using the DOS system calls. I do not want to give the impression that I am somehow down on the DOS operating system, however. DOS represents a large body of largely bug free code. While some versions of DOS are known to have bugs, these bugs are rare and well documented. This large body of working code should not be overlooked easily.

In addition, future protected mode operating systems, such as OS/2, may make many of the direct access techniques which we will examine impossible. Turbo C programs which begin reading and writing memory all over the machine will not be tolerated and will require extensive revision. Programs which, by and large, limit themselves strictly to DOS calls will be easier to port over to these new executives than applications which do not.

Accessing DOS

As we mentioned earlier, when confronted with a problem the programmer should first examine the Turbo C library for his solution. If the programmer needs to open a file, for example, he should first look towards Turbo C's *open()* or *open()*. Each is well documented and their arguments are adapted to the C language. Not only is this the safest, but by staying with the UNIX calls, can provide a certain amount of portability beyond the DOS operating system. Only when that does not work, either because the library function does not exist, is too slow, or does not provide exactly the correct arguments, should the programmer turn to direct access to the DOS system calls.

The DOS functions are intended to be called effeciently from all languages, but they are primarily laid out for thc assembly language programmer. Arguments to these functions are assigned to the registers of the 8086 microprocessor rather than on the stack as are arguments to C functions. To mate the two interfacing techniques properly, Turbo C provides a library routine *intdos()*. *Intdos()* accepts two arguments: a structure containing the registers to be loaded before entering the DOS call and a structure into which to store the registers upon returning.

Before we can call *intdos()* we should include the *.H* file, *DOS.H*. Within this file are the following definitions:

```
struct WORDREGS
        {
         unsigned int ax, bx, cx, dx, si, di, cflag, flags;
        };

struct BYTEREGS
        {
         unsigned char al, ah, bl, bh, cl, ch, dl, dh;
        };

union   REGS    {
        struct  WORDREGS x;
        struct  BYTEREGS h;
        };
```

As we can see, *REGS* is declared to be the union of two structures, one of characters and the other of integers. A union is the C way to gain access to the same location in memory in different formats. For example, in the simpler declaration below, the integer *WORD* and the two characters *BYTE1* and *BYTE2* both refer to the same word in memory.

```
union {
       unsigned word;
       char byte1, byte2;
      } double_up;
```

Storing a *0x12* into *DOUBLE_UP.BYTE1* and a *0x34* into *DOUBLE_UP.BYTE2* results in *DOUBLE_UP.WORD* containing the value *0x3412*. While you might have expected 0x1234, Intel microprocessors store the byte of lower significance at the lower address. Therefore, *BYTE1* corresponds to the lower byte of *WORD* and *BYTE2* to the upper. It is only at times such as these, when addressing the same location as both a byte and a word, that programmers need concern themselves with the storage order.

Figure 5.2

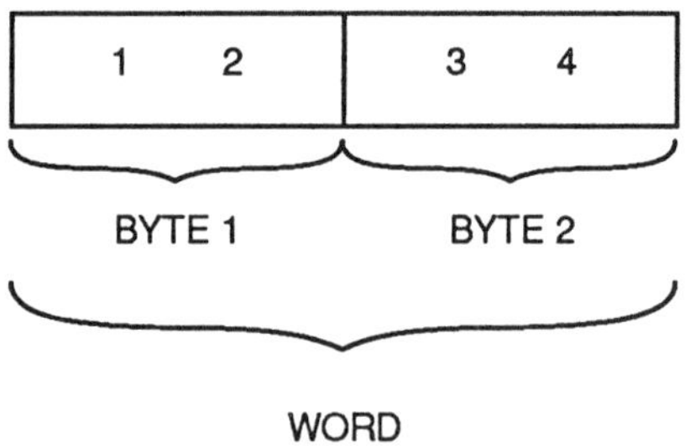

Of course, the names of the elements in these two structures are not accidental. The names *AX, BX,* etc. in structure *WORDREGS* are the same as the names of the 16-bit registers in the 8086 and 80286 class of microprocessors. The elements *AH, AL, BH,* and so on in the structure *BYTEREGS* are the same as the 8 bit registers in these microprocessors.

The union of the character declarations BYTEREGS and the integer declarations WORDREGS allows the first four words of each to be accessed as either words (integer) or pairs of bytes (character). This corresponds to the fact that the first four 16 bit registers in the 8086 can also be accessed as pairs of 8-bit registers. Thus, the two bytes in AX may be independently referred to as *AH* and *AL, BX* as *BH* and *BL,* etc. The union *REGS* represents in C the register architecture of the 8086.

The programmer declares one or more variables of type *REGS*. Rather than load values into a register, which the C programmer cannot do, he loads them into the element of REGS with the same name. Once all of the values are set up, he calls *intdos()* passing to it the address of *REGS*. *Intdos()* loads the registers from this union and performs the system call. Upon returning from the call, *intdos()* stores the registers back into the same (or another) union where they can be easily accessed from C again.

Each DOS call is assigned a unique number to differentiate it. The caller indicates to the system the DOS call he is trying to make by placing its number in the AH register. All of the other registers are defined uniquely to the individual DOS calls. While many DOS functions assign similar meanings to the individual registers, there is no rule of thumb that can be made other than the AH rule. The different DOS functions are best documented in Microsoft's MS-

DOS *Programmer's Reference*. They are also described in several popular books on the subject. I have included a short description of them in *Appendix 1*.

For example, one of the simplest of the DOS calls is system call *0x2e, Set/Reset Verify Flag*. (If the *Verify Flag* is set, DOS automatically verifies all disk writes by performing a subsequent read and comparing the results.) Passing the *Set/Reset Verify Flag* function a 0 in register *AL* resets the flag, while a 1 sets it. Assuming that the union *REGS* has already been defined, the following code segment sets the *Verify flag ON*.

```
regs.h.ah = 0x2e;          /*Set Verify Flag*/
regs.h.al = 1;             /*set the flag on*/
intdos (&regs, &regs);
```

While access to the 8 *common* registers is sufficient for the majority of DOS calls, a few also require that the segment registers be initialized to particular values. For this purpose, a separate library routine *intdosx()* is provided. This function is identical to *intdos()* except that it accepts one extra argument, a structure of type *SREGS*. This structure has the following definition in the include file *DOS.H*.

```
struct  SREGS   {
        unsigned int es;
        unsigned int cs;
        unsigned int ss;
        unsigned int ds;
        };
```

Just as the members of *BYTEREGS* and *WORDREGS* corresponded to the *normal* registers of the *8086*, the elements of this structure correspond to the segment registers of the processor. Say that a particular DOS function required that *DS:DX points to the variable to be written*, for example. This would be accomplished with the following C example:

```
#include <dos.h>
union REGS reg;
struct SREGS sreg;
char *string;
        .
        .
        .
reg.x.dx = FP_OFF ((char far *)string);
sreg.ds  = FP_SEG ((char far *)string);
        .
        .
        .
```

The DOS calls fall into two groups: the DOS 1.x calls and the DOS 2.x (and later) calls. As we mentioned earlier, the original DOS mimicked very much its predecessor, CPM. At the time of the PC's introduction, the CPM machines were king. Since all of the existing software was designed to run on CPM machines, DOS made every effort to make the job of porting programs from CPM to DOS 1.x as simple as possible. The table on the next page gives a cursory comparison of the CPM-like DOS calls to their CPM equivalents.

Many of these system calls, like their CPM equivalents before them, are clumsy and difficult to use. This is especially true of the file related system calls which required the user program to build a File Control Block before handing it over to the system. (File Control Blocks are explained in the *Programmer's Reference Manual* also.) Besides, these file access routines do not provide support for the UNIX-like directory structure which was adopted with DOS 2.x. Those system calls marked with an asterisk above have been retained in DOS only for compatibility purposes. Microsoft no longer recommends their use. In fact, most of them could probably be removed from DOS today without the majority of programs even being aware.

The second set of system calls are the so-called UNIX-like DOS calls. While not resembling the system calls found in the UNIX operating system, these services were given this name primarily because they introduce support for DOS' UNIX-like features such as hierarchical directories, redirection, and the like. These DOS 2.x enhancements are listed in Table 5.2.

These system calls tend to be the ones we access when making Turbo C library calls. They are also the ones we should attempt to use when making our own *intdos()* calls. They are both easier to use and more powerful.

Some DOS Concepts

Let us examine some DOS concepts. Many of these will already be familiar to UNIX programmers, but many will not. A firm understanding of these concepts will be necessary to write effective C programs in the DOS environment.

Table 5.1
CPM-like DOS System Calls

System Call	Function	Corresponding CPM Call	Function
0*	Terminate	0	System Reset
1	Keyboard Input w/ Echo	1	Console Input
2	Display Output	2	Console Output
3	Serial Input	3	Reader Input
4	Serial Output	4	Punch Output
5	Printer Output	5	List Output
6	Direct Console I/O	6	Direct Con I/O
7	Direct Keyboard Input w/o Echo	–	
8	Keyboard Input w/o Echo	–	
9	Display String	9	Print String
A	Buffered Keyboard Input	A	Read Con Buffer
B	Check Keyboard Buffer Status	B	Get Con Status
C	Clear Keyboard and DO Function	–	
D	Reset Disk	D	Reset Disk
E	Select Drive	E	Select Disk
F*	Open File	F	Open File
10*	Close File	10	Close File
11*	Find First	11	Find First
12*	Find Next	12	Find Next
13*	Delete File	13	Delete File
14*	Read Sequential	14	Read Sequential
15*	Write Sequential	15	Write Sequential
16*	Create File	16	Make File
17*	Rename File	17	Rename File
19	Report Current Drive	19	Retn Current Disk
1A	Set Disk Transferr Address	1A	Set DMA Addr
1B	Get Default Disk Data	–	
1C	Get Disk Data	–	
21*	Read Random	21	Read Random
22*	Write Random	22	Write Random
23*	Get File Size	23	File Sizc
24*	Set Relative Record	24	Set Random Record
25	Set Interrupt Vector	–	
26*	Create New PSP	–	
27*	Read Random Block	–	
28*	Write Random Block	28	Write Random w/Fill
29	Parse Filename	–	
2A	Get Date	–	
2B	Set Date	–	
2C	Get Time	–	
2D	Sot Time	-	
2E	Set/Reset Verify Flag	–	

Those system calls marked with an asterisk have been replaced by DOS 2.x calls and are included only for compatibility.

Table 5.2
DOS 2.x System Calls

SystemCall	Function	Replaces
2F	Get Disk Transfer Address	
30	Get DOS Version Number	
31	Terminate and Stay Resident	Interrupt 27
33	Get/Set Control Break Check	
35	Get Interrupt Vector	
36	Get Disk Free Space	
38	Get Country Data	
39	Create Directory (MKDIR)	
3A	Remove Directory (RMDIR)	
3B	Change Current Directory (CHDIR)	
3C	Create Handle (Create File)	16
3D	Open Handle (Open File or Device)	F
3E	Close Handle (Close File or Device)	10
3F	Read Handle (Read File or Device)	14,21,27
40	Write Handle (Write File or Device)	15,22,28
41	Delete Directory Entry (Delete File)	13
42	Move File Pointer	24
43	Get/Set File Attributes	
44	I/O Control	
45	Duplicate File Handle	
46	Force Duplicate File Handle	
47	Get Current Directory	
48	Allocate Memory	
49	Free Memory	
4A	Set Block	
4B	Load and Execute Program	26
4C	End Process	0
4D	Get Return Code of Child Process	
4E	Find First File	11
4F	Find Next File	12
54	Get Verify State	
56	Change Directory Entry (Rename File)	17
57	Get/Set Date/Time of File	
58	Get/Set Allocation Strategy	
59	Get Extended Error	
5A	Create Temporary File	16
5B	Create New File	16
5C	Lock/Unlock	
5E	Get Machine Name	
5F	Nextword Assign List Entry Access	
62	Get PSP	
65	Get Extended Country Information	
66	Get/Set Global Code Page	
67	Set Handle Count	
68	Committ File	

Note that system calls beginning with 59 were first introduced with DOS 3.0. System calls 65 through 68 are only defined under DOS 3.3.

The first and easiest of these concepts is that of version number. While DOS 2.x will be sufficient for most of the programs in this book, some of these programs rely on the enhanced capabilities of DOS 3.x. If 3.5 inch floppy disk or LAN support or any of the other features unique to the newer versions of DOS are important to your program, it should check the DOS version number before proceeding. (Technically, a program should check the version number even before using the 2.x enchancements, but today we can safely assume DOS 2.0 as a minimum.)

Notice that our concern goes only one way. So far, Microsoft has not removed support for any feature of DOS. For example, all of the CPM-like system calls that have been replaced are still supported today. Therefore, if a program relies on a capability introduced in a particular version of DOS, it need only worry that the current DOS being executed is not too old. It does not have to worry, that the version of DOS is too new and that the critical feature has been removed.

Prg5_1 shown in the listing below checks the version number as reported from Turbo C against that reported from DOS itself. Of course, they agree, but this is a simple example of accessing the same capability from Turbo C and via the *intdos()* call. Turbo C maintains a global variable *_VERSION* which contains the major and minor version numbers. The major version is the number in front of the decimal point and the minor version the number after. For example, in DOS 3.1, the major version is 3 and the minor is 1. To pull apart the two halves of the version number we have used the union *WORD2BYTE*.

```
/*Prg5_1 - Check DOS Version Number
   by Stephen R. Davis

  This is the most rudimentary form of access to DOS and, yet, it
  is sometimes necessary to make sure that the DOS supports alls
  the facilities we intend to use.
*/

#include <stdio.h>
#include <dos.h>

/*some prototype definitions*/
unsigned dos_from_TC (void);
unsigned dos_from_intdos (void);
void main (void);

/*declare some global variables*/
union REGS regs;

/*Main - fetch the current version from Turbo C and from DOS and
         make sure they agree*/
void main (void)
{
     int dosversion1, dosversion2;
     union {
```

```
                unsigned int  word;
                unsigned char byte [2];
              } WORD2BYTE;

    /*first get the version from Turbo C*/
    dosversion1 = dos_from_TC ();

    /*and display it as two bytes*/
    WORD2BYTE.word = dosversion1;
    printf ("According to Turbo C Library,"
            "you are using DOS %d.%d\n",
            WORD2BYTE.byte [0],
            WORD2BYTE.byte [1]);

    /*now get the version direct from DOS*/
    dosversion2 = dos_from_intdos ();

    /*and display it as two bytes also*/
    WORD2BYTE.word = dosversion2;
    printf ("while according to DOS itself,"
            "you are using DOS %d.%d\n",
            WORD2BYTE.byte [0],
            WORD2BYTE.byte [1]);

    /*now compare the two*/
    if (dosversion1 == dosversion2)
         printf ("The two sources agree\n\n");
    else
         printf ("DOS and Turbo C don't agree!\n\n");
}

/*Dos_from_TC - return the DOS version number from the Turbo C Library
                global value*/
unsigned dos_from_TC (void)
{
    return _version;
}

/*Dos_from_intdos - fetch the version number using the DOS function*/
unsigned dos_from_intdos (void)
{
    regs.h.ah = 0x30;
    intdos (&regs, &regs);
    return regs.x.ax;
}

```

The function *dos_from_intdos()* loads the *Get Version Number* system call into register *AH* before making a call to *intdos()*. The major version number is returned from the call in *AL* and the minor in *AH*. Again, we make use of the union *WORD2BYTE* to separate the two. *Get Version Number* returns a 0 for versions of DOS prior to 2.0.

Another DOS concept all too often ignored is that of *Return Status*. Whenever a program executes and then completes, it returns a single integer *Return Status* back to the operating system. The operating system does not do anything with this status except store it in case anyone wants to know what it is. The intent is that a program use the *Return Status* to indicate whether it was successful or not in doing whatever is was supposed to do.

A Turbo C program sets the *Return Status* by exiting the program with a call to the Turbo library routine *exit()*. *Exit()* accepts a single integer argument, which it passes back to DOS as the *Return Status*. Since there are no rules, the user can assign whatever meaning he desires to the return value. It is, however, convention that a successful program returns a 0. A nonzero return status indicates a failure of some sort, with the actual value perhaps indicating the nature of the failure.

When a program is executed from the IDE or from the DOS prompt, the Return Status is not obvious. Since presumably the program also generates error messages in the event of a problem, it does not need to be. If the program failed, the user should be aware of that fact already by reading the messages on his screen. He does not need a cryptic single digit number to tell him the problem. The operator can decide what to do next on the basis of the messages generated by the application.

Batch files are another matter. It is not possible for a *.BAT* batch file to *read* the messages appearing on the screen to decide if a particular step executed as desired. Most batch files are written *blind*, assuming that each step worked to perfection and blundering on to the next command. Alternatively, the batch file can access the *Return Status* via the label *ERRORLEVEL*. For example, the following batch file executes a two pass process. If *PASS1* is unsuccessful, *PASS2* should not be executed. This batch file fits the bill.

```
        pass1 %1
        if errorlevel 1 goto :exit
        pass2 %1
:exit
```

This batch file executes the program *PASS1* on its first argument. Upon completion, *PASS1* sets the *Return Status* to 0 for success and 1 or greater for failure. The test *IF ERRORLEVEL* 1 is true if the *Return Status* is 1 *OR GREATER*. Since there is no test for equality, if more than one type of failure is to be differentiated, they must be tested for in descending order of value. If the *Return Status* is 1 or greater, the command *GOTO :EXIT* is executed to jump around executing *PASS2* on the same first argument.

We can put *Return Status* to other uses, however. Since it has no meaning to the operating system at all, we can assign meanings other than success and failure. For example, examine Prg5_2 below.

```
/*Prg5_2 - Return Status upon Exit
   by Stephen R. Davis, 1987

  Use the return of status to indicate to a .BAT file what character
  was depressed.
*/

#include <stdio.h>
#include <ctype.h>
#include <process.h>

/*Main - pose the question and await the response*/
void main (argc, argv)
     unsigned argc;
     char *argv [];
{
     /*provide the question*/
     if (argc <= 1)
          printf ("Yes or No?");
     else
          while (**++argv)
               printf ("%s ", *argv);

     /*now get the response*/
     if (tolower (getchar ()) == 'y')
          exit (0);
     else
          exit (1);
}
```

This program is quite simple. First, it checks to see if it has any arguments or not. If it does, it prints these arguments in their entirety on the display. If not, it simply prints *Yes or No?*. Either way, it waits for a single letter response from the keyboard. If that response is a *Y* or *y*, it exits with a *Return Value* of 0; otherwise, with a value of 1.

A batch file such as the following puts this to good use.

```
echo off
prg5_2 Do you want RAM resident software installed?
if errorlevel 1 goto :dont
echo Installing Ram residents
goto :exit
:dont
echo Not installing Ram resident programs
:exit
```

Prg5_2 views each of the words appearing after it as a separate argument, all of which it copies to the display. It then awaits a response to the question. If the user enters *Y*, *Return Status* returns as a 0 and the *IF ERRORLEVEL 1* fails causing the batch file to fall through to the *Installing RAM residents* section. Presumably, in a real batch file, ram resident programs would actually be installed here. If some other response is entered to the question, the *IF*

ERRORLEVEL 1 clause passes, causing the batch file to branch to the *:DONT* section.

```
C:\USER\C
C>example
Do you want RAM resident software installed? y
Installing Ram residents
```

Although Prg5_2 only differentiates between 2 different responses, it is conceivable that a similar program might be written which differentiated between several different inputs. For example, *Y*es, *N*o and the first 10 letters of the alphabet. Such programs allow menuing systems to be built around DOS batch files.

These niceties aside, what usually pops to mind when thinking of an operating system is its handling of the file system. How does a program get at the disk? Before we examine how to use Turbo C's file support routines, let's take just a minute to see how to avoid them. Up until now, we have written numerous programs without resorting to any of the normal file access facilities. This is particularly remarkable when you consider that, like UNIX, DOS considers both the screen and the keyboard to be special types of files!

For most of the screen and keyboard routines we have used so far, an analogous *file* version exists. For example, *printf()* is the same as *fprintf()* with the file specifier removed. It has been removed, because *printf()* assumes that output is to be directed at the *stdout* file. In fact, in most systems, *printf()* does nothing more than invoke *fprintf()* with the console output specifier.

Treating the hardware devices like files leads to some pleasing simplifications in the way the operating system is built and in the command structure. It does lead to a problem, however. A file must be opened before it can be read from or written to. If an error occurs on the open, the program should print an error message to the screen and give up. But if an error occured on the open of the screen itself, where could the program go to alert the operator?

Besides which fact, it would be an awful bother to be forced to open the keyboard and screen at the beginning of every program. Not only would programmers be forced to include the same silly open calls in almost every one of their programs, but the rest of us would be forced to read them. To save us the bother, C opens three files by default: *stdin* (standard input), *stdout* (standard output) and *stderr* (standard error). *Stdin* defaults to the keyboard, while *stdout* and *stderr* default to the display.

DOS allows the standard output and standard input to be redirected to other files, however. Including the statement *<FILE1* on the command line redirects standard input away from the keyboard and to *FILE1*. Similarly, the command *>FILE2* redirects standard output to *FILE2*. The single redirection arrow deletes *FILE2*, if present, and creates a new one. The similar double redirection arrow appends output onto the end of *FILE2*, if it already exists. The standard error device cannot be redirected for reasons we will see shortly.

It is sometimes desirable to tie the output of one program with the input of another. This is done via the pipe |. The command *DIR|MORE* sends the output of *DIR* to the program *MORE* rather than to the default display. *MORE* in its turn, accepts the input from directory and outputs 25 lines at a time on the display. (Try it.)

We first used this trick back in Chapter 3, in Prg3_1, to put off the discussion of DOS files until now. Prg3_1 takes C programs as input and generates the listing files which we have been using in this book. Instead of doing so directly, however, Prg3_1 took its input from the standard input device and sent its output to the standard output. I pointed out back then that all you had to do was to enter a command such as

```
prg3_1 <prg3_1.c >lpt1
```

to generate perfectly suitable output to the printer. It is interesting to note that we could have used pipes back then also with commands such as

```
prg3_1 <prg3_1.c | more
```

or

```
type prg3_1.c | prg3_1 | more
```

to display one screenworth of program listing at a time. (Notice that the two DOS statements above have the same effect. Why?)

We used redirection and pipes back then to avoid discussing file handling until now. It is, however, a worthwhile tool to keep in our arsenal all of the time. If our program has simple input/output needs, using redirected input and output gives the programmer one less thing with which to worry. This gets simple programs up and working in less time.

Programs without such simple input/output requirements will need to access the DOS file system. Before doing so, the programmer should have a basic understanding of DOS files. There are four parts to every DOS file name: the disk, the path, the name and the extension. The disk is a single letter followed by a colon, such as *A:*. This specifies which disk drive contains the file. The second part is the subdirectory path. This is string of directory names beginning, ending and separated with a backslash (\). The file name is a string of up to 8 letters or numbers. A zero length file name is not legal. Finally, the extension is a string of up to 3 letters or numbers. A zero length extension is legal. The filename and extension are separated by a period (.).

Most of the parts of a DOS file name are pretty straightforward, probably not requiring much discussion. UNIX users will have to get used to the fact that DOS considers the period to be a special file name divider instead of just another character. Users of simpler file systems, however, may not be familiar with the second part of the file name, the file path.

There are several types of files which DOS recognizes. One of the special types is the subdirectory. The subdirectory contains pointers to other files contained within it. One might view this as an octopus with the subdirectory file at the head and the individual files at the ends of the legs. Pictorially this might look like the following:

Figure 5.3

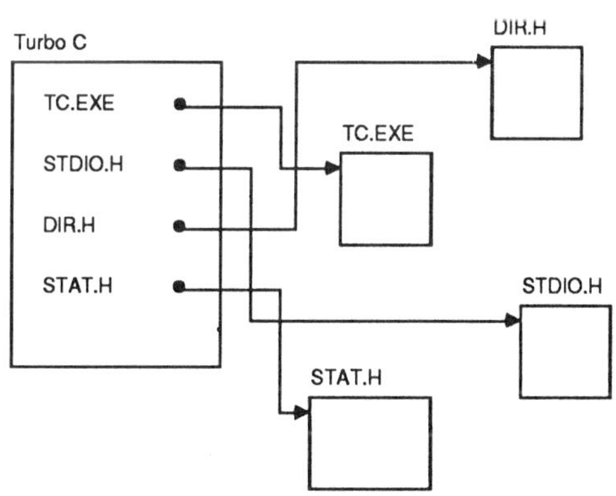

A directory is a file containing pointers to other files

Since subdirectories are nothing more than a special type of file, a subdirectory itself may be contained within other subdirectories leading to a multilevel file system. Pictorially, this more resembles a tree as in the following:

Figure 5.4

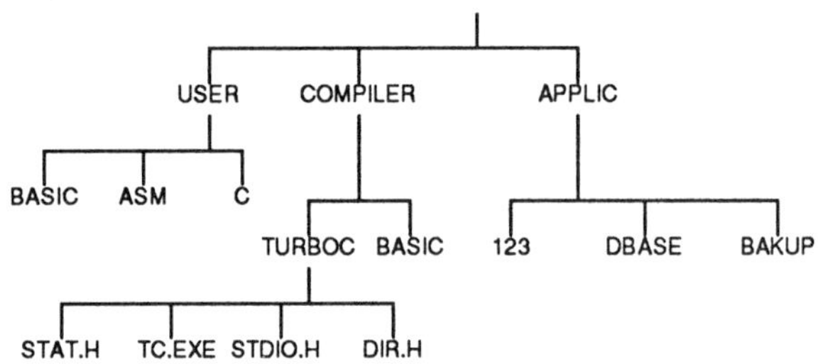

A portion of the hierarchical structure of the author's hard disk

A file's path name specifies all of the subdirectories the operating system must traverse to get from the disk's base level (the so-called root) to the file. For example, in the file *A:\DOG\CAT\CHICKEN.BRD,* the file *CHICKEN.BRD* is found in the directory CAT which is in turn found in the directory *DOG* which is found in the root of disk *A:*.

It is not usually necessary to specify the entire path. A default disk drive and directory path, often called the *current disk* and *current directory,* are known to the system. If the current default path were *A:\DOG\CAT,* it would only be necessary to specify the simple file name, *CHICKEN.BRD*. DOS would automatically append the default path onto the front. If the default were *A:\DOG,* it would only be necessary to specify *CAT\CHICKEN.BRD*. Any path which does not begin with a \ is assumed to be relative to the default directory path. Those which do begin with \, however, specify the entire path. That is, *CAT\CHICKEN.BRD* is assumed to be relative to the default *A:\DOG,* whereas *\CAT\CHICKEN.BRD* is assumed to be the full path name.

When specifying a path name in C, the programmer must remember that the character backslash already has a meaning. Thus, specifying a \ will confuse C into thinking that the next character has special meaning, as in *\n* or *\0x0d*. Two backslashes are required within a C character string. Therefore, for the above pathname, a C program must specify *A:\\DOG\\CAT\\CHICKEN.BRD*.

As you will see in the example programs, the Turbo C library is very helpful in handling pathnames in programs. In particular, the routines *fnsplit()* and *fnmerge()* parse DOS filenames into their constituent parts.

Now that we understand DOS file naming conventions, let's examine our *pretty print* program, Prg3_1, rewritten now to accept a file name as input and a different file name as output in Prg5_3.

```
/* Prg5_3 -- Pretty print (2nd vers)
    by Stephen R. Davis, 1987

  Accepts up to two arguments which are assumed to be file names.
  Prints first argument to second argument after adding line
  numbers and noting the "nesting level".  If the second file name
  is missing, assumes 'stdout'.  If first argument is missing, this
  is assumed to be an error and an error message is given.
*/

#include <stdio.h>
#include <process.h>
#include <errno.h>

/*the system error list is known at link time*/
extern char *sys_errlist [];

/*define a few macros we can use*/
#define min(x,y) ((x)<(y)) ? (x):(y)
#define lpp 66

/*prototype definitions --*/
void main (int, char **);
void nesting (unsigned *, char *);
char *fgetstr (char *, int, FILE *);
void errexit (unsigned);

/*Main - open the first and second arguments and proceed
         as in Prog1*/
void main (argc, argv)
    int argc;
    char *argv[];
{
    FILE *input,*output;
    char string[256];
    unsigned linenum,level,newlevel;

    if (argc > 3 || argc < 2)           /*wrong number args?*/
         errexit (1);

    if ((input = fopen (argv[1], "r")) == 0) /*get input file*/
         errexit (2);

    if (argc == 2)                      /*if no output file...*/
         output = stdout;               /*...use stdout, else...*/
    else {                              /*...open output file*/
         if ((output = fopen (argv[2], "r")) != 0)
              errexit (3);              /*file exists already!*/
         fclose (output);
         if ((output = fopen (argv[2], "w")) == 0)
```

```
[ 2]:               errexit (4);
[ 1]:     }
[ 1]:
[ 1]:     linenum = 0;
[ 1]:     newlevel = 0;
[ 1]:     while (fgetstr(string, 255, input)) {
[ 2]:          level = newlevel;
[ 2]:          nesting(&newlevel, string);
[ 2]:          string[70] = '\0';
[ 2]:          if (fprintf (output, "%3u[%2u]: %s\n", ++linenum,
[ 2]:                              min(level, newlevel), string) < 0)
[ 2]:               errexit (5); /*note: '\n' removed for fgets*/
[ 1]:     };
[ 1]:
[ 1]:     while (linenum++ % lpp)            /*<--use this...*/
[ 1]:          fprintf (output, "\n");
[ 1]:     /*fprintf (output, "\f\n");*/      /*<--...or this */
[ 1]:
[ 1]:     if (fclose (input))                /*put our toys away*/
[ 1]:          errexit (6);
[ 1]:     if (fclose (output))
[ 1]:          errexit (7);
[ 1]:
[ 1]:     /*exit normally*/
[ 1]:     exit (0);
[ 0]: }
[ 0]:
[ 0]: /*Nesting - examine the given string for "{" and "}".  Increment
[ 0]:             level for every "{" and decrement for "}"s.*/
[ 0]: void nesting (levelptr,stringptr)
[ 0]:     unsigned *levelptr;
[ 0]:     char *stringptr;
[ 0]: {
[ 1]:     do {
[ 2]:          if (*stringptr == '{')
[ 3]:               *levelptr += 1;
[ 2]:          if (*stringptr == '}')
[ 2]:               *levelptr -= 1;
[ 1]:     } while (*stringptr++);
[ 0]: }
[ 0]:
[ 0]: /*fgetstr - 'gets' does not return '\n' -- 'fgets' does.
[ 0]:             this routine makes 'fgets' like 'gets'*/
[ 0]: char *fgetstr (string, n, filptr)
[ 0]:     char string[];
[ 0]:     int n;
[ 0]:     FILE *filptr;
[ 0]: {
[ 1]:     char *retval, *ptr;
[ 1]:     if (retval = fgets (string, n, filptr))
[ 1]:          for (ptr = string; *ptr; ptr++)
[ 1]:               if (*ptr == '\n') {
[ 2]:                    *ptr = '\0';
[ 2]:                    break;
[ 1]:               }
[ 1]:     return retval;
[ 0]: }
[ 0]:
[ 0]: /*Errexit - handle errors as they arise*/
[ 0]: char *errlist[] =
[ 0]:     {"invalid error",
[ 1]:
[ 1]:      "wrong number of arguments."
[ 1]:      " Try: prg5_3 input_file [output_file]",
```

```

        "input file does not exist",
        "output file already exists",
        "output file cannot be created",
        "error on output file write",
        "error on closing input file",
        "error on closing output file",
        "debug error"};

void errexit (errnum)
    unsigned errnum;
{
    if (errnum > 7)
        errnum = 7;
    fprintf (stderr, "pretty printer error:  %s\n"
                     "system error:          %s\n",
                     errlist[errnum],
                     sys_errlist [errno]);
    exit (errnum);
}
```

This program accepts either one or two arguments. The first argument is assumed to be the input file. The second argument, if present, is the output file. If the output file already exists, it is not rewritten and the program aborts. If the output file name is not given then output is directed to *stdout* as before. As mentioned previously, *stdout* is a perfectly good file handle that has already been opened.

For example, the command *PRG5_3 PRG5_3.C OUTPUT* will cause Prg5_3 to generate a listing of itself and place it in a file called OUTPUT. Prg5_3 will not overwrite an existing output file to avoid inadvertantly overwriting something of importance. Therefore, to list directly to the printer, it is still necessary to use redirection, as in *PRG5_3 PRG5_3.C >LPT1*.

The program is very similar to its smaller sibling. At a functional level, it is identical. Notice the calls to *fprintf()* and *fgets()*, replacing *printf()* and *gets()* in the simpler example. The primary difference is the complexity introduced by opening the input and output files and the associated error checking which must be done. The *open()* and *fopen()* Turbo C routines either return handles with which to subsequently access the files or an error code. These error returns must be checked. As tempting as it might be, a C programmer cannot just assume the file routine executed properly.

The routine *errexit()* has been written here to handle reporting of the different error conditions. Prg5_3 has invented an error code and associated a message with each one. If an error does arise, you do not want the error message appearing on *stdout* as that may have been redirected to a file. The user wants to see error messages, whether *stdout* has been redirected or not. Therefore, Prg5_3 directs its error output to *stderr*, which cannot be redirected away from the screen.

Notice also that after displaying its own error message, Prg5_3 references the array *SYS_ERRLIST* with the index *ERRNO*. *SYS-ERRLIST* is a list of all the different system errors with which Turbo C is familiar. In our above example, *fopen()* did not tell us what the problem was, only that an error had occured which kept the request from being fulfilled. In such a case, the Turbo C library sets the externally defined variable *ERRNO* to the index of the error within *SYS_ERRLIST*. We can use this to output a more complete explanation of the problem. (We must do this immediately or save *ERRNO* away, as the next system call which has a failure will overwrite *ERRNO* with its own error message.)

In our example, we accessed *SYS_ERRLIST* ourselves. The Turbo C library provides two routines to simplify error reporting. *Strerror()* accepts the address of a user message and returns a pointer to that message with the proper error message from *SYS_ERRLIST* tacked to the end. *Perror()* accepts a user string and prints it with the proper error message to stderr. (*Perror()* is equivalent to *fprintf(stderr, strerror())*.) Which to use is largely a matter of taste. I have used each of the three approaches in different programs as examples.

When opening files, remember that in versions of DOS prior to 3.3, it is not allowed for programs to have more than twenty files open at the same time. While this may seem like a lot, database applications can easily attempt to exceed this number. Users are often confused into thinking that the *FILES=* specifier in the *CONFIG.SYS* file allows this limit to be raised at boot up, but this is not the case. The *FILES* statement specifies the number of files that can be opened in the entire system. The per program limit is still 20. (DOS 3.3 does allow the per program limit to be raised up to that of the *FILES* specifier via the *Set Handle Count* system call. In addition, there is a programming trick to lift the 20 file limit in other versions of DOS, the details of which are beyond this text. For more information, see *Dr. Dobb's Journal of Software Tools,* #130, page 114.)

As an aside here, the Turbo C programmer should be very careful about the naming of his functions. Do not give one of your own procedues the same name as a function documented in the Turbo C library reference. By its presence the user program will keep the linker from loading the proper routine out of the Turbo C library. As we know, routines such as *printf()* make calls to the more fundamental routines like *fprintf()*. The entire structure of Turbo C library routines is interconnected in less than obvious ways. Replacing any of the Turbo C library routines may be disastrous even if it is not obvious that your program calls that routine.

For example, on one of the later programs I inadvertantly named a function *read()*. Of course, I new that there was a Turbo C routine *read()*, but as I did not call it anywhere, I thought that all would be safe. Unfortunately, my program did contain a call to *getchar()*. What I did not realize is that *getchar()* simply performs a *read()* call to *stdin*. Since my function did not perform at all like the Turbo C *read()*, my program did not run. Worse, the error generated was very peculiar and did not relate at all to reality. This problem took the better part of a day to track down, so be careful.

Table 5.3
DOS File Attributes

Bit	Meaning
ReadOnly	File may not be written or deleted
Hidden	File will not be listed in a directory listing (or in a FindFirst/FindNext system call unless specifically requested)
System	File is considered part of the DOS operating system (gets transferred with SYS command)
Volume	specifies volume identifier entry in root directory
Subdirectory	file is a subdirectory
Archive	file has been backed up since the last time it was written (maintained for backup purposes)

One final topic when discussing simple files is that of attributes. While UNIX maintains a complete set of access bits, DOS maintains six attribute bits. These bits and their explanations appear in Table 5.3.

The desired bits are set whenever a file is created. To enhance portability (and confuse the programmer) the Turbo C library maintains two different concepts for doing this: permission and attributes. Permission is implemented to be as compatible with UNIX as possible.

For example, *open()* uses permission bits while *_open()* uses attributes. If the *O_CREAT* access flag is set, the *open()* library call will create the file if it does not already exist. There are two permission flags: *S_IWRITE* and *S_IREAD*. These may be ORed together into one field, if desired. In actual fact, *S_IREAD* is not implemented, as a file is always readable in DOS. If the *S_IWRITE* bit is set then the file is created with the *RD_ONLY* attribute cleared. Otherwise, the *RD_ONLY* attribute is set. *_Open()* allows the user program to pass the attributes to be used with the new file directly. Equates exist in *DOS.H* for the both sets of bits.

Be sure to specify either permission or attributes on system calls which might create a file. Inadvertantly creating *RD_ONLY* files is one of the more common sources of file problems. Problems relating to *RD_ONLY* files are difficult to track down as the program tends to run correctly the first time and incorrectly on subsequent attempts for no apparent reason. To be safe, you may want to specify a permission of *S_IWRITE|S_IREAD* or attribute of 0x00 (normal) on all such calls—if they are not needed, they are simply ignored.

Unfortunately, DOS does not display a file's attributes. In fact, it will not even display hidden files at all. Fortunately, once a file has been created, its attributes can still be modified using the system call. (Otherwise, *Read-Only* files would be permanently stuck onto a disk until reformatted.) Prg5_4 below uses this system call to access and, potentially, change the attributes of DOS files. This program can be used not only as an example of accessing these flags, but also as a utility for accessing file attributes. (One use for Prg5_4 is to clear the *Read-Only* bit, so that a file accidentally created as *Read-Only* can be deleted.)

```
/*Prg5_4 - Access File Attributes
   by Stephen R. Davis, 1987

  Use the _chmod() Turbo C library routine to access (both read
  and write) the attribute bits of a file
*/

#include <stdio.h>
#include <io.h>
#include <process.h>
#include <ctype.h>

/*prototype definitions*/
void display (unsigned);
void main (unsigned, char **);
unsigned gethval (char *);
unsigned getyval (char *);
void error (unsigned);

/*define global data*/
char *labels[] = {"read_only",
                  "hidden",
                  "system",
```

```
                       "volume",
                       "subdirectory",
                       "archive"};

char *errors[] = {"illegal",
                       "Wrong number of arguments\n"
                       "Try 'prog5_3 <filename>' to access attribute bits",
                       "Failure accessing file attributes",
                       "File attributes not changed"};


/*Main - read the attribute bits and try to change them*/
void main (argc, argv)
     unsigned argc;
     char *argv [];
{
     unsigned attrib;

     /*first check for proper number of arguments*/
     if (argc != 2)
          error (1);

     /*now attempt to read the attributes of given file*/
     attrib = _chmod (argv [1], 0);
     if (attrib == -1)
          error (2);

     /*interpret them for the user*/
     printf ("Current attributes of %s are:\n", argv [1]);
     display (attrib);

     /*now let him change them*/
     do {
          attrib = gethval ("Enter new attribute");
          printf ("This would be:\n");
          display (attrib);
        } while (!getyval ("Is this ok? (Y/N)"));

     /*change the file's attributes*/
     if (attrib != _chmod (argv [1], 1, attrib))
          error (3);
     printf ("File's attributes are now:\n");
     display (_chmod (argv [1], 0));

     /*exit normally*/
     exit (0);
}

/*Display - interpret the attributes of a file*/
void display (attrib)
     unsigned attrib;
{
     unsigned count, bit, empty;

     /*first display numerically*/
     printf ("%x -> ", attrib);

     /*and then interpret*/
     empty = 1;
     for (bit = 1, count = 0; count < 5; bit <<= 1, count++)
          if (attrib & bit) {
               empty = 0;
               printf ("%s  ", labels [count]);
          }
```

```
 88[ 1]:        if (empty)
 89[ 1]:             printf ("<none>");
 90[ 1]:        printf ("\n");
 91[ 0]: }
 92[ 0]:
 93[ 0]: /*Gethval - prompt the user and get a hex value*/
 94[ 0]: unsigned gethval (prompt)
 95[ 0]:        char *prompt;
 96[ 0]: {
 97[ 1]:        unsigned answer;
 98[ 1]:
 99[ 1]:        printf ("%s: ", prompt);
100[ 1]:        scanf ("%x", &answer);
101[ 1]:        getchar ();
102[ 1]:        return answer;
103[ 0]: }
104[ 0]:
105[ 0]: /*Getyval - prompt user and return a 1 for Yes response, else 0*/
106[ 0]: unsigned getyval (prompt)
107[ 0]:        char *prompt;
108[ 0]: {
109[ 1]:        printf ("%s: ", prompt);
110[ 1]:        return tolower (getchar ()) == 'y';
111[ 0]: }
112[ 0]:
113[ 0]: /*Error - print error number and quit*/
114[ 0]: void error (number)
115[ 0]:        unsigned number;
116[ 0]: {
117[ 1]:        printf ("error #%d: %s\n", number, errors [number]);
118[ 1]:        exit (number);
119[ 0]: }
```

An example run of Prg5_4 shows:

```
prg5_4 prg5_4.c
Current attributes of prg5_4.c are:
20 -> <none>
Enter new attribute: 22
This would be:
22 -> hidden
Is this ok? (Y/N): y
File's attributes are now:
22 -> hidden
```

The program first reads the existing file attributes using the call to *_chmod()* on line 47. If an error occurs, the attributes are returned as –1 and the program stops. The program then interprets them using the function *display()*. The user may then enter whatever hex attribute desired, which the program also interprets using *display()*. Once the proper attributes have been selected, the program assigns these to the file using the *_chmod()* call on line 66. The attributes actually assigned are reinterpreted at that time.

Notice that it is not desirable nor possible to change the attributes arbitrarily. Files which have the subdirectory flag set may not have any of the other attributes set, nor may they have that attribute cleared. A subdirectory should stay a subdirectory and not be modified into some other type of file. Try changing the access bits of existing files and directories. (Better try it on a scratch floppy, lest you somehow succeed.)

DOS Directories

As we saw in the previous section, DOS directories like their UNIX cousins, are really nothing more than special files containing pointers to other files. Along with these pointers, certain other information is also stored such as date last written and attributes. Since one of the files within a directory may itself be another directory type file, directories may chain to each other in a tree like fashion. Not only is this hierarchical approach to directories possible, it is desirable. Such directory structures are the only practical method for managing the large amounts of on-line storage offered by rigid disk devices.

The names of all the directories the operating system must traverse to get to a file is called its path. As we have seen, a path name consists of a series of directory names, each separated by a \ character. The entire address of a file is completed by adding to the front of this the letter of the disk drive on which this path is found followed by a colon. For example, *C:\COMPILER\TURBOC\TC.EXE* is the full name of my Turbo C compiler— it is the *TC.EXE* file pointed at by the directory TURBOC which is in turn pointed at by the directory *COMPILER* that is found in the root of disk C.

Typically a user tends to put files which somehow belong together into the same directory (all the data files, at least). It would be tiring indeed to be forced to type *C:\COMPILER\TURBOC* in front of every file in the Turbo C library. Therefore, DOS allows the operator to specify a default disk and a default path. Any file name which is specified without a disk or path in front gets the default values tacked onto it.

To aid in traversing the directory tree, two special directories are defined in every directory except the root. These are the subdirectory '.' (called dot) and '..' (known as dot-dot). The directory dot is the current directory, while directory dot-dot is the parent of the current directory.

The user level *CHDIR* (*CD*) command sets or changes this default. When using this command, the user usually has a mental image of *moving* from one directory to another, but, of course, there is no movement at all, only a change in the default. Programs may also change the default using the *chdir()* Turbo C library routine which in turn invokes the Change Current Directory (0x3b) system call.

The user may change the default disk drive by entering the disk letter followed by a colon and nothing else.

Interestingly the user cannot change the default disk and directory in the same command. This action must always be taken in two separate commands. The example program Prg5_5 below not only demonstrates how a program can change the default directory, but it serves a useful purpose. Prg5_5 allows the user to change default disk and directory in the same command.

```
/*Prg5_5 - Change Disk and Directory
   by Stephen R. Davis, 1987

  Change disk and directory at the same time.  Both disk and directory
  are optional.  If either is missing, the current disk or directory
  is assumed.  If both are missing, the value of the environment
  label DEFAULT is used.
*/

#include <stdio.h>
#include <stdlib.h>
#include <dir.h>
#include <process.h>
#include <ctype.h>

#define MAXDISK 5

/*prototype definitions*/
void main (unsigned, char **);
unsigned parse (char *);

/*global variables*/
unsigned disk;
char *directory;
char defaultdir [132];

/*Main - load up default fcb, then parse the input argument and
         finally set the disk and directory*/
void main (argc, argv)
     unsigned argc;
     char *argv[];
{
     /*check the number of arguments*/
     if (argc > 2) {
          printf ("Wrong number of arguments\n"
                  "  try '%s [pathname]'\n",
                  argv [0]);
          exit (1);
     }

     /*if no argument provided, get the argument from the environment*
     if (argc == 1)
          if (argv [1] = getenv ("DEFAULT"))
               printf ("Using default directory\n");

     /*if no argument present, just display the defaults*/
     if (!argv [1]) {
          disk = getdisk ();
          getcurdir (disk + 1, defaultdir);
          printf ("%c:%s", (char)(disk + 'A'), defaultdir);
```

```
51[ 2]:        } else {
52[ 2]:
53[ 2]:              /*if present, parse the input argument into drive and direc
54[ 2]:             if (parse (argv [1])) {
55[ 3]:                 printf ("Illegal input: %s\n", argv [1]);
56[ 3]:                 exit (1);
57[ 2]:             }
58[ 2]:
59[ 2]:             /*now set the disk and directory*/
60[ 2]:             setdisk (disk);
61[ 2]:             if (chdir (directory)) {
62[ 3]:                 printf ("Directory %s does not exist\n", directory);
63[ 3]:                 exit (1);
64[ 2]:             }
65[ 1]:        }
66[ 1]:
67[ 1]:        /*exit normally*/
68[ 1]:        exit (0);
69[ 0]: }
70[ 0]:
71[ 0]: /*Parse - parse out the disk from the file name*/
72[ 0]: unsigned parse (ptr)
73[ 0]:        char *ptr;
74[ 0]: {
75[ 1]:        /*first check for the presence of a disk*/
76[ 1]:        if (ptr [1] == ':') {
77[ 2]:             disk = (unsigned)(toupper (ptr [0]) - 'A');
78[ 2]:             if (disk > MAXDISK)
79[ 2]:                 return -1;
80[ 2]:             directory = ptr + 2;
81[ 1]:        }
82[ 1]:        else {
83[ 2]:             disk = getdisk ();
84[ 2]:             directory = ptr;
85[ 1]:        }
86[ 1]:
87[ 1]:        /*if no directory present, change to '.'*/
88[ 1]:        if (*directory == '\0') {
89[ 2]:             directory = ".";
90[ 1]:        }
91[ 1]:
92[ 1]:        /*return success*/
93[ 1]:        return 0;
94[ 0]: }
```

Prg5_5 first checks the number of arguments, like usual. If the number of arguments is incorrect, a message is displayed prompting the user as to what type of input is expected. Notice that in printing out the user prompt on line 36, the name of the program is not hard coded. Instead, *ARGV[0]* is used. Under DOS 3.0 and later, *ARGV[0]* points to the full pathname of the executing program. This technique has the advantage that the proper name of the program is used in the error message, even if the program is renamed after compiling. It has the disadvantage that it only works under Version 3.x of DOS. Under Version 2.x, the name of the program must be hardcoded.

Let's skip the special code involving the *DEFAULT* and concentrate on the *normal* cases. If no argument is present, then Prg5_5 simply asks for the current disk and the current directory and displays these just as *CHDIR* or *CD* do when presented no arguments. If one argument is present, the function *parse()* is used to pull the path name apart. *Parse()* takes a somewhat simplistic approach. If the second character is a colon, it assumes that the first letter is the disk letter. It converts this disk letter into a number, using a 0 for A, a 1 for B, etc. If no disk is present it uses the *getdisk()* routine to fetch the current disk number. Anything after the disk letter is assumed to be the target path. If there is nothing left after the disk, then *parse()* supplies the default path of '.', the current directory.

Upon returning from *parse()*, Prg5_5 uses the *setdisk()* and *chdir()* library routines to change the defaults to the target value. Prg5_5, renamed to something more reasonable such as CDD (Change Disk and Directory), is now in position to replace the DOS *CHDIR* and *CD* command, relieving their limitation.

```
D:\                         <--old disk and directory
D>prg5_5 c:\user\c

C:\USER\C                   <--note the new disk and directory
C>
```

In Prg5_3 and Prg5_4 we were provided with a single file for which the complete pathname was given, either explicitly or implicitly using the directory and disk defaults. One of the more powerful features of DOS filenames are the so-called wildcards, the * and *?*, which allow more than one file at a time to be specified. The question mark in a file name stands for any single legal file name character. For example, *C?T.* stands for *CAT, CBT,* etc through *CZT* and then *C1T* and so on. The asterisk stands for any number of question marks from that point onwards in the name.

Consider the following examples:

```
F?.    -> matches any two letter file name beginning with an F
          and w/ null extensions
F?.*   -> matches any two letter file name beginning with an F
F*.*   -> matches any file name beginning with an F
*.*    -> matches any file name
```

Be careful, however:

```
*F.*     -> also matches any file name (the letter after the
            asterisk is ignored)
```

Therefore, while the command *COPY CAT. B:* might copy the file *CAT* in the current directory to the default directory on drive B, *COPY C*.* B:* would copy all files in the current directory beginning with a C to the default directory on drive B. Just as with simple file names, a path name can be used with the wildcards so that *COPY \DOG\C*.* B:* would copy all of the files in the directory *\DOG* which begin with a C. Programs gain access to the list of files which match wild cards by using the DOS *Find First* and *Find Next* system calls or the equivalent Turbo C library routines, *findfirst()* and *findnext()*.

Findfirst() accepts three arguments: the pathname plus wild cards, a buffer of type *FFBLK*, and the attribute flags. *Findfirst()* finds the first filename which matches the given path and has attributes matching those in the third argument. It stores the name of the file into *FFBLK.FF_NAME* as an ASCII string. It also stores away extra information into *FFBLK* which it uses to find the next filename passing the same criteria when the user program calls *findnext()*. The user program continues to call *findnext()* until it returns a –1, indicating there were no more found. If there are no files at all matching the criteria, *findfirst()* returns the –1 itself.

As an example of its use, let's look at another program designed to expand upon the capabilities of DOS, Prg5_6. In DOS, the *ERASE* command erases a file from disk. *ERASE* allows the use of wild cards, so that one might erase all C source files in the current directory by simply entering the command *ERASE *.C*. This, however, is a dangerous thing to do. If the user happens to be in the wrong directory or if he enters the command incorrectly (for example, *ERASE *. C*) the results can be disasterous. Most systems either require or allow a verify option on the erase command to keep users from inadvertently deleting useful files.

Prg5_6 represents just such an *erase with verify* command. Prg5_6 expects a single argument consisting of an optional drive and pathname attached to a filename possibly containing wildcards. The program begins by parsing out the drive and pathname of the argument for later use. Rather than make our own parsing function as we did in Prg5_5, this time we use the much more able *fnsplit()* library routine. Notice that *fnsplit()* splits a full pathname into its four consituent parts (disk, path, filename and extension) and writes these into different buffers. The labels *MAXDRIVE, MAXDIR, MAXFILE* and *MAXEXT* can be used to define buffers which are guaranteed to be large enough to accept the four output strings. Providing *fnsplit()* a 0 address for any of the four buffer addresses indicates the program is not interested in that particular string.

The program then presents the input filename to *findfirst()*. If no match is found, the message *error in path* along with the system error is printed on the display on line 49. (This time we used the *fprintf(stderr, strerror ())* call.)

```
 1[ 0]: /*Prg5_6 - Erase w/ Question
 2[ 0]:    by Stephen R. Davis, 1987
 3[ 0]:
 4[ 0]:   One of the more glaring deficiencies in MS-DOS is the absence
 5[ 0]:   of a verify option on the delete command.  Several public
 6[ 0]:   domain utilities have been created to rectify this problem.
 7[ 0]:   This program recreates that solution.  It also serves as a
 8[ 0]:   simple example of the FindFirst/FindNext system calls.
 9[ 0]:
10[ 0]:   This program searches for any file which matches the first
11[ 0]:   argument, which may contain disk drive, path and or wild-cards.
12[ 0]:   The names of any files which match are presented to the user.  If
13[ 0]:   he enters a 'Y' or 'y', the file is deleted.  Anything else, skips
14[ 0]:   to the next file.  Read_only files are not deleted and hidden files
15[ 0]:   are not found.
16[ 0]: */
17[ 0]:
18[ 0]: #include <stdio.h>
19[ 0]: #include <dos.h>
20[ 0]: #include <dir.h>
21[ 0]: #include <ctype.h>
22[ 0]: #include <errno.h>
23[ 0]: #include <process.h>
24[ 0]: #include <conio.h>
25[ 0]:
26[ 0]: /*define our global data*/
27[ 0]: struct ffblk control_block;
28[ 0]: char path [MAXPATH], drive [MAXDRIVE], dir [MAXDIR], file [MAXFILE];
29[ 0]: char ext [MAXEXT];
30[ 0]:
31[ 0]: /*Main - search the given path; for all those found ask the user
32[ 0]:          whether to delete them or not*/
33[ 0]: void main (argc, argv)
34[ 0]:      unsigned argc;
35[ 0]:      char *argv [];
36[ 0]: {
37[ 1]:      /*check argument count (better be just one)*/
38[ 1]:      if (argc != 2) {
39[ 2]:           printf ("Wrong number of arguments\n"
40[ 2]:                   "   try 'prg5_6 pattern' to erase w/ question\n");
41[ 2]:           exit (1);
42[ 1]:      }
43[ 1]:
44[ 1]:      /*split the argument into file and directory*/
45[ 1]:      fnsplit (argv [1], drive, dir, 0, 0);
46[ 1]:
47[ 1]:      /*look for files which match the path provided*/
48[ 1]:      if (findfirst (argv [1], &control_block, 0)) {
49[ 2]:           fprintf (stderr, strerror ("error in path"));
50[ 2]:           exit (1);
51[ 1]:      }
52[ 1]:
53[ 1]:      /*use this (and subsequent) files combined with our path*/
54[ 1]:      do {
55[ 2]:           /*build up the current file's name*/
56[ 2]:           fnsplit (control_block.ff_name, 0, 0, file, ext);
57[ 2]:           fnmerge (path, drive, dir, file, ext);
58[ 2]:
```

```
59[ 2]:          /*prompt user*/
60[ 2]:          printf ("\nErase %s? ", path);
61[ 2]:          if (tolower (getche ()) == 'y')
62[ 2]:              if (unlink (path))
63[ 2]:                  fprintf (stderr,
64[ 2]:                      strerror ("    error erasing file"));
65[ 1]:      } while (!findnext (&control_block));
66[ 1]:
67[ 1]:      /*exit normally*/
68[ 1]:      exit (0);
69[ 0]: }
```

If a match is found, only the filename is given in *FF_NAME* and not the entire path. We must first split the filename into name and extension using the *fnsplit()* function and then recombine the two parts along with the disk and pathname saved back on line 45 using the *fnmerge()* call. *Fnmerge()* takes the four character strings and combines them into the single full pathname. The label *MAXPATH* is provided to define a buffer large enough to accommodate any path generated by *fnmerge()*. Pictorially it looks like this:

```
original argument:
          ----------------------|
          |                     |
          |      ----------------------     Complete file name
          |      |              |     |
          - ---------           V     V
   prg5_6 c:\dos\cat\*.c        c:\dos\cat\prg10_1.c
                                             ^
                                             |
                                             |
   findfirst() finds:                        |
                    prg10_1.c-------------------
```

Having constructed the entire filename, including directory and path, Prg5_6 then presents this to the user along with the prompt *Erase?*. If the user enters a *Y* or a *y* to this prompt, the program erases the file by presenting its complete pathname to the library routine *unlink()*. (We could have used the equivalent library routine *remove()*, but this Turbo C library function is not documented in the original *Turbo C Reference Guide* except for an oblique reference on page 11.)

```
C>prg5_6 *.c

Erase PRG5_3.C? y
Erase PRG5_2.C? y
Erase PRG5_11.C? n              <--this file not deleted
Erase PRG5_1.C? y
Erase PRG5_4.C? y
Erase PRG5_5.C? y
Erase PRG5_6.C? y
Erase PRG5_7.C? y
Erase PRG5_12.C? y
Erase PRG5_8.C? y
```

```
Erase PRG5_10A.C? y
Erase PRG5_10B.C? y
Erase PRG5_9.C? y
```

If the user enters anything other than a *Y* or *y*, the file is not erased and the program skips over to the next. Prg5_6 quits when the last file which matches is found. If the file is marked as Read-Only, the *unlink()* will return an error and the program will spit out a message to the right of the file explaining the problem. (Use Prg5_4 above to clear the *Read-Only* flag if you still want to delete it.)

When given a more mnemonic name, such as *ERQ* (*ER*ase w/ Question), this program can make a valuable addition to any set of DOS utilities. Perhaps I am being over cautious, but I have not used anything but *ERQ* to erase files off of my disks in well over a year.

In the example above, we specified an attribute of 0 for our *findfirst()/findnext()* requests. This indicates we are interested in files with none of the special attribute flags set. Had we wanted to include Read-Only, Hidden or System files, we need only have set the Read-Only, Hidden or System bits in the attribute argument of *findfirst()* (the labels *FA_RDONLY*, *FA_HIDDEN* and *FA_SYSTEM* are defined in the include file DOS.H).

By the way, notice that setting the *FA_RDONLY* flag in the attribute field does not keep normal files from being listed, it merely includes *Read-Only* files in with the others. If we wanted to list *ONLY* the *Read-Only* files, for example, we would skip over files found without the *FA-RDONLY* bit set in the attribute field in the *FFBLK* returned from *findfirst()/findnext()*, *FFBLK.FF_ATTRIB* as shown below. Depending on the conditional, we could devise a program to only list any given subset of files matching the wild-card pattern.

```
                  .
                  .
                  .
/*only consider Read-Only files*/
if (ffblk.ff_attrib & FA_RDONLY) {
        /*continue process*/
                  .
                  .
                  .
```

In similar fashion, setting the *FA_DIREC* bit in the attributes field results in any subdirectories being displayed along with other files in the directory. Being able to list subdirectories leads to several interesting possibilities, none of which are explored by the DOS commands. The power of subdirectories is the ability to subdivide storage space into manageable parts. Their weakness lies in finding individual files within that multidivided storage space. Often the user knows that somewhere on his hard disk is a file he wants, but without knowing which subdirectory to look into, the *DIR* command does him no good. As attractive as hierarchical storage is, it is sometimes desirable to act on the entire disk with one command as if the various subdivisions did not exist.

Prg5_7 uses the subdirectory find feature to provide just such a capability. This program is a global find and copy command. It is ideal both for finding that errant file which just doesn't seem to be in the proper subdirectory and for putting it there. Prg5_7 starts at the specified directory and searches all subdirectories for the pattern supplied. If a second directory name is supplied, then all files found are copied to that directory. If no second directory name is present, then the full path of the file found is printed without copying anything. This forms a sort of global *DIR* command.

For example, suppose that I cannot find a particular data file which I feel sure is somewhere on my hard disk. Being a reasonable sort, I am pretty sure that I named it with the extension *.DAT* for data. The command *PRG5_7 C:*.DAT* will perform a search of every subdirectory of drive C for files with the extension *.DAT*. If I was quite certain that it must be in one of the subdirectories off of directory *LABDATA*, then I might have saved some search time by entering *PRG5_7 C:\LABDATA*.DAT* instead. This would cause Prg5_7 to search *LABDATA* and all of its subdirectories, but not the remainder of the disk.

If I really just wanted to copy all of the *.DAT* files found in directory *LABDATA* and all of its subdirectories to a floppy disk, perhaps for backup purposes, entering a separate *COPY* command in each of the subdirectories which Prg5_7 presented me can still be quite laborious. Entering the single command PRG5_7 *C:\LABDATA*.DAT B:* saves me the trouble by automatically copying each file found to the target directory. If two files with the same name are found, only the first one gets copied over—the second file generates an error message.

It is not necessary to specify the disk drive and full path every time, but be careful on one point. Entering *PRG5_7 *.DAT* searches the current directory and any of its subdirectories for *.DAT* files—it does not search the entire disk as you might think. The \ is necessary in front to start the search at the disk root if the entire disk is to be searched (*PRG5_7 *.DAT*).

The operator must specify the target path, even if it is the current directory. Leaving it off would cause Prg_7 to simply perform a search. However, we can use the dot directory here. The command *Prg5_7 D:*.BAS .* would copy all of the BASIC files on drive D to the current directory.

The operator must specify the target path, even if it is the current directory. Leaving it off would cause Prg5_7 to simply perform a search. However, we can use the dot directory here. The command *PRG5_7 D:*.BAS .* would copy all of the BASIC files on drive D to the current directory.

```
/*Prg5_7 - Copy/Find all files matching a pattern
   by Stephen R. Davis, 1987

  Search all subdirectories for a particular file pattern.  All files
  found matching that pattern are copied to the target path, if presen

  If a file is found on the target disk with the same name, it is not
  overwritten.  Thus, if more than one file exists in the subdirectory
  tree with the same name, only the first one will get copied.

  It is possible to specify a starting point.  For example,
           prg5_7 c:\user\*.* b:
  copies all of the files found in \USER and all of its subdirectories
*/

#include <stdio.h>
#include <dir.h>
#include <io.h>
#include <dos.h>
#include <process.h>
#include <fcntl.h>
#include <conio.h>
#include <ctype.h>

/*prototyping definitions*/
void main (unsigned, char **);
void copyall (char *, char *, char *);
void copy (char *, char *);
void append (char *, char *, char *);

/*Main - parse user input and start the ball rolling*/
void main (argc, argv)
     unsigned argc;
     char *argv [];
{
     char sourcedisk [MAXDRIVE], sourcedir [MAXDIR];
     char sourcefile [MAXFILE], sourceext [MAXEXT];
     char fromdir [MAXPATH], pattern [MAXFILE+MAXEXT];

     /*check the argument count*/
     if (argc == 1 || argc > 3) {
          printf ("Wrong number of arguments\n"
                  "  try 'prg5_7 <source> [<dest>]' to copy all"
                  "  files from source and all of it's \n"
                  "  subdirectories to destination.\n"
                  "  e.g., prg5_7 c:\*.* d: to copy the entire\n"
                  "  contents of C disk to D.\n"
                  "  (Simply find if no destination present)\n");
          exit (1);
     }

     /*parse argument 1 into its two halves*/
```

```
     fnsplit (argv [1], sourcedisk, sourcedir, sourcefile, sourceext);

     /*now reconstruct the two halves*/
     fnmerge (fromdir, sourcedisk, sourcedir,          0,         0);
     fnmerge (pattern,          0,          0, sourcefile, sourceext);

     /*now just copy them all over*/
     copyall (fromdir, pattern, argv [2]);

     /*exit normally*/
     exit (0);
}

/*Copyall - copy all files matching a given pattern from the
            current directory and all subdirectories*/
void copyall (fromdir, pattern, todir)
     char *fromdir, *pattern, *todir;
{
     char spath [MAXPATH], tpath [MAXPATH];
     struct ffblk block;

     /*first copy all files patching the pattern*/
     append (spath, fromdir, pattern);
     if (!findfirst (spath, &block, 0))
          do {
               append (spath, fromdir, block.ff_name);
               append (tpath,   todir, block.ff_name);

               /*if destination present, copy; else just find*/
               if (todir) {
                    printf ("\nCopying %s -> %s", spath, tpath);
                    copy (spath, tpath);
               } else {
                    printf ("\nFound %s    -- continue?", spath);
                    if (tolower (getche ()) == 'n') exit (1);
               }


          } while (!findnext (&block));

     /*now check all subdirectories*/
     append (spath, fromdir, "*");
     if (!findfirst (spath, &block, FA_DIREC))
          do {

               /*only pay attention to directories*/
               if (block.ff_attrib & FA_DIREC)

                    /*ignore directories '.' and '..'*/
                    if (block.ff_name [0] != '.') {

                         /*now tack on name of directory + '\'*/
                         append (spath, fromdir, block.ff_name);
                         append (spath, spath, "\\");

                         /*and copy its contents too*/
                         copyall (spath, pattern, todir);
                    }
          } while (!findnext (&block));
}

/*Copy - given two patterns, copy the source to the destination file*/
#define NSECT 17
void copy (from, to)
```

```
     char *from, *to;
{
     int fhandle, thandle, number;
     char buffer [NSECT*512];

     /*open the source for reading binary*/
     _fmode = O_BINARY;
     if ((fhandle = open (from, O_RDONLY)) == -1) {
          perror ("\nError opening source file");
          return;
     }

     /*now open the destination*/
     if ((thandle = creatnew (to, 0)) == -1) {
          perror ("\nError opening target file");
          close (fhandle);
          return;
     }

     /*now perform the copy*/
     while (number = read (fhandle, buffer, NSECT*512))
          if (number != _write (thandle, buffer, number)) {
               fprintf (stderr, "\nError on writing target file");
               break;
          }
     close (fhandle);
     close (thandle);
}

/*Append - concatenate two strings together*/
void append (to, from1, from2)
     char *to, *from1, *from2;
{
     /*copy the first string*/
     while (*from1)
          *to++ = *from1++;

     /*now the second*/
     while (*from2)
          *to++ = *from2++;

     /*and then tack on a terminator*/
     *to = '\0';
}
```

For example, to copy all *.DAT* files from the author's hard disk to drive *D:* enter:

```
C>prg5_7 \*.dat d:\
Copying \BENCH\BENCH07.DAT -> d:\BENCH07.DAT
Copying \DOS\DBUGUTIL\DIRN-DBU.DAT -> d:\DIRN-DBU.DAT
Copying \USER\BOOK\PROGRAMS\PRG4_2G.DAT -> d:\PRG4_2G.DAT
```

Now we will take a quick look at how Prg5_7 works. After first checking the number of arguments in routine fashion, Prg5_7 divides the first argument into two halves: the disk/path and the filename. This it does quite simply by calling *fnsplit()* to parse the argument into its four constituent parts and then combining the two pairs back together again with *fnmerge()*. It then calls the function *copyall()* to copy all of the files from the given directory which match the given pattern to the second argument, if present.

Copyall() recombines the directory and pattern to come up with a search pattern which it passes to *findfirst()*. All files found are either copied over if the pointer to the second argument is not *NULL*, or simply listed to *stdout* if it is. Having found all of the files, it then makes a search of all subdirectories from this directory. This it does by calling *findfirst()* again using the wild card *, which matches all directory names, and the attribute *FA_DIREC*. The test on line 99 filters out all non-directories found during this second search. The test on line 102 filters out the special directories dot and dot-dot. The names of any directories which *copyall()* finds are added to the end of the search directory (with an extra \) and the result is passed to *copyall()* for searching.

In this way, *copyall()* looks through all of the subdirectories of all the hard disk in a depth before breadth exhaustive search. Calling *copyall()* from within *copyall()* itself may seem like a strange thing to do. After all, isn't this going to lead eventually to an infinite loop? As it turns out, this is a perfectly acceptable thing to do as long as the function is written properly. The technique is called recursive programming and is ideal for these types of repetitive applications. We will study recursion in more detail in Chapter 8 when we discuss speed and space optimization techniques.

The actual copy is performed in the function *copy()*. *Copy()* accepts two arguments, the full pathname of the source file and the pathname of the target file. It opens the source for reading and creates the target. An error on either aborts the copy. Errors are reported to *stderr* using the *perror()* routine. The copy is performed by performing sector reads followed by writes until the number of bytes read from the source file is 0, indicating an end of file. The handles returned from the *opens* must be subsequently used on the *reads* and *writes* to access the file. Finally, both file handles are closed and the function returns.

There are two points of interest here. First, remember to close the first file if an error is encountered on the second open. Otherwise, the file will stay open until the program has completed. Although not harmful, this file will count against the 20 file per program limit. Second, reading and writing a single sector at a time is not particularly fast. We make the copy faster by increasing the block size and the number of bytes read at a time. The number of bytes read and written should always be a multiple of 512, as this is the size of a single sector. The *#define NSECT* specifies the number of sectors tranferred at a time.

Copy() takes the conservative approach by creating the target file. If this file exists, the call to *createnew()* generates an error. *Copy()* could just as easily have overwritten the target file by using *open()* with the *truncate* option selected.

Remember that output from prg5_7 can be redirected to another file. Although probably not useful in the copy mode, this can be very useful in the find mode to provide an image of the entire contents of a disk.

A similar *Erase All* command could have be written just as easily by combining Prg5_7 with Prg5_6. (Although doing so should be trivially easy, given the example programs provided, I will not present such a program lest a reader carelessly delete his entire hard disk.) If you do decide to create your own *Erase All*, please make it an *Erase All w/ Question*. The ability to erase the entire contents of a disk with a single command is not one that I would want lying about unguarded.

(In fact, Prg5_7 can be made into quite a useful utility. Often the details of such a *real world* utility obscure the principles of operation. However, it is interesting to see this done at leat once. Appendix 5 shows the development of such a DOS utility, *KOPY,* from Prg5_7.)

Dividing a hard disk up into many small directories brings with it another problem. Many programs require auxiliary files to run properly. These files may contain data, overlays, or configuration information. The classic example here was the earlier versions of the word processor and editor WordStar, which required two extra files to run properly. The problem was that we might reasonably want to execute WordStar from any directory which contains text files, which is most of them. Of course, we could do this by entering the entire path for WordStar. Unfortunately, if we were not actually in the WordStar directory, it would not execute properly since it could not find its helper files.

The solution in those days was to put copies of the helper files for WordStar in just about every directory on the hard disk. Not only was this wasteful of disk space, but it spoiled much of the elegance of hierarchical directories. As authors of software, if our program requires support files, we do not want our users to be compelled to make dozens of copies of them all over their hard disk. Under DOS 3.x, there is a solution.

As we have noted before, a Turbo C program executed under DOS 3.x has access to its own name in argument 0. In the past we have used this as the name of the program, preferring this over hardcoding its name in case the user renames the program without recompiling. However, not only is the name of the program itself present their, but its complete pathname.

Prg5_8 is a simple example of how a program can use this to find its helper files. Prg5_8 accepts one argument, which is taken to be the name of a file. The program first attempts to open a file of that name. If that attempt is unsuccessful, Prg5_8 looks for the file in the directory from which Prg5_8 itself was executed, the so-called *home directory.*

This is best explained by example. Suppose the current default directory is *C:\USER\C* and suppose that PRG5_8 is in directory *D:\UTILS*. If the user enters *PRG5_8 EXAMPLE,* the program will first attempt to open *EXAMPLE* in directory *C:\USER\C*. If it is found, it is printed on the display. But if it is not found, the program does not give up. Instead it uses the *fnsplit()* library routine to split the disk and path, *D:\UTILS*, off of the program name in *ARGV[0]* on line 41. It then peels the simple filename off of any path which may have been attached to it on line 42. Finally, it constructs a new pathname from the two parts, resulting in this case with *D:\UTILS\EXAMPLE*. If the program can open this file, it uses it instead.

```
 1[ 0]: /*Prg5_8 - Opening a file in the "Home Directory"
 2[ 0]:     by Stephen R. Davis, 1987
 3[ 0]:
 4[ 0]:    When a file is not found to be present in the current directory,
 5[ 0]:    it is usually advisable to look in the directory in which the
 6[ 0]:    program resides before giving up.  Note that this program requires
 7[ 0]:    DOS 3.x to function.
 8[ 0]: */
 9[ 0]:
10[ 0]: #include <stdio.h>
11[ 0]: #include <dir.h>
12[ 0]: #include <fcntl.h>
13[ 0]: #include <io.h>
14[ 0]: #include <dos.h>
15[ 0]: #include <process.h>
16[ 0]:
17[ 0]: /*globally defined data*/
18[ 0]:
19[ 0]: char path [MAXPATH], drive [MAXDRIVE], dir [MAXDIR], file [MAXFILE];
20[ 0]: char ext [MAXEXT];
21[ 0]:
22[ 0]: /*Main - try and open the file specified as the first argument.
23[ 0]:          If an error is returned, look in the home directory.*/
24[ 0]: void main (argc, argv)
25[ 0]:      unsigned argc;
26[ 0]:      char *argv [];
27[ 0]: {
28[ 1]:      unsigned handle, number;
29[ 1]:      char buffer [512];
30[ 1]:
31[ 1]:      /*if error on opening in current directory...*/
32[ 1]:      if ((handle = open (argv [1], O_RDONLY)) == -1) {
33[ 2]:
34[ 2]:           /*...and if this is running under DOS 3.x...*/
```

```
        if (_osmajor < 3) {
            printf ("Can't find file (try using DOS 3.x)\n");
            exit (1);
        }

        /*...look in home directory*/
        fnsplit (argv [0], drive, dir,    0,    0);
        fnsplit (argv [1],     0,    0, file, ext);
        fnmerge (    path, drive, dir, file, ext);
        if ((handle = open (path, O_RDONLY)) == -1) {
            perror ("Can't find file");
            exit (1);
        }
    }

    /*now copy the file to the screen*/
    while (number = read (handle, buffer, 512))
        fwrite (buffer, number, 1, stdout);

    /*and exit normally*/
    exit (0);
}
```

In our case, Prg5_8 did not *need* the file it was printing to the screen, per se. However, the entire program could be rewritten as a *globalopen()* function which future programs use to provide the same service. Under DOS 3.x, your programs need never trouble their users with the necessity of keeping multiple copies of helper files again.

Finally, as part of the housekeeping chores of maintaining a tree of disk directories, it often becomes necessary to move a file from one directory to another. This is either because the file was not placed in the proper directory in the first place or because the host directory is being done away with and its contents divided among the remaining directories. Normally, moving a file is accomplished by copying it from the source to the target directory and then deleting the file from the source directory.

We can use the DOS Rename system call to perform the move operation in one step. Rename accepts two pathnames, the old name and the new name. During a rename operation, only the simple filename is different between the old and new names. The pathname stays the same. However, this need not be the case. If the pathname is different between the old and new names, the Rename system call will relink the file from the old directory path into the new one, in effect, *moving* the file.

Of course, the file has not moved at all. It is only that it is now accessible through a different path. This is actually desirable. Not only is this quicker, but it avoids some of the disk storage space fragmenting, which accompanies copying and deleting files back and forth. (Notice how the time required to move a file is not a function of its size, while it is when copying.)

Prg5_9 below demonstrates the principle.

```
/*Prg5_9 - Move a File from a Directory to Another
   by Stephen R. Davis, 1987

  Normally, moving a file from one directory to another involves
  copying it and then deleting the original.  Not only is this
  clumsy, but it adds to disk fracturing.  This program uses the
  rename function to actually move a file.
*/

#include <stdio.h>
#include <dir.h>
#include <process.h>
#include <string.h>

/*define global data*/
char path [MAXPATH];
char drive1 [MAXDRIVE], dir1 [MAXDIR], file1 [MAXFILE], ext1 [MAXEXT];
char drive2 [MAXDRIVE], dir2 [MAXDIR], file2 [MAXFILE], ext2 [MAXEXT];

/*Main - parse the first argument, assumed to be the source, and the
        second, assumed to be the target.  Check for validity and the
        attempt the rename*/
void main (argc, argv)
     unsigned argc;
     char *argv [];
{
     char *dptr, *fptr, *eptr;

     /*check the number of arguments first*/
     if (argc != 3) {
          printf ("Wrong number of arguments\n"
                  "  try 'prg5_9 source dest' to move file 'source'\n"
                  "  to file 'dest'\n");
          exit (1);
     }

     /*parse out the two file names*/
     fnsplit (argv [1], drive1, dir1, file1, ext1);
     fnsplit (argv [2], drive2, dir2, file2, ext2);

     /*if present, the disks must match*/
     if (*drive2)
          if (strcmp (drive1, drive2)) {
               printf ("Drives must match\n");
               exit (1);
          }

     /*if second directory not present, assume the first*/
     dptr = dir2;
     if (!*dptr)
          dptr = dir1;

     /*if second file not present, assume the first*/
     fptr = file2;
     if (!*fptr)
          fptr = file1;

     /*if the second extension not present, assume the first*/
     eptr = ext2;
```

```
    if (!*eptr)
        eptr = ext1;

    /*now execute the rename*/
    fnmerge (path, drive1, dptr, fptr, eptr);
    printf ("\nRenaming %s -> %s\n", argv [1], path);
    if (rename (argv [1], path)) {
        perror ("Rename error");
        exit (1);
    }

    /*exit normally*/
    exit (0);
}
```

Prg5_9 is written as a general move utility. The program accepts two arguments, the source filename and the target filename. The source filename must completely specify the file. The target filename may be incomplete, however. If the target pathname is missing, the source pathname is used instead. If the filename is missing, the source filename is used and if the extension is not present, the source extension is pressed into service.

Therefore, all of the commands below are equal.

```
1) prg5_9 \user\c\file1.c \programs\file1.c

2) prg5_9 \user\c\file1.c \programs\file1

3) prg5_9 \user\c\file1.c \programs\

4) chdir \user\c
   prg5_9 file1.c \programs\
```

Renamed, Prg5_9 can be used as a general rename utility, capable of renaming a program or moving it from one directory to another or both.

The Environment

Simply put, the environment is a series of 0 terminated ASCII strings terminated by a 0 length string to which the user program can gain access. Each of these strings is of the format *LABEL=STRING*. These strings are saved in the operating system and provide another communication path between DOS and the user program. At least three labels are defined in any environment: *COMSPEC*, *PATH* and *PROMPT*. Let us start by reviewing the functions of these.

As I mentioned at the beginning of the chapter, *COMMAND.COM* is the program which puts up the *A>* prompt and which accepts and interprets the usual *DIR*, *TYPE* and *ERASE* type commands. Occasionally during normal operation parts of *COMMAND.COM* get overwritten. Upon completion of a program which has overwritten some part of *COMMAND.COM,* DOS reloads it from disk. In a hierarchical file system, this can be a problem. In which subdirectory is *COMMAND.COM* anyway?

We could simply make up a rule and say, for instance, *COMMAND.COM* must always be located in the root directory. But then the question becomes, *of which disk?* In any case, such rules are too inflexible and are not accepted well by such liberal thinkers as programmers. The label *COMSPEC* in the environment specifies the full pathname of *COMMAND.COM.* If *COMSPEC* says that DOS should reload *C:\DOS\COMMAND.COM,* then we have no misunderstanding, even if the default directory happens to be *D:\UTIL.*

The *PATH* specifier solves a slightly different problem. Easy access to common utilities and commands is a problem with hierarchical files systems. The user probably has a set of favorite utilities, some of which came from the original DOS disk, but many of which are of his own making, such as the *Erase w/Question* and *Copy All* utilities presented above. These commands are of such general use that the user would like to have access to them at all times, irrespective of what the default directory might be.

No problem, you might say, the user can always enter the full pathname instead of relying on the default path. That is, even while in directory *\USER\C,* the user can still enter *\DOS\DOSUTILS\COPYALL* to gain access to his *COPYALL* utility. While this is true, being compelled to type in the entire pathname removes much of the luster of hierarchical file systems. Besides, this solution presupposes that the user even remembers exactly what directory the utility is in. Many users, myself included, keep their utilities divided into several small directories on the basis of function. Remembering exactly which directory houses a particular utility can be a real chore.

The solution to this problem in DOS is the very same solution used in UNIX, that of *PATH.* The *PATH* consists of a string of directories, separated by semicolons. If a particular command is not found in the current default directory, then each of the directories specified in the *PATH* is searched until either the command is found or the path is exhausted.

Just as an aside, notice that the directories in the *PATH* are interpreted when they are needed and not when entered. This causes casual users some confusion in the following case. Suppose we keep most of our utilities in directory *\UTIL* and our DOS files in directory *\DOS* on drive C. Having read up on the *PATH,* we dutifully set our *PATH* to *\UTIL;\DOS.* All works as planned as long as we default to drive C. Every time we invoke one of our utilities, DOS correctly looks for and finds it in either directory *C:\DOS* or *C:\UTIL*. As soon as we move to drive D, however, nothing works. Since we did not specify a drive for our *PATH* directories, DOS will now look for *D:\UTIL* and *D:\DOS* when we attempt to invoke one of our utilities. Since these directories do not exist, they certainly do not contain them. To avoid this problem, we should have set our *PATH* to *C:\UTIL;C:\DOS*.

The final string, *PROMPT*, allows users to customize their prompts. My personal preference is to display the default directory as well as drive before the >. Interested readers should refer to the DOS Users' Manual for details.

Each program is provided with its own copy of the environment when it is executed. There are several ways for a program to access its copy. First of all, the segment address of the environment is contained at offset *0x2c* of the first *0x100* bytes of a program. (This section of a program is called the Program Segment Prefix [PSP].) Prg5_10a shows a general purpose function *getenv()*, which uses the Turbo C library routine *getpsp()* to fetch a pointer to this area from which it returns the far address of the environment. The remainder of the program simply prints out the contents of the environment on the display. (*Note:* It is necessary to copy the environment to a local buffer so that its address matches the type expected by *print()*.)

```
/*Prg5_10a - Display the Environment
   by Stephen R. Davis, 1987

  Display the entire current environment.  This program
  gets the environment address directly from offset 0x2C in
  the Program Segment Prefix.  The environment consists of a
  series of ASCII strings, each terminated with a 0, with the
  entire thing terminated by a 0.
*/

#include <stdio.h>
#include <dos.h>

/*prototyping definitions*/
char far *getenv (void);
void main (void);

/*Main - dump the environment on the screen*/
void main (void)
{
     char far *envptr;
     char localbuf [128];
     char *localptr;
     unsigned count;

     count = 0;
     envptr = getenv ();
     while (*envptr) {

```

```
                localptr = localbuf;          /*xfer this to a local buffer*/
                while (*envptr)
                     *localptr++ = *envptr++;
                *localptr = '\0';
                printf ("entry %d: %s\n", count++, localbuf);
                envptr++;
           }
}

/*Getenv - return a pointer to the environment strings*/
char far *getenv (void)
{
     unsigned far *envseg;
     unsigned pspseg;

     pspseg = getpsp ();                /*get the psp segment*/

     /*at offset 2C in the PSP is the segment address of
       the environment*/
     envseg = (unsigned far *)MK_FP ( pspseg, 0x2C);
     return   (char far *)    MK_FP (*envseg, 0x00);
}
```

Accessing the envitonment using *ENVPTR[]* is much like acessing the arguments via *ARGV[]*. Both are declared similarly. Both point to standard C strings.

Although this routine has the advantage of being accessible from anywhere within a program, it is actually a bit of overkill. I have been ignoring it up until now, but *main()* actually is provided with a third parameter. After the array of pointers to the program arguments is another array of pointers. This array points to the individual strings which make up the program's environment. Prg5_10b below uses this array of pointers to gain access to the environment and display it on the screen.

```
/*Prg5_10b - Display the Environment
   by Stephen R. Davis, 1987

  Display the entire current environment.  Use the environment
  pointer passed to us in main().
*/

#include <stdio.h>

/*Main - dump the environment on the screen*/
void main (argc, argv, envptr)
     unsigned argc;
     char *argv[];
     char *envptr[];
{
     unsigned count;

     count = 0;
     while (*envptr[0]) {
          printf ("entry %d: %s\n", count++, envptr[0]);
          envptr++;
     }
```

```
23[ 0]: }
```

Accessing the environment using *ENVPTR[]* is much like accessing the arguments via *ARGV[]*. Both are declared similarly. Both point to standard C strings. In actual fact, you need neither program to display the contents of the environment. Simply entering the DOS command *SET* will cause DOS to dump the current environment to the display.

```
C>SET
COMSPEC=C:\COMMAND.COM
PROMPT=$p$_$n$g
PATH=C:\DOS\DOSUTIL;C:\DOS;C:\DOS\RAMUTIL;
DEFAULT=C:\USER\BOOK
```

Reading the environment is only half the battle. How can we write to the environment? From the DOS command prompt, we simply enter *SET <label>=<string>* where label is any label of 8 characters or less and string is any ASCII string. The *SET* command will add our label to the current environment. Entering *SET <label>=* will remove a label which already exists in the environment.

From within a program, labels can be added and removing using *putenv()*. The syntax here is similar to the *SET* command. Unfortunately, *putenv()* only affects the program's copy of the environment. When the program completes, the environment returns to its previous value. The communication path established by the environment is, by and large, one way.

The *getenv()* library routine is useful for searching the environment for the value of a particular label. For example, the call *getenv(PATH)*would return a pointer to the value of the label *PATH*. If the label is not found, *getenv()* returns a *NULL* pointer.

A professional package can use the environment in many different ways. Prg5_8 used the path specified argument 0 to solve the problem of auxiliary files, but, as we noted, this technique only works for DOS 3.0 and later. You might just as well have equated a label to the home directory. The program could then have used this label to find its auxiliary files. Although this technique has the disadvantage that it requires the user or a batch file to enter another command (the SET command) to define the label, it has the advantage that it works even under DOS 2.x. Besides, with this trick we have the added flexibility that the auxiliary files could even be in some third directory apart from the executable file itself.

Turbo C itself uses the environment to affect how it handles floating point numbers. Turbo C programs that are linked with the emulation library contain the code either to use an *8087 Numerical Processor* or to emulate its presence in software. If you set the label *87* to *N* before running such a program, it will not use the *8087* coprocessor even if one is present. On the other hand, setting the label *87* to *Y* forces such a program to attempt to use the *8087* coprocessor, even if one is not present (which hangs the system, by the way).

You have already seen an example program which uses the environment. If no argument was presented it, Prg5_5, the change drive and directory utility, looked in the environment for a label called *DEFAULT*. If present, Prg5_5 used the value of that label as its argument. That was the meaning of the call to *getenv(DEFAULT)* on line 43. I found this particularly useful in preparing this book. My *AUTOEXEC* file defined the label *DEFAULT* to *C:\USER\BOOK*, the directory containing the chapters of this book. No matter where I might be, entering *CDD*, the name I gave to Prg5_5 in use, returned me to that directory to continue work. (Notice the definition of *DEFAULT* in my previous environment dump.)

Batch files can also access individual entries out of the environment by the way. Although not documented until recently, a label between percent signs within a batch file is replaced by that label's value out of the environment. For example, *%PATH%* within a batch file is replaced by the list of directories which make up the path. Since a batch file can also add labels to the environment using the *SET* command, the environment forms something of a random storage area for batch files. This provides further communication paths between batch files and your programs.

With all this use, the environment might quickly run out of room. Individual environment strings are limited to 128 bytes in length, but fortunately, you can specify the overall size of the environment at boot up under DOS 3.0 and later. You do this with the SHELL command in the *CONFIG.SYS* file. Originally intended to allow companies to write their own *COMMAND.COM* type shells with different names, the SHELL command is most often used for other purposes. For example, entering the command *SHELL=C:\DOS\COMMAND.COM /P* causes DOS to load *COMMAND.COM* from that subdirectory rather than from the root.

At the same time that the directory is being specified, the size of the environment can also be adjusted by adding the switch */E:xx*. Under DOS 3.0, this feature was undocumented and the value *xx* was in units of paragraphs (one paragraph = 16 bytes). In DOS 3.1 and later, this feature is documented but the units were changed to bytes and not paragraphs. Specifying a larger environment size might use up a small amount of additional memory, but it provides a great deal more space for label definitions.

With a large and flexible environment space, it is a shame that the communications path it represents is only one way. DOS presents copies of the environment to user programs and not *the real thing* as a means of self protection. If a program defines a label using the *putenv()* library call, that label will not be defined when the program exits. Usually this is a good thing, since if the user program inadvertently destroys its own copy, the original is still safely tucked away back in the bank. Sometimes you would like your program to be able to define labels that DOS or a batch file could read after the program completed, however. With such a mechanism, the program could tell you exactly what it did or what it expects us to do. In addition, one invocation of the program could communicate with future invocations by leaving such labels behind.

There are two ways to do this, neither of them completely satisfactory. One approach is to not exit at all, but instead to execute a new version of *COMMAND.COM* (you will see how you might do this at the end of this chapter). Since a daughter process always inherits the environment of its parent, this new version of *COMMAND.COM* will inherit any labels which your program defined. If that version of *COMMAND.COM* then executes your program again, it can read the labels from it previous invocation. The problem here is that loading new versions of *COMMAND.COM* on top of older versions can use up a lot of memory quickly. In any case, you have not solved the problem, only diverted it.

Another approach which shows promise was presented by Charles Petzold in *PC Magazine's* PC Tutor Volume 6, Number 8. It seems that there is an undocumented DOS system interrupt *0x2e* that can be used to execute user-type commands under the current version of *COMMAND.COM*. This system call is quite skittish. First of all, *COMMAND.COM* is no more reentrant than DOS is. If your program were executed from a batch file, executing system interrupt *0x2e* would probably prove fatal. Second, since this system call does not restore the *SS* and *SP* registers upon returning, it cannot be invoked using the normal *intdos()* mechanism.

If you do not mind writing your own inline assembly language function to do so, you can pass a *SET <label>=* command to the current version of *COMMAND.COM* using this system interrupt (we will study inline assembly language in Chapter 8). This command should be formatted exactly as it would appear in the PSP; that is, the first byte should indicate the number of characters in the string. Since this is the same *COMMAND.COM* from which your program was invoked, the label will continue to be defined even after the program terminates. (In fact, the label will only be defined in the original—the currently executing program's copy will not get updated.) Of course, undocumented system calls may disappear from future versions of DOS without warning, so including such a command within your program may not enhance its future portability.

Executing other Programs

It is possible for a Turbo C program to execute other programs, including *COMMAND.COM*. This technique is variously known as shelling or spawning and comes in three forms in Turbo C. Before we examine these forms, however, we must concern ourselves with a small problem. Internal RAM memory is not the problem it used to be, but no matter how much is available, programs will be written which can exceed what is available. In a simple program, the situation is generally handled by DOS. If the program even started, then we are assured that sufficient memory is available for its use. (The only exception to this that you have seen so far lies in the program's dynamic use of the heap.)

When executing subprograms, however, it is not clear just because the first program loaded that there will be sufficient room to load the second program. If the programs are small, we can just continue on and hope for the best. We are not likely to run out of memory, and DOS will tell us if we do, anyway. If the programs are large, however, this is not entirely satisfactory. Our program might get several levels deep before deciding that it cannot continue. This will not only waste time, but is likely to leave the program and any files it has open in a state from which it will be difficult to recover. It would be much better if the program could decide at the very beginning whether sufficient memory exists to continue or not.

DOS maintains a few system calls for communicating this information to user programs. Prg5_11 shows how a program can examine the amount of internal RAM and disk space, both available and total. Prg5_11 does nothing more with this information than display it, but a user program with extensive RAM or disk requirements could check the amount available before beginning.

```
/*Prg5_11 - Get disk and memory information
   by Stephen R. Davis, 1987

  Get the current disk and memory information and display in
  a comfortable format
```

```
*/

#include <stdio.h>
#include <dos.h>
#include <alloc.h>

#define membios 0x12

/*allocate some local structures*/

struct dfree dfres;                         /*for the getdfree() call*/
union REGS regs;                            /*for the int86() call*/

/*Main - perform the necessary system calls and format the
         results for output*/
int main ()
{
     long totdisk, availdisk, totmem, availmem;
     unsigned currseg;
     double percentdisk, percentmem;

     /*first accumulate the information*/
     getdfree (0, &dfres);                  /*uses system call 0x36*/
     availdisk = (long)dfres.df_avail * (long)dfres.df_sclus *
                 (long)dfres.df_bsec;
     totdisk =   (long)dfres.df_total * (long)dfres.df_sclus *
                 (long)dfres.df_bsec;
     percentdisk = ((double)availdisk / (double)totdisk) * (double)100

     int86 (membios, &regs, &regs);     /*use BIOS call 0x12*/
     totmem    = (long)regs.x.ax * (long)1024;
     availmem = (long)farcoreleft ();
     percentmem = ((double)availmem / (double)totmem) * (double)100.;

     currseg = FP_SEG ((int (far *)())main);

     /*now print these values out in a reasonable form*/
     printf ("Display available disk and memory\n"
             "\n"
             "Disk:\n"
             "    %9ld bytes available (%6ldk)\n"
             "    %9ld bytes total     (%6ldk)\n"
             "    (%2.0f%% free)\n"
             "\n"
             "Memory:\n"
             "    %7ld bytes available (%4ldk)\n"
             "    %7ld bytes total     (%4ldk)\n"
             "    (%2.0f%% free)\n"
             "\n"
             "Current segment is %X\n",
                 availdisk, availdisk / (long)1024,
                 totdisk,   totdisk   / (long)1024,
                 percentdisk,
                 availmem,  availmem  / (long)1024,
                 totmem,    totmem    / (long)1024,
                 percentmem,
                 currseg);
}
```

An example run of Prg5_11 on the author's system:

```
C>d:prg5_11
Display available disk and memory

Disk:
     5718016 bytes available (  5584k)
    21213184 bytes total     ( 20716k)
   (27% free)

Memory:
    360976 bytes available ( 352k)
    655360 bytes total     ( 640k)
   (55% free)

Current segment is 3371
```

Notice that both the RAM and disk sizes are too large for conventional integer variables. Instead all of these values have been stored into variables declared to be of type *long int*. Also notice that while the amount of available memory is found easily using the library routine *farcoreleft()*, the call to examine the total memory in the system is not a DOS call at all. Rather this is a BIOS call. You may want to return to this program once you have finished Chapter 6's coverage of BIOS calls.

There are three different ways to execute another program from within a Turbo C program. If all that you really want to do is to execute a common DOS command, such as *DIR *.C*, then the library routine *system()* is straightforward. In this case, *system(DIR *.C);* is just the ticket. Why, you may ask, is this considered executing another program? Because, to perform this function, you must actually load and execute another copy of *COMMAND.COM* in memory. This new version of *COMMAND.COM* executes the command and then exits back to your program upon completion. The value returned by *system()* is the same as the return status from the last command executed.

When executing other programs from within one of your own programs, there are two things that you might want to do. You might want the other program to replace your program. This is usually called *chaining*. In chaining, there are usually a series of programs which are to be executed. *Program A* chains to *Program B*, which chains to *Program C*, and so on.

For example, suppose we are executing a process such as the linked list sorting back in Chapter 4. At any given time, we are either entering data, sorting data or outputting data. We are never performing two of these functions at any one time. While sorting data, for example, the code to input and output the data is just sitting about taking up memory. Instead we could have written the input, sort and output functions as three separate programs. *Program A* would input the data and save it away in the necessary structures, usually on disk. When all the data was in, it would invoke *Program B* to sort it which then invoked *Program C* to print it out. No code sitting around in memory doing nothing means no wasted space.

Even when there is looping envolved, this can still be accommodated with chaining. For example, once ProgramC has completed output, it could just as easily execute ProgramA again to restart the whole process. It may be necessary to communicate to ProgramA that this is the second time around, lest it put up the opening banner which the user saw the first time he executed the program. This technique also works for menu systems. After a particular menu item has been executed, the program chains back to the central menu program to restore the the menu to the screen and wait for the user's next selection.

The other alternative is that a program might execute another program using whatever memory is left over. In this technique, known as either *shelling* or *spawning,* the program makes a *call* to what is actually a program, rather than a function. The operating system leaves the calling program intact and loads the called program above it in memory. Once the called program completes, the operating system returns control back to the calling program.

This technique is easier to work, since each program returns to the caller which can then decide what action to take, much more like a normal program. Not only can the subprogram return a *return status* to indicate success or failure, but the calling programs variables and data space are still intact.

The space saving with spawning can be almost as great, however. For example, we might have written our menu program with each of the menu options housed in a separate program and with a small nucleus program to call them. Even though the nucleus is always in memory, we can keep its size small by limiting its function. In our menu example, the only job of the nucleus is to put up the menu, accept user input and spawn the appropriate subprogram.

In Turbo C, chaining is performed using the *exec()* function call, while spawning is performed with the *spawn()* call. Both routines actually come in a variety of versions. All of the versions are quite similar, however, differing only in the way arguments and environment are passed to the subprogram and whether the *PATH* is automatically searched in the event the subprogram is not in the current directory.

Besides saving memory, spawning can also be used to add functionality to existing programs. For example, our move program, Prg5_9, was used to move programs from one subdirectory to another. Unfortunately, Prg5_9 was only written to move one file. If we needed to move an entire directory using Prg5_9, we would have to execute Prg5_9 once for each file. This would quickly run into more work than Prg5_9 was trying to save us in the first place.

To save effort, we could easily rewrite Prg5_9 so that it accepted wild cards and moved large blocks of files with a single command. But let's assume that Prg5_9 was given to you and that you do not have access to the code or for whatever other reason we do not want to change the program. You could construct another program that accepts wild-card specifications for files and then spawns Prg5_9 to move each file it finds. Prg5_12 below is just such a program.

```
/*Prg5_12 - Execute another Program
   by Stephen R. Davis, 1987

  In addition to invoking simple functions, a C program may also
  invoke other programs.  While this may be costly in terms of
  time, the technique is useful for programs which otherwise
  will not fit into memory in their entirety.  User shells which
  surrond DOS to provide a more user friendly interface also use
  this approach.

  This program provides a "move all" capability to Prg5_9, which
  can only move one file at a time.
*/

#include <stdio.h>
#include <dir.h>
#include <process.h>

/*define global data areas*/
char path [MAXPATH], drive [MAXDRIVE], dir [MAXDIR];
char file [MAXFILE], ext [MAXEXT];
struct ffblk block;

/*we also need the name of the program to execute*/
char *pname = {"prg5_9.exe"};
char *pathname;

/*Main - Find all of the files matching argument 1 and pass
         each one to Prg5_9 in turn*/
void main (argc, argv, env)
     int argc;
     char *argv [];
     char *env [];
{
     /*as always, check the argument count*/
     if (argc != 3) {
          printf ("Wrong number of arguments\n"
                  "  try prg5_12 <source dir><pattern> <dest dir>\n"
                  "  to move all files matching pattern from dir\n"
                  "  source to dir destination\n");
          exit (1);
     }

     /*search for prg5_9 either in current directory or path*/
     if (!(pathname = searchpath (pname))) {
          printf ("Prg5_9 must be current directory or path\n");
          exit (1);
```

```
    }

    /*pull argument 1 apart to separate directory and filename*/
    fnsplit (argv [1], drive, dir, 0, 0);

    /*now search for all files matching pattern*/
    if (findfirst (argv [1], &block, 0)) {
         printf ("No files found\n");
         exit (0);
    }
    do {
         /*assemble the first file name*/
         fnsplit (block.ff_name, 0, 0, file, ext);
         fnmerge (path, drive, dir, file, ext);

         /*and pass this file off to prg5_9*/
         if (spawnle (P_WAIT, pathname, pname, path, argv [2],
                                           NULL, env)) {
              printf ("\nError detected in subprocess\n");
              exit (1);
         }
    } while (!findnext (&block));

    /*exit normally*/
    exit (0);
}
```

An example run of Prg5_12 shows:

```
prg5_12 \sources\*.c \user\c\
Renaming \sources\PRG5_11.C -> \user\c\PRG5_11.C
Renaming \sources\PRG5_1.C -> \user\c\PRG5_1.C
Renaming \sources\PRG5_5.C -> \user\c\PRG5_5.C
Renaming \sources\PRG5_6.C -> \user\c\PRG5_6.C
Renaming \sources\PRG5_7.C -> \user\c\PRG5_7.C
Renaming \sources\PRG5_12.C -> \user\c\PRG5_12.C
Renaming \sources\PRG5_8.C -> \user\c\PRG5_8.C
Renaming \sources\PRG5_10A.C -> \user\c\PRG5_10A.C
Renaming \sources\PRG5_10B.C -> \user\c\PRG5_10B.C
```

After the obligatory check of the number of arguments, Prg5_12 searches for the file *PRG5_9.EXE,* which it will need. The library function *searchpath()* first looks in the current directory. If not found there, it then looks in every subdirectory specified in the *PATH.* (Therefore, we can execute Prg5_12 from any directory as long as both it and Prg5_9 are in the *PATH* or the default directory.) Having found it, *searchpath()* returns the full pathname of Prg5_9.

Prg5_12 first saves off the disk and directory of the first argument. It then performs a search for files matching the specified filename containing wild cards. For every filename found, Prg5_12 tacks the disk and directory name to the front and passes this, along with the target directory, to Prg5_9 for execution using the Turbo C library routine *spawnle()*.

Examine carefully the arguments to *spawnle()*. The first argument must always be *P_WAIT*, indicating that the caller intends to wait for the subprogram to complete before resuming execution. The alternative, *P_NOWAIT*, is not legal under a single tasking executive like DOS. The second argument is the pathname of Prg5_9, found on line 45. This is preferrable to using the *spawnp()* form of the call in this case. *Spawnp()* would have to search the *PATH* for Prg5_9 for each file moved, adding considerably to the execution time. Following that, we send over *ARGV[0]*, *ARGV[1]*, etc. As always you set *ARGV[0]* to the path of Prg5_9 itself. You must be sure to add an extra NULL argument after the last *real* argument. The target program might be expecting it (many of the programs we have written so far do). Finally you pass the environment. In this case, you could have dispensed with the environment and removed the *e* from *spawnle()* as it is not being used.

Notice when executing Prg5_12, that this is much slower than it might have been had you written it completely internally. The spawn process adds a considerable amount of overhead to the process and increases execution time accordingly. On the other hand, Prg5_12 is much faster than entering the individual calls to Prg5_9 yourself, so the overall effect is a great improvement.

Conclusion

As maligned as the IBM's PC-DOS and MS-DOS operating systems might be, they still harbor quite a considerable array of capabilities. Almost all of these capabilities are reflected in a function in the Turbo C support library. Careful perusal of the documentation for the library will reveal many tidbits with which the programmer might interest himself. Hopefully this chapter has touched on a sufficient number of these capabilities to get the beginning DOS programmer started in his search.

Many readers will be completely satisfied with the functions found in the Turbo C library. Some, however, will want for either additional capabilities or speed. This is particularly a problem when it comes to screen output, perhaps the most speed critical part of any program. Such readers will not be happy until they have peeled the DOS operating system back to have a look at the BIOS underneath. For these readers, there is Chapter 6.

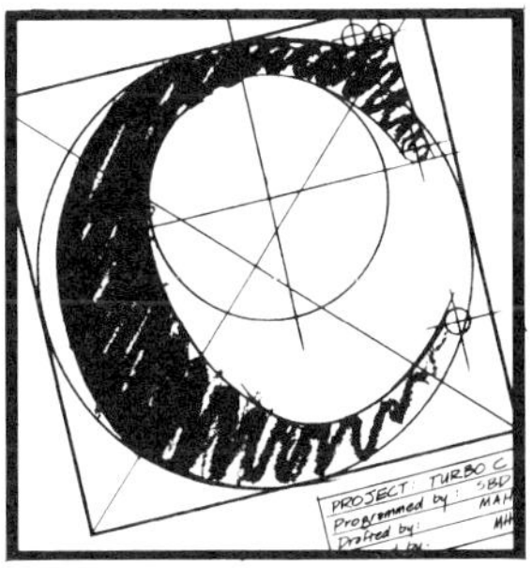

6 Accessing the PC's BIOS

From a programming point of view, the Turbo C library and DOS support routines form a user friendly interface to the PC, a shell over the harsh realities of computer hardware. (Proponents of other operating systems might wish to debate me on the*user friendly* aspects of DOS, but remember that I am referring to DOS and not *COMMAND.COM*, the user interface.) It is precisely this user friendliness that sometimes forces the programmer down to the next level in the PC's software hierarchy: the *Basic Input/Output Service*, the BIOS.

User friendliness almost always brings with it a certain amount of overhead. It takes time for the system to do all those things for you. This slows down the user application. Sometimes the reduction in speed is imperceptible, but it can be frustratingly noticeable. This is especially true on a machine with marginal performance in the first place, such as a 4.77 MHz PC.

In addition, operating systems try to remove the applications software from the details of the hardware as much as possible. Normally this is good. Writing your program so that it runs equally well under PC-DOS and UNIX, which is possible using the Turbo C library routines, opens it up to a larger audience of users. Even when programs do not port from one operating system to another entirely without change, the job is much easier when the programmer has stuck with high level operating system calls.

But there is a down side to this also. Removing the user program from the underlying hardware dulls its perception of what the machine is doing. For example, commercially successful applications, such as those which *pop up* windows of different colors on the PC's display, could not do so if they only utilized DOS calls; there is no *window* system call in the current versions of DOS.

What is the BIOS?

The BIOS is the next level of software support beneath the DOS operating system. It is actually a collection of independent hardware support routines—a separate one for each different piece of hardware. The interface to each of these routines is standardized and documented. Each of the arguments to each of the interface routines is strictly spelled out. The BIOS collectively makes up a rational interface (this has nothing to do with whether it is logical or not).

Theoretically, any 8086-based machine which supports the same BIOS interface as the PC can run all of the same applications, including DOS itself, irrespective of exactly how the hardware is configured. Many of the early PC clone manufacturers, such as Columbia, Seequa and Eagle, shattered on problems with this for reasons that we will see in Chapter 7. Nevertheless, there is still a large amount of truth to the statement. Today, different models of PC compatibles use different keyboards, different programmable interval timers and different communications adapters. This is true even among IBM machines (actually, this is true among IBM machines). Because the BIOS interface rationalizes these different hardware fixtures, software can run without even knowing that there is a potential problem.

With DOS it was straightforward: we put in a disk marked DOS or something similar, turned the power on, the red disk light flickered on, we heard the crunching sound of a floppy disk's stepper motor and DOS was loaded. When we thought about the DOS operating system, at least, we knew more or less where it came from, even if its files were hidden from our view. But there is no disk marked BIOS. No crunching sound or red lights to mark its arrival. Where does it come from?

The BIOS is contained in a Read-Only Memory (ROM) located on the PC's system board itself. When the PC is first switched on, the CPU begins executing code out of this ROM. The ROM starts by performing power-on diagnostics. It is this diagnostic routine which puts that annoying memory counter on your screen as it checks system memory (and which takes so long doing it). Once the hardware has been checked out, the power-up program installs the address of the support routine for each of the different pieces of hardware into its assigned interrupt.

Exactly what an interrupt is and how it gets handled by the PC's microprocessor will have to wait for our low-level discussions in Chapter 9. For now, let's suffice to say that there are 256 interrupts numbered *0x00* through *0xff*. Each has associated with it the address of a function. When we invoke the interrupt by number, control gets passed to that function, much as if we had called it.

We associate some of these interrupts with different pieces of the PC's hardware. For example, during power-up the address of the screen handler function gets placed into interrupt *0x10*. Therefore, we say that interrupt *0x10* is the screen BIOS interrupt. When we want to access the screen BIOS function, we execute an interrupt *0x10*. A complete list of the BIOS interrupts is found in *Appendix 2*.

This all seems somewhat round about. We call other functions directly—we don't load their addresses into interrupts and then interrupt to them. Why not just assign each BIOS function to some fixed address? We might then have called some far location, say *0xfe000100,* when we wanted to perform screen output. Of course, we would have been very clever about it, perhaps defining some constant of the proper type; e.g.

```
#define screenBIOS ((void (far *)(union REGS *)) 0xfe000100)
```

That is, declaring a constant *screenBIOS* to be a far pointer to a function which accepts a pointer to a union of type *REGS* as its argument and returns nothing (*VOID*) (isn't it wonderful!). When it came time to invoke *screenBIOS* we would simply have called it like any other function. After all, isn't this exactly what we are doing when we access DOS via the *intdos()* call?

This would have been a very bad idea. Let's take the very example of the screen BIOS function to see why. The original PC supported two different types of display. The *Monochrome Display Adapter* (MDA) was a green-screen display intended solely for text processing. Although it was completely incapable of graphics, its high persistence phosphor and high resolution character box made it pleasing, if slightly smallish, for the eye. This was intended to be the primary display for PC applications. The *Color Graphics Adapter* (CGA) was a lower resolution, color monitor intended as a supplement to supply the user with the graphics capability lacking in the MDA. The two cards were designed so that both could be present in the same system at the same time. The original BIOS, the one still supplied with PC's and AT's shipped today, supports both of these two displays.

As electronics improved, two things became apparent. First, buyer's did not want to forgo color graphics ability. Although a superior display, few PC's were being purchased with the MDA. The CGA was always a better seller. Even at that, an early third party supplier in the PC market built a display adapter which provided the monochrome screen with graphics capability. Sales of this plug-in card, the Herculese card, and its clones eventually outstripped sales of the IBM card. Second, the resolution and color capability of the CGA (*320x200* w/four colors or *640x200* w/one color) needed improving. Never intended as a primary display, it was giving the entire PC line a bad name. To address these concerns, IBM introduced a new display adapter, the *Enhanced Graphics Adapter* (EGA).

The EGA had resolution almost as good as that of the MDA for comfortable text processing as well as graphics and color capabilities beyond that of the CGA. While not up to CAD/CAM standards, its *640x350* resolution with 16 colors was acceptable for most applications. The only problem was that it was not completely compatible with the other two displays. How could it be and offer any improvement? The existing screen BIOS routines in the PC would not support this new display with its extended modes of operation.

Our *screenBIOS()* function would have been in serious trouble about now. By calling the old screen BIOS function directly, we have insured that our program is not compatible with the new displays. Okay, so we busily design and implement our own BIOS routines. Ones that are capable of handling the newer display adapters. We issue a software upgrade and all is well. Unfortunately, we are doomed to repeat ourselves every time a new display adapter appears on the market that is the least bit different, and in the PC clone world that's just about every day.

To address this problem, the EGA (and other new cards) come with its own ROM. This ROM contains the code for a new screen handler capable of handling not only the older CGA and MDA, but also the new EGA displays. During power-up, the PC first installs all of its BIOS normally. It then makes a search of certain fixed locations for the presence of ROMs, such as the one on the EGA card. When it finds these, it calls them to allow them to initialize their particular hardware. The EGA ROM installs the address of its display routine into interrupt *0x10,* replacing that of the older routine. The same old programs which previously called the old screen handler via interrupt *0x10* to display text and graphics on the older CGA and MDA displays, now use interrupt *0x10* to access the new screen handler to write to the new EGA display. It's the perfect con—they are not even aware of the switch.

This trick is not limited to replacing existing interface functions with those of higher capability. It can also be used to add capabilities that did not previously even exist. The original PC did not offer a hard disk, even as an option. The cost of such disks was prohibitive when the PC was introduced. Installing a hard disk into these older machines, however, is no more difficult than plugging in the hard disk controller card and connecting the cables. The hard disk contains its own support ROM. Just like the EGA, this ROM installs itself into one of the PC's interrupts during power-on to add the hard disk support previously missing.

Even when the implementation of the BIOS support functions leaves something to be desired, as we will see, there is nothing wrong with the idea itself. The PC's BIOS represents one of the most important cases of *forward looking* embodied in the PC.

Using the BIOS

Although not as easy as the Turbo C library, the PC's BIOS routines are certainly nothing to be scared of. The main difficulty is that the BIOS functions are less user friendly than DOS or Turbo C. Each BIOS call requires more arguments and usually gets less work done than an equivalent Turbo C might. Being forced to set more different hardware parameters for each and every call also means that the user program has more different ways to influence the hardware, however. You will find that the simpler BIOS routines execute faster than the equivalent higher level routines.

Invoking a BIOS call from Turbo C is quite simple. As BIOS calls were primarily intended to be accessed from assembly language programs, they accept arguments in the registers rather than on the stacks. Therefore, the first thing you must do is include the *.H* file *DOS.H*. You then load the intended registers into the union *REGS* defined there. The actual interrupt is performed by calling the Turbo C library routine *int86()*.

Let's take a very simple example. Prg6_1 shows the source code for a very simple program. This program invokes the BIOS function reboot (interrupt *0x19*). This BIOS function takes and returns no arguments.

```
/*Prg6_1 - Perform a simple BIOS request
   by Stephen R. Davis, 1987

  This program merely serves as an example of a program which
  performs a simple BIOS request: the bootstrap interrupt 0x19.
  Since this interrupt does not go through a complete reset,
  it may or may not be effective.  It merely serves as a simple
  but immediately apparent system call.
*/

#include <stdio.h>
#include <dos.h>

union REGS reg;

main ()
```

```
{
    printf ("\nreboot!\n");
    int86 (0x19, &reg, &reg);
}
```

Notice how we declare the variable *REG* to be of type *REGS*. Since this BIOS call takes no arguments, we do not bother to initialize any of the registers. The call to *int86()* follows the standard pattern. The first argument specifies the number of the BIOS interrupt, *0x19*. The second is the address of the *REGS* union from which to load the registers before making the call. The third is the address of the union in which to store the registers upon returning. It is not uncommon to specify the same union address for both of these arguments as we have done.

This should have seemed like deja vu. Haven't we been through this all before? In fact, we did almost exactly the same thing to execute DOS calls directly back in Chapter 5. The only difference is that back then we did not specify an interrupt number. This was only a bit of Turbo C slight of hand. Calling *intdos()* is exactly the same as calling *int86()*, passing it an interrupt number of *0x21*.

`intdos (&reg, &reg)` <==is equivalent to==> `int86 (0x21, &reg, &reg)`

Just as there was an *intdosx()* earlier to handle cases where you needed to load the segment registers before making a call, so there is also an analogous *int86x ()* with the same correspondence.

Interrupt *0x21* is known as the DOS system call interrupt and provides access to the DOS calls which you examined earlier. So you see, your argument was complete. You have never defined some typed constant to call, even when it seemed like it earlier. In a way, the DOS operating system is just another set of BIOS calls, which happen to be loaded from disk instead of being resident in ROM.

As we noted already, the different BIOS interrupts are centered around the different pieces of hardware. For example, interrupt *0x10* is our access to the display support routines. Of course, there are several things that can be done with a device such as the display. There must be some indicator as to exactly what service is being requested on the particular device. Just as with DOS calls, it is convention to indicate the specific subfunction by the value of the AH register upon entry. While invoking interrupt *0x10* with *AH* set to 6 might cause the screen to scroll up, doing so with *AH* set to *0x0e* will cause characters to be written to the display.

Because the various pieces of hardware are so unalike, there are no generalities for the meanings of the subfunctions for different BIOS calls. Subfunction 2 for the screen BIOS function has nothing in common with subfunction 2 for the keyboard BIOS routine. Likewise, there are no generalities concerning the remainder of the registers. Each subfunction for each BIOS interrupt in *Appendix 2* assigns its own meaning to the registers.

Simple BIOS Functions

The program above was too small to be useful. In fact, rebooting the system via interrupt *0x19* may not even be successful depending upon what pop-up programs have been installed. The important thing is that the call is simple and the effects are immediate and unmistakable. I'll now examine some of the more useful BIOS functions.

One of the simpler of these is the *Equipment Status*. Like the *Boot* call above, *Equipment Status* has no subfunctions and requires no arguments. Unlike reboot, *Equipment Status* does return to the caller, however, returning a single integer. This integer describes the hardware as determined during power-on initialization, both by examining the system board switches and by direct determination. It has the following significance:

Binary representation of *Equipment Status* flag:

```
PPxGCCCxDDVVRR8I
```

where

```
PP - number of printers attached
G  - 1 -> game port attached
CCC- number of RS232 COM: ports
DD - number of disk drives - 1 (if I = 1)
VV - video mode
      00 -> none or EGA
      01 -> 40x25 CGA
      10 -> 80x25 CGA
      11 -> monochrome
RR - system board RAM
     on original 64k PC:
       00 -> 16k
       01 -> 32k
       10 -> 48k
       11 -> 64k
8  - 0 -> 8087 present
I  - 1 -> system booted from floppy
x  - don't care
```

This system call is actually useful for programs which have specific hardware requirements. You should notice, however, that many of the fields in the *Equipment Status* word have been replaced by newer system calls. For example, memory size should be determined by BIOS interrupt *0x12* and display adapter type by direct inspection or by checking the display mode (both of which we will do later), but the other fields are pretty trustworthy. If your program needs to know if a particular piece of hardware is present, using the Equipment Status is better than asking the operator. Don't ask the operator what you can determine for yourself. Doing so reflects poorly on the resulting program.

```
/*Prg6_2 - Read the Hardware Status
   by Stephen R. Davis, 1987

  Get the equivalent hardware status via BIOS request 0x11
  and interpret it according to the format:

         PPxGCCCxDDVVRR8I

  where
      PP - number of printers
      G  - 1 -> game port present
      CCC- number of RS232 COM ports
      DD - number of disk drives - 1 (if I = 1)
      VV - video mode:
             00 -> none or EGA
             01 -> 40x25 CGA
             10 -> 80x25 CGA
             11 -> monochrome
      RR - system board RAM
      8  - 0 -> 8087 present
      I  - 1 -> booted from floppy

  This is a simple example of performing BIOS calls.
*/

#include <stdio.h>
#include <dos.h>

/*prototype definitions*/
int main (void);
unsigned getstatus (void);
void interpret (unsigned);

/*define global data structures*/
union REGS reg;

/*Main - make the BIOS call to get status and then interpret it*/
main ()
{
     printf ("\nEquipment as reported by BIOS:\n");
     interpret (getstatus ());
}

/*Getstatus - get the equipment status via BIOS call 0x11*/
unsigned getstatus (void)
{
     int86 (0x11, &reg, &reg);
     return (unsigned)reg.x.ax;
}
```

```

/*Display routines which we need for Interpret()*/
void dispnum (i)
     unsigned i;
{
     printf ("%d", i);
}

void dispdsk (i)
     unsigned i;
{
     printf ("%d", i + 1);
}

char *modes [] = {"No monitor or EGA attached",
                  "Color/Graphics in 40 x 25 mode",
                  "Color/Graphics in 80 x 25 mode",
                  "Monochrome monitor"};
void dispmode (i)
     unsigned i;
{
     printf (modes [i]);
}

char *mems [] = {"16k", "32k", "48k", "64k"};
void dispmem (i)
     unsigned i;
{
     printf (mems [i]);
}

char *yn [] = {"Yes", "No"};
void dispyn (i)
     unsigned i;
{
     printf (yn [i]);
}
void dispny (i)
     unsigned i;
{
     printf (yn [1 - i]);
}

/*Interpret - interpret the IBM status word*/
struct DICT {
     unsigned mask;
     unsigned shiftvalue;
     char *string;
     void (*disp) (unsigned);
     } dictionary [] = {{0xc000, 14, "Printers =            ", dispnum},
                        {0x1000, 12, "Game I/O ports =      ", dispnum},
                        {0x0e00,  9, "Serial ports =        ", dispnum},
                        {0x00c0,  6, "Disk drives =         ", dispdsk},
                        {0x0030,  4, "Video mode =          ", dispmode}
                        {0x000c,  2, "System board RAM =    ", dispmem},
                        {0x0002,  1, "8087/287 NDP =        ", dispny},
                        {0x0001,  0, "IPL from diskette =   ", dispyn},
                        {0x0000,  0, "Terminator", dispnum}};
void interpret (value)
     unsigned value;
{
     unsigned maskvalue;
     struct DICT *ptr;

```

```
        ptr = dictionary;
        while (ptr -> mask) {
             maskvalue = value & ptr -> mask;
             maskvalue >>= ptr -> shiftvalue;
             printf (ptr -> string);
             (*(ptr -> disp)) (maskvalue);
             printf ("\n");
             ptr++;
        }
}
```

The important part of this program is the 2 line function *getstatus()*. This invokes the Equipment Status BIOS call and then returns the equipment status returned in AX. Notice that the Turbo C library routine *biosequip()* does the same thing. In fact, there is a BIOS—()routine for many of the major BIOS functions; however, looking up and calling a different routine for each different BIOS call strikes me as an unnecessary complication. I prefer to use *int86()* and provide the proper number from the list in *Appendix 2*. Not only is this clearer to me, but it is actually more portable. Almost all C compilers for the PC provide an *int86()* library function and most of them are invoked in this very same way. The function *biosequip()* is unique to the Turbo C library. Invoking *int86* (*0x19, &reg, &reg*) is likely to work with any C compiler for the PC; calling *biosequip()* is not.

The remainder of Prg6_2 merely serves to interpret the flags returned by *getstatus()*. I chose to do this by building a table of masks and right shift values, but in this particular case it might have been just as easy to handle each different field explicitly.

Another simple, but useful, BIOS interrupt is *0x1a*, the *Time of Day* request. The PC family of personal computers is equipped with an *8253* or *8254A Programmable Interval Timer* (PIT). The PIT acts as a clock, *ticking* at reqular, processor controlled intervals. The power-on ROM initializes the PIT in the PC to tick at 1092 times per minute or 18.2 times per second. Once the PC has read the current time, either via operator input or from a battery backed up clock chip, it maintains the proper time throughout the remainder of the day using this regular beat. The date and time are maintained by DOS for such functions as the time stamping of files.

Unlike *Equipment Status, Time of Day* has two subfunctions. Entering with *AH = 1* sets the *Time of Day* clock. This subfunction is used by COMMAND.COM to set the clock anytime the DOS *TIME* command is used to change the current time. Units are clock ticks since midnight. A quick calculation shows that the number of clock ticks in 24 hours is larger than the maximum 16-bit integer (65535):

```
clock ticks/day = 24 * 60 * 60 * 18.2 = 1,572,480
                  ^    ^    ^     ^
                  |    |    |     |
                  |    |    |     |- ticks/second
                  |    |    |------- seconds/minute
                  |    |------------ minutes/hour
                  |----------------- hours/day
```

It is therefore necessary to pass the time in two 16-bit registers, in this case, *CX* and *DX*.

Calling the *Time of Day* function with *AH = 0* reads the current time of day, also in units of number of clock ticks since midnight. Just as with set subfunction, the upper 16 bits of the time are returned in the *CX* register and the lower 16 bits in the *DX* register. In addition, the *AL* register is set to 0 if the date has not changed since the last time the time of day function was called (the date changes if the user program is running as the time goes beyond midnight).

Measuring time takes on two forms in user programs. Either you are interested in the absolute time, i.e., displaying the time of day, or in elapsed time. Programs often use elapsed time to allow the operator to read data displayed on the screen which might otherwise slip by too rapidly for human eyes. They might also allow users a limited amount of time to provide critical input (such as passwords). The most straightforward method of *killing time* is for the program to enter a *do-nothing FOR* loop. Indexing a count and performing a multiplication a few thousand times will generally be enough to let the user see what is on the screen.

The problem with such *do-nothing* loops is that the amount of time they use up is a function of the speed of the host computer. A *FOR* loop which waits a comfortable amount of time on a stock PC will flash by in an instant on an 80386 based machine. Set the loop counter properly for an *AT* and the program drags on the PC. Prg6_3 demonstrates a much better way to delay. This program watches the PC's clock tick off using repeated invocations of the *Get Time of Day* subfunction.

```
/*Prg6_3 - Delay Specified Number of Seconds
   by Stephen R. Davis, 1987

  Many programs must delay for short periods of time.  Often this
  is done by executing an "empty" FOR loop.  The Time-of-Day BIOS
  routine provides a more accurate means of delaying.
*/

#include <stdio.h>
#include <dos.h>

```

```
/*prototype definitions*/
void main (void);
unsigned getval (char *);
void wait (unsigned);
unsigned getime (void);

/*global data definitions*/
union REGS reg;
union  {
        int stime [2];
        long int dtime;
       } both;

/*Main - ask the user for length of time to delay (0 terminates)*/
void main (void)
{
     unsigned delay;

     printf ("This program simply delays the user specified number\n"
             "of seconds.  Entering a zero terminates the program.\n"
             "\n"
             "Seconds are counted down to provide output so that\n"
             "the user can break out prematurely, if desired\n"
             "\n");
     for (;;) {

         /*get the specified delay and wait () that long*/
         if ((delay = getval ("Enter delay time [seconds]")) == 0)
              break;

         /*now call our wait function to perform the delay*/
         printf ("Start delay:\n");
         wait (delay);
         printf ("Finished\n");
     }
}

/*Getval - output a prompt and get an integer response*/
unsigned getval (prompt)
     char *prompt;
{
     unsigned retval;

     printf ("%s - ", prompt);
     scanf ("%d", &retval);
     return retval;
}



/*Wait - wait the specified length of time*/
void wait (delay)
     unsigned delay;
{

     unsigned previous, current;

     /*every time the time changes - decrement count*/
     previous = getime ();
     for (;;) {
          if (previous != (current = getime ())) {
               previous = current;
               if (!--delay)
                    return;
```

```

                        /*remove this print statement in actual use*/
                        printf ("count - %d\n", delay);
                }
        }
}

/*Getime - return the current time in seconds since midnight*/
unsigned getime (void)
{
                /*use the BIOS Time-of-Day to read the current time*/
                reg.h.ah = 0;
                int86 (0x1a, &reg, &reg);
                both.stime [0] = reg.x.dx;
                both.stime [1] = reg.x.cx;

                /*now convert the clock ticks into seconds (fudge factor
                  is the difference between 18.2 and 18*/
                return (unsigned)(both.dtime / 18) -
                       (unsigned)(both.dtime / 1638);
}
```

In this program *main()* prompts the user for the number of seconds to delay. Once entered, the program delays that length of time before prompting the operator again. The program is terminated by entering a 0. The important parts of the program are the functions *wait()* and *getime()*.

Getime() uses the *Time of Day* interrupt, *0x1a,* to get the number of clock ticks since midnight. The *Get* subfunction is indicated by setting the *REG.H.AH* to 0. The returned time is loaded from *REG.X.CX* and *REG.X.DX*. *Getime()* uses the union both to convert the two 16-bit integers into a 32-bit long integer. Be very careful here: transfer the lower 16-bits into the first word of the long integer and the upper 16-bits into the second, not the other way around.

While Turbo C supports 32-bit long integers, the 8086 microprocessor being a 16-bit machine does not support them well. Much more efficient machine code is generated by staying with normal, 16-bit integers whenever possible. To this end, *getime()* converts the long *BOTH.DTIME* into the number of seconds since midnight, which can be accommodated in a single unsigned integer variable. The conversion itself involves another small trick. Converting a number to floating point and back just to execute a floating point division is quite a bit slower than an integer division. A little algebra shows that:

$$\frac{x}{18} - \frac{x}{1638} = \frac{x}{18.2}$$

Although perhaps not important here, in general, avoiding floating point operations can make a sizable difference in the speed and size of a program, especially if an 8087 or 80287 numerical co-processor is not present. Such algebraic relationships can convert division by a floating point value into the sum or difference of two integer relationships. (The alternative of multiplying and dividing runs the risk of overflow on simple integers.)

The function *wait()* uses *getime()* to read the current time in a loop. Every time the current time changes it decrements the count of seconds to delay. Once the count has decremented to 0, it returns to the caller. The *printf()* to display the number of seconds left to delay serves as a *count down*. It may be removed as required.

Getime() can also be used to measure time critical sections of code to the nearest second. Given that the user wished to time the execution of a subroutine, *critical()*, he might use the following C code:

```
before = getime ();                  /*note the time*/
critical ();                         /*call the function*/
printf ("Time elapsed = %d\n", getime () - before);
```

Moving up one step in complexity we come to the keyboard BIOS handler. It has three subfunctions: read the next character, check for the presence of a character, and read the current shift status. The *Read* subfunction reads a single character from the keyboard buffer. The *Presence* subfunction checks the keyboard buffer to see if there is a character to be read. This subfunction is necessary since the *Read* subfunction is a blocking read; i.e., if a character is not present, the call waits until a key is pressed. The *Status* subfunction returns a byte with indicator bits for each of the shift and lock keys.

Not all keys have an ASCII equivalent associated with them. Programs must have some way of identifying them. In addition, some ASCII characters, such as the * and +, are generated by more than one key. It would be advantageous if a program could distinguish which key generated the character. To this end, every key on the PC's keyboard is assigned a so-called scan code. This is a number that corresponds to its location on the keyboard and is unique to the key. Unlike the ASCII character, the scan code of a key does not change when the *Shift* or *Control* key is depressed.

Prg6_4 below is an example program that reads the keyboard status in a loop. Whenever the status changes, the new status is displayed on the monitor. If one of the other keys is pressed, the ASCII character associated with that key is printed along with the scan code.

```
/*Prg6_4 - Read the Keyboard Status
    by Stephen R. Davis, 1987

```

```
   Read the status of the keyboard in a continual loop.  If the
   status changes or a character appears, display this on the screen.
   (Print both the character and its scan code.)
*/

#include <stdio.h>
#include <dos.h>
#include <process.h>
#define TRUE 1
#define FALSE 0

/*define the keyboard BIOS subfunctions*/
#define readchar 0x00
#define typeahead 0x01
#define readstatus 0x02

/*prototype definitions*/
void decode (unsigned);
unsigned charpresent (void);
unsigned getstatus (void);
int main (void);

/*data definition*/
union REGS reg;
char lineclear;

/*Main - constantly display keyboard status*/
main()
{
     unsigned oldstatus, newstatus, charandscan;
     char currchar, scancode;

     printf ("\nDepress shift, control, etc. keys in any\n"
             "and all combinations.  Program prints when\n"
             "keyboard status changes or character appears.\n"
             "Program prints both ASCII and scan code.  To\n"
             "terminate enter capital X\n");

     oldstatus = 0;
     lineclear = FALSE;
     for (;;) {
          if (charandscan = charpresent ()) {
               lineclear = FALSE;
               currchar = (char) (charandscan & 0x00ff);
               scancode = (char) ((charandscan & 0xff00) >> 8);
               printf ("%c %d,", currchar, scancode);
               if (currchar == 'X')
                    exit (0);
          }
          if ((newstatus = getstatus ()) != oldstatus)
               decode (newstatus);
          oldstatus = newstatus;
     }
}

/*Charpresent - check for the presence of a character.  If none presen
                return a 0, otherwise return the character and scan co
                entered.*/
unsigned charpresent (void)
{
     /*first check for the presence of a character*/
     reg.h.ah = typeahead;
     int86 (0x16, &reg, &reg);

```

```
 68[ 1]:        /*if the zero flag returned is clear...*/
 69[ 1]:        if (reg.x.flags & 0x0040)
 70[ 1]:             return 0;
 71[ 1]:
 72[ 1]:        /*...then read the character and scan code*/
 73[ 1]:        reg.h.ah = readchar;
 74[ 1]:        int86 (0x16, &reg, &reg);
 75[ 1]:        return reg.x.ax;
 76[ 0]: }
 77[ 0]:
 78[ 0]: /*Getstatus - read the keyboard status*/
 79[ 0]: unsigned getstatus (void)
 80[ 0]: {
 81[ 1]:        reg.h.ah = readstatus;
 82[ 1]:        int86 (0x16, &reg, &reg);
 83[ 1]:        return (unsigned)reg.h.al;
 84[ 0]: }
 85[ 0]:
 86[ 0]: /*Decode - decode the keyboard status bits*/
 87[ 0]: unsigned bits [] = {0x80, 0x40, 0x20, 0x10,
 88[ 0]:                     0x08, 0x04, 0x02, 0x01};
 89[ 0]: char *meaning[] = {"Insert on  ",
 90[ 1]:                    "Caps lock  ",
 91[ 1]:                    "Num lock  ",
 92[ 1]:                    "Scroll lock  ",
 93[ 1]:                    "Alt  ",
 94[ 1]:                    "Control  ",
 95[ 1]:                    "Left-shift  ",
 96[ 0]:                    "Right-shift  "};
 97[ 0]: void decode (bitpattern)
 98[ 0]:        unsigned bitpattern;
 99[ 0]: {
100[ 1]:        unsigned index;
101[ 1]:
102[ 1]:        if (!lineclear)
103[ 1]:             printf ("\n");
104[ 1]:        for (index = 0; index < 8; index++)
105[ 1]:             if (bitpattern & bits [index])
106[ 1]:                  printf (meaning [index]);
107[ 1]:        printf ("\n");
108[ 1]:        lineclear = TRUE;
109[ 0]: }
```

Like the delay program before, the critical parts of Prg6_4 are embodied in its functions (as they should be). *Main()* calls *charpresent()* which performs a nonblocking read of the keyboard buffer. This it does by first checking for the presence of a character using the *Presence* subfunction. If a character is not present, it returns to the caller a character and scan code of 0 (line 69 and 70) a scan code of 0 is not legal. If a character is present, it and its scan code are read using the *Read* subfunction and returned to the caller. If a character is returned from *charpresent()*, it and its scan code are separated and printed.

From this point, *main()* then calls *getstatus()* to read the keyboard shift bits using the *Status* subfunction. If the status returned matches the status the last time *getstatus()* was called then *main()* takes no action but returns back up and starts the process over. If it is different, *main()* calls *decode()* to display the meaning of the new shift status.

Decode() has two arrays, one a series of bytes with one bit set and the other a series of character strings. *Decode()* ANDs the bit fields in with the shift status. If a bit is set then the corresponding string is printed. The variable *LINECLEAR* is used to clean up the display a bit and is not critical to the program.

Try the program by depressing the shift keys and control key. Notice how the status gets printed both when the key is pressed and when it is released (both events represent a change of status). Notice how the program differentiates between left and right shift key. Try holding down more than one shift key plus the control and alternate at the same time. To see how the scan codes are location dependent try entering a few keys that are next to each other from side to side, such as the A, S, D, and F.

All of the remaining BIOS functions follow the same pattern. Use *Appendix 2* to describe the individual subfunctions and their arguments. Use a variable of type *UNION REGS* to load the registers with the proper values. Having made the call, fetch the returned register values from the same union. If at all possible, make the call to each BIOS routine into a separate function by itself. This not only makes documenting the call easier, but makes the program easier to modify if, for some reason, the BIOS call does not work out and requires replacement. Two of the BIOS functions are particularly important and require special discussion. These make up the balance of this chapter.

The BIOS Screen Handler

The most popular and yet most complicated of the BIOS interrupts is the screen handler. The BIOS screen handler provides uniform, rapid access to all of the different display adapters available for the PC. As we noted above, this is true because each display adapter can either conform to the MDA or CGA standards or bring its own BIOS code, in ROM or on floppy, to support it.

The screen BIOS interrupt is *0x10*. A list of its subfunctions is provided in *Appendix 2*. A condensed list appears in Table 6.1. A few of the video concepts behind these subfunctions may not be familiar. *Mode,* for example, refers to whether the display adapter is programmed to send B&W text, color text, graphics or monochrome text. Table 6.2 represents the different video modes supported by the PC. Notice that not all of them (in fact none of them) are supported by any

Table 6.1
Screen BIOS Handler

Subfunction	Meaning
0	Set CRT Mode
1	Set Cursor Type
2	Set Cursor Position
3	Read Cursor Position
4	Read Light Pen Position
5	Select Active Page
6	Scroll Active Page Up
7	Scroll Active Page Down
8	Read Attribute/Character at cursor
9	Write Attribute/Character at cursor
A	Write Character at cursor
B	Set Color Palette
C	Write Dot
D	Read Dot
E	Write Teletype to Active Page
F	Get Current Video State
*10	Set Palette Registers
*11	Character Generator Routine
*12	Alternate Select
*13	Write String

Those subfunctions marked with a * are present on EGA only.

Table 6.2
Video Modes of the IBM PC

Mode	Meaning	Adapters that support it
0	40x25 BW text	CGA,EGA,PCjr,VGA
1	40x25 color text	CGA,EGA,PCjr,VGA
2	80x25 BW text	CGA,EGA,PCjr,VGA
3	80x25 color text	CGA,EGA,PCjrVGA
4	320x200 4 color graphics	CGA,EGA,PCjr,VGA
5	320x200 BW graphics	CGA,EGA,PCjr,VGA
6	640x200 BW graphics	CGA,EGA,PCjr,VGA
7	monochrome text	MDA,EGA,VGA
8	160x200 16 color graphics	PCjr
9	320x200 16 color graphics	PCjr
A	640x200 4 color graphics	PCjr
B	internal use	
C	internal use	
D	320X200 16 color graphics	EGA,VGA
E	620x200 16 color graphics	EGA,VGA
F	640x350 monochrome graphics	EGA,VGA
10	640x350 16 color graphics	EGA,VGA
11	640X480 2 color graphics	VGA
12	640x480 16 color graphics	VGA
13	320x200 256 color graphics	VGA

Note: modes B and C are used for loading of custom fonts and are not display modes. Mode 10 is only supported by EGA cards with 128k or more memory.

one display adapter. If we ignore the special modes of the now defunct PCjr, however, the EGA and the PS/2's VGA support the majority of them.

This raft of different video modes stems from the fact that, from the beginning, the PC was designed to work with television sets equipped with RF modulators as well as the two different monitors already described. A television set does not have sufficient bandwidth (resolution) to comfortably display 25 lines of 80 column text, hence the special *40x25* modes. In addition, the black-and-white modes of operation are designed to support the less expensive black-and-white monitors.

In practice, a CGA connected to a color monitor displaying text will be set to mode 3. Its text resolution (the size of the pixel matrix assigned to each character) is *5x7* pixels with a one pixel descender within a box of *8x8* pixels. While serviceable, this resolution gives characters a tightly packed and *blocky* appearance. To enhance compatibility with the CGA, the EGA also uses mode 3 to display text, but at a considerably higher *7x9* pixel resolution within an *8x14* pixel box. The text-only MDA is always in mode 7 and uses a *7x9* character matrix within a *9x14* box. The effective overall screen resolution of the MDA is *720x348*.

Although the EGA can emulate the CGA's graphics modes, the popular *EGA mode* is the *640x350* pixel mode *0x10* with its 16 colors. This resolution cannot be supported by the older color graphics monitors and requires either IBM's Enhanced Display or equivalent or one of the very popular, high bandwidth multisynch monitors.

Outputting text to any of the displays is merely a matter of invoking the BIOS screen handler with subfunction *0x9, 0xa* or *0xe.* Subfunctions *0x9* and *0xa* output character/attribute or character at the current cursor location, while subfunction *0xe* outputs a character and then updates the cursor's location. The character to be output is one of the standard ASCII characters. The attribute is a one byte field that is used to control that character's color, intensity, whether is blinks, etc. The following attributes are defined for the different monitors:

Text Mode Character Attributes for CGA, EGA,VGA -
attribute uses the following bit mask -

```
BIT   7   6   5   4   3   2   1   0
      BL  R   G   B   I   R   G   B
          background      foreground
```

where

```
BL - blinking
I  - 0 -> half bright, 1 -> full bright
R  - red
G  - green
B  - blue
```

for example, an attribute of *0x07,* the default attribute, specifies half-bright white on a black background

for MDA

the attribute mask is roughly the same, except that since monochrome has no color capability, setting any one of the color bits results in white. The one exception is specifying a blue foreground results in underlined.

Thus:

Setting Value	**Meaning**
0x00	black on black (no display)
0x01	underlined
0x07	normal
0x0f	high intensity
0x70	inverse
0x87	blinking normal
0x8f	blinking high intensity
0xf0	blinking inverse

Prg6_5 uses the BIOS subfunction *0xe* to define a new console output routine, *qprintf(),* which is slightly faster then C *printf()* function. *Qprintf()* accepts one argument, the pointer to a null-terminated ASCII string. *Qprintf()* invokes the BIOS screen handler for each successive character until the null is encountered, at which point it returns to the caller. The only character which *qprintf()* checks for is *\n*. *Qprintf()* does not print this to the screen, but, instead, scrolls the screen up one line.

```
/*Prg6_5 - Screen Output via BIOS calls
   by Stephen R. Davis, 1987

  Perform screen output using BIOS calls.  This may not
  be all that much faster than 'printf' output, since 'printf'
  uses BIOS calls itself.
*/
```

```

#include <stdio.h>
#include <dos.h>

#define white 0x07
#define screenheight 25

/*add the screen BIOS subfunctions*/
#define scrollup 0x06
#define setcursor 0x02
#define writetele 0x0e
#define getmode 0x0f

/*define global variables*/
unsigned v_pos, h_pos, screenwidth;
union REGS regs;

/*prototype declarations*/
void init (void);
void scroll (unsigned);
void qprintf (char *);
void pcursor (unsigned, unsigned);

/*Main - test the output routines*/
int main ()
{
    int i, j;

    init ();
    for (i = 0; i < 20; i++) {
         for (j = 0; j < screenheight; j++) {
              qprintf ("this is BIOS output");
              pcursor(v_pos, 30+j);
              qprintf ("and this\n");
         }
         for (j = 0; j < screenheight; j++)
              printf ("this is normal printf output\n");
    }
}

/*Init - clear the screen*/
void init ()
{
    regs.h.ah = getmode;
    int86 (0x10, &regs, &regs);
    screenwidth = (unsigned)regs.h.ah;

    scroll (screenheight);
    pcursor (0, 0);
}

/*Scroll - scroll up N lines using function 6*/
void scroll (nlines)
    unsigned nlines;
{
    if (nlines >= screenheight)
```

```
            nlines = screenheight;

        h_pos = 0;
        if ((v_pos += nlines) >= screenheight) {
            nlines = (v_pos - screenheight) + 1;
            regs.h.ah = scrollup;
            regs.h.al = nlines;
            regs.h.bh = white;
            regs.x.cx = 0;
            regs.h.dh = screenheight;
            regs.h.dl = screenwidth;
            int86 (0x10, &regs, &regs);
            v_pos = screenheight - 1;
        }
}

/*Qprintf - output a string using the BIOS screen handler.  If
            an attribute is not provided, use the default.*/
void qprintf (c)
    char *c;
{
    for (; *c; c++)
        if (*c == '\n')
            scroll (1);
        else {
            if (h_pos++ < screenwidth) {
                regs.h.ah = writetele;
                regs.h.al = *c;
                int86 (0x10, &regs, &regs);
            }
        }
    pcursor (v_pos, h_pos);
}

/*PCursor - place the cursor at the current x and y location.
            To place the cursor, and subsequent output, to any
            arbitrary location, set 'v_pos' and 'h_pos' before
            calling pcursor.*/
void pcursor (y, x)
    unsigned x, y;
{
    v_pos = y;
    h_pos = x;

    regs.h.ah = setcursor;
    regs.h.bh = 0;
    regs.h.dh = v_pos;
    regs.h.dl = h_pos;
    int86 (0x10, &regs, &regs);
}
```

The accompanying *pcursor()* and *scroll()* functions call other subfunctions to place the cursor and scroll the screen. Scrolling the screen by 0 lines, clears it. *Init()* must be invoked before any of the others so that it can check the display for screen width. *Main()* merely calls *qprintf()* and *printf()* in a loop to demonstrate their use and compare output speed.

Notice that accepting only a single string may seem like a severe limitation compared to *printf()*. Look closely at the documentation for *printf()*. This routine is capable of a considerable array of reformatting options for displaying characters, integers, floating points as well as simple character strings.

However, *qprintf()* is not really at such a disadvantage. Programmers can always use the related *sprintf()* to first translate the output into a string, which they can then output using *qprintf()* as shown below. (This is equivalent to the conventional use of *printf()*, as shown in the next output.) *Sprintf()* has all of the reformatting capabilities of *printf()*. Output from *qprintf()* cannot be redirected, however. By accessing the BIOS directly, we are avoiding DOS and its redirection. Output is supported in all video modes.

```
char buffer [80];
int a, b, c;

/*first generate a simple character string*/
sprintf (buffer, "results are: a = %d\n"
                 "             b = %d\n"
                 "             c = %d\n",
                 a, b, c);


/*now output it using qprintf*/
qprintf (buffer);
```

```
printf ("results are: a = %d\n"
        "             b = %d\n"
        "             c = %d\n",
        a, b, c);
```

Outputting to the screen in graphics mode is similar. The write dot (*0x0c*) and read dot (*0x0d*) subfunctions view the entire screen as a matrix of pixels. The legal range of column and row values are dependent on the screen mode and are given in the mode table earlier. The color value to the write dot subfunction is also mode dependent.

In modes 4 and 5, the color value is a number between 0 and 3. This selects a color out of the current palette, which is specified with subfunction *0x0b*. Only one palette may be active at a time. In mode 4 there are two standard palettes with the following colors listed in Table 6.3.

Table 6.3
Mode 4 Palettes

value	color (Palette 0)	color (Palette 1)
0	black	black
1	green	cyan
2	red	magenta
3	brown	white

In the EGA and VGA modes *0x0d, 0x0e* and *0x10,* color is a value between 0 and 15, inclusive. This value specifies that the dot should have the color of the corresponding palette register. The palette registers are set to one of 64 colors using the set palette register subfunction (*0x10*). That is, the programmer can select between 64 different colors, but only 16 of them can be on the display at any one time. In the VGA's mode *0x13*, the color is a value between 0 and 255. Each value selects a color from a palette of 256,000. The Herculese-style monochrome graphics cards support two colors (black and white) on a *720x348* pixel screen.

There is a problem represented by the different modes with their different pixel resolutions. If you draw a line 200 pixels long, it might reach from one end of the screen to another or it might reach barely a third of the way across, depending on the video mode and orientation. The most versatile solution to this problem is to define a *virtual* screen which is square and some 1,000 pixels on a side. All graphing functions can then be performed on this virtual screen. A different driver is constructed for each different graphics video mode which translates pixel coordinates from this virtual screen into the real pixel address for this display. Although slightly less efficient, the algorithms are simpler and need not vary with video mode, both present and future.

Besides just greater resolution and 16 independently adjustable palette registers, the EGA offers further capabilities. These include alternate character fonts and hardware smooth scroll, both vertically and horizontally. Unfortunately, most of these extended capabilities are not accessible via the BIOS screen handler. It is useful to be able to detect the presence of an EGA using the standard BIOS calls before attempting to directly access these extended functions. Further, an EGA can be equipped with between 64k and 256k of RAM. A 64k EGA does not have all the capabilities of its bigger sibling (for example, mode *0x10* graphics). It is sometimes necessary to check the amount of on-board memory before selecting some of the fancier modes of operation.

When the screen BIOS handler is presented with a subfunction to which it has not assigned any meaning, the handler returns with all registers intact without taking any action at all. Scanning the list of screen BIOS subfunctions, you should notice that four of those listed are not defined in the older *CGA/MDA BIOS*. If a program attempts to execute one of them in a machine not equipped with an EGA card and its superset BIOS, it will have no effect on either the screen or the registers.

Prg6_6 uses this fact to detect the presence of an EGA display. Subfunction 0x12 allows the user to read, among other things, the amount of memory on the card as a number between 0 and 3. Prg6_6 sets the *REG.X.BX* to 0x10, indicating it wishes to make such a read, and then executes the subfunction. If the register comes back unchanged, then the program knows that an EGA BIOS is not installed. If, on the other hand, it comes back with one of the four legal values, the program can assume that the extended BIOS is present. The program goes on to interpret the amount of memory as well as the switch values, although this may not always be necessary.

```
/*Prg6_6 - Detect presence of Enhanced Graphics Adapter
   by Stephen R. Davis, 1987

  Check for the presence of the EGA by invoking one of the EGA
  BIOS subfunctions.  The normal CGA BIOS will treat this as a
  No-Operation, returning to us the registers we supplied.
*/

#include <stdio.h>
#include <dos.h>
#include <process.h>

/*prototyping definitions*/
void main (void);

/*define global data*/
union REGS reg;

char *colorvals [] = {"color", "monochrome"};
char *memvals [] = {"64k", "128k", "192k", "256k"};
char *switchvals [] = {
               /*0*/   "monochrome w/ 40x25 EGA secondary",
               /*1*/   "EGA emulation mode w/ monochrome secondary",
               /*2*/   "40x25 CGA w/ monochrome EGA secondary",
               /*3*/   "illegal value",
               /*4*/   "monochrome w/ EGA emulation mode secondary",
               /*5*/   "monochrome EGA w/ 40x25 CGA secondary",
               /*6*/   "40x25 EGA w/ monochrome secondary",
               /*7*/   "illegal value",
               /*8*/   "monochrome w/ 80x25 EGA secondary",
               /*9*/   "hi res EGA w/ monochrome secondary",
               /*a*/   "80x25 CGA w/ monochrome EGA secondary",
               /*b*/   "illegal value",
               /*c*/   "monochrome w/ hi res EGA secondary",
               /*d*/   "monochrome EGA w/ 80x25 CGA secondary",
               /*e*/   "80x25 EGA w/ monochrome secondary",
               /*f*/   "illegal value"};
```

```

/*Main - Test for EGA.  If present, display memory and switch
         settings.*/
void main (void)
{
     reg.h.ah = 0x12;
     reg.h.bl = 0x10;
     int86 (0x10, &reg, &reg);
     if (reg.h.bl > 3) {        /*illegal value implies no EGA present*/
          printf ("No EGA present!\n");
          exit (1);
     }
                                /*dump out all of the other info*/
     printf ("EGA attached in %s mode with %s memory installed\n",
                    colorvals [reg.h.bh],
                    memvals [reg.h.bl]);
     printf ("Switch settings indicate: %s\n", switchvals [reg.h.cl]);
}
```

One facet of display adapters that is often overlooked is that of display pages. A color/graphics adapter contains 16k bytes of memory to handle the graphics modes of display (640 x 200 = 128,000 bits = 16,000 bytes). However, only some 4,000 bytes are required to store a screen's worth of video data (80 x 25 = 2,000 characters, with 1 byte for the character and 1 byte for the attribute = 4,000 bytes). Therefore, there is sufficient memory on the CGA to hold some four screens worth of text.

Table 6.4
Number of Pages Available in Display Modes

Mode	MDA	CGA	EGA
0	–	8	8
1	–	8	8
2	–	4	8
3	–	4	8
4	–	1	1
5	–	1	1
6	–	1	1
7	1	–	8
D	–	–	8
E	–	–	4
F	–	–	2
10	–	–	2

These different screens are called *pages*. In mode 3, the CGA supports four pages while the EGA supports 8 (though it has enough memory, it does not bother to support more than 8). Table 6.4 shows the number of pages supported in the different display modes. Most applications stay in the default page, page 0, but the currently displayed page can be changed via the subfunction *0x05*.

The write subfunctions of the BIOS screen handler either require the page to be specified or they write to the currently active page. Writing to one page does not affect the contents or cursor position of other pages. This is often used as a type of *poor man's* windows. Manipulating windows requires the CPU to read and write large blocks of data to and from the display. In addition, window operations cannot be perfomed with simple block moves. Instead the CPU must calculate the constrains of the windows, perform clipping, etc. Changing pages by comparison requires little overhead.

A menu program might, for instance, place its opening menu on page 0 of the display. When an option is selected, the program would change windows displaying the second menu on page 1. When the operator then wants to return to the main menu, it is not necessary to rewrite it as it is still intact back on page 0. Once all of the menus are loaded into pages, the operator can move among them virtually instantaneously, thus giving the program very rapid response time.

It is possible to write to pages which are not currently selected. Of course, the text written there will not be displayed until the page has been selected in a subsequent subfunction *0x05* call. A program can use this fact to improve user response time. While waiting for user input, the program can fill the other pages of display memory with the menus for all the possible selections the operator might make. As operators are usually quite slow in making choices, there is usually sufficient time. Once the choice is made, the program changes to the proper page without delay.

Prg6_7 below demonstrates how rapidly a page may be selected in comparison with the time it takes to write to it. The program first loops through the existing pages, filling each very densly with text. The displayed page is indicated by the text as well as its color. The program then waits for the operator to enter a single digit. The program switches to that page. The response is immediate.

Notice that Prg6_7 does not use *printf()* to fill the different pages, instead relying on direct calls to the screen BIOS. This is because, *printf()* does not appear to support pages other than 0. (*Qprintf()* supports the current page, no matter which that might be.) As mentioned above, the program could have filled the various pages without displaying them.

```
/*Prg6_7 - Demonstrate Video Adapter Display Pages
   by Stephen R. Davis, 1987
```

```

   Many programmers forget that their display adapter has more
   than it is showing them.  This program allows the programmer
   to select through the display pages of their adapter.  It will
   only work in color or BW 80 column mode - when running from DOS
   it may require a CLS to reset the video controller completely.
*/

#include <stdio.h>
#include <dos.h>
#include <process.h>
#include <conio.h>

/*prototype definitions*/
void main (void);
unsigned egapresent (void);
void selectpage (unsigned);
void fillpage (unsigned);
unsigned getmode (void);
void outstring (char *);
void scroll (unsigned, unsigned);

/*global data definitions*/
union REGS reg;

/*Main - Put data on each of the screens, then await user input
         to select the "current" screen*/
void main (void)
{
     unsigned i, no_pages;

     if ((getmode () & 0xfe) != 2) {
          printf ("Must be in Color or BW 80 mode\n");
          exit (1);
     }

     /*CGA has 4 pages, EGA has 8*/
     no_pages = 4;
     if (egapresent ()) no_pages = 8;

     /*put something on each of the pages*/
     for (i = 0; i < no_pages; i++) {
          selectpage (i);
          fillpage (i);
     }

     /*no prompt the operator for input*/
     selectpage (0);
     printf ("Enter page number (>%d terminates):", no_pages);
     for (;;) {
          i =  (unsigned)(getche () - '0');
          if (i > no_pages) {
               selectpage (0);
               exit (0);
          }
          selectpage (i);
     }
}

/*Egapresent - check for the presence of an EGA card*/
unsigned egapresent (void)
{
     reg.h.ah = 0x12;
     reg.h.bl = 0x10;
```

```
     int86 (0x10, &reg, &reg);
     if (reg.h.bl > 3)
          return 0;
     return 1;
}

/*Getmode - return the current video mode*/
unsigned getmode (void)
{
     reg.h.ah = 0x0f;
     int86 (0x10, &reg, &reg);
     return (unsigned)reg.h.al;
}

/*Selectpage - select the video page*/
void selectpage (page)
     unsigned page;
{
     reg.h.ah = 5;
     reg.h.al = page;
     int86 (0x10, &reg, &reg);
}

/*Fillpage - fill the current page with text*/
char *strings [] = {
"Page 0        Page 0         Page 0         Page 0         Page 0",
"Page 1        Page 1         Page 1         Page 1         Page 1",
"Page 2        Page 2         Page 2         Page 2         Page 2",
"Page 3        Page 3         Page 3         Page 3         Page 3",
"Page 4        Page 4         Page 4         Page 4         Page 4",
"Page 5        Page 5         Page 5         Page 5         Page 5",
"Page 6        Page 6         Page 6         Page 6         Page 6",
"Page 7        Page 7         Page 7         Page 7         Page 7"};

void fillpage (page)
     unsigned page;
{
     unsigned row;

     scroll (0, page);
     for (row = 0; row < 25; row++) {
          outstring (strings [page]);
          scroll (1, page);
     }
}

/*Outstring - put a string on the current page*/
void outstring (string)
     char *string;
{
     while (*string) {
          reg.h.ah = 0x0e;
          reg.h.al = *string++;
          int86 (0x10, &reg, &reg);
     }
}

/*Scroll - scroll the current screen up N lines*/
void scroll (n, page)
     unsigned n, page;
{
     reg.h.ah = 0x06;          /*scroll the current page N lines*/
     reg.h.al = n;
     reg.h.ch = 0;
```

```
        reg.h.cl = 0;
        reg.h.dh = 25;
        reg.h.dl = 80;
        reg.h.bh = page + 1;     /*make each page a different color*/
        int86 (0x10, &reg, &reg);

        reg.h.ah = 0x02;         /*put cursor at bottom left hand corner*/
        reg.h.dh = 25;
        reg.h.dl = 0;
        reg.h.bh = page;
        int86 (0x10, &reg, &reg);
}

```

Absolute Disk Access

There are actually two different sets of disk service interrupts: interrupt *0x13* and interrupts *0x25* and *0x26*. In fact, the latter two are not truly BIOS interrupts, not being defined in any ROM. These are part of the DOS operating system and are not initialized until DOS has been booted. I treat them as BIOS routines, however, as their interface and the approximate level of user friendliness is the same. The distinction between what belongs to DOS and what to the BIOS is not important for our purposes.

Interrupt *0x13* references sectors on the disk by physical address. Before a sector may be read or written, the user must specify the sector, cylinder, and surface (Figure 6.1). These concepts smack too much of hardware for any dedicated software person to be comfortable with them. Storing and recovering these values is also somewhat inconvenient.

Figure 6.1

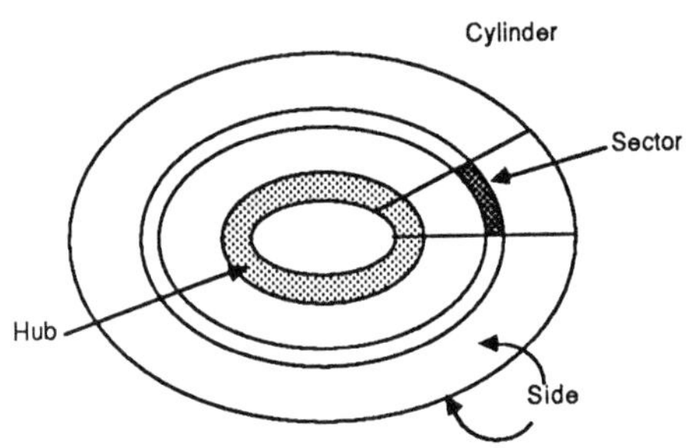

Structure of disk

Interrupts *0x25* and *0x26* use a logical sector numbering scheme. Sectors are numbered starting at 0 and continuing on the disk until the last sector. This is much more convenient for C programs to manipulate. The sector number very much resembles a one word pointer onto the disk. A second word offset within the sector completes the address of every byte on the disk. There is a pleasant symmetry between this and addresses in memory. Physical sector address may be converted to logical sector address using the following formula:

```
logical = sector + sectors/track *  (side +  (cylinder * side/cylinder)) - 1
```

where

```
logical = logical sector address
 sector = sector number on the track (1 relative)
 sectors/track = number of sectors per surface per cylinder
                (9 for floppies, 17 for most hard disks)
 side = disk head number
 cylinder = cylinder number measured from hub
 side/cylinder = same as number of recording heads
```

As an aside, the fact that the logical sector number is limited to 16 bits is the source of the 32 Megabyte disk limit for current versions of DOS. A sector in DOS is 512 bytes in length. This multiplied by the largest unsigned number (65535) gives you your 32-Megabyte limit (actually, 33,553,920 bytes). While the practice is discouraged in general, accessing sectors via interrupt *0x25* and *0x26* is no more difficult than any other BIOS interrupt. Normal file accesses should always go through the more refined DOS file functions discussed back in Chapter 5. When getting down to the disk is necessary, these interrupt services are the best.

Writing directly to the disk is too dangerous to include in a book intended for the general market; however, Prg6_8 below reads sectors directly from the disk and displays them on the screen. Simple utilities such as this are very useful when attempting to learn the mysteries of DOS directories and the FAT (*File Allocation Table*).

```
/*Prg6_8 - Sector Read
   by Stephen R. Davis, 1987

  Read sectors by logical sector number using interrupt 0x25.
  This can be used to inspect a hard disk or floppy.
*/

#include <stdio.h>
#include <ctype.h>
#include <dos.h>
#include <conio.h>
#include <string.h>

#define sector_size 512
#define chars_per_line 16
```

```
#define max_disk 5

/*prototype definitions*/
void main (void);
unsigned readsector (unsigned, unsigned, char *);
void disperr (unsigned);
void display (char *, unsigned, unsigned);
void disphex (char *, unsigned);
void dispascii (char *, unsigned);
unsigned getval (char *);

/*global data*/
char buffer [sector_size];
union REGS reg;
char *drives [] = {"A", "B", "C", "D", "E", "F"};

/*Main - prompt the user for input and read the indicated sector*/
void main (void)
{
     unsigned diskno, sector;
     char character;

     /*program preamble*/
     printf ("Disk examiner -\n"
             "   Enter disk and sector number to start (both hex);\n"
             "   thereafter, just enter + and - to move one sector.\n"
             "   Anything else returns to disk/sector question.\n"
             "   Exit by entering a drive number greater\n"
             "   than %d\n", max_disk);

     /*read the disk number to examine*/
     for (;;) {
          diskno = getval ("Enter disk number (0 = A, 1 = B, etc)");
          if (diskno > max_disk)
               break;
          sector = getval ("Enter new sector number (0 relative)");

          /*keep spitting out sectors as long as enters '+' or '-'*/
          for (;;) {
               if (readsector (diskno, sector, buffer))
                    break;

               printf ("\nDrive = %s, Sector = %4.4x\n",
                              drives [diskno], sector);
               display (buffer, sector_size, chars_per_line);

               character = getche ();
               if (character == '-')
                    sector--;
               else
                    if (character == '+')
                         sector++;
                    else
                         break;
          }
     }
}

/*Getval - display a prompt and input the response*/
unsigned getval (prompt)
     char *prompt;
{
     unsigned value;

```

```
     printf ("%s - ", prompt);
     scanf ("%x", &value);
     return value;
}

/*Read - read a sector from the specified disk.  Return a 0
          if successful, else display the error*/
unsigned readsector (diskno, sector, bufptr)
     unsigned diskno, sector;
     char *bufptr;
{
     reg.h.al = diskno;
     reg.x.bx = (unsigned)bufptr;
     reg.x.cx = 1;
     reg.x.dx = sector;
     int86 (0x25, &reg, &reg);

     if (reg.x.cflag)
          disperr (reg.h.al);
     return reg.x.cflag;
}

/*Disperror - display the error from DOS disk read*/
char *errlist [] = {"Attempt to write on write-protected disk",
                    "Unknown unit",
                    "Drive not ready",
                    "Unknown command",
                    "CRC error",
                    "Bad drive request structure length",
                    "Seek error",
                    "Unknown media type",
                    "Sector not found",
                    "Printer out of paper",
                    "Write fault",
                    "Read fault",
                    "General failure"};

void disperr (errnum)
     unsigned errnum;
{
     printf ("\n%s\n", errlist [errnum]);
}

/*Display - display a buffer on the user's screen in both hex
            and ASCII format.  Suppress displaying a line if it
            is the same as its predecessor.*/
void display (bufptr, number, per_line)
     char *bufptr;
     unsigned number, per_line;
{
     unsigned count;
     char *oldptr;

     count = 0;
     oldptr = "something very unlikely";
     while (count < number) {
          if (strncmp (oldptr, bufptr, per_line)) {
               printf ("%4x: ", count);
               disphex (bufptr, per_line);
               printf (" - ");
               dispascii (bufptr, per_line);
               printf ("\n");
          }
          oldptr = bufptr;
```

```
                bufptr += per_line;
                count += per_line;
        }
}

/*Disphex - display data in hex format*/
void disphex (bufptr, count)
        char *bufptr;
        unsigned count;
{
        for (; count; count--)
             printf ("%2.2x ", 0xff & *bufptr++);
}

/*Dispascii - display data in ASCII format*/
void dispascii (bufptr, count)
        char *bufptr;
        unsigned count;
{
        for (; count; bufptr++, count--)
                if (isprint (*bufptr))
                        printf ("%c", *bufptr);
                else
                        printf ("%c", '.');
}
```

Figure 6.2

```
Drive = B, Sector = 0005
   0: 42 45 4e 43 48 20 20 20 45 58 45 20 00 00 00 00  - BENCH   EXE ....
  10: 00 00 00 00 00 00 01 20 41 0d 02 00 34 88 00 00  - ....... A...4...
  20: 42 45 4e 43 48 30 37 20 45 58 45 20 00 00 00 00  - BENCH07 EXE ....
  30: 00 00 00 00 00 00 02 20 41 0d 25 00 09 20 00 00  - ....... A.%.. ..
  40: 42 45 4e 43 48 30 37 20 44 41 54 20 00 00 00 00  - BENCH07 DAT ....
  50: 00 00 00 00 00 00 02 20 41 0d 2e 00 25 0e 00 00  - ....... A...%...
  60: 42 45 4e 43 48 30 38 20 45 58 45 20 00 00 00 00  - BENCH08 EXE ....
  70: 00 00 00 00 00 00 03 20 41 0d 32 00 89 1b 00 00  - ....... A.2.....
  80: 42 45 4e 43 48 30 39 20 45 58 45 20 00 00 00 00  - BENCH09 EXE ....
  90: 00 00 00 00 00 00 03 20 41 0d 39 00 49 19 00 00  - ....... A.9.I...
  a0: 42 45 4e 43 48 31 30 20 45 58 45 20 00 00 00 00  - BENCH10 EXE ....
  b0: 00 00 00 00 00 00 04 20 41 0d 40 00 e9 14 00 00  - ....... A.@.....
  c0: 42 45 4e 43 48 31 32 20 42 41 53 20 00 00 00 00  - BENCH12 BAS ....
  d0: 00 00 00 00 00 00 04 20 41 0d 46 00 00 15 00 00  - ....... A.F.....
  e0: 42 45 4e 43 48 31 37 20 45 58 45 20 00 00 00 00  - BENCH17 EXE ....
  f0: 00 00 00 00 00 00 05 20 41 0d 4c 00 d9 48 00 00  - ....... A.L..H..
 100: 42 45 4e 43 48 31 38 20 45 58 45 20 00 00 00 00  - BENCH18 EXE ....
 110: 00 00 00 00 00 00 05 20 41 0d 5f 00 d6 20 00 00  - ....... A._.. ..
 120: 42 45 4e 43 48 32 30 20 45 58 45 20 00 00 00 00  - BENCH20 EXE ....
 130: 00 00 00 00 00 00 06 20 41 0d 68 00 6a 2b 00 00  - ....... A.h.j+..
 140: 42 45 4e 43 48 32 31 20 45 58 45 20 00 00 00 00  - BENCH21 EXE ....
 150: 00 00 00 00 00 00 07 20 41 0d 73 00 9e 29 00 00  - ....... A.s..)..
 160: 42 45 4e 43 48 32 31 41 45 58 45 20 00 00 00 00  - BENCH21AEXE ....
```

A hexadecimal dump of the directory for a benchmark floppy disk

In this program, *main()* displays an explanatory preamble to the operator and then awaits a disk and logical sector number. Disks are numbered starting with 0 (A = 0, B = 1,...). *Main()* uses the functions *readsector()* to actually read the sector and *display()* to put it on the screen. Once displayed, the operator may continue by entering a + for the next sector, a – for the previous sector or anything else for a new disk/sector number prompt.

Readsector() performs the actual read using interrupt *0x25*. An error is indicated upon return from the interrupt if the carry flag is set. If set, the error number is contained in *REG.H.AL*. The routine *disperr()* is used to display an error message. *ERRLIST* represents the list of possible errors returned from the direct disk interrupts. *Readsector()* returns a 0 if no error occurred, otherwise it returns a 1.

Display() is a general usage display routine which prints a buffer first in hex and then in ASCII across a line. *Display()* uses the *strncmp()* function to suppress the display of lines that are identical to their predecessors. This is to keep from displaying line after line of 0's or blanks. *Display()* continues printing *PER_LINE* characters per line until *NUMBER* of characters total has been printed. (*NUMBER* should be a multiple of *PER_LINE*.)

Notice in the display ASCII function, *dispascii()*, the use of the *IS* function *isprint()*. *Isprint()* returns a 1 if the character provided it is printable, i.e. other than line feeds, carriage returns, tabs and the like, and a 0 if not. If the current character is not printable, a dot is printed in its place. This keeps a control character from cluttering up the display. The *IS* functions are intended for just these sorts of chores and should be kept in mind.

A truly useful hacker's utility can be built easily from this start. Adding a simple editing capability to allow the user to change the hex data in the sectors just read and a sector write capability results in a hacker's bit-picking utility. While the program presented might satisfy the programmer's curiosity, such a utility can be used to put a crashed disk back together.

Conclusion

Really nothing to be afraid of, the BIOS interrupt routines are easily accessible from Turbo C and can provide intimate access to the PC's hardware. This can result in faster execution and more exciting effects than is possible strictly through DOS function calls. Of course, this capability comes at the price of more details with which to worry.

If this is still not enough power (or not enough details to worry about) then continue on into Chapter 7, where you bypass even the BIOS to access the machine hardware yourself.

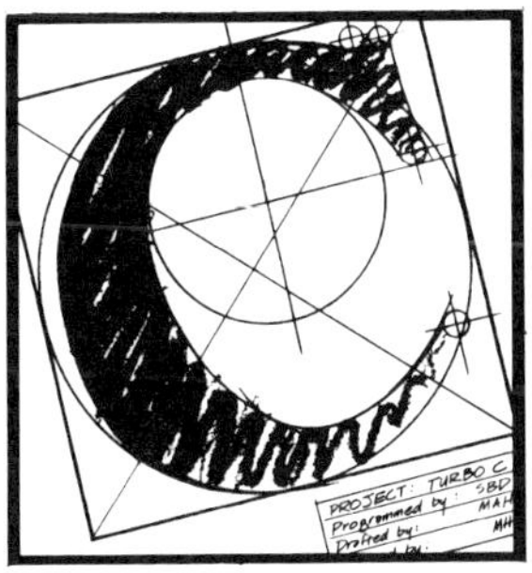

7 Accessing the PC's Hardware

Users of microprocessors suffer many disadvantages in comparison with their mainframe-based cousins. Slow processors, small memories, and slow hard disks (or, worse yet, floppies!) all conspire to drag down the user's application. For this, the micro user does gain a few advantages: no time sharing or file access protection to worry with, no fighting for terminals and complete control of the computer.

One of the biggest advantages the micro programmer has is the ability to access the hardware directly. When programs are time-sharing back and forth, swapping in and out of memory, if one of them decided to simply take over the printer, for instance, things would quickly become quite a mess. Lines from different programs would become interspersed in a hieroglyphic jumble. No self-respecting multiuser system can allow this sort of thing to happen.

To protect against such things, the user program cannot be allowed to access things it shouldn't. The system designer can make a rule: "No accessing the hardware directly!" and paste it right up on the very first page of the programmer's manual, but without some mechanism to preclude it from happening, someone is going to try it. The system must protect itself.

It is not possible in software to watch every instruction that a user program is executing to be sure it isn't doing something unallowed. The underlying computer must provide hardware protection mechanisms. In a protected system, user programs cannot access the printer directly, not because it's *against the rules,* but because the computer instructions necessary to do so, are not accessible. In addition, programs which try to access memory beyond the bounds assigned to them, are kicked off of the machine in short order.

Single tasking microcomputers do not have such problems. There is only one user running a single program. If it wants to go out and start talking directly to the printer, who cares? Even if it does bring the computer into silent, unresponsive confusion, no one else is injured by the crash. Typically, microprocessors and their operating systems do not implement protection mechanisms to keep user programs away from the hardware. There's still that rule on the first page of the programmer's manual, of course, but programs are free to ignore it (and so, of course, they do).

When programs decide to bypass even the BIOS, nothing is done for them. They must concern themselves with all the trivial details that their DOS-calling siblings can ignore. Besides, such programs must be updated every time a new display or disk controller is introduced if they are going to *keep up with the Microsofts*. With all this difficulty, there must be some overriding reason why programmers are so eager to make all this work for themselves. The answer is obvious: speed and power.

The software within the BIOS is not particularly fast. BIOS calls are much faster than DOS calls because they don't do nearly as much. Print something out to the screen using a DOS call and it must check for potential console redirection, interpret special characters, and constantly be on the lookout for *Control-Breaks*. The BIOS routine does none of these things (besides, the DOS call uses the BIOS routine to perform the actual output). However, the BIOS routines are written very conservatively. For example, most of the them push the entire register set onto the stack upon entering and pop them all back off before exiting. This is the safe thing to do, but if none of these registers are being used for anything in the user program, it is a complete waste of time.

A program which handles the hardware itself need not be so conservative. It knows which registers contain data worth saving and those which do not. A particularly efficient routine that has side effects that would make it unsuitable for general application, can be accommodated in a custom application.

Further, the BIOS routines in the PC are quite weak compared to more modern machines. The screen output handler does not include any of the drawing primitives you would expect of a more graphically oriented machine. Not even a fill subfunction is included. Filling a large area by setting each and every dot using the *Write Dot* subfunction gives an all new meaning to the term *response time*. Programs which access the hardware themselves can define and implement whatever primitives they choose. Nothing is beyond their reach.

Still, I do not want to give the impression that every program you write should callously skip over the DOS and BIOS and begin grappling with the machine on its own. As I have noted, these two services represent a large body of debugged code which I would not want to repeat. Besides, there are other ways to get increased BIOS speed and power.

Almost as soon as it became clear that applications were avoiding the BIOS routines because they were too slow, third party vendors began writing replacements. Today, there are dozens of such packages, many of which are in the public domain. (Public-domain programs are either free or Shareware packages available through public bulletin board systems and through services such as CompuServe, BIX, and the Source.)

The user installs one of these programs in the *CONFIG.SYS* file using the *DEVICE=* directive. At boot up, these packages replace the existing BIOS routines just as our EGA screen handler replaced the old CGA/MDA handler. The new BIOS routines are usually simply faster, but some are both faster and more capable. One such package, marketed by a company called Metaware, actually defines a full set of graphics primitives, much like those on the Apple Macintosh computer. If you find that you routinely need more than the BIOS has to offer, purchasing or downloading one of these programs is undoubtedly quicker and less expensive than writing one yourself.

Having read this, very few readers will decide they are no longer interested in direct machine access and skip over to Chapter 8. There are always times and places when direct machine access is required. What areas benefit the most and which the least?

File systems are complicated affairs. While DOS's is no worse than any other, it is certainly not the type of thing that a programmer should capriciously diddle with. Make a mistake during debug and write an incorrect block out to the disk randomly and you risk a disk crash that only a complete reformat can recover from. Further, there are the problems of different types of disk formats, not to mention the various disk controllers out there, which would have to be supported. While it is done, this is definitely not an area for amateurs.

On the other hand, direct display output is one area which can benefit a program greatly. No matter what gyrations your program might be undergoing internally, the user perceives its performance in only two ways: the screen and the keyboard. Of course, if the data is not ready to be printed, a faster display program will not help, but simply doubling the output speed of a program with lots of screen output will make a big difference in user acceptance. Fortunately, the display is both simple and forgiving and, therefore, very amenable to experimentation.

O/S2 and the Future

When I said earlier that microcomputers were not equipped with the types of hardware protection features normally found on minicomputers and mainframes, that was not quite true. In fact, the 80286 and 80386 microprocessors have an involved and powerful protection mechanism. The problem lies not with the chip, but with the operating system.

DOS was designed at the close of an earlier era of microcomputers. A 64k machine was standard fair. I remember distinctly having a RAM disk on a machine equipped with only 192k bytes of RAM. Operating systems in those days were both simpler and smaller. Besides, the 8088 and 8086 microprocessors, for which DOS was designed, have none of the protection mechanisms of their younger brothers. There was no point in trying to design protection into DOS.

Time is catching up with DOS. The 640k byte of RAM limit imposed by DOS which once seemed like a basketball court now feels like a broom closet. The IBM AT years ago introduced microcomputers equipped with the 80286 processor and today the 80386 is not uncommon. While improvements are added to DOS in a continuing evolutionary process, nothing can be done to address the underlying design deficiencies. The newer chips are forced to execute DOS in their 8086-emulating *real mode,* in which the protection mechanisms are disabled. DOS is not a protected mode operating system and it cannot be made into one.

As of this writing, not all the details of OS/2 are known. A few things are certain, however. OS/2 is a multitasking, virtual memory executive which uses (and requires) the full protection capabilities of the 80286 and 80386 microprocessors. As such, OS/2 will not look kindly upon an application which begins playing with OS/2's precious hardware. Any application attempting to pull the tricks described in this chapter, will find itself relegated to the garbage-can icon under OS/2.

Lower Memory

It is well known that the BIOS maintains all of its variables in lower memory in segment *0x40*. (The main reason this is so well known is that IBM published source code listings for all of the BIOS routines—one need only read the listings to determine what is stored where.) Table 7.1 is a summary of key low memory locations and their meanings:

Table 7.1
Key Low Memory Locations

Location	Size	Meaning
0x10	2	equipment status flag
0x13	2	size of memory in kbytes
0x17	1	keyboard shift status
0x49	1	current video mode
0x4a	I	number of columns on current screen
0x50	16	cursor position for each of 8 pages
0x62	1	active page
0x63	1	I/O address of active 6845
0x66	1	current pallette setting
0x6c	4	timer [clock ticks since midnight]
0x70	1	1 -> roll over since timer last read
0x71	1	1 -> break key has been depressed

All of the above addresses are offsets into segment 0x40.

The easiest method of accessing these locations is to define a far pointer of the proper type and initialize it to the proper value taken from the table above. For example, suppose that we wanted to read the equipment status by direct examination instead of using the proper BIOS call back in Chapter 6. Prg7_1 represents just such a program.

```
/*Prg7_1 - Read the Hardware Status (Direct Access)
   by Stephen R. Davis, 1987

  Get the equivalent hardware status by directly addressing
  the keyboard status word in lower memory.  See Prg6_2 for
  interpretation of status word.
*/

#include <stdio.h>
#include <dos.h>

/*prototype definitions*/
int main (void);
void interpret (unsigned);

/*define global variables*/

unsigned far *equip_flag = {(unsigned far *)0x00400010};
```

```

/*Main - make the BIOS call to get status and then interpret it*/
main ()
{
     printf ("\nEquipment as reported by 'equip_flag' variable:\n");
     interpret (*equip_flag);
}

/*Display routines which we need for Interpret()*/
void dispnum (i)
     unsigned i;
{
     printf ("%d", i);
}

void dispdsk (i)
     unsigned i;
{
     printf ("%d", i + 1);
}

char *modes [] = {"No monitor or EGA attached",
                  "Color/Graphics in 40 x 25 mode",
                  "Color/Graphics in 80 x 25 mode",
                  "Monochrome monitor"};
void dispmode (i)
     unsigned i;
{
     printf (modes [i]);
}

char *mems [] = {"16k", "32k", "48k", "64k"};
void dispmem (i)
     unsigned i;
{
     printf (mems [i]);
}

char *yn [] = {"Yes", "No"};
void dispyn (i)
     unsigned i;
{
     printf (yn [i]);
}
void dispny (i)
     unsigned i;
{
     printf (yn [1 - i]);
}

/*Interpret - interpret the IBM status word*/
struct DICT {
     unsigned mask;
     unsigned shiftvalue;
     char *string;
     void (*disp) (unsigned);
     } dictionary [] = {{0xc000, 14, "Printers =           ", dispnum},
                        {0x1000, 12, "Game I/O ports =     ", dispnum},
                        {0x0e00,  9, "Serial ports =       ", dispnum},
                        {0x00c0,  6, "Disk drives =        ", dispdsk},
                        {0x0030,  4, "Video mode =         ", dispmode}
                        {0x000c,  2, "System board RAM =   ", dispmem},
                        {0x0002,  1, "8087/287 NDP =       ", dispny},
                        {0x0001,  0, "IPL from diskette =  ", dispyn},
```

```
                              {0x0000,  0, "Terminator", dispnum}};
void interpret (value)
     unsigned value;
{
     unsigned maskvalue;
     struct DICT *ptr;

     ptr = dictionary;
     while (ptr -> mask) {
          maskvalue = value & ptr -> mask;
          maskvalue >>= ptr -> shiftvalue;
          printf (ptr -> string);
          (*(ptr -> disp)) (maskvalue);
          printf ("\n");
          ptr++;
     }
}
```

The most remarkable feature of this program is how similar it is to its BIOS calling brother. The only real difference is that the call to *getstatus()* has been replaced by a reference to the variable *EQUIP_FLAG*. *EQUIP_FLAG* is declared to be of type *UNSIGNED FAR* * and set to the value *0x00400010* in accordance with the table above.

Notice once again how a far pointer is initialized. The first 4 hex digits are assigned to the segment portion of the pointer and the lower 4 hex digits to the offset portion. If this feels uncomfortable, you can also use the *MK_FP()* call in the Turbo C library to *build* the far pointer from the two unsigned values 0x40 and 0x10.

Values in lower memory need not be static. We can just as well read data which is changing. For example, Prg7_2 below is a *direct access* translation of our time delay program also from Chapter 6.

```
/*Prg7_2 - Delay Specified Number of Seconds (Direct Access)
   by Stephen R. Davis, 1987

  Many programs must delay for short periods of time.  Often this
  is done by executing an "empty" FOR loop.  Use the clock counter
  in lower memory as a more accurate clock.
*/

#include <stdio.h>

/*define a clock tick -> seconds macro*/
#define GETIME (unsigned)(*timer / 18 - *timer / 1638)

/*prototype definitions*/
void main (void);
unsigned getval (char *);
void wait (unsigned);

/*global data definitions*/
volatile long far *timer = {(long far *)0x0040006c};

```

```
/*Main - ask the user for length of time to delay (0 terminates)*/
void main (void)
{
        unsigned delay;

        printf ("This program simply delays the user specified number\n"
                "of seconds.  Entering a zero terminates the program.\n"
                "\n"
                "Seconds are counted down to provide output so that\n"
                "the user can break out prematurely, if desired\n"
                "\n");
        for (;;) {

            /*get the specified delay and wait () that long*/
            if ((delay = getval ("Enter delay time [seconds]")) == 0)
                 break;

            /*now call our wait function to perform the delay*/
            printf ("Start delay:\n");
            wait (delay);
            printf ("Finished\n");
        }
}

/*Getval - output a prompt and get an integer response*/
unsigned getval (prompt)
        char *prompt;
{
        unsigned retval;

        printf ("%s - ", prompt);
        scanf ("%d", &retval);
        return retval;
}

/*Wait - wait the specified length of time*/
void wait (delay)
        unsigned delay;
{
        unsigned previous, current;

        /*every time the time changes - decrement count*/
        previous = GETIME;
        for (;;) {
             if (previous != (current = GETIME)) {
                  previous = current;
                  if (!--delay)
                       return;

                  /*remove this print statement in actual use*/
                  printf ("count - %d\n", delay);
             }
        }
}
```

Here I have defined the macro *GETIME*, which appears much as the call to *getime()* did in Prg6_3; however, *GETIME* translates to a direct access to the data pointed at by *TIMER*. The definition of *TIMER* is slightly different than *EQUIP_FLAG* above. Why the descriptor *VOLATILE?*

First, you should analyze a little more closely what is meant by *changing data*. In this particular program, the CPU is in a very tight loop examining the variable **TIMER*. How can anything be changing? In fact, there are many things going on inside the PC even when programs are sitting in tight loops. For one thing, every tick of the *Programmable Interval Timer,* the CPU is being interrupted from its tight loop and is running off into the timer interrupt service handler. One of the functions of this handler is to increment the time of day variable in low memory.

The timer interrupt is *transparent* to the user program; i.e., it comes and goes without the user program ever being aware. Programmers try to visualize things using the simplest model possible, so we act as if the CPU is always in the program loop and someone or something else is incrementing the clock for us. By repeatedly reading the timer location in memory, the program can watch time *pass by*.

There is only one problem. We have to be sure that our program is, in fact, watching the memory location. Turbo C attempts to perform certain optimizations in translating our C programs into assembly language to generate faster programs. One of these is to not load memory locations that it knows are already stored in a register of the microprocessor. Turbo C assumes that all variables retain their value unless it changes them. It does not know about variables that click along in the background.

If we are not careful, Turbo C is likely to load **TIMER* one time. On the next pass, Turbo C might note that the value of **TIMER* is already stored in a register some place and not reload it from memory. This would be disasterous for our program. The location **TIMER* might in fact be ticking along, but the value of **TIMER* which Turbo C has stashed away in a register somewhere will not. To avoid this we add the descriptor *VOLATILE* to **TIMER*. This alerts Turbo C to reload the value of **TIMER* even if Turbo C thinks it knows what it is already.

I want to point out here that you do not *know* that Turbo C is going to make some optimization on **TIMER* which will mess up your program. You only know that it *might*. Adding the descriptor *VOLATILE* removes any possibility.

The second program above has a much better justification for existing than the first. Reading the equipment status is not typically a time critical operation. The *BIOS* call does not take long to execute and provides much better assurance of functioning properly on all machines. One could argue that the *Get Time of Day BIOS* call does take a certain amount of time. When measuring the execution time of programs very accurately, one does not want the execution time of the stop watch to appreciably add to the over all time.

The resolution of a clock ticking 18.2 times per second is not going to lead to timings which could be appreciably thrown off by two *Get Time of Day BIOS* calls. It is possible to increase the accuracy of such measurements by speeding up the clock to, say, 100 times per second by writing to the PIT. In such cases, the minimum time resolution becomes short enough that it may be necessary to access the location directly as we have done in Prg7_2.

In other words, unless there is some overriding reason, don't access the lower memory words directly. The arguments to the BIOS routines are documented. This means that they are not likely to change. New ones are sure to come along, but the old BIOS calls will certainly continue to be supported in new machines. The address locations in low memory are not documented. There is no assurance that these variables will stay put. In fact, although the above two programs have been tested on an IBM PC and AT, we have no assurance that they will function properly on PC's from other companies.

Direct Screen I/O

Of all the forms of direct access to the PC's hardware, direct screen I/O is by far the most common. Whether this is a testament to how important good display performance is or how inadequate the BIOS routines are, I do not know. Or, perhaps, it is merely an indication of how easy it is to access the screen yourself.

It is this fact which doomed some of the clone manufacturers of the early days. The BIOS was supposed to rationalize the interface to the display hardware. In principle, it did not make any difference how the details of the video adapter were arranged as long as all the BIOS calls were adequately supported. Believing that and noticing several gaping inadequacies the the color/graphics adapter, several companies decided to go off and make their own. These new cards were equipped with more resolution or more colors or both. Sure they were different, but the BIOS was supposed to handle these little problems.

Unfortunately, when programs began routinely skipping over the BIOS, these small hardware differences began to seem quite important indeed. One of the most hardware sensitive of these programs was a game known as *Flight Simulator*. Ninety-nine percent of programs for the PC did not care about the minutiae of graphics design that *Flight Simulator* did, but that didn't matter.

Flight Simulator was the acid test for graphics compatibility. If a computer's video adapter could not run *Flight Simulator,* then it did not sell.

Let's start by reviewing a few basics. A computer display consists of two parts: the monitor and the video controller graphics card. The front surface of the display tube of the monitor is coated with a thin film of a phosphor containing substance. This material normally appears dark when viewed from the front of the tube, but glows when it is excited by high velocity electrons impacting it. Fortuitously enough, right in the back of the display tube is an electron gun which can spew out a controlled supply of such electrons. This gun is capable of turning on and off the supply of electrons very rapidly (from on to off in rougly 0.1 microsecond in a CGA display). Large coils located on all four sides of the tube immediately in front of the electron gun generate magnetic fields which cause the beam of energized electrons to both focus and deflect to a spot on the screen, a pixel.

As the electron gun sweeps from left to right for each of the CGA's 200 vertical lines, it paints the image by turning the electron supply on and off. Wherever it is on, the pixel glows; wherever it remains off, it remains dark. In a color monitor, there are 3 sets of pixels, each of which glows with one of the primary colors. Each set has its own electron gun. The 3 beams are swept together but each is aligned with its own color. If a particular spot is to be red, only the red gun is turned on. If white, all three are energized.

If the beam sweeps the screen fast enough, the retention in both the phosphor and in the user's eye will cause the entire screen to appear equally bright. The user experiences no perception of the sweeping going on. How fast is fast enough? The CGA monitor scans the screen vertically 60 times per second. Since there are 200 vertical lines on the CGA's display and each must be swept 60 times per second, then the electron beam must sweep from left to right at least 12,000 times per second (60 * 200). In fact, the horizontal sweep rate, as it is called, is almost 16,000 Hertz (Hertz sounds better than times per second). This extra is to allow for details such as overscan and sync pulses. The figures for the MDA and EGA are accordingly higher because of their higher resolution.

All that activity going on within the monitor means that there is a constant stream of information being sent to the monitor screen. This is true, even if nothing on the screen is changing. Since monitors have no memory, this information must be continuously supplied from the video card. (This is the fundamental difference between a monitor and a terminal. A terminal, which has

Figure 7.1

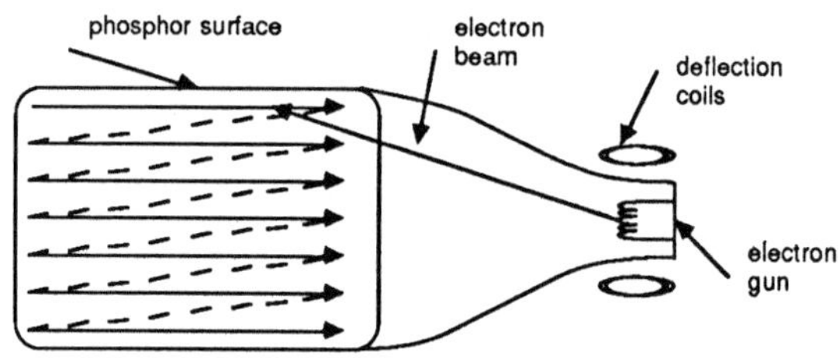

Inside of computer monitor

its own memory, will continue to display information on the screen even when unplugged from the computer.)

In a raster scan monitor such as we have been describing, all the video card has to send are the gun instructions. The monitor is going to sweep back and forth and up and down without instructions from the computer. The card merely sends a chain of bits, one for each pixel, telling the monitor whether to make that pixel glow or not. Just to keep the monitor and card talking about the same pixel, the card sends a sync pulse at the end of each horizontal and vertical sweep.

Just as the monitor has a large matrix of pixels on its front surface to scan, the graphics card scans a large block of internal memory for the information to display. In graphics mode 6, it's quite simple. The card views its memory as a large matrix of bits, each one corresponding to one of the pixels on the monitor's display. If the bit is set, the pixel glows. In graphics mode 4 and 5, the card associates each pixel with 2 bits in memory. These two bits indicate the 4 colors of a pallette.

When displaying characters in one of these graphics modes, each character must be painted in memory, setting each of the appropriate bits to form the character image on the screen. Even though this is very flexible, it is not easy, involving lots of overhead. Fortunately, in the character modes of operation, the card makes the translation from character to pixel pattern for us. In these modes, the card views memory as a matrix of character/attributes. The first 80 words of display memory correspond to the first row (assuming 80 characters across), the next 80 to the next row and so on.

Figure 7.2

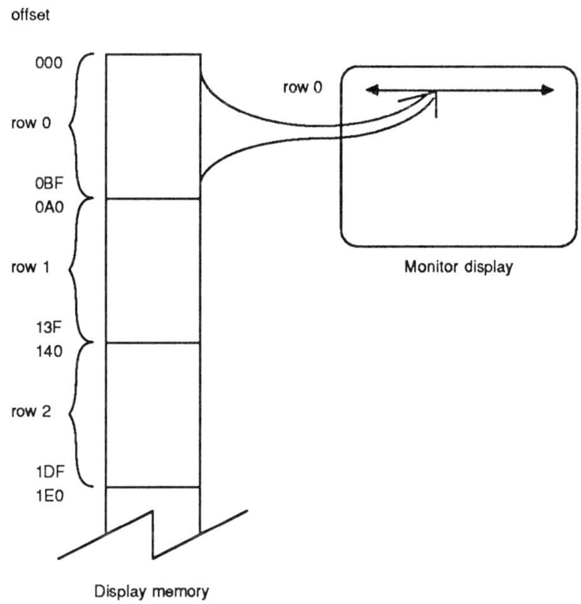

Mapping video memory to monitor display

Except for maybe being very fast to allow the video card rapid access, video memory is identical to other memory within the system. So where is this memory? Physically, it's located on the video card itself. (In the PCjr, the video card borrows some of the system memory.) Logically, each of the different monitors is assigned its own address. Table 7.2 shows the segment addresses for each of the major video displays. To enhance compatibility with the CGA and MDA, the EGA and VGA cards use the their addresses in some modes.

Why all these different addresses? Because, as we mentioned above, the CGA and MDA were designed to both work within the same computer. By assigning them different addresses, the PC can address them independently. The EGA and VGA require more memory in their higher resolution modes, but attempt to emulate the older cards as much as possible in modes 0 through 7. Notice that because of memory overlap, it is not possible to have an MDA, a CGA and an EGA, all in the same machine, but any two are allowed.

Table 7.2
Segment Address for Video Memory

Monocrome Display Adapter	0xB000
Color Graphics Adapter	0xB800
Enhanced Graphics Adapter and Video Graphics Array	0xB800 (modes 0 thru 6) 0xB000 (mode 7) 0xA000 (other modes)

Now prove to yourself that this isn't just so much clap trap. If the display adapters have memory, then you must be able to write to it. The most direct way to write to memory is via the *DEBUG* debugger supplied with your DOS disks (any debugger will do, if you don't like *DEBUG*). Be sure your video adapter is in one of the character modes. Enter *DEBUG* and attempt to edit memory, entering for example the following command:

```
- E B800:0000

    xx 41 xx 42 xx 43 xx 44 etc.
```

where – is the debugger prompt and *xx* is some numerical value. The B8000 will be a B000 for a monochrome display.

The hex codes for the letters of the alphabet are 41, 42, 43, etc. Before you go too far, look up in the upper left-hand corner of the display. What's this? Every other character of the alphabet is appearing, but with strange colors (or characteristics on a monochrome). The *E* command writes bytes to the screen. The first byte we write is the character, but the second becomes its attribute, the third the next character, the fourth its attribute, and so on. (The printed page cannot do the effect justice—try it yourself.)

As soon as you enter *return,* everything you've written scrolls off the screen. Maybe we should have written on one of the other rows. If the first row is 80 characters across, then the second row should start at address B800:00A0. This we get by remembering that each character is 2 bytes and that 160 decimal = 00A0 hexadecimal. This should work exactly the same, except that it takes two line feeds to remove it from the screen. You may want to go back and use the attribute table in Chapter 6 to play with the different attribute values to see their effect on the screen.

Figure 7.3

```
A EGIKM Q UWY[]█
C>DEBUG
-E B800:0000
B800:0000  20.41   07.42   20.43   07.44   20.45   07.46   20.47   07.48
B800:0008  20.49   07.4A   20.4B   07.4C   20.4D   07.4E   20.4F   07.50
B800:0010  20.51   07.52   20.53   07.54   20.55   07.56   20.57   07.58
B800:0018  20.59   07.5A   20.5B   07.5C   20.5D   07.5E   20.5F   07.60
-
```

Editing screen memory from DEBUG

Accessing screen memory from a program is just about as simple as accessing it from *DEBUG*. Of course, there will be details to worry about, such as scrolling and the like. Let's start with a simple example that avoids all that. If the screen consists of simple memory, then it must be possible to save it to disk, just like any other buffer. Having done that, it should then be possible to read the file back from disk to the display.

Prg7_3 in the listing below shows a program which does exactly that. You should examine it carefully. First, two constants have been defined and one pointer *SCREEN*. Both have been declared as *UNSIGNED FAR **. The *UNSIGNED* is because each character on the screen has both the character byte and the attribute byte. The *FAR* because segments *0xb000* and *0xb800* must be specified explicitly.

```
/*Prg7_3 - Save the screen area to disk and recall it
   by Stephen R. Davis, 1987
```

```

   The user screen can be saved off to disk to be recalled
   at a later time.  The effect is almost instantaneous as the
   example program demonstrates.  This program must be compiled
   under the compact or large memory models.
*/

#include <stdio.h>
#include <io.h>
#include <process.h>
#include <dos.h>
#include <fcntl.h>
#include <stat.h>
extern char *sys_errlist [];
extern int errno;

/*define screen related constants*/
#define cga  (unsigned far *)0xb8000000
#define mono (unsigned far *)0xb0000000
#define screenheight 25

/*prototyping definitions*/
void main (void);
void init (void);
void errexit (void);
void pattern (char, unsigned);
char gtcr (char *);

/*define global variables*/
unsigned far *screen, size, screenwidth;
union REGS regs;
char *fname = {"screen.sav"};
unsigned waccess = {O_RDWR | O_CREAT | O_TRUNC | O_BINARY};
unsigned raccess = {O_RDONLY | O_BINARY};
unsigned normfile = S_IWRITE | S_IREAD;

/*make sure that we are in the compact or large memory model*/
#if (sizeof (int far *) - sizeof (int *))
     #error Compile with compact or large memory model!
#endif


/*Main - save the screen directly to disk and recall it*/
void main ()
{
     int handle;

     init ();
     pattern ('0', 10);
     if ((handle = open (fname, waccess, normfile)) == -1) {
          printf ("error opening 'screen'\n");
          errexit ();
     }
     gtcr ("Press any key to save number screen to disk\n"
            "and copy over with a character screen\n");

     if (size != write (handle, (void *)screen, size)) {
          printf ("error writing 'screen'\n");
          errexit ();
     }
     close (handle);
     pattern ('a', 26);

     gtcr ("Press any key to read character number "
```

```
            "screen back from disk");
        if ((handle = open (fname, raccess)) == -1) {
            printf ("error reopening 'screen'\n");
            errexit ();
        }
        read (handle, (void *)screen, size);
        exit (0);
}

/*Init - initialize screen pointer and width*/
void init ()
{
        regs.h.ah = 0x0f;                           /*get mode*/
        int86 (0x10, &regs, &regs);
        screenwidth = regs.h.ah;
        size = screenwidth * screenheight * sizeof (*screen);

        if (regs.h.al == 7)
            screen = mono;
        else
            screen = cga;
}

/*Gtcr - display a prompt and fetch character response*/
char gtcr (prompt)
        char *prompt;
{
        printf (prompt);
        return (char)getchar ();
}

/*Errexit - display disk error*/
void errexit ()
{
        printf ("DOS error: %s\n", sys_errlist [errno]);
        exit (1);
}

/*Pattern - fill screen with an incrementing pattern*/
void pattern (c, modulo)
        char c;
        unsigned modulo;
{
        unsigned i, j;
        char tchar;

        for (j = 0; j < (screenheight - 1); j++) {
            tchar = c + (char)(j % modulo);
            for (i = 1; i < screenwidth; i++) {
                printf ("%c", tchar);
                if ((++tchar - c) >= modulo)
                    tchar = c;
            }
            printf ("\n");
        }
}

```

Main() in this program first calls *init()* which checks the video mode using the BIOS call. First, the number of bytes in the current screen display is calculated. This calculation assumes that the display is in one of the text modes. A check is then made of the mode. If the mode is 7, then the address of the monochrome display is stored in *SCREEN;* otherwise, the address of the *CGA/EGA* is used. No check is made for the graphics modes above 7.

From this point *main()* puts a pattern up on the screen and saves it to disk. Once saved, *main()* closes the file and puts another pattern up on the screen. *Main()* waits for a key to be depressed. When released, *main()* reopens the saved file and reads into to screen memory, restoring the screen to it previous state. Notice how rapidly the screen is restored to its original pattern (much less time than the pattern required to place there in the first place).

There is one trick, however, which must be observed. As pointed out, *SCREEN* must be a far pointer since the segment of the screen is explicitly indicated. In order to pass *SCREEN* to the Turbo C library routines *read()* and *write()*, you must make sure that they are prepared to accept far pointers to data. This you do by selecting either the *COMPACT* or *LARGE* memory models from the Options menu of the *IDE*. The check on line 40 insures this by comparing the default address size with that of a far address. If they are different, then the compilation model is wrong and the compilation is aborted with the *#error* directive. If the default size for a pointer is far, then the model is correct. You also could have explicitly checked for the labels *__TINY__*, *__SMALL__*, etc. These labels are defined by Turbo C to indicate the compilation mode. If either *__COMPACT__* or *__LARGE__* is true then all is okay, otherwise abort the compilation.

Now you are ready to try your hand at writing text to the screen yourself. Prg7_4a represents our BIOS screen output program from Chapter 6, rewritten as a direct access routine. The similarities are great, the main differences being in the routines *scroll()* and *qprintf()*.

Just as before, the actual write operation is performed by the function *qprintf()*, which accepts as an argument a single character string. *Qprintf* first calculates the memory address of the current cursor position, which is stored in the variables *V_POS* and *H_POS*. It then uses the lines

```
for (; *c; c++)
     *sp++ = (attrib << 8) + *c;
```

to copy the character string into screen memory after adding the proper attribute. Extra code is added to the above to properly update the cursor position and to check for an embedded *\n*. Newline is the only special character the program checks for.

Scroll() handles the scrolling operation. Scrolling the screen up involves copying each character on the screen to the location of the character on the row above it and then writing blanks to the last line of the display. Basically this is handled as follows:

```
/*scroll the screen up 1 row*/
dest = address of first row of screen
source = address of second row of screen
number = the number of characters on the screen minus one row

for (temp = number; temp; temp--)
     *dest++ = *source++;

/*now blank the last line*/
dest = address of last row of screen
number = number of characters across screen

for (temp = number; temp; temp--)
     *dest++ = blank;
```

Your *scroll()* routine is complicated slightly by the fact that it can scroll any number of lines at one time. This can result in substantial time savings as it takes slightly less than half as long to scroll 2 lines than it does to scroll 1 line twice.

The complete program appears in listing Prg7_4a below.

```
/*Prg7_4a - High Speed Screen Output
    by Stephen R Davis, 1987

  Perform direct screen output by accessing screen memory directly
  via the screen pointer 'screen'.  Scroll using standard C
  statements.
*/

#include <stdio.h>
#include <dos.h>
#include <stdlib.h>

#define cga  (unsigned far *)0xb8000000    /*same for ega*/
#define mono (unsigned far *)0xb0000000
#define space 0x20
#define attrib 0x07
#define screenheight 25

/*add the screen BIOS functions*/
#define setcursor 0x02
#define getmode 0x0f

/*define global variables*/
unsigned v_pos, h_pos, screenwidth;
union REGS regs;
unsigned far *screen;                      /*screen pointer*/

/*prototype declarations*/
```

```
void init (void);
void scroll (unsigned);
void qprintf (char *);
void pcursor (unsigned, unsigned);

/*Main - test the output routines*/
int main ()
{
     int i, j;

     init ();
     for (i = 0; i < 20; i++) {
          for (j = 0; j < screenheight; j++) {
               qprintf ("this is BIOS output");
               pcursor(v_pos, 30+j);
               qprintf ("and this\n");
          }
          for (j = 0; j < screenheight; j++)
               printf ("this is normal printf output\n");
     }
}

/*Init - set the screen address and clear the screen*/
void init ()
{
     short mode;

     regs.h.ah = getmode;
     int86 (0x10, &regs, &regs);
     mode = regs.h.al;
     screenwidth = regs.h.ah;

     if (mode == 7)
          screen = mono;
     else
          if (mode == 3 || mode == 2)
               screen = cga;
          else
               abort ();

     scroll (screenheight);
     pcursor (0, 0);
}

/*Scroll - scroll up N lines using function 6*/
void scroll (nlines)
     unsigned nlines;
{
     unsigned far *source, far *dest, number, temp;

     if (nlines >= screenheight)
          nlines = screenheight;

     h_pos = 0;
     if ((v_pos += nlines) >= screenheight) {
          nlines = (v_pos - screenheight) + 1;

          /*scroll the screen up 'nlines' amount*/
          source = screen + (nlines * screenwidth);
          dest = screen;
          number = (screenheight - nlines) * screenwidth;
          for (temp = number; temp; temp--)
               *dest++ = *source++;

```

```
            /*now blank the lines abandoned*/
            dest = screen + number;
            number = nlines * screenwidth;
            for (; number; number--)
                 *dest++ = (attrib << 8) + space;

            v_pos = screenheight - 1;
      }
}

/*Qprintf - output a string using the BIOS screen handler.  If
              an attribute is not provided, use the default.*/

#define SCREENLOC screen + ((screenwidth * v_pos) + h_pos)

void qprintf (c)
     char *c;
{
     unsigned far *sp;

     sp = SCREENLOC;
     for (; *c; c++)
          if (*c == '\n') {
               scroll (1);
               sp = SCREENLOC;}
          else
               if (h_pos < screenwidth) {
                    h_pos++;
                    *sp++ = (attrib << 8) + *c;
               }
     pcursor (v_pos, h_pos);
}

/*PCursor - place the cursor at the current x and y location.
             To place the cursor, and subsequent output, to any
             arbitrary location, set 'v_pos' and 'h_pos' before
             calling pcursor.*/
void pcursor (y, x)
     unsigned x, y;
{
     v_pos = y;
     h_pos = x;

     regs.h.ah = setcursor;
     regs.h.bh = 0;
     regs.h.dh = v_pos;
     regs.h.dl = h_pos;
     int86 (0x10, &regs, &regs);
}
```

Just as with prg6_5 before, *main()* calls *qprintf()* and *printf()* in a loop to compare their performance and their speed.

Routines that directly write graphics to the screen follow the same pattern. In this case, it is simply a matter of calculating the address of the dot we wish to access and *OR*ing it set or *AND*ing it clear. To result in reasonable writing speeds, the programmer must often resort to enmasse block settings and clearings of large areas of the screen.

Besides screen memory, it is also possible to directly access the 6845 CRT controller chip in the CGA and MDA graphics adapters themselves. This is the heart of the video adapter and performs most of the work of transforming video memory into the bit stream the monitor sees. Although crude by modern graphics chip standards, it contains a series of registers which user programs may access. Table 7.3 is a partial listing of these:

Table 7.3
Ports on the 6845 CRT Controller of the CGA and MDA

Port	Access	Meaning
3x4	W/O	Address register
3x5	R/W	Data register
3x8	W/O	Mode select
		Bit 0 - 80 col mode
		Bit 1 - graphics mode
		Bit 2 - B&W select
		Bit 3 - Video enable
		Bit 4 - 640x200 mode select
		Bit 5 - blink enable
3x9	W/O	Color select
		Bit 0 - blue border
		Bit 1 - green border
		Bit 2 - read border
		Bit 3 - Intense border
		Bit 4 - Alt. background color (alph modes only)
		Bit 5 - mode 4 color pallette select
3xa	R/W	Status register
		Bit 0 - 1 -> ok to access display
		Bit 1 - light pen trigger set
		Bit 2 - light pen switch

where x = B for monochrome displays and D for CGA displays

The address register is actually a selector to one of 18 data registers within the chip. The data registers are specified in Table 7.4. For example, writing a *0x01* to port *0x3d4* gives the program access to the Horizontal displayed register at port *0x3d5*.

Table 7.4
Data Registers in the 6845 CRT Controller

Number	Access	Name	Meaning
*0	W/O	Hor. Total	Total number of chars. across
*1	W/O	Hor. Dsplyd	No. of cols. on screen
2	W/O	H Sync Pos	Col. number of hor. sync pulse
3	W/O	H Sync Wdth	Width of sync pulse in col.s
4	W/O	Ver. Total	Total number of lines vertically
5	W/O	Ver. Adjust	No. of scan lines adjust to above
6	W/O	Ver Dsplyd	No. of rows on screen
7	W/O	V Sync Pos	Row number of ver. sync pulse
8	W/O	Interlace	Display interlace
9	W/O	Max Scn Ln	Maximum scan line address
*A	W/O	Cursor start	Vert. scan line to start cursor
*B	W/O	Cursor end	Vert. scan line to end cursor
*C	W/O	Start addr-H	Offset in video memory of display
*D	W/O	Start addr-L	(Lower byte of same)
*E	R/W	Cursor addr-H	Cursor address
*F	R/W	Cursor addr-L	(Lower byte of same)
*10	R/O	Light pen-H	Light pen position
*11	R/O	Light pen-L	(Lower byte of same)

Each of the above registers is selected by outing the proper value to the adress register and then reading or writing the data register. Those marked with * are common to EGA displays.

Programs may access these registers using the Turbo C library routines *outport()* and *inport()*, which write and read word values to the 8086 ports. The related *outportb()* and *inportb()* are macros which invoke the corresponding word routines to return byte sized values. Alternatively *outportb()* and *inportb()* may be *UNDEF*ed, in which case different byte routines with the same function will be loaded at link time.

Playing with the different registers can lead to some very interesting effects. For example, decreasing the total number of columns across the display or increasing the number of rows (there is enough memory in both MDA and CGA displays to accommodate one more albeit incomplete row). The most useful of the above registers is the *Start Address*. This register is used by the BIOS to select the active page. Its value can be changed to that of any of the active pages from Table 7.5.

Table 7.5
Offsets for Different Video Pages

Page Number	Offset
	40 x 25 mode
0	0x0000
1	0x0800
2	0x1000
3	0x1800
4	0x2000
5	0x2800
6	0x3000
7	0x3800
	80 x 25 mode
0	0x0000
1	0x1000
2	0x2000
3	0x3000
4	0x4000
5	0x5000
6	0x6000
7	0x7000

It can also be changed to intermediate values, displaying the last half of page 0 and the first half of page one (with half a line not otherwise displayed in the middle). As we will learn in the next few chapters, scrolling the display up is a time consuming job. Rather than move the entire display memory up one line, I have written scroll routines which performed the scroll operation by moving the *start of display* pointer down by one line. *Qprintf()* wrote all the way through memory eventually wrapping around at the bottom, with *scroll()* always keeping the *start of display* address 25 lines behind it.

Unfortunately, I can not present those routines in this book. Although incredibly fast at output, they leave the screen in a state from which only they know how to access it. Only a CLS restores sanity to the display. Worse yet, it is possible, although unlikely, to burn up a monitor when changing some of these values. The *Starting Offset* register can be modified with impunity, but I would not want a reader to incorrectly key in a program from this book and destroy his or her monitor.

The status register is especially useful to owners of older CGA displays. They may have noticed that every time these programs accessed the display memory, a great deal of static, generally known as *snow*, appeared on their screens. This snow is caused by the fact that the memory in the CGA can only be accessed by one piece of hardware at a time. If the CPU is busy accessing the screen, it can get in the way of the CRT controller's ability to read display memory. If the controller cannot read display memory, it does not know what to send to the monitor, so it stutters. The monitor displays this stammering as small brightly colored or white streaks.

We cannot actually avoid this interference, but we can arrange it so that the streaks only appear during the horizontal retrace period. During this time the electron beam is returning to the left side of the display and no video is going to the monitor. Streaks here will not be seen. The listing below shows the same Prg7_4 with extra checks added to make sure that screen memory is only accessed during a full retrace cycle. Even though virtually identical, the entire listing is presented so that the additions can be noted.

```
/*Prg7_4b - High Speed Screen Output w/ CGA Retrace check
   by Stephen R Davis, 1987

  Perform direct screen output by accessing screen memory directly
  via the screen pointer 'screen'.  Scroll using standard C
  statements.  Check for CGA retrace before accessing screen to
  prevent "snow" from appearing.
*/

#include <stdio.h>
#include <dos.h>
#include <stdlib.h>

#define cga  (unsigned far *)0xb8000000
#define space 0x20
#define attrib 0x07
#define screenheight 25

/*define the "check for retrace" function*/
#define trace   while (  inportb (0x3da) & 0x01)
#define retrace while (!(inportb (0x3da) & 0x01))

/*add the screen BIOS functions*/
#define setcursor 0x02
#define getmode 0x0f

/*define global variables*/
unsigned v_pos, h_pos, screenwidth;
union REGS regs;
unsigned far *screen;                          /*screen pointer*/

/*prototype declarations*/
void init (void);
void scroll (unsigned);
void qprintf (char *);
void pcursor (unsigned, unsigned);

```

```
/*Main - test the output routines*/
int main ()
{
     int i, j;

     init ();
     for (i = 0; i < 20; i++) {
          for (j = 0; j < screenheight; j++) {
               qprintf ("this is BIOS output");
               pcursor(v_pos, 30+j);
               qprintf ("and this\n");
          }
          for (j = 0; j < screenheight; j++)
               printf ("this is normal printf output\n");
     }
}

/*Init - set the screen address and clear the screen*/
void init ()
{
     int mode;

     regs.h.ah = getmode;
     int86 (0x10, &regs, &regs);
     mode = regs.h.al;
     screenwidth = regs.h.ah;

     if (mode == 7)
          abort ();
     else
          if (mode == 3 || mode == 2)
               screen = cga;
          else
               abort ();

     scroll (screenheight);
     pcursor (0, 0);
}

/*Scroll - scroll up N lines using function 6*/
void scroll (nlines)
     unsigned nlines;
{
     unsigned far *source, far *dest, number, temp;

     if (nlines >= screenheight)
          nlines = screenheight;

     h_pos = 0;
     if ((v_pos += nlines) >= screenheight) {
          nlines = (v_pos - screenheight) + 1;

          /*scroll the screen up 'nlines' amount*/
          source = screen + (nlines * screenwidth);
          dest = screen;
          number = (screenheight - nlines) * screenwidth;
          for (temp = number; temp; temp--) {
               trace; retrace;
               *dest++ = *source++;
          }

          /*now blank the lines abandoned*/
          dest = screen + number;
          number = nlines * screenwidth;
```

```
            for (; number; number--) {
                trace; retrace;
                *dest++ = (attrib << 8) + space;
            }

            v_pos = screenheight - 1;
        }
}

/*Qprintf - output a string using the BIOS screen handler.  If
            an attribute is not provided, use the default.*/

#define SCREENLOC screen + ((screenwidth * v_pos) + h_pos)

void qprintf (c)
    char *c;
{
    unsigned far *sp;

    sp = SCREENLOC;
    for (; *c; c++)
        if (*c == '\n') {
            scroll (1);
            sp = SCREENLOC;
        }
        else
            if (h_pos < screenwidth) {
                h_pos++;
                trace; retrace;
                *sp++ = (attrib << 8) + *c;
            }
    pcursor (v_pos, h_pos);
}

/*PCursor - place the cursor at the current x and y location.
            To place the cursor, and subsequent output, to any
            arbitrary location, set 'v_pos' and 'h_pos' before
            calling pcursor.*/
void pcursor (y, x)
    unsigned x, y;
{
    v_pos = y;
    h_pos = x;

    regs.h.ah = setcursor;
    regs.h.bh = 0;
    regs.h.dh = v_pos;
    regs.h.dl = h_pos;
    int86 (0x10, &regs, &regs);
}
```

The macro definition *TRACE* examines the retrace flag of the CGA status register to make sure that the video adapter is not initially in the retrace mode. If the adapter is performing retrace, *TRACE* waits in a loop until it is through. The similar macro *RETRACE* performs the opposite test, hanging in a tight loop until the adapter is retracing.

By invoking *TRACE* followed immediately by *RETRACE*, the program is assured that it has found the leading edge of the retrace pulse, the beginning of the retrace cycle. This ensures that the entire retrace period is available for outputting a character. The program must perform this text immediately prior to any access of display memory (lines 95, 103, and 130). (It is not sufficient to only check for horizontal retrace by invoking *RETRACE* alone. The display adapter may be just completing a retrace cycle the first time the program checks. This would not leave sufficcient time for the processor to get a character onto the screen.)

This version of Prg7_4 is only designed to work with CGA cards. Monochrome adapters have arbitrating hardware and do not display *snow*. Besides, monochrome adapters do not have a status register at port *0x3da*. The *TRACE/RETRACE* combination would wait forever for the leading edge of a signal that is not even present, hanging the machine. To avoid this, *init()* aborts prematurely of the video mode is 7 (lines 65–66).

Notice that the vertical retrace period is very short, only a few microseconds long. This is not very much time for a 4.77 MHz PC. Even though correct in principle, the C program presented here will not actually have the desired effect on these machines. The 8088 microprocessor takes too long making the two calls to *inportb()* to react within the retrace interval. The program works correctly on a 6 MHz AT or faster machine. Inline assembly code to perform the same test is necessary for this to work properly on a PC. We will study inline assembly in Chapter 8.

Notice further that being compelled to wait for horizontal retrace puts quite a cramp in Prg7_4b's perfomance. So much so, that it might actually be slower than some other display routines, particularly those which do not wait for retrace, but instead turn the video off when writing to avoid screen snow. These latter programs suffer from a screen flicker which are almost as bad as the snow they avoid. As many video controls as the 6845 CRT controller in the CGA and MDA displays have, the EGA has more. The EGA does not use the 6845 controller and so is not completely compatible with the CGA and MDA at the register level. In fact, the EGA consists of several intelligent chips to which the program may talk. A brief overview of the EGA's registers and their meanings appears in Table 7.6.

As you can see, the EGA is quite a complicated device. From feature connectors to bit planes, the details of accessing the EGA hardware are beyond the scope of this chapter. Programmers interested in the details of the EGA display should purchase the technical reference manual titled *IBM Enhanced Graphics Adapter* (part number 6280131) from IBM's document service (1-800-IBM-PCTB, see *Bibliography).*

Table 7.6
EGA Registers

Port		Access	Name	Meaning
3C0		W/O	Attrib Cntrl	output a selector followed by one of following:
	0-F			Color value of Pallette register
				Bit 0 - blue
				Bit 1 - green
				Bit 2 - red
				Bit 3 - scndry blue/mono
				Bit 4 - scndry green/intensity
				Bit 5 - scndry red
	10			Mode control
				Bit 0 - 1 -> graphics 0 -> alphanumeric
				Bit 1 - 1 -> color display 0 -> monochrome
				Bit 2 - 1 -> enable line graphics
				Bit 3 - 1 -> enable blink
	11			Border color select
	12			Color plane enable
	13			Hor pixel panning control number of bits to pan to left
3C2		W/O	Misc reg	following bit pattern:
				Bit 0 - 1->CGA emulation, else mono
				Bit 1 - enable RAM to processor
				Bit 2,3 - clock select
				Bit 4 - disable video drivers
				Bit 5 - odd/even 64k select
				Bit 6 - hor retrace polarity
				Bit 7 - ver retrace polarity
3C2		R/O	Inp Status 0	following bit pattern: Bit 7 - 0 -> ver retrace active
3C4		W/O	Sequencer Addr	selects meaning of 3C5
3C5		W/O	Sequencer Cntrl	sequencer command
3CA		W/O	Graphics 2 Pos	graphics 2 position
3CC		W/O	Graphics 1 Pos	graphics 1 position
3CE		W/O	Gr. 1 & 2	selects meaning of 3CF
3CF			Graphics Cntrl	following registers:
	0	W/O		Set/Reset register
	1	W/O		Enable Set/Reset
	2	W/O		Color compare
	3	W/O		Data rotate count
	4	W/O		Read map select
	5	W/O		Mode register
	6	W/O		Misc. register
	7	W/O		Color don't care
	8	W/O		Bit mask register
3x4		W/O	Control Addr	selects meaning of 3x5
3x5		R/W	CRT control	largely the same as listed for CGA/MDA above
3xA		W/O	Feature control	used to comm. w/ feature connector
3xA		R/O	Inp Status 1	same as Status Reg of CGA plus Bit 3 - 1 -> ver retrace active

x may be either B or D depending on the type of display emulated

Windows

When you write to the display adapter, we are free to define whatever functions we like, whether they were originally supported by the BIOS or not. One of the most common functions to introduce is that of windows. In a windowed interface, the user application is capable of writing to subsets of the screen which are arranged to appear as small mini-screens within the screen itself.

There is nothing particularly difficult about managing windows. The programmer must merely keep the mental image of screen memory fixed firmly in his mind. Before going any further, I should point out that there are commercial packages which add windowing functions either to the Turbo C library in the form of C toolboxes or to the BIOS. While the coding of windowing functions is not tricky, it is tedious to get all of the parameters just right. Purchasing a ready made package may be the better bet.

Having said that let's examine Prg7_5. This program is a simple example of text windows. Normally windows are surrounded by a framing of special characters so that the user can differentiate the window from the background clearly. This program does not include that as it adds lots of needless complexity.

Notice the structure definition *WINDOW* and the three declarations *FULL, WIN1*, and *WIN2*. *FULL* represents the entire screen whereas the other two represent some window within the screen. All of our favorite functions are there in their windowed form: *wscroll(), wprintf()* and *wpcursor()*. Two new routines have been introduced: *openwindow()* and *closewindow()*.

Openwindow() uses a *WINDOW* definition to determine the bounds of the new window. It must also be provided a buffer, into which it stores the current cursor position, window dimensions and the background color. Added to that, it stores all of the text on the screen which is about to be overwritten by the window. In place of the data saved, *openwindow()* writes the new window's color plus any fill pattern desired. Finally, it places the cursor properly within the window and calculates the new window dimensions.

Closewindow() reverses the steps, restoring the cursor position, window dimensions and color before restoring the text covered up by the window to the screen.

Figure 7.4

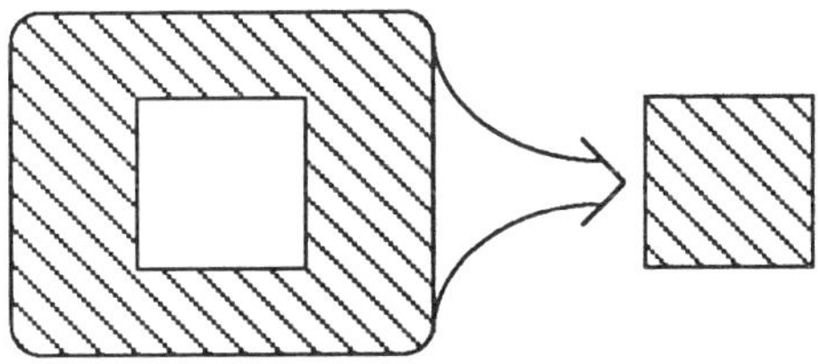

Saving window from screen to internal buffer

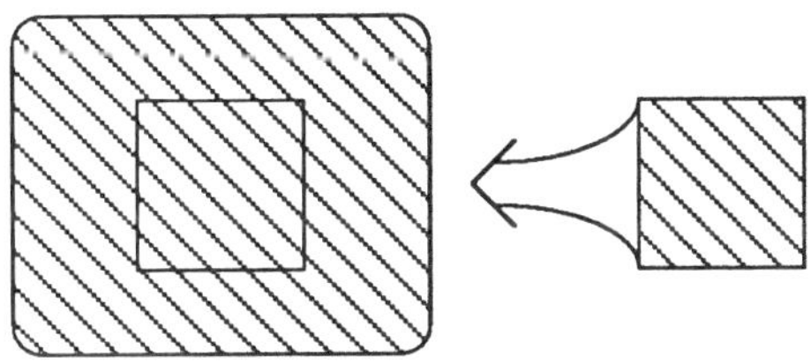

Restoring buffer to screen

The older routines, *wscroll()* and *wprintf()* are basically the same, except that the variables *V_POS* and *H_POS* have now been redefined to be the vertical and horizontal positions within the window and not within the entire screen. In addition, no assumptions can be made about the window height or width. The macro *SCREENLOC*, defined immediately before function *wscroll()*, performs the majority of the brain work, calculating the screen memory location of a row/column position within the current window.

```
/*Prg7_5 - Open/Close Screen Windows
    by Stephen R. Davis, 1987

  Example of using our screen writing skills to open and close
  windows on the screen
*/

#include <stdio.h>
#include <dos.h>
#include <stdlib.h>
#include <process.h>

/*define screen parameters*/
#define height 25
#define width 80
#define cga  (unsigned far *)0xb8000000    /*same for ega*/
#define mono (unsigned far *)0xb0000000
```

```
/*define screen BIOS functions*/
#define setcursor 0x02
#define getmode 0x0f

/*define the colors - 'b'ackground and 'f'oreground*/
#define bred   0x4000
#define bgreen 0x2000
#define bblue  0x1000
#define bwhite bred+bgreen+bblue
#define fred   0x0400
#define fgreen 0x0200
#define fblue  0x0100
#define fwhite fblue+fgreen+fred

/*type definitions*/
struct WINDOW {
               unsigned x0, y0;        /*upper, left hand corner*/
               unsigned x1, y1;        /*lower, right hand corner*/
              };

/*our prototype definitions*/
void main (void);
char gtcr (struct WINDOW *, char *);
void openwindow  (struct WINDOW *, unsigned *, unsigned);
void closewindow (struct WINDOW *, unsigned *);
void wscroll (struct WINDOW *, unsigned);
void wprintf (struct WINDOW *, char *);
void wpcursor (struct WINDOW *, unsigned, unsigned);
void init (void);

/*data definitions*/
union REGS regs;
unsigned far *screen;
typedef unsigned SCREEN [height * width + 5];
unsigned windowwidth, windowheight, color;
unsigned v_pos, h_pos;

/*Main - exercise the window routines*/

struct WINDOW full = { 0, 0, 79, 24};
struct WINDOW win1 = {10, 5, 60, 20};
struct WINDOW win2 = {20, 0, 40, 24};
SCREEN buff1, buff2;

void main (void)
{
     unsigned i;

     /*initialize the works*/
     init ();

     /*put pattern up before opening first window*/
     for (i = 1; i < height; i++)
          wprintf (&full, "***************************************"
                          "***************************************\n")
     wpcursor (&full, 0, 0);

     /*open first window with pattern and then scroll it*/
     gtcr (&full, "This is the main screen\n"
                  "Press Enter key to open first window");
     openwindow (&win1, buff1, bred+fwhite);
     for (i = 1; i < 50; i++)
          wprintf (&win1, "Window #1   ---    scrolling\n\n");
```

```

     /*now open window #2 and scroll it also*/
     gtcr (&win1, "Press Enter key for #2");
     openwindow (&win2, buff2, bblue+fgreen);
     for (i = 1; i < 50; i++)
          wprintf (&win2, "Window #2 --\n"
                          "          scrolling\n\n");

     /*now, prepare to close*/
     gtcr (&win2, "Press Enter key");
     closewindow (&win2, buff2);
     gtcr (&win1, "Press Enter key");
     closewindow (&win1, buff1);
}

/*Gtcr - output a prompt and then await a character response*/
char gtcr (window, prompt)
     struct WINDOW *window;
     char *prompt;
{
     char buffer [80];

     /*build the message string and write it into current window*/
     sprintf (buffer, "%s :\n", prompt);
     wprintf (window, buffer);

     /*now await a response*/
     return (char)getchar ();
}

/*Openwindow - save off a specified box from the screen and set
               to a box of the given box*/
void openwindow (window, buffer, fill)
     struct WINDOW *window;
     unsigned *buffer, fill;
{
     unsigned line, column, far *screenptr;

     /*first save the cursor and window info*/
     *buffer++ = h_pos;
     *buffer++ = v_pos;
     *buffer++ = windowwidth;
     *buffer++ = windowheight;
     *buffer++ = color;

     /*now save off the window and cover it with 'fill'*/
     for (line = window -> y0; line < window -> y1; line++) {
          screenptr = screen + ((line * width) + window -> x0);
          for (column = window -> x0; column < window ->x1;
                         column++, screenptr++, buffer++) {
               *buffer = *screenptr;
               *screenptr = fill;
          }
     }

     /*calculate new width and height*/
     h_pos = 0;
     v_pos = 0;
     windowwidth  = window -> x1 - window -> x0;
     windowheight = window -> y1 - window -> y0;
     color = fill & 0xff00;
}

/*Closewindow - restore the previously saved window to the screen*/
```

```
void closewindow (window, buffer)
     struct WINDOW *window;
     unsigned *buffer;
{
     unsigned line, column, far *screenptr;

     /*first restore the cursor position and screen dimensions*/
     h_pos = *buffer++;
     v_pos = *buffer++;
     windowwidth  = *buffer++;
     windowheight = *buffer++;
     color = *buffer++;

     /*now restore the window area of the screen*/
     for (line = window -> y0; line < window -> y1; line++) {
          screenptr = screen + ((line * width) + window -> x0);
          for (column = window -> x0; column < window ->x1; column++)
               *screenptr++ = *buffer++;
     }
}

/*WScroll - scroll current window up N lines*/

#define SCREENLOC(y,x) screen + ((width * (y + window -> y0)) \
                              +  (window -> x0 + x))

void wscroll (window, nlines)
    struct WINDOW *window;
    unsigned nlines;
{
    unsigned far *source, far *dest, number, i, j;

    if (nlines >= windowheight)
         nlines = windowheight;

    h_pos = 0;
    if ((v_pos += nlines) >= windowheight) {
         nlines = (v_pos - windowheight) + 1;

         /*scroll the screen up 'nlines' amount*/
         number = windowheight - nlines;
         for (i = 0; i < number; i++) {
              source = SCREENLOC (i + nlines, 0);
              dest   = SCREENLOC (i, 0);
              for (j = 0; j < windowwidth; j++)
                   *dest++ = *source++;
         }

         /*now blank the lines abandoned*/
         for (i = number; i < windowheight; i++)
              dest = SCREENLOC (i, 0);
              for (j = 0; j < windowwidth; j++)
                   *dest++ = color + 0x20;

         v_pos = windowheight - 1;
    }
}

/*Wprintf - output a string using the BIOS screen handler.  If
            an attribute is not provided, use the default.*/
void wprintf (window, c)
    struct WINDOW *window;
    char *c;
{
```

```
    unsigned far *sp;

    sp = SCREENLOC (v_pos, h_pos);
    for (; *c; c++)
         if (*c == '\n') {
              wscroll (window, 1);
              sp = SCREENLOC (v_pos, 0);
         }
         else
              if (h_pos < windowwidth) {
                   h_pos++;
                   *sp++ = color + *c;
              }
    wpcursor (window, v_pos, h_pos);
}

/*WPCursor - place the cursor at the current x and y location.*/
void wpcursor (window, y, x)
    struct WINDOW *window;
    unsigned x, y;
{
    v_pos = y;
    h_pos = x;

    regs.h.ah = setcursor;
    regs.h.bh = 0;
    regs.h.dh = v_pos + window -> y0;
    regs.h.dl = h_pos + window -> x0;
    int86 (0x10, &regs, &regs);
}

/*Init - set the screen address and clear the screen*/
void init ()
{
    short mode;

    regs.h.ah = getmode;
    int86 (0x10, &regs, &regs);
    mode = regs.h.al;

    /*we are only set up for 80 column widths...*/
    if (regs.h.ah != width)
         abort ();

    /*...and one of the character modes*/
    if (mode == 7)
         screen = mono;
    else
         if (mode == 3 || mode == 2)
              screen = cga;
         else
              abort ();

    /*now initialize the cursor and screen dimensions*/
    windowheight = height;
    windowwidth  = width;
    color = fwhite;
    h_pos = v_pos = 0;

    /*and clear the screen*/
    wscroll (&full, height);
    wpcursor (&full, 0, 0);
}
```

Figure 7.5

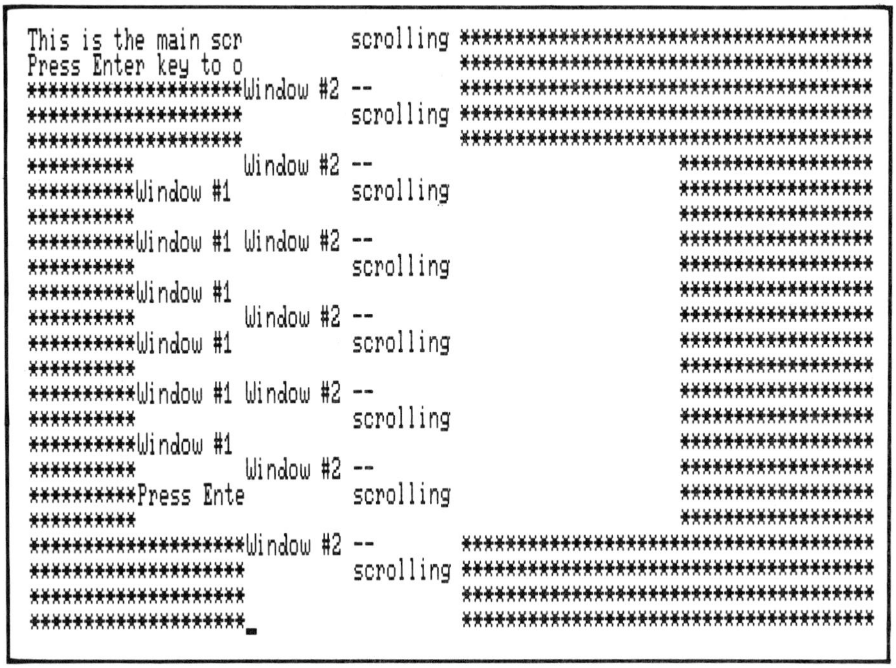

Two windows opened up by Prg7_5

Execute the program. Notice how the windows seem to appear almost instantaneously and how each window scrolls without disturbing the screen behind it. (The effect is much more striking on a color monitor.) What improvements could be made? Prg7_5 could easily be made to allow the windows to be panned about the screen. Not so easy is the task of allowing text to scroll behind a foreground window.

You can combine this concept of windows with that of pages already mentioned. As was pointed out before, you can write to pages other than page 0 using the offsets provided in Table 7.5. (This is most easily accomplished by adding the instructions *+PAGEOFFS[PAGE]* to the definition of *SCREENLOC*. In this definition, *PAGEOFFS* is a table of the offsets from Table 7.5, and *PAGE* is the current page.) The techniques are the same as those presented in Chapter 6 when discussing writing to pages using the screen interrupt. While one screen presents the operator with a menu, write the screens associated with each of the choices to the other pages. When the operator makes his decision, simply select the page containing the proper submenu.

In fact, now that you are expert in direct screen access, you can combine windowing with paging and direct screen to disk transfer to create a veritable managerie of colors and effects.

Conclusion

Programmers should not write programs which access the PC's hardware directly for no reason. Not only can it lead to programs that are difficult to port to other machines, but it can lead to programs which don't even port among other members of the PC family. Direct access to the underlying hardware can sometimes be justified by the increased performance it brings, both in terms of effects and throughput.

In Chapter 8, we take a slightly different tack and begin to examine techniques we can use to speed up programs in other ways.

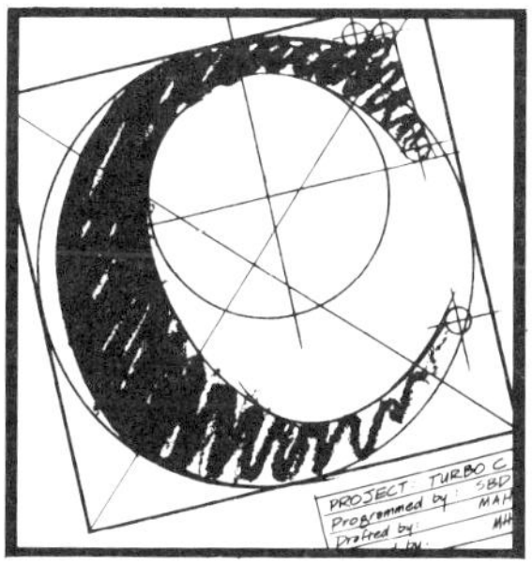

8 Maximum Performance

One of the sexiest topics in advanced programming texts is that of program performance. Something of a software machismo surrounds the entire field. People add accelerator cards to their personal computers to increase performance. Magazines rate software performance, in some cases to two *significant* digits. Suites of benchmarks are devised to measure the speed of machines and compilers—winners of such comparisons invariably feature that fact predominantly in their advertising. Just as with cars, it's not a question of fast enough to do the job; faster is better, period.

Although overblown, not all such concern over performance is frivolous. Specifications for large, professional software systems stipulate not only what the program is supposed to do, but how fast it is able to do it. There is no sense in providing the answer if the user has forgotten the question out of boredom.

To a real extent, this entire book has been devoted to producing efficient, compact software. Many writers chastise readers not to worry about program performance. To them, legibility and machine independence are the only concerns. I have taken the approach that the underlying machine should be considered, at least peripherally, at every step. Following good programming practices usually results in programs that are both legible and reasonably swift. But what if you follow good programming techniques and your program still doesn't run fast enough or is too large to fit into existing memory? What can be done?

One answer is to make use of assembly language programming. Even though Turbo C is very good at generating assembly language from C source statements, all compilers suffer from a problem: they are generalists. When a particular C construct appears, compilers must convert it into machine instructions that work in every case where that construct might legally appear. Compilers understand the individual C statements, but not their underlying meaning.

Human programmers understand the context (hopefully!) of their assembly language. As a result, they can generate more intelligent code that uses fewer instructions. The particular instruction sequence may not work in every case, but it works in this case and that's what is important. An experienced assembly language programmer can out perform a compiler in generating code for a small function, on the average about two to one in terms of both size and speed.

People who build microprocessors are engineers. As engineers, they enjoy packing in as much capability as possible. In addition to the mundane types of instructions, most microprocessors include a few special purpose instructions. It is very difficult for compilers to use these *trick* instructions, since thaey require some understanding of the context of the problem. Additionally, the number of applications for some of these instructions is quite small, so that it doesn't pay to spend a lot of effort in the compiler design to generate them. When human programmers can use such special purpose instructions to solve their problems, the savings can be dramatic. We will examine such a case later in this chapter.

So how do you know whether it will be worthwhile to write some functions in assembly language and how do you know which ones? This question can't usually be answered at the beginning of a program. A programmer can't easily examine a program design and point out the memory or time hogs at a glance. Even careful analysis may not make the answer obvious.

The best approach is to forget the question in the beginning. Formulate the best design possible and code the entire program in C. Turbo C might surprise you with what it can do. The program might be fast enough and small enough the first time. If it isn't, those places that need performance improvement will usually be obvious. A few minutes behind the keyboard of a working prototype can give a programmer a better feel for performance problems than weeks of analysis on paper.

If a module must be rewritten later in assembly language, the programmer has a block diagram in the form of a working C routine of what the function is supposed to do. The inputs and outputs are already defined as well. When it comes time to debug this function—always a difficult task with assembly language—the programmer has a working program surrounding the routine. Problems which arise can reasonably be attributed to the new assembly function. This simplifies the debug job immensely.

In larger jobs, it is almost as important that the other members of the project already have a working program with which to continue their efforts. This all-C version may not be as fast as required, but at least it works. This helps to give the assembly programmer the extra time needed to get more time critical routines functioning properly.

Sometimes it isn't even necessary to write assembler routines from scratch. Taking the assembly output of the Turbo C compiler and optimizing it manually, a practice known as hand optimizing, can result in appreciably faster code.

The programmer should not be too quick to reach for assembly language. There are plenty of tools in the Turbo C arsenal for optimizing programs. Rewriting a well written C module into a slightly less clear but quicker routine may be all that is required. Assembly language should be a last resort, to be used when all other approaches have failed.

(*Note*: The number of C statements is not the only determining factor in either the overall performance or the overall size of the resulting program. I have seen programmers combine multiple source statements into one very large statement, thinking that this will execute faster since it results in *few statements*. What counts is not the number of source statements, but the number of machine instructions they generate.)

Execution Speed

There are several techniques that can be used to speed up routines in Turbo C. Some of these will work in all languages, some are specific to the C language, and some are specific to Turbo C. Let's consider a few.

One older but more effective trick is that of saving common expressions. The idea here is to not perform the same work over and over. For example, suppose we are transforming a point specified by the coordinates *X1, Y1* into another frame of reference rotated by some angle *W* and we wish to calculate the new coordinates *X2, Y2*. The equation for such a transformation is:

```
X2 = X1 cos W + Y1 sin W

Y2 = -X1 sin W + Y1 cos W
```

This can be implemented using the following C routine:

```
void xform (omega, x1, y1, x2, y2)
      float omega, *x1, *y1, *x2, *y2;
{
```

```
        *x2 =  *x1 * cos (omega) + *y1 * sin (omega);
        *y2 = -*x1 * sin (omega) + *y1 * cos (omega);
}
```

Although straightforward, this is not the best that we can do. In the above program, the sine and cosine of omega are calculated twice. The following routine will perform faster with identical results:

```
 void xform (omega, x1, y1, x2, y2)
        float omega, *x1, *y1, *x2, *y2;
{
       float tcos, tsin;

       *x2 =  *x1 * (tcos = cos (omega)) +
              *y1 * (tsin = sin(omega));
       *y2 = -*x1 * tsin + *y1 * tcos;
}
```

Further gains can be made by making use the power of C. Although they might have the same effect, the following three constructs do not necessarily generate the same number of machine instructions.

```
i = i + 1;          /*the normal form*/
i += 1;              /*the assignment operator form*/
i++;                 /*the autoincrement*/
```

Use the simplest construct available to you. Assignment operators almost always generate less code than the *normal* form of the same instruction and autoincrement even less.

C also allows the operator to define a variable to be stored permanently in a machine register via a register declaration. Since microprocessors can access their registers much faster than memory, declaring an often used variable to be register can save a lot of machine cycles with no effort on the part of the programmer. Turbo C allows a function to define up to two register variables. Subsequent register declarations are treated the same as automatic declarations. Register variables can only be of type integer.

Using register variables in Turbo C might not have as great an effect as you might think, however. Since Turbo C is an optimizing compiler, it attempts to keep often used values loaded into the cache registers *SI* and *DI* (unless register optimization has been turned off in the *Options* menu). Declaring a register variable deprives Turbo C of a register in which to keep active values. Making an unwise choice of register variable can result in a slower executing program.

To demonstrate this, let us examine Prg8_1, the famous *Sieve of Eratosthenes* computer benchmark. This benchmark is ideal because it is highly computational and does not use many variables.

```
/*Prg8_1 - The Sieve of Eratosthenes Prime Number Program
    adapted from  Byte Magazine, January 1983.

  This is the classic, non-floating point benchmark.  Although
  no benchmark can do it all, the Sieve measures how well a
  machine can access and manipulate integer data.  In our case,
  we will use it to measure the effect of register variables and
  register optimization in Turbo C.
*/

#include <stdio.h>
#include <stdlib.h>

#define TRUE     1
#define FALSE    0
#define ITER     10
#define SIZE     8190

/*define our Boolean sieve*/
char flags [SIZE+1];

/*Main - the sieve program*/
main () {
    /*register*/ int i,k;
    /*register*/ int iter, count;

    printf ("%d iterations.  "
             "Hit enter and start stop watch\n", ITER);
    getchar ();
    printf ("Start...");

    for (iter = 1; iter <= ITER; iter++) {
         count = 0;
         for (i = 0; i <= SIZE; i++)       /*init flags true*/
              flags[i] = TRUE;

         for (i = 2; i <= SIZE; i++)
              if (flags[i]) {               /*found a prime*/
                   for ( k = i + i; k <= SIZE; k += i )
                        flags[k] = FALSE; /*cancel multiples*/
                   count++;
              }
    }

    printf ("stop!\n\n%d primes\n", count);
}
```

I have benchmarked this program in various modes and compiled the results in Table 8.1 for comparison. Several cases were considered: 1) no register variables declared, but Turbo C allowed any register optimizations it could make; 2) cleverly declared register variables (*I* and *K*); 3) unfavorably declared register variables (*ITER* and *COUNT*); 4) no register variables declared and no register optimization allowed.

Table 8.1

Register optimization On -		
1)	- no register variables declared	6.1 sec
2)	- register i, k	6.1 "
3)	- register iter, count	11.8 "
4) Register optimization Off -		11.8 "

Notice the similarity in times between cases 1 and 2. Since *I* and *K* are being used so often and in such a tight loop, Turbo C tends to cache these variables into registers, so that the register declaration does not help as much as you might think it would.

On the other hand, declaring infrequently accessed variables to be of register type can adversely affect performance. This case shows identical times with that of no register optimization at all! By declaring *ITER* and *COUNT* to be register variables, Turbo C is deprived of the two cache registers for its own use. It cannot cache *I* and *K* by itself, as in case 1, because these registers were already in use. From a performance standpoint, case 3 and case 4 are identical.

Even without declaring variables to be register, some improvement can be gained by declaring them to be external by defining them outside of any function. Locally declared automatic variables are stored on the stack, whereas globally defined variables are assigned a fixed location in memory. The address of stack variables must be calculated by the microprocessor each time the variable is accessed. This calculation is very quick in the 80186, 80286 and 80386 processors with their address calculation hardware; it is not so quick on the 8086 with its microcoded subroutines. If reentrancy is not a problem, declaring a variable globally can speed up execution on 8086 and 8088 based machines.

This is also true for arguments to functions, especially if they are complex. The same improvements can be gained by transferring arguments to globally declared variables. Saving off array and structure elements can avoid even more time consuming address calculations being performed more than once. These are probably minor savings, unless the code section is within a loop of some kind.

Turbo C has some of its own offerings in the Options menu. One of the biggest improvements is in the selection of memory model. Always select the smallest memory model capable of performing the task. Far pointers are 32 bits in length, whereas near pointers are only 16-bits. Using a smaller memory model avoids the overhead of loading double word addresses if the smaller address will do. This goes for both program and data addresses. Remember that it is not necessary to use the large memory model just because one pointer variable must be of type *FAR*. Declare the specific variable to be *FAR* and let the rest default to *NEAR*.

Allow Turbo C to generate 186 instructions if possible. The 8086 and 8088 microprocessors are the oldest members of the 86 processor family. Later members, such as the 80186, 80286 and 80386, include instructions which the older members do not have. Some of these new instructions can replace several of the older instructions at a considerable savings in time. Although Turbo C Version 1.0 will generate neither 80286 nor 80386 specific instructions, it will use the 80186 specific instructions, which both of the other chips understand.

Of course, including 80186 specific instructions means that the resulting program won't run on a PC equipped with the earlier 8086 and 8088 microprocessors. However, if you know that a particular program is only going to be executed on a 186 based machine or on a PC AT type machine with its 80286, then selecting the 186 option can result in a faster executing program. (The new NEC V20 and V30 processors can execute most of the 186 instructions, so they can probably handle programs compiled with the 186 option.)

All members of the 8086 family, except the 8088 and little used 80188, access memory in 16 bit chunks. The processor hardware can only access words on even addresses. Whenever a word of memory happens to fall on an odd address, the processor must actually make two memory fetches. It loads one word to get one byte and then loads the next word to get the other byte. To avoid this double load, Turbo C can be instructed to automatically insure that variables declared to be one word or larger are allocated on even byte boundaries. This is done by selecting *Word Alignment* in the Compiler *Options* menu. This results in slightly better perfomance on 16 bit bussed machines. The 8088 based machines, such as the IBM PC, must always perform two memory fetches per word so this option has no effect on their performance.

To increase the numerical performance of its line of microprocessors, Intel built the 8087 and functionally equivalent 80287 *Numerical Data Processors* (NDP). These NDPs internally perform various floating point functions, such as tangent and logarithms. Turbo C can properly instruct the NDP to carry out floating point (float and double) calculations. For use in computers not equipped with an NDP, Turbo C includes an emulation library which emulates the function of the numerical processor using normal 8086 instructions. This emulation library executes slower than the NDP instructions. Consider the standard matrix multiply benchmark below:

```
/*Prg8_2 - Floating point benchmark
  by Stephen R. Davis

  The matrix multiply is something of a floating point
  performance standard.  The size may be varied at will, but
  the default is 50 x 50.  To execute this program without
  using the 8087 in a machine equipped with one, issue the
  DOS command SET 87=N before starting.  SET 87=Y will reenable
  the 8087.
*/

#include <stdio.h>
#include <stdlib.h>

#define msize 50

/*define our data requirements*/
unsigned i, j, k;
float x [msize][msize], y [msize][msize], z[msize][msize];
double accum;

/*Main - perform the benchmark*/
main ()
{
    /*begin by initializing the matrices*/
    printf ("Initializing matrices\n");
    for (i = 0; i < msize; i++)
        for (j = 0; j < msize; j++) {
            x [i][j] = rand () / 10000.;
            y [i][j] = rand () / 10000.;
        }

    /*now begin the benchmark*/
    printf ("Enter return and start stop watch at same time\n");
    getchar ();
    printf ("Start...");

    for (i = 0; i < msize; i++)
        for (j = 0; j < msize; j++) {
            accum = 0;
            for (k = 0; k < msize; k++)
                accum += x [i][k] * y [k][j];
            z [i][j] = accum;
        }

     printf ("stop!\n");
}
```

Without an 8087 present, a 4.77 MHz IBM PC required a whopping 436 seconds to multiply a 50 x 50 floating point matrix. With an 8087 NDP, the same machine required 26.3 seconds, some 16 times as quick. (Prg8_2 was convinced to use or ignore the 8087 present in my machine by using the DOS commands *SET 87=Y* and *SET 87=N*, respectively.) Adding an 8087 or 80287 NDP to the target machine will improve floating point performance many fold.

An executable program generated by Turbo C does not normally know whether an NDP is present or not when it is first executed. The first time a floating point operation is performed, the library tests for the NDP's presence. If present, the library uses it. If not, it emulates it. This test requires some time. If it is known that the target machine has an NDP installed, the test can be avoided by selecting the 8087 library in the options menu. This library will not perform any tests, resulting in only slightly improved floating point performance. This measure is more worthwhile as a space savings measure, as the straight NDP library does not include the emulation software. This option is selected from the options menu.

The same effect can be achieved in programs already linked with the normal emulation library by executing the DOS command *SET 87=Y* before executing the program. The presences of the 87 variable in the environment suppresses the test for an NDP. The programmer should be careful, however. Executing a program intended for an NDP in a machine not equipped with a numerical processor will result in a system crash requiring a complete reboot.

While on the subject of floating point operations, I should mention that C has a peculiarity which can cost the unsuspecting programmer a lot of performance. Float is not a resolution type—double is. This means that calculations between single precision floating point values are actually performed in double precision. The following C statement actually performs 3 conversions:

```
float a, b, c;

a = b * c;
```

First *B* and *C* are converted to double and the multiplication is carried out. The resulting double precision values are then converted back to single precision and stored in the variable *A*. These automatic type conversions can result in a significant performance degradation in floating point operation, especially if an NDP is not present. Whenever possible, declare floating point variables to be double to avoid these conversions.

Some optimization techniques, especially those contained in older texts, are not helpful, however. These suggestions were intended for the non-optimizing compilers of earlier years. For example, Turbo C automatically resolves constant expressions at compile time so that multiplying out constants in expressions yourself does not increase performance at all. Similarly, rearranging arithmetic expressions to reduce the number of multiplies is also not effective, again because, Turbo C performs these optimizations itself.

Assembly Language Optimizations

When these techniques still don't sufficiently increase performance, it may be necessary to resort to the use of assembly language. Fortunately, statistics show that in the typical program, 10 percent of all code is executed 90 percent of the time. Restated, this means that most of the C code in any given program is only occasionally executed. Therefore, it is not necessary to recode the entire program in assembly language. Significant improvement can only be gained by recoding those routines which are executed a significant percentage of the time. Consider the following case:

```
Module A  -  100 msec     10 times      =  1,000 msec
Module B  -  100 msec      1 time       =    100 msec
Module C  -   10 msec     10 times      =    100 msec
                                          -------------
                                Total   =  1,200 msec
```

This program consists of three modules. Modules A and C are executed 10 times, each iteration requiring the length of time specified. Module B is executed once. From this we see that the total execution time for the program is 1.2 seconds. It is also clear from these figures that it would be a waste of time to attempt to optimize either Module B or C to affect overall performance.

Suppose that through clever use of assembly language, we were able to make Module B twice as fast, reducing its execution time from 100 msec to 50 msec. This would only reduce the execution time by the same 50 msec from 1.2 seconds to 1.15 seconds, less than a 5 percent improvement! The same is true for Module C. Only efforts at reducing Module A's execution time will show any significant results. Doubling its speed would drop the program's execution time by 500 msec from 1.2 to 0.7 seconds, an improvement of 42 percent.

How does the programmer decide which modules are taking up most of the time? Sometimes examination of the C source code will reveal the culprits. This examination can be augmented by examining the executing program (another reason for completing the program first). Those areas which are executing quickly enough need no further inspection; concentrate on those areas which appear to have problems.

When simple inspection does not solve the problem, it may be necessary to examine the machine code generated by the C source code. The command line version of Turbo C, TCC, is very helpful. By including the –B switch during compilation, TCC can be coaxed into providing an optional assembly language output. It is often not easy to decide which assembly statements go with which

C source statements. In this case, however, TCC includes the source code line number as a comment in front of the assembly it generated. These line numbers match the line numbers generated by the C pretty print format program used throughout this book, Prg3_1.

Not all microprocessor instructions execute in the same amount of time. An 8086 processor can move a value from one register to another more than 100 times faster than it can execute an integer division. *Appendix 4* includes a list of the 8086 instructions followed by their execution times. Instruction times are measured in units called clock cycles. To convert clock time, divide the number of clock cycles by the clock rate of your machine (4.77 million in the case of the IBM PC). Comparisons of execution time are often left in units of clock cycles.

Be sure that the numbers you have are those for your machine. Different members of the 8086 processor family execute the same instructions in different numbers of clock cycles. Appendix 4 includes the times for different members of the processor family.

As an example, I have broken down our direct screen write program generated in Chapter 7 (Prg7_4a) into numbers of machine cycles on an 8088 equipped machine. In performing these analyses, one must take a *typical* example. In my case, I assumed a 40 character string being output to the bottom of a 25 line by 80 column display, requiring the display to be scrolled up one line. My base microprocessor is the 8088. The results appear below.

routine/line numbers	# cycles	# loops	total cycles
scroll			
75 - 89	578	1	578 (0%)
90 - 91	216	1,920	414,720 (96%)
92 - 95	240	1	240 (0%)
96 - 97	98	80	7,840 (2%)
99 -101	70	1	70 (0%)
qprintf			
102 -113	300	1	300 (0%)
114 -122	120	40	10,000 (2%)
121 -123	144	1	144 (0%)
		Total =	433,892

numbers of clock cycles to output a single 40 character string using qprintf() and scroll an 80 x 25 screen 1 row using scroll(). Does not include time to reposition cursor using BIOS routine.

To save space, I have not broken out the numbers for each separate instruction. Instead, I have added up the clock cycles for each stretch of code. Code contained within loops has been broken out separately and the average number of times through the loop has been used as a multiplier.

We see that it does not pay to worry too much about routines that are called only once, no matter how complicated they might be, when other routines are being executed many hundreds or thousands of times. Too many times programmers expend heroic effort to shrink the execution time of some particularly slow module, only to find that it has little or no effect on overall performance.

In this case, *scroll()* is consuming the lion's share of the execution time, and, more specifically, just the scroll operation itself (lines 92–93). Although this loop is quite short—only some 7 machine instructions—it must be executed for each column of each line, some 1,920 times (= 80 x 24).

(In reality, the situation is even worse than pictured. Access to the display memory invariably involves contention with the CRT controller chip, resulting in a large number of memory wait states. There is, unfortunately, nothing that can be done to rectify this problem.)

Occasionally, this type of analysis cannot be performed. Usually this is because not all of the source code is available to the programmer. Even in the rather simple analysis above, it was not possible to include the code executed to place the cursor at the end of the string because the BIOS listings were not available. Even if they had been, it would have been different for other display adapters. Since the cursor positioning code is only executed once per line, it was relatively safe to ignore its contribution to the overall throughput. Had there been any doubt, however, the routine *pcursor()* could have been completely commented out during the analysis.

The BIOS version of this same program would be impossible to analyze in this way without detailed listings of the screen output BIOS routines. Occasionally we can analyze programs which make a large number of BIOS or DOS calls by a process known as *selective removal.* We begin by measuring the performance of the program. We then remove or stub out each major module of the program in turn, measuring the performance of the resulting system. Removing the most time-consuming module will result in the greatest overall improvement. This technique is only possible when the individual modules are loosely coupled so that removing one does not so adversely affect the others that statistics become meaningless.

When these techniques fail, it is necessary to resort to commerically available software profilers. Profilers work in several different ways, but all help to give the programmer an accurate view of where the software is spending the majority of its time and, thus, where improvements should be made. However, unlike the pen and paper analysis above, profilers give no clue as to what improvements should be made.

A profiler might indicate that a program is spending all of its time in the operating system. This might indicate that the operating system is the weak link in the performance chain or, more likely, that some section of code is invoking the operating system too often. Perhaps some program is going to the disk more than it needs to. In this case, the profiler will not show the actual offender, since the amount of time it takes to make a disk call is very short. Only a hand analysis of the user program can show the reasons, but a profiler can put you on the right track.

Inline Assembly Code

Once you have decided which sections of code need optimizing with assembly language, the question becomes a matter of how. There are two options open to the Turbo C programmer, each with its own advantages. The first is inline assembly. In this technique, assembly code is inserted directly into the object output of the Turbo C compiler by use of the ASM directive.

Normally, the Turbo C compiler inspects each succeeding C source statement and converts it into the equivalent assembly language instructions, which it places in the *.OBJ* file output. The ASM directive allows users to write their own assembly statements to be inserted among those generated by Turbo C. Time critical sections of C functions can be handwritten for efficiency using inline assembly without the need to resort to writing separate assembly language modules.

Inline assembly is only indicated when there is a particularly good reason, such as a particular routine using up a large amount of time. The other justification for inline assembly is when a particular instruction or set of instructions is well adapted to your problem. Analysis of the assembly generated by Turbo C from Prg7_4a showed that the scroll operation was by far the largest user of time. It also showed, however, that with only seven instructions generated, there may not be too much that can be done to optimize this code section. This might be the case were it not for the existence of the 8086 string instructions.

The string instructions are designed to manipulate large blocks of memory. They can scan a large block for a particular value, compare two blocks, initialize a block or move a block of memory. It is these last two capabilities which are ideal for our needs. The block move instruction can perform the scroll move in fewer clock cycles than Prg7_4a's *FOR* loop.

Of course, the good people at Borland have not been asleep. It did not go unnoticed that such a useful instruction was hiding in the 8086 instruction set. Even though it would have been ideal, it would have been very difficult to make the compiler so smart that it generated the block move instruction automatically when it saw the first *FOR* loop or the set block instruction for the second. Instead, Turbo C includes the library routines *movmem()* and *setmem()* which specifically provides access to these instructions to the Turbo C programmer.

This is a specific example of the "don't be too quick to use assembly" principle. By making use of these documented and debugged library routines, we can get the benefits of the assembly language instructions without the difficulties. An example of Prg7_4a rewritten to use the library routine appears below as Prg8_3a.

```
/*Prg8_3a - High Speed Screen Output
  by Stephen R Davis, 1987

  Perform direct screen output by accessing screen memory directly
  via the screen pointer 'screen'.  Scroll using the movmem()
  library function which uses the 8086 block move instruction (this
  must be compiled under the compact or large memory models).
*/

#include <stdio.h>
#include <dos.h>
#include <stdlib.h>
#include <mem.h>

#define cga  (unsigned far *)0xb8000000 /*same for ega*/
#define mono (unsigned far *)0xb0000000
#define space 0x20
#define attrib 0x07
#define screenheight 25

/*add the screen BIOS functions*/
#define scrollup 0x06
#define setcursor 0x02
#define writetele 0x0e
#define getmode 0x0f

/*define global variables*/
unsigned v_pos, h_pos, screenwidth;
union REGS regs;
unsigned far *screen;                    /*screen pointer*/

/*test to make sure that we are under Compact or Large
  memory models*/

```

```
[ 0]: #if sizeof (screen) - sizeof (int *)
[ 0]: #error Must compile under Compact or Large memory models
[ 0]: #endif
[ 0]:
[ 0]: /*prototype declarations*/
[ 0]: void init (void);
[ 0]: void scroll (unsigned);
[ 0]: void qprintf (char *);
[ 0]: void pcursor (unsigned, unsigned);
[ 0]:
[ 0]: /*Main - test the output routines*/
[ 0]: int main ()
[ 0]: {
[ 1]:     int i, j;
[ 1]:
[ 1]:     init ();
[ 1]:     for (i = 0; i < 20; i++) {
[ 2]:          for (j = 0; j < screenheight; j++) {
[ 3]:               qprintf ("this is BIOS output");
[ 3]:               pcursor(v_pos, 30+j);
[ 3]:               qprintf ("and this\n");
[ 2]:          }
[ 2]:          for (j = 0; j < screenheight; j++)
[ 2]:               printf ("this is normal printf output\n");
[ 1]:     }
[ 0]: }
[ 0]:
[ 0]: /*Init - set the screen address and clear the screen*/
[ 0]: void init ()
[ 0]: {
[ 1]:     short mode;
[ 1]:
[ 1]:     regs.h.ah = getmode;
[ 1]:     int86 (0x10, &regs, &regs);
[ 1]:     mode = regs.h.al;
[ 1]:     screenwidth = regs.h.ah;
[ 1]:
[ 1]:     if (mode == 7)
[ 1]:          screen = mono;
[ 1]:     else
[ 1]:          if (mode == 3 || mode == 2)
[ 1]:               screen = cga;
[ 1]:          else
[ 1]:               abort ();
[ 1]:
[ 1]:     scroll (screenheight);
[ 1]:     pcursor (0, 0);
[ 0]: }
[ 0]:
[ 0]: /*Scroll - scroll up N lines using function 6*/
[ 0]: void scroll (nlines)
[ 0]:     unsigned nlines;
[ 0]: {
[ 1]:     unsigned far *source, far *dest, number, i;
[ 1]:
[ 1]:     if (nlines >= screenheight)
[ 1]:          nlines = screenheight;
[ 1]:
[ 1]:     h_pos = 0;
[ 1]:     if ((v_pos += nlines) >= screenheight) {
[ 2]:          nlines = (v_pos - screenheight) + 1;
[ 2]:
[ 2]:          /*scroll the screen up 'nlines' amount*/
[ 2]:          source = screen + (nlines * screenwidth);
```

```
         dest = screen;
         number = (screenheight - nlines) * screenwidth;
         movmem (source, dest, number << 2);

         /*now blank the lines abandoned*/
         dest = screen + number;
         number = nlines * screenwidth;

       /*setmem (dest, number << 2, 0); /*messes up 'normal' scroll*/
         for (i = 0; i < number; i++)
              *dest++ = attrib << 8;

         v_pos = screenheight - 1;
    }
}

/*Qprintf - output a string using the BIOS screen handler.  If
            an attribute is not provided, use the default.*/
#define SCREENLOC screen + ((screenwidth * v_pos) + h_pos)
void qprintf (c)
    char *c;
{
    unsigned far *sp;

    sp = SCREENLOC;
    for (; *c; c++)
         if (*c == '\n') {
              scroll (1);
              sp = SCREENLOC;
         }
         else {
              if (h_pos++ < screenwidth)
                   *sp++ = (attrib << 8) + *c;
         }
    pcursor (v_pos, h_pos);
}

/*PCursor - place the cursor at the current x and y location.
            To place the cursor, and subsequent output, to any
            arbitrary location, set 'v_pos' and 'h_pos' before
            calling pcursor.*/
void pcursor (y, x)
    unsigned x, y;
{
    v_pos = y;
    h_pos = x;

    regs.h.ah = setcursor;
    regs.h.bh = 0;
    regs.h.dh = v_pos;
    regs.h.dl = h_pos;
    int86 (0x10, &regs, &regs);
}
```

This program is very similar to its parent, both in principle and structure. Only the specific *FOR* loops have been replaced by the appropriate library routines.

The *FOR* loops were copying integers which are 2 bytes in length. Since *movemem()* and *setmem()* accept the number of bytes to move instead of the number of integers, the variable *NUMBER* has been shifted left by 1 bit.

The address being passed to these routines is *SCREEN*, which is a *FAR* pointer. To insure that *movmem()* and *setmem()* accept *FAR* pointers as their arguments, Prg8_3a must be compiled under either the compact or the large memory model. Because they default all data pointers to large, the libraries for these models accept *FAR* data pointers. To enforce this, we have used the same trick as in Prg7_3, comparing the *SIZEOF* a default pointer to a known value.

Try executing Prg7_4a and Prg8_3a back to back. Despite their similarities, Prg8_3a is quicker than its predecessor. Our analysis was correct. We improved performance by use of the block move routines.

Okay, so maybe this isn't fair. We were lucky that the Turbo C library had just the routine we needed, but it wasn't all luck. The routines exist because the block instructions are so useful. Had they not existed, the library routines would not have existed, but then the benefits of assembly language for this application would not have been nearly so great. This fits with our assertion that assembly language is usually not necessary. But what if these library routines did not exist? How might we have generated our own inline code to make use of the block instructions?

The actual mechanism for inserting inline assembly is pretty clumsy by Turbo C standards. The normal interactive Turbo C, TC, cannot handle inline assembly (at least not in Version 1.0). So we must resort to the clumsier command line version of the compiler, TCC. Since we will already have gotten the first pass of our program up and running without inline assembly, we will only have the relatively small section of inline assembly to get working with TCC.

Inline assembly is indicated by the Turbo C directive ASM, followed by a single assembly language statement. It is conventional to place each ASM directive on a separate line and to not follow them by a semicolon. Assembly statements may be followed by comments.

Turbo C understands the normal Intel mnemonics for the 8086 instructions. Fortunately, it is not necessary to worry how to reference Turbo C variables, as they are automatically referenced. (This was a major problem in using the INLINE directive in Turbo Pascal.) The following demonstrates the problem:

```
unsigned count;
void proc ();
{
     unsigned index;
```

```
asm mov count,10          /*init count*/
asm mov ax,index          /*and load up index*/
    .
    .
    .
```

By virtue of one variable having been declared globally and the other locally, *COUNT* and *INDEX* are not accessed from assembly language in the same way. One is stored on the stack and the other in direct memory. Fortunately, the user of inline assembly doesn't have to worry with this problem. Turbo C makes the necessary additions to properly access the two different variables.

Unfortunately, Version 1.0 of Turbo C has no built-in assembler. The output from TCC is not a normal object file, but rather an assembly language source code. TCC will automatically generate this source file when it first encounters an ASM directive, but it must restart compiling from the beginning to generate the assembly source code for C statements already encountered. To avoid this waste of time, the user should include the *–B* switch in the command line. This tells TCC that ASM statements appear in the C source file being compiled and that it should compile assembly source statement from the very beginning.

(Hackers might be curious at the output generated by the *–B* option. Even programs containing no ASM directives may be compiled with this switch (or the *–S*) to generate an assembly source file. It is interesting to see how various C constructs are decoded into 8086 instructions.)

One problem with this method, however, is that the resulting assembly source file must then be assembled to get the *.OBJ* file, which we must have to link. Borland specifies Microsoft's Macro Assembler (MASM) Version 3.0 or later. Since MASM is the default standard assember in the IBM PC world, there are several assemblers which are MASM compatible. Even some assemblers in the public domain are reasonably MASM compatible. Many of these will assemble the output of TCC -B, but to be effective an assembler must at least support the *GROUP* and *SEGMENT* directives. Extensive macro capability does not seem to be a consideration.

Once the compilation is complete, TCC will automatically attempt to execute MASM. If it cannot find MASM, it will generate an error message. This is not a problem, however, as the user can manually execute MASM on the assembly source file generated. In fact, this manual method might be preferable since it allows the user to pass any desired switches to the assembler, such as directing the creation of a listing file or inclusion of line numbers in the *.OBJ* file. The

.OBJ file created in this manner is normally linked using either the Microsoft LINK or Borland TLINK linkers.

Debugging inline assembly presents its own unique problems. Assembly language is more finicky than C and always more difficult to debug. The hybrid of C and inline assembly language together is even worse. The debug process is complicated by the multiple step compilation process, which greatly slows turnaround time. This makes it even more important that a 100 percent C version of the program be completely debugged before attempting the inline sections. Inline code is hard enough to get working, even when the remaining C program works. If the C program has problems of its own, it is virtually impossible.

To debug inline assembly, you will need an assembly language debugger, such as DEBUG, which is supplied with DOS. A debugger with symbolic capability is helpful, but not required. You should first print out a copy of the assembly source generated by TCC or the listing file of the same which MASM created. Follow this with the C source listing generated from our pretty print program. Cross reference the C source line numbers with those contained in the assembly program comments.

In order to find your way around the *.EXE* file, you should be certain that you generate a load map during the link step. Instructions for using TLINK are contained in the Turbo C User's Guide. LINK generates a load map if a name other than NULL is provided to the load map question. It may be helpful to include line numbers in the load map by using the */LI* switch. If you have any experience debugging assembly programs, you should have little problem finding your way equipped with these listings.

Prg8_3b is our same old screen writing program, rewritten to use inline assembly to perform the critical block move and block clear operations. Once again, notice how similar Prg8_3b is to its predecessors. Only the two critical operations have been converted to assembly code.

```
/*Prg8_3b - High Speed Screen Output
  by Stephen R Davis, 1987

  Perform direct screen output by accessing screen memory directly
  via the screen pointer 'screen'.  Scroll using the 8086 block
  move instruction using the #asm directive.
*/

#include <stdio.h>
#include <dos.h>
#include <stdlib.h>
#include <mem.h>

```

```
#define cga  (unsigned far *)0xb8000000 /*same for ega*/
#define mono (unsigned far *)0xb0000000
#define space 0x20
#define attrib 0x07
#define screenheight 25

/*add the screen BIOS functions*/
#define scrollup 0x06
#define setcursor 0x02
#define writetele 0x0e
#define getmode 0x0f

/*define global variables*/
unsigned v_pos, h_pos, screenwidth;
union REGS regs;
unsigned far *screen;                    /*screen pointer*/

/*prototype declarations*/
void init (void);
void scroll (unsigned);
void qprintf (char *);
void pcursor (unsigned, unsigned);

/*Main - test the output routines*/
int main ()
{
    int i, j;

    init ();
    for (i = 0; i < 20; i++) {
         for (j = 0; j < screenheight; j++) {
              qprintf ("this is BIOS output");
              pcursor(v_pos, 30+j);
              qprintf ("and this\n");
         }
         for (j = 0; j < screenheight; j++)
              printf ("this is normal printf output\n");
    }
}

/*Init - set the screen address and clear the screen*/
void init ()
{
    short mode;

    regs.h.ah = getmode;
    int86 (0x10, &regs, &regs);
    mode = regs.h.al;
    screenwidth = regs.h.ah;

    if (mode == 7)
         screen = mono;
    else
         if (mode == 3 || mode == 2)
              screen = cga;
         else
              abort ();

    scroll (screenheight);
    pcursor (0, 0);
}

/*Scroll - scroll up N lines using function 6*/
void scroll (nlines)
```

```
    unsigned nlines;
{
    unsigned far *source, far *dest, number;

    if (nlines >= screenheight)
         nlines = screenheight;

    h_pos = 0;
    if ((v_pos += nlines) >= screenheight) {
         nlines = (v_pos - screenheight) + 1;

         /*scroll the screen up 'nlines' amount*/
         source = screen + (nlines * screenwidth);
         dest = screen;
         number = (screenheight - nlines) * screenwidth;

         asm push ds
         asm mov dx,si                /*not necessary to store...*/
         asm mov bx,di                /*...si and di with -Z switch*/
         asm les di,dest
         asm lds si,source
         asm mov cx,number
         asm cld
         asm rep movsw
         asm pop ds
         asm mov si,dx
         asm mov di,bx

         /*now blank the lines abandoned*/
         dest = screen + number;
         number = nlines * screenwidth;

         asm mov ax,0700H
         asm mov bx,di
         asm les di,dest
         asm mov cx,number
         asm rep stosw
         asm mov di,bx

         v_pos = screenheight - 1;
    }
}

/*Qprintf - output a string using the BIOS screen handler.  If
               an attribute is not provided, use the default.*/
#define SCREENLOC screen + ((screenwidth * v_pos) + h_pos)
void qprintf (c)
    char *c;
{
    unsigned far *sp;

    sp = SCREENLOC;
    for (; *c; c++)
         if (*c == '\n') {
              scroll (1);
              sp = SCREENLOC;
         }
         else {
              if (h_pos++ < screenwidth)
                   *sp++ = (attrib << 8) + *c;
         }
    pcursor (v_pos, h_pos);
}

```

```
142[ 0]: /*PCursor - place the cursor at the current x and y location.
143[ 0]:              To place the cursor, and subsequent output, to any
144[ 0]:              arbitrary location, set 'v_pos' and 'h_pos' before
145[ 0]:              calling pcursor.*/
146[ 0]: void pcursor (y, x)
147[ 0]:      unsigned x, y;
148[ 0]: {
149[ 1]:      v_pos = y;
150[ 1]:      h_pos = x;
151[ 1]:
152[ 1]:      regs.h.ah = setcursor;
153[ 1]:      regs.h.bh = 0;
154[ 1]:      regs.h.dh = v_pos;
155[ 1]:      regs.h.dl = h_pos;
156[ 1]:      int86 (0x10, &regs, &regs);
157[ 0]: }
```

This program demonstrates the advantage of inline assembly over other forms of assembly language. First, as we mentioned earlier, the inline assembly programmer does not have to worry about the storage class of the variables being accessed. Stack variables and global variables are accessed the same way. Turbo C makes the necessary conversions to the assembly output.

Second, we were able to keep the amount of written assembly code to an absolute minimum. Analysis had shown that the contributions of lines 75–89, 95, and 99–101 to the execution time of Prg7_4a are completely insignificant. Therefore, we left these in C. When writing routines using sections of inline assembly, try to keep the more complicated code sections, such as complex calculations, in C. This is especially important when manipulating floating point numbers. It is even possible to use the Turbo C pseudo variables to initialize the registers in C before some inline assembly section uses them.

One warning: be sure that any section of inline assembly code that you might write retains the value of the *SI* and *DI* registers if you intend to leave register optimization turned on. Consider the following *do nothing* code segment:

```
a = b * 10;
asm mov si,1
c = b * 5;
```

In the first line, some variable *B* is loaded from memory into a register, multiplied by 10, and stored in the variable *A*. Since accessing of registers is so much faster than memory accessing, Turbo C tries to retain the value of *B* in the *SI* register for later use in line 3. In line 3, the value of *B* is not reloaded from memory, but is assumed already to be present in *SI*. Turbo C does not know that the inline assembly in line 2 wiped out the value of *B* stored there. Inline assembly sections which need to use the *SI* and *DI* registers should push them onto the stack at the beginning and then pop them off at the end, or, better yet, save them into other, unused registers, as we have done. (The alternative, disabling register optimization or declaring *B* to be of type *VOLATILE* in order to force *B* to be reloaded from memory on each line, may actually slow execution more than the inline assembly improved it.)

You might think that the Turbo C pseudo variables provide us with another solution to the problem. If Turbo C knew that the value of register *B* was no longer contained in *SI,* it would be forced to reload its value from memory in line 3. We could easily do this by inserting the line *_SI = 1* between lines 2 and 3, where the actual constant is not important. It is only important that Turbo C know that *SI* has been modified. Curiously, this does not work. Turbo C does not make the association between the assignment to the pseudo variable and the value of *B* which it has stashed there. Apparently, this is a bug in the Turbo C compiler which the reader should be aware of when using the pseudo variables *_SI* and *_DI*.

Errors involving register optimization, such as the one presented above, are to be watched out for, since they are so difficult to find. The C source code looks okay, but the answer is wrong. Anytime you suspect such a problem, try recompiling and running the program with register optimization deselected in the *Options* menu. If the results are different, then you have a register problem.

Separate Assembly Modules

The inline assembly technique is ideal when the amount of time critical code is fairly small, as was the case with Prg7_1a. In such cases, the programmer can perform the necessary calculations and initialize the proper variables in C and then drop into assembly language for the critical sections. When this is not the case, however, inline assembly becomes unwieldy. It is then better to separate the time critical functions into separate modules written entirely in assembly language.

Assembly language modules must be assembled into *.OBJ* files by a separate assembler. We will use Microsoft's MASM assembler, but any assembler capable of generating *.OBJ* files and supporting the *SEGMENT* and *GROUP* directive can be used. Since none of the assembly source module is written by the Turbo C compiler, this technique is not nearly so tied to any particular assembler as was inline assembly.

The *.OBJ* file created from the assembly language module is combined with that generated by Turbo C during the linking process. Fortunately, almost all compilers and assemblers for the IBM PC generate the same object file format, so the linker is not even aware that the two *.OBJ* files were generated from different compilers.

Functions written in assembly language modules and linked together with Turbo C modules can be called from those modules as if they were written in C. As long as the assembly language functions follow the rules of program interfacing, the calling program does not need to make any special concessions. By the same token, assembly language routines can also call Turbo C functions. This is an ideal way to include larger sections of assembly language in a Turbo C program. Since the assembly language is more or less the same (depending on what assembler you are using), how does one write assembly language functions to be interfaced with Turbo C?

The first thing to remember is also the easiest. Turbo C attaches a _ onto the beginning of all externally defined variable and function names, so that if a C routine is to call an assembly function *print()*, the assembly module which defines it should call it *_print*. Although rules differ, the Microsoft assembler does not automatically make a function name global, as does C. Somewhere in the module a *PUBLIC* declaration must also be made so that the function is known outside of the module. Otherwise, the C modules will not be able to find it. The only other rules of interfacing C with assembly languages are those which deal with the stack.

I have been a little free up to now with the term *stack,* never having really defined it. The stack is an area of memory which is pointed to by the stack pointer. Some instructions automatically place things on the stack. For example, when a microprocessor calls a function, it must have some way of knowing how to return to the point after the call. The *CALL* instruction automatically stores the address of the next instruction (the so-called return address) at the location pointed at by the stack pointer. To keep that value safe, this instruction then decrements the stack pointer. When the called function is ready to return to the caller, it executes a *RET* instruction which increments the stack pointer and then jumps to the address it points to. This puts the program back at the instruction following the original *CALL.*

The details differ from one microprocessor to the next, but the principle is the same. In the 8086 family of microprocessors, the stack pointer is a special register abbreviated *SP*. In this architecture, the decrement is actually performed before the return address is saved on the stack, and the return address is loaded before the stack pointer is incremented. Figure 8.1 shows pictorially how the *CALL* and *RET* instructions work in the 8086.

Figure 8.1

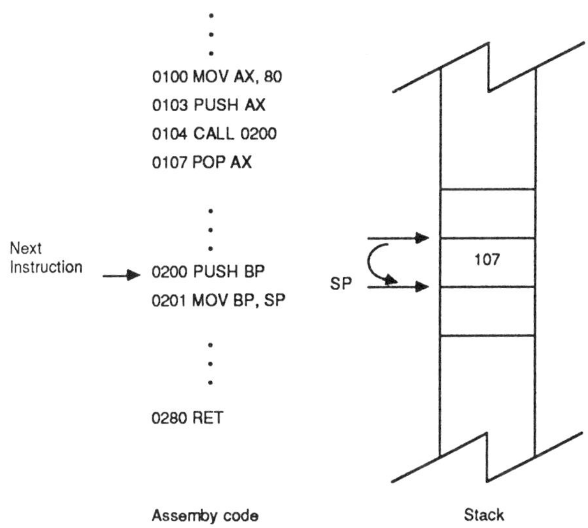

Immediately after executing CALL at 0104

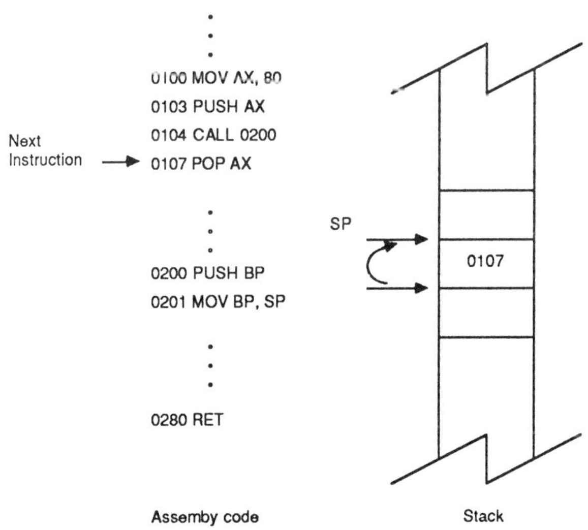

Immediately after executing RET at 0280

Besides return addresses, other things can be saved on the stack. The 8086 instructions *PUSH* and *POP* save and restore register values in the same way that *CALL* and *RET* save and restore the return address. For example, *PUSH AX* decrements the stack pointer and then saves the contents of the *AX* register on the stack. The inverse instruction, *POP AX*, loads the value pointed at by the stack pointer into the *AX* register and then increments the stack pointer.

Return addresses and local variables are stored on the stack to provide a capability known as *reentrancy*. If the return address for a call to a function were stored in some fixed location, as was the case in some older computers, then that function must make sure that a) it is never called twice at the same time, and b) it does not call itself. If it did, the second return address would overwrite the first and the information would be lost. It may not sound like reentrancy is that big of a deal, but, as we shall see, it often can be.

Turbo C also uses the stack to pass arguments from one function to another. To make a call, the value of the last argument to the called function is pushed onto the stack, then the next to last, and so on, until the first argument has been pushed before the actual call is made. The calling routine restores the stack pointer after the called function returns either by executing the proper number of pops or by direct addition to the stack pointer. For example, examine the stack which the C function *called()* sees after it has been called.

Pushing and popping variables on and off the stack is fine for passing arguments to functions, but is not really adequate for variables used within functions. Variables and arguments must be accessible in any order, unlike the serial order of pushes and pops. To place such variables on the stack and still retain random access to them, Turbo C (and most other compilers) uses a concept called the stack frame. The stack frame uses the base pointer register (*BP*) in combination with the stack pointer to allocate stack space at the beginning of Turbo C functions using the following assembler sequence:

```
PUSH    BP                      ;SAVE CALLER'S BP
MOV     BP,SP                   ;POINT BP TO TOP OF FRAME
SUB     SP,<frame size>         ;ALLOCATE THE STACK FRAME
```

and the following code sequence to *pull down* the stack frame:

```
MOV     SP,BP                   ;RESTORE SP TO TOP OF FRAME
POP     BP                      ;RESTORE CALLER'S BP
RET                             ;RETURN TO CALLER
```

Figure 8.2

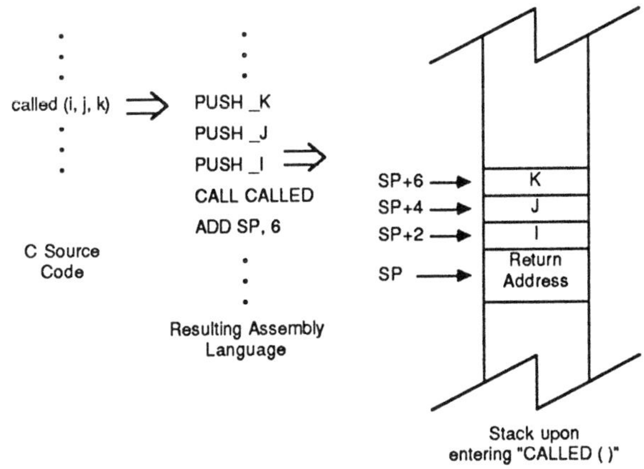

PUSHing arguments on stack in C

The entire stack, including stack frame, has the following appearance within a Turbo C function:

Figure 8.3

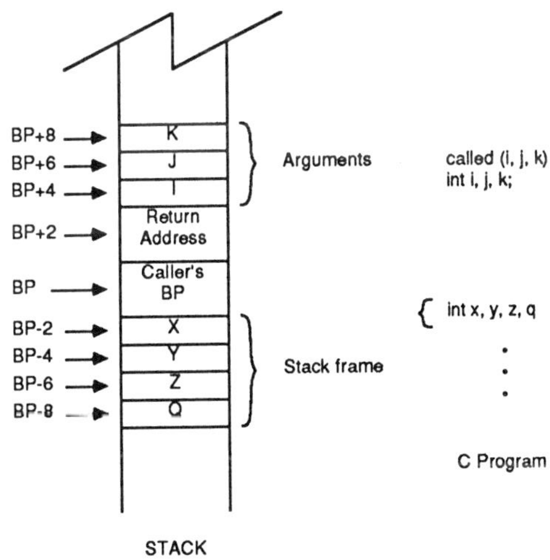

Stack frames in C procedures with both arguments and automatic variables

This stack frame technique is almost *built into* the 8086 instruction set. In fact, later members of the 8086 family can erect and tear down stack frames in a single instruction. In addition, the 8086 can reference indirectly off of the base pointer register (something it cannot do off of the stack pointer). Thus, a function which has erected a stack frame can reference arguments as positive offsets off of the base pointer, and locally declared automatic variables as negative offsets off of the base pointer.

The value returned from a function is not pushed on the stack, but simply returned in the *AX* register. For example, examine the following assembly language function written for the Microsoft MASM assembler and designed to be called from Turbo C. Notice how it performs the calls to other Turbo C routines and compare it against the diagram of the complete stack above:

```
;  int poly (x, a, b)
;       returns the value of the equation f(a,x) + g(b,x)
;       where f() is a C function
;
; define the variables we will need
;
x       equ     4                       ;first the arguments
a       equ     6
b       equ     8

temp    equ     -2                      ;now the temporary variable

        public _poly
        extern _f, _g                   ;declare the C functions
                                        ;remember to include "_"

_poly proc near
        push    bp                      ;set up the stack frame
        mov     bp,sp
        sub     sp,2

                                        ;first call f(a,x)
        push    x[bp]                   ;pass x...
        push    a[bp]                   ;...and a
        call    _f
        pop     dx                      ;fix the stack from...
        pop     dx                      ;...the above pushes

        mov     temp[bp],ax             ;save the results locally

                                        ;now call g(b,x)
        push    x[bp]                   ;pass x...
        push    b[bp]                   ;...then b
        call    _g
```

```
        pop     dx
        pop     dx

        add     ax,temp[bp]         ;generate the results in ax

        mov     sp,bp               ;tear down stack frame
        pop     bp
        ret                         ;and return the results in ax
_poly   endp
```

This is a particularly good style for writing such routines. The arguments are declared at the very front of the routine as positive equates and the local variables as negative equates. This allows argument X to be referred to in the body of the program as *X[BP]*, which is much clearer to the reader than the equivalent *04[BP]*. (The above argument offsets assume that the calls are all near calls—add 2 to each offset for far functions.)

The last argument to *f(a,x)* is pushed onto the stack first followed by the first argument and then the function is called with the _ preceding the name. We assume that *f()* and *g()* are both near functions. After *f()* returns, the result is saved into a local variable while *g()* is called. Once *g()* returns, the two values are added together and the result is left in the *AX* register to be returned to the calling C function. The *SI* and *DI* registers were not saved since they were not modified. (Remember that Turbo C functions always restore *SI* and *DI* before returning.) If this routine had intended to use these registers, and if the calling routine was to be compiled with register optimization or register variables enabled, they would have needed to be saved.

As you can see, writing an assembly function to be called from C is not a trivial exercise. The above code section does not even include the proper *SEGMENT* and *GROUP* declarations, which differ for each of the memory models. Fortunately there is a trick which can be helpful in writing these routines. Write a C module containing a single function which has the same name, same local variables you will need, and the same number of arguments. The body of the function should access each of the arguments and variables in turn in some trivial way. Now compile this module using TCC with the *–B* or *–S* switch to generate an assembly source code output. Be sure to compile it under the proper model.

If you now take the *.ASM* output from TCC, you will find an assembly source file containing all the proper segment and function declarations. Since you accessed each of the variables and arguments in the C program, this source should contain assembly statements to access them also. By comparing the line numbers on the assembly output with the source code line numbers, you determine by example the proper offset for each argument and local variable.

You can now use this assembly source generated by Turbo C as the starting point for your program. First edit it and add equates for each of the variable and argument offsets. Then delete any assembly language generated by the trivial C assignments. Finally, add your own program body using the stack equates you have just defined. You do not need to remember all of the details of C stack structure, since you can just trick Turbo C into telling you what you need to know. Although not a job for someone unfamiliar with 8086 assembly language, this is much simpler than trying to recreate such a routine from scratch.

If reentrancy is not a consideration, then the assembly language program can be made even simpler by declaring all local variables in the data or BSS segments and by not passing any arguments. When neither arguments nor stack variables are present, the assembly language subroutine does not even need to set up a stack frame. The entire stack issue can be ignored.

The restriction of no arguments may seem like a severe one, but remember that data can be passed to the assembly language subroutine through globally declared variables into which the caller can store data which the subroutine can retrieve. Turbo C declares the variables outside of any functions, leaving them of storage class extern. The assembly module uses the same variable name, but with a _ attached to the beginning, declaring it externally defined with the *EXTERN* directive.

```
/*Noarg - a C function which uses globally defined
          variables to pass arguments*/

int arg1, arg2, *array1;
void noargs (void)
{
        int i, j, k[10];

        /*set up arg.s in globals and make the call*/
        arg1 = i;
        arg2 = j;
        array1 = k;
```

```
            assem ();
            i = arg1;
            j = arg2;
      }
```

I hesitate to mention this technique, since it breaks the rules of good programming. If you are going to play the game, you should play by Turbo C's rules. Problems arising from globally declared variables being set unexpectedly in some function, especially an assembly function, are very difficult to trace. On the other hand, this technique can simplify the demands on a programmer ill-at-ease with 8086 assembly language in the first place.

Once the assembly language module has been written and assembled, its object file must be included in the link with the Turbo C generated object modules. If you are using the Microsoft linker, you must name the assembly object in the list of the other object files being linked (refer to the PC-DOS or MS-DOS manual). However, you can still enjoy the benefits of the *Interactive Development Environment,* if you desire. The assembly module is simply added to the project file. Since it did not originate from a C source file, its name should include the *.OBJ* extension. Turbo C will not attempt to compile the assembly language file during the compile phase of the make process, but it will include the object file during the link. The project file is specified in the *Project* menu.

Program Prg8_3c is our old favorite screen write program rewritten as a separate assembly language module called from Turbo C. Notice how similar the actual assembly code appears to its inline assembly equivalent above. The proper segment and group declarations were discovered by assembling a dummy Turbo C module with TCC –B and examining the output. Notice that both functions save and restore the *SI* and *DI* registers in case register optimization is enabled in the calling function. Register optimization errors can be very difficult to track down.

The associated project file necessary to build the executable screen write program from the IDE is also shown below.

```
/*Prg8_3c - High Speed Screen Output
  by Stephen R Davis, 1987

  Perform direct screen output by accessing screen memory directly
  via the screen pointer 'screen'.  Scroll using the 8086 block
  move instruction this encased in separate assembler subroutines
  linked in as .OBJ files.  The assembler name is Prog9d1.asm and
  the project file name is Prog9d.prj.  This must be compiled under
  the Small or Tiny memory models (otherwise, the stack offsets in
  the assembler routine must be changed).
*/

```

```
#include <stdio.h>
#include <dos.h>
#include <stdlib.h>

#define cga  (unsigned far *)0xb8000000 /*same for ega*/
#define mono (unsigned far *)0xb0000000
#define space 0x20
#define attrib 0x07
#define screenheight 25

/*add the screen BIOS functions*/
#define scrollup 0x06
#define setcursor 0x02
#define writetele 0x0e
#define getmode 0x0f

/*define global variables*/
unsigned v_pos, h_pos, screenwidth;
union REGS regs;
unsigned far *screen;                    /*screen pointer*/

/*prototype declarations*/
void init (void);
void scroll (unsigned);
void qprintf (char *);
void pcursor (unsigned, unsigned);

/*prototype declarations for external assembler routines*/
/*(remember that MASM generates uppercase symbols)*/
void MOVS (unsigned far *, unsigned far *, unsigned);
     /*move from first pointer to second, third arg words*/
void STOS (unsigned far *, unsigned);
     /*clear at pointer, unsigned words*/

/*be sure compile model is correct*/
#if sizeof(MOVS)-2
#error Must compile under Small or Tiny models
#endif

/*Main - test the output routines*/
int main ()
{
    int i, j;

    init ();
    for (i = 0; i < 20; i++) {
         for (j = 0; j < screenheight; j++) {
              qprintf ("this is BIOS output");
              pcursor(v_pos, 30+j);
              qprintf ("and this\n");
         }
         for (j = 0; j < screenheight; j++)
              printf ("this is normal printf output\n");
    }
}

/*Init - set the screen address and clear the screen*/
void init ()
{
    short mode;

    regs.h.ah = getmode;
    int86 (0x10, &regs, &regs);
    mode = regs.h.al;
```

```
    screenwidth = regs.h.ah;

    if (mode == 7)
        screen = mono;
    else
        if (mode == 3 || mode == 2)
            screen = cga;
        else
            abort ();

    scroll (screenheight);
    pcursor (0, 0);
}

/*Scroll - scroll up N lines using function 6*/
void scroll (nlines)
    unsigned nlines;
{
    unsigned far *source, far *dest, number;

    if (nlines >= screenheight)
        nlines = screenheight;

    h_pos = 0;
    if ((v_pos += nlines) >= screenheight) {
        nlines = (v_pos - screenheight) + 1;

        /*scroll the screen up 'nlines' amount*/
        source = screen + (nlines * screenwidth);
        dest = screen;
        number = (screenheight - nlines) * screenwidth;
        MOVS (source, dest, number);

        /*now blank the lines abandoned*/
        dest = screen + number;
        number = nlines * screenwidth;
        STOS (dest, number);

        v_pos = screenheight - 1;
    }
}

/*Qprintf - output a string using the BIOS screen handler.  If
              an attribute is not provided, use the default.*/
#define SCREENLOC screen + ((screenwidth * v_pos) + h_pos)
void qprintf (c)
    char *c;
{
    unsigned far *sp;

    sp = SCREENLOC;
    for (; *c; c++)
        if (*c == '\n') {
            scroll (1);
            sp = SCREENLOC;
        }
        else {
            if (h_pos++ < screenwidth)
                *sp++ = (attrib << 8) + *c;
        }
    pcursor (v_pos, h_pos);
}

/*PCursor - place the cursor at the current x and y location.
```

```
               To place the cursor, and subsequent output, to any
               arbitrary location, set 'v_pos' and 'h_pos' before
               calling pcursor.*/
void pcursor (y, x)
    unsigned x, y;
{
    v_pos = y;
    h_pos = x;

    regs.h.ah = setcursor;
    regs.h.bh = 0;
    regs.h.dh = v_pos;
    regs.h.dl = h_pos;
    int86 (0x10, &regs, &regs);
}
```

```
;  Prg8_3d  - Fast Screen Output Using Assembler Subroutines
;    by Stephen R. Davis, 1987
;
;  Here we have taken a dummy .C program consisting only
;  of the statement 'main{}' and compiled it to assembler
;  source using 'TCC -B' command.  We then go in and remove
;  the main program found there and insert our own routines
;  being careful to attach a "_" to the front of our
;  routine names.
;  (I have only commented out the original code so that you
;  can see what was there.)
;
        name    Prog9d1
_text   segment byte public 'code'
dgroup  group   _data,_bss
        assume  cs:_text,ds:dgroup,ss:dgroup
_text   ends
_data   segment word public 'data'
_d@     label   byte
_data   ends
_bss    segment word public 'bss'
_b@     label   byte
_bss    ends
_text   segment byte public 'code'
;
;Here is the original code generated by empty main()
; Line 2
;_main  proc    near
; Line 3
;@1:
;       ret
;_main  endp
;
;Now we insert our own routines
;Movs - scroll the screen via the movs instruction

msource equ 4                          ;first argument is int *source
mdest   equ 8                          ;second argument is int *dest
mnumber  equ 12                        ;third argument is int number

msaveds  equ -2                        ;declare local storage
msavesi  equ -4
msavedi  equ -6

_movs  proc near
        push    bp                     ;set up stack frame
```

```
        mov     bp,sp
        sub     sp,6

        mov     msaveds[bp],ds          ;save reg.s on frame
        mov     msavesi[bp],si
        mov     msavedi[bp],di

        les     di,mdest[bp]            ;fetch arg.s from stack
        lds     si,msource[bp]
        mov     cx,mnumber[bp]
        cld
        rep     movsw

        mov     ds,msaveds[bp]          ;restore regs
        mov     si,msavesi[bp]
        mov     di,msavedi[bp]

        mov     sp,bp                   ;pull down frame
        pop     bp
        ret
_movs   endp

;Stos - clear the bottom lines via the stos instruction

sdest   equ     4                       ;first arg is int *dest
snumber equ     8                       ;second arg is int

ssavedi equu    -2

_stos   proc    near
        push    bp
        mov     bp,sp
        sub     sp,2

        mov     ssavedi[bp],di

        mov     ax,0700H
        les     di,sdest[bp]
        mov     cx,snumber[bp]
        rep     stosw

        mov     di,ssavedi[bp]

        mov     sp,bp
        pop     bp
        ret
_stos   endp

_text   ends
_data   segment word public 'data'
_s@     label   byte
_data   ends
_text   segment byte public 'code'
;       public  _main                   ;from TC
        public  _movs                   ;our own inserted
        public  _stos
_text   ends
        end
```

Project File for Above:

```
prg8_3c
prg8_3d.obj
```

Interfacing Turbo C with Other Languages

In general, interfacing Turbo C with other languages is discouraged. In the case of assembly language, it was argued that the benefits of increased performance outweighed the disadvantages, but few high level languages are as efficient as Turbo C. Writing a package in multiple languages merely serves to increase obfuscation.

If you have some overriding reason for combining Turbo C with another programming language, there are several hurdles to overcome. First is the function interface embodied in the treatment of the stack by different languages. If the other language uses the same calling sequence, then there is no problem. Minor stack problems can be *worked around.*

It is very unlikely that other languages push *SI* and *DI* onto the stack at the beginnings of functions as does Turbo C, so it will almost certainly be necessary to disable register optimization during compilation to suppress these pushes. Some languages push arguments in the opposite order from Turbo C. This can be overcome by calling the foreign language function with the arguments in the reverse order from the way they are specified in the other language. The C program must also be sensitive to whether the foreign language passes arguments by reference (that is, by address) or by value.

For example, assume that we want to interface Turbo C with a FORTRAN compiler which pushes function arguments from front to back. We might have the following situation:

in Turbo C:

```
fortfunc (&i, &j, &k);       /*FORTRAN always passes by
                               reference so we must pass
                               address, not value*/
```

in FORTRAN:

```
        Subroutine _fortfunc (k, j, i)
C
C       Remember to include "_" in front of name and to name
C       arguments in opposite order
C
```

If the arguments don't line up correctly because the other language and Turbo C don't set their stack frames up in quite the same manner, it will be necessary to pad either the calling sequence or the called function with dummy arguments. It may be necessary to run a few experiments to decide whether this is the case or not. For example, we might have started our Turbo C/FORTRAN interface exercise by compiling, linking, and executing something similar to the following program:

in Turbo C:

```
main ()
{
        fortest (&1, &2, &3, &4, &5);
}

ctest (i, j, k, l, m)
        int *i, *j, *k, *l, *m;
{
        printf ("%u %u %u %u %u", *i, *j, *k, *l, *m);
}
```

in FORTRAN.

```
        Subroutine _fortest (i, j, k, l, m)

        write (6, 100) i, j, k, l, m
100     format (6I6)

        call _ctest (1, 2, 3, 4, 5)
```

We might discover that when *_fortest()* printed out the values it received, the values 1 through 4 appeared, preceeded by garbage, indicating a minor stack misalignment. This could be overcome by adding a dummy argument to every call of a FORTRAN function from Turbo C.

Much more serious is the question of how the foreign computer language restores the stack after returning from a function from the pushes of the arguments. As noted in the assembly language examples above, C restores the stack in the calling function either by executing a series of POP instructions or by direct addition to the stack pointer register. Some languages correct the stack pointer in the called function, either immediatly before returning or as part of the return itself. If a routine from such a language is called from Turbo C, the resulting program will crash, since the stack will get corrected twice and lose important data in the process.

To address this problem, Turbo C defines the descriptor *PASCAL*, since Pascal is the most common language which restores the stack in the called function. This descriptor may be added to the prototype definition of any function, whether it is actually written in Pascal or not. When Turbo C calls such a Pascal-type function, it will not correct the stack after returning. It will also push the arguments to the function in the reverse order, since this is another property of the Pascal language. (Merely declaring a *FUNCTION* to be of type *PASCAL* does nothing to address *PASCAL*'s other peculiarities. For example, remember that *PASCAL* strings place the length in the first byte instead of ending with a *NULL*.)

If the stack interconnection still can not be made to work, it will be necessary to write an interface routine in assembly language to weld the two languages together. Two such routines will be necessary: one to make the C to other language bridge and another for other language to C connection. Such a routine might accept as its first argument the address of the function to be called, followed by any arguments to pass. This routine would then set the stack up the way the other language likes to see it and make the call. When the other language returns, the assembly routine could restore the stack to match C customs before returning. Although difficult to write, these routines would only have to be written once, since they would serve for all C to other language connections.

Once again, although I hesitate to mention it, the problem of function interconnections can be greatly reduced by not passing any arguments at all. Data can be passed by storing them in globally declared variables which are then accessed by the other language routine. Again, this simplifies the stack interface problem, but makes the eventual job of debugging more difficult by inviting difficult to trace errors.

Libraries represent another problem. It is usually desirable to only make library calls from one language, avoiding them in the other. Using our FORTRAN example above, use either Turbo C's *printf()* or FORTRAN's *WRITE* to perform output, but not both. If this is not possible, it will be necessary to name both libraries in the link step.

Again, the link step is again a tricky problem. Turbo C expects object files with which it links to have the proper code and data segment names. It will be necessary to name the code segments of C and the other language to some common group. This problem can also be solved by an assembly language interface program which can make the jump from the C code segment to the foreign language and back.

There are a few tricks to avoid the problems of direct interfacing. If only a small number of functions from the other language are necessary, it may be more economical to complete the foreign language functions as a stand alone program. When those functions are needed, the Turbo C program can then chain to the foreign language program using the DOS *exec()* or *spawn()* studied in Chapter 5.

Yet another approach is for the independently compiled foreign language program to *install itself* into one or more of the 8086 interrupt vectors. The Turbo C program can then easily access the foreign language functions by executing the library routine *int86()*. Keep this in mind when we discuss installing code into interrupts in Chapter 9.

Program Size

Increasing a program's performance is difficult, but reducing its size is even more so. I should first define what I mean by size. I do not mean the number of C source code statements or even the size of the resulting *.EXE* executable file. Size refers to the number of bytes of random access memory a program requires to execute.

There is a strong correlation between the program's source code size and the amount of memory it consumes, but it is not 100 percent. Novice programmers have been known to go to great pains to reduce the number of source code statements in their programs, not realizing that the resulting object code was actually increasing in size due to the increased code complication.

The most obvious solution is to buy more memory. Saving a few bytes of code is not nearly as important as it once was given today's sinking memory prices. Even with DOS' limit of 640k, a lot can be done before memory starts to become tight. It is not uncommon for commercial packages today to specify a minimum memory requirement of 320k, an unheard of amount just a few years ago.

A program's memory requirements can be greatly reduced if its functionality can be divided up among several different programs. Suppose, for example, that we have been tasked with writing a database program. There are several functions which our package must offer the user, including the ability to add entries, remove entries, sort entries, etc. We could write our package as one very large program containing all of the required capabilities; however, it is never the case that more than one of these is ever exercised at any given time. Therefore, it is not necessary that more than one be resident in memory at a time.

With this fact, we might build our package out of several different executable programs. One of the programs is resident at all times, acting as the band director for the others. This shell program provides the user with a menu of choices, and accepts the response, deciding which of the others to call to handle the request. Having decided, this master program invokes the subordinate program as a subprocess. This causes DOS to load the program from disk into memory immediately above the master program.

Once the command has been carried out, the subprocess terminates, releasing the memory it occupies back to the operating system to be used for other subprocesses. The subprogram can return a termination value which the master program can use to decide whether the subprocess was successful, and, if not, what problem was encountered. The subject of program chaining was discussed in greater detail in Chapter 5.

Sometimes it is desirable for the master program to provide information or capabilities to the subordinate programs which would not normally be present. It can do this by installing data or function addresses into some of the interrupt vectors much as the BIOS routines are installed into certain interrupts at power on to handle the hardware. In our database example, extracting individual fields out of a database entry is so common that a function to perform this function might be installed into one of the user interrupts by the master program. This function can be invoked from either the master or any of the subordinate programs. While this may not have any effect on memory requirements, it can reduce the amount of redundant code that would otherwise be repeated in each of the subordinate programs.

Figure 8.4

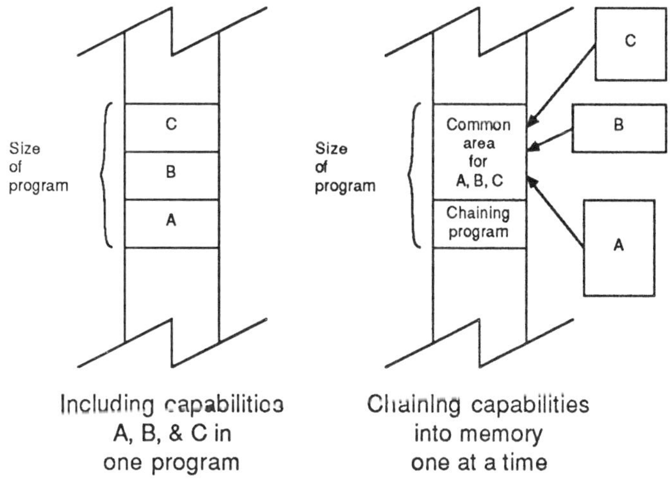

For programs which cannot be so easily subdivided, there are a few tricks to achieve relatively modest decreases in code size. First, we can minimize the number of different library functions that are called. Remember how the linker handles *.LIB* files: functions which are not called are not loaded from the *.LIB* file; those that are called are loaded even if they are only called once. If we can substitute library routines which have already been called for a new one, we can keep the new library routine from being loaded.

Compiling under the smallest possible memory model helps. *NEAR* pointers are only 16 bits, as opposed to a *FAR* pointer's 32 bits. Not only do we save the 16 bits per address, but also the extra instructions necessary to load and store these larger addresses. Be careful , however, as *NEAR* pointers can be counter-productive. *NEAR* pointers can only address 64k, even if more memory than that is available in the machine. It makes no sense to convert *FAR* pointers to *NEAR* pointers to save 10k of data requirement if it is going to cost you 512k of memory which you can no longer address.

Declaring and accessing data structures globally can also save a small amount of memory. Object code must be generated to pass variables to functions and to access them there. Accessing variables globally saves that space. It is questionable whether this is a good idea, however, as the resulting code is often much more difficult to debug. Besides, globally declaring a variable that is used only once ties up that variable's space. Variables declared on the stack only use memory when they are *active*.

If possible avoid the use of floating point numbers for the same reason that calls to extra functions were avoided above. The floating point libraries are not loaded if there are no floating point numbers in the application. When floating point numbers are used, if the target machine is known to have an 8087 or 80287 numerical data processor, select the 8087/287 library from the *Options* menu. It is much smaller than the default emulation library.

Aside from these simplistic approaches, we can reexamine the original problem to find different approaches which require less space. One such approach is the technique of state tables presented in Chapter 4. State table solutions to problems tend to be very small in comparison to what they can achieve.

Judicious use of reiterative functions can also result in a considerable decrease in object code size. Like the state table solutions to problems, reiterative solutions tend to be difficult to find, since they are generally not obvious. Even worse than state table solutions, they are sometimes difficult to read, even when the reader is familiar with the technique.

The classic example of reiterative solutions is the factorial. The factorial of an integer *N*, written *N!*, is equal to that number multiplied by all of the smaller integers greater than zero. For example, *5! = 5 * 4 * 3 * 2 * 1*. In many texts this is implemented by a subroutine which calls itself in a reiterative fashion. The C equivalent is shown below.

```
int factorial (number)
     int number;
{
     if (number = 1)
          return 1;
     else
          return number * factorial (number - 1);
}
```

Had we invoked *factorial()* with the constant 5, the second branch of the *IF* statement is taken since 5 is not equal to 1. This calls *factorial()* with the value 4. This continues until eventually we work our way down to 1. 1! is 1 so *factorial()* returns the value 1. This gets multiplied by the 2 waiting from the previous invocation, which gets multiplied by the 3 from the one before that, and so on until we work our way back up to 5.

In fact, this is a terrible example. The factorial function is so much more easily and clearly solved through the use of a *FOR* loop. For example:

```
int factorial (number)
     int number;
{
     int accum;

     accum = 1;
     for (; number > 1; number --)
          accum *= number;
     return accum;
}
```

Better examples of the use of reiterative solutions can be found in the areas of look ahead searches, such as those accompanying game playing and decision making.

Take, for example, a simple maze problem. Assume we have a maze with walls and passage ways. Somewhere within the maze is a piece of cheese. Our program is to search the maze until it can find a path to the cheese. To make the problem simpler, let's assume that for any given legal location in the maze, there is only one legal path. In other words, there are no circles in the maze in which we might get permanently lost. (These multipaths can be handled, but at the cost of extra complexity which only obscures the principle being demonstrated here.) Dead ends are allowed.

This problem is much simpler if we start by placing ourselves at some random location in one of the hallways. From that position there are four different directions open to us which might lead to the cheese. In fact, one of those directions can't possibly have the cheese, since we just came from there in the previous step. Of the other three directions, all are equally likely so we must try each one in turn.

Those selections which end up *in* the wall are immediately precluded, just as those which end up *in* the cheese are immediately successful. But for the remaining selections, those down one of the hallways, we don't know if they end up at the cheese or not. The only way that we can know is to continue searching along those paths.

However, as soon as we have made a jump in any legal direction, we are presented with exactly the same problem as before: that of searching for cheese. Alarms should go off in your head. Such problems invite reiterative solutions. Such a solution to the maze problem appears as Prg8_4.

```
/*Prg8_4 - The Maze Problem
   by Stephen R. Davis, 1987

  Notice how small this reiterative solution to the maze problem
  is.  The routine evaluate() checks the current location for
  cheese (success) or wall (failure).  If the answer is neither,
  it then calls itself in each of the 3 directions open to it
  (we forbid it from looking in the direction from which it came)
  until success or failure is attained.  The successful path is
  marked with '.'s.

  Create mazes with any ASCII file editor.  Rules for mazes are:
  - no loops
  - halls marked with spaces
  - cheese marked with '&' (need not be present)
  - halls must be single space wide
  - must have a single opening at the top; search starts here
*/

#include <stdio.h>
#include <dos.h>
/*use 0xb0000000 for monochrome and Hercules screens*/
#define screenaddr ((unsigned far *)0xb8000000L)
#define screen(y,x) screenaddr [(y * 80) + x]

#define space ' '
#define cheese '&'
#define path '.'
#define VISIBLE 1

/*define prototypes for routines used*/

int main (int, char **);
void readmaze (FILE *);
int evaluate (unsigned, unsigned, unsigned);
int value (unsigned, unsigned);
void clrscrn (void);

/*Main - if one argument provided, read it up onto the screen and
         evaluate it for a maze solution*/
main (argc, argv)
    int argc;
    char *argv[];
{
    FILE *fp;
    unsigned x;

    /*clear the screen - first line of maze must be at top of screen*/
    clrscrn ();

    if (argc == 2) {
         if (fp = fopen(argv[1], "r")) {
              readmaze (fp);

              /*solve maze by finding a space in the top and
                searching from there*/
              for (x = 0; (char)screen (0, x) != space; x++);
              if (evaluate (0, x, 2))
                   printf ("solution!\n");
              else
                   printf ("no solution found\n");
         } else
              printf ("File not found\n");
    } else
```

```
        printf ("Enter 'Prg8_4 <filename>'\n"
                "  where filename contains the maze to be solved\n");
}

/*Readmaze - read a maze from a file onto the screen.  Transfer
             only the character part to the screen.*/
void readmaze (fptr)
    FILE *fptr;
{
     char buffer [81];

     while (fgets (buffer, 80, fptr))
          printf (buffer);
}

/*Evaluate - solve the maze*/

int deltax [] = {0, 1, 0, -1};          /*define the directions*/
int deltay [] = {-1, 0, 1, 0};
int noallow [] = {2, 3, 0, 1};

int evaluate(yloc, xloc, prevmove)
    unsigned yloc, xloc, prevmove;
{
    int i, val;
    int value();

    if ((val = value(xloc, yloc)) == -1)   /*wall*/
         return 0;
    if (val == 1)                          /*cheese!*/
         return 1;

    for (i = 0; i < 4; i++)                /*4 possible moves*/
         if (i != noallow[prevmove])       /*don't go backwards*/
              if (evaluate(yloc+deltay[i], xloc+deltax[i], i)) {
                   (char)screen (yloc, xloc) = path; /*found it!*/
                   return 1;
              }
    return 0;                  /*nothing down this path*/
}

/*Value - evaluate the current location*/
int value (xloc, yloc)
    unsigned xloc, yloc;
{
    char curr;
    int i;

    curr = (char)screen (yloc, xloc);
#if VISIBLE                                /*make the search visible*/
    (char)screen (yloc, xloc) = '#';
    for (i = 0; i < 10000; i++) ;
    (char)screen (yloc, xloc) = curr;
#endif
    switch (curr) {
         case cheese: return  1;        /*cheese -> success*/
         case space : return  0;        /*space -> keep looking*/
         default    : return -1;        /*else -> can't go that way*/
    }
}

/*Clrscrn - clear the screen*/
struct REGS regs;
void clrscrn (void)
```

```
{
        regs.h.ah = 6;
        regs.h.al = 0;
        regs.h.bh = 7;
        regs.x.cx = 0;
        regs.x.dx = 0x1950;
        int86 (0x10, &regs, &regs);

        regs.h.ah = 2;
        regs.h.bh = 0;
        regs.x.dx = 0;
        int86 (0x10, &regs, &regs);
}
```

Figure 8.5

```
*******,******************************************
*,,,,,,,                                         *
*,****************** ********* *******************
*,,,,,,,,*,,,,,,,,,* *       * *                 *
****** *,*,*******,* * ***** * * *****************
*      *,*,*&,,,,,,* * * * * *   *               *
* ******,*,********* * * * * * *** ***************
*      *,,,*         *   *         ***************
**************************************************

solution!









Press any key to return to Turbo C . . . .
```

Successful search of maze for *cheese*

Notice that once *main()* has read the maze onto the screen, the remaining solution consists of only two functions. *Value()* accepts an *x* and *y* location. It then looks at that location on the screen and returns an indication of what it finds there. A 1 indicates that the location contains cheese (the character &). A 0 indicates that we are in a hallway (a space). Anything else is assumed to be the wall and illicits a –1 response.

The function *evaluate()* is the heart of the solution and the reiterative part of the program. Given a location, *evaluate()* first calls *value()* to determine whether or not this location is on the correct path. If this location is in the wall, then it is not part of the correct path and *evaluate()* returns a *FALSE*. If this location contains the cheese then it obviously is the correct path, and *evaluate()* returns a *TRUE*.

If this location is in a hallway, however, then the answer is not clear. *Evaluate()* calls itself to evaluate each of its 3 neighbors (it does not evaluate the position from which it just came). This reiterative loop continues until either success or failure can be found. If each of the 3 paths returns a failure, then *evaluate()* returns a failure to its caller. If any one of the three returns a success, then *evaluate()* returns a success also.

In practice, it is helpful to make *evaluate()*'s quest for cheese visible. To this end, I added a few extra lines to *value()* to place a # at the location being evaluated, leave it there long enough to be visible and then replace whatever character that was originally there. This should be left in the program, since it is very educational to watch the #s crawl around the maze as the program searches the halls for a scrap of cheese.

You should examine the program's source code and watch it execute until you fully understand why it searches where and when. You truly understand the program when you can examine a given maze and predict how Prg8_4 will search it. Currently, Prg8_4 first looks up, then right, then down and finally left. Even without examining the program you can know this by watching the # move through the maze. As an exercise, try changing the order that directions are searched and watch the result.

You can design your own mazes as you like and let the program solve them. They do not even have to contain any cheese—the program will figure this out. Use any editor you like which can generate a straight ASCII file (if you use WordStar, be sure to use it in the nondocument mode). Build the maze with one hole anywhere along the top. Prg8_4 will start from that point. Be sure that there are not two legal paths to any given spot in the hall, or the program will get permanently stuck. This means that halls can't be more than one space in width (walls can be as wide as you like).

Unfortunately, neither reiterative nor state table solutions are a panacea for the storage problem. Most problems can't be easily adapted to either technique (especially reiterative programming). The rewards are so great, however, when the opportunity does arise that all C programmers should keep these tools in their toolkits.

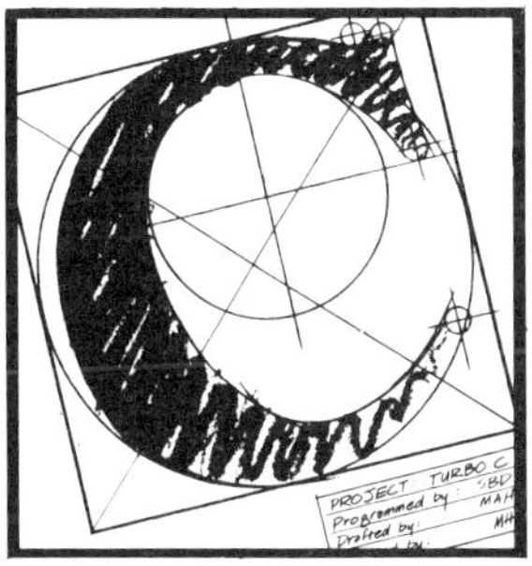

9 Terminate and Stay Resident "PopUp" Programs

Programs are usually written in a continuous flow, from top to bottom, beginning to end. Each statement leads inexorably to the following statement. Although the flow may be convoluted by a call to a function or by an *IF* statement, the path is nonetheless predictable. There is a class of programs that is not so predictable because these programs react to outside events that occur at unpredictable intervals. This class is known as interrupt handlers.

Because programmers are so accustomed to thinking of their programs as having a specific beginning and end, interrupt handlers often seem ominous. Programmers skilled in the art of such software are raised to the status of guru.

It is not true that interrupt handlers must be written in assembly language. Although it is often the case that the entry into, and exit out of such programs must involve a few assembler instructions, these can be written in almost any compiled language. In fact, the first article I ever published described the writing of such routines in Turbo Pascal (*see Micro/Systems Journal*, Sept. 1985). Turbo C accommodates interrupt handlers so well that no assembly language is required at all.

A special subset of this group are the Terminate-and-Stay Resident (TSR) programs. These are the "PopUp" utilities such as SideKick and Homebase that have become popular in the DOS world. Although you might not think of TSRs as being interrupt handlers, they are, both in structure and in execution. I will approach the writing of such utilities from this standpoint.

TSR programs are very popular. The ability to add some capability to the DOS environment is a powerful one. Every programmer thinks about writing one at least once. The fact that such utilities can be constructed out of Turbo C opens up this class of program to a much larger audience.

Do not think, however, that these programs are easy to write. Writing and debugging a TSR program is about the most painful project one can undertake. Every bit of programming intuition gets called into play before it works properly. Each of the examples in this chapter took many hours to debug. By modeling your own TSRs after the examples presented here, perhaps you can be spared much of the difficulty such programs normally present.

Control Break

The first and easiest of the interrupt handlers is the *break handler*. A *break* is ellicited when the operator depresses the *break key* in the upper right hand corner of the keyboard while simultaneously holding down the *control key*. (While more accurately described as *control-break*, I will call it *break* for brevity's sake.) A *break* is intended as a "wake up call" for a program that has otherwise gone off on an errant path. For example, if the user has begun listing a large file to the screen, he may want to stop the listing prematurely, which he or she can do by entering *break*. To enhance compatibility with CPM, entering *control C* also generates a *break*.

The DOS operating system has no idea what might be going on when the *break* is entered. It must be designed to terminate the current application, whatever it is doing. The DOS *break handler* starts by closing all open files. It then terminates the executing program and reloads *COMMAND.COM*, which restores the expected *A>* prompt. If the *broken* program was executed from a batch file, DOS puts up the *Terminate Batch File (Y/N)?* message to decide whether it should continue or drop back to the *COMMAND.COM* level immediately or continue with the next command in the batch file.

Depending on the type of program, it may not be too desirable for the broken program to return immediately to the DOS level. Since DOS automatically closes all open files, the file structure is preserved from a DOS standpoint, but not necessarily from an application standpoint. Files may be in the middle of being updated with some entries containing new data and others left with older data. Returning to DOS is almost never acceptable from a user standpoint either. If the user enters *break* to stop some operation, he usually wants to return to the current program's prompt or menu, not that of DOS.

It is almost always preferable if the user program can handle the *break* itself, perhaps stopping the current operation and placing the user back at the last command prompt. This gives the program a more orderly interface and a professional appearance. Turbo C makes writing a *break handler* a fairly simple thing to do.

There is no wire to the processor known as the *break line*. *Break* is a condition that must be searched for. DOS must examine the keyboard input to determine if a *control break* (or control C) has been entered. It does this on every I/O operation. Programs that do not perform I/O operations cannot be broken

When DOS detects a *break*, it executes an *INTERRUPT 0x23*, much as you executed an *INTERRUPT 0x10 BIOS* call back in Chapter 6 to perform screen I/O. Unlike a *BIOS* call, however, *INTERRUPT 0x23* is not defined until shortly before the program is given control. DOS initializes this location as one of the chores it performs when executing a *.COM* or *.EXE* program. DOS uses the address of its own built-in *break handler*. It is this handler which, if left in place, returns the user to the DOS prompt when a break is detected. Fortunately, you are free to redefine this *INTERRUPT 0x23* address to any *break handler* you define.

To do this, Turbo C defines the library function *ctrlbrk()*. *Ctrlbrk()* has the following prototype definition:

```
void ctrlbrk (int (*fptr)(void));
```

That is, *ctrlbrk()* returns no value and accepts the address of a function that takes no arguments and returns an integer. *(*Fptr)()* is not invoked directly off of the interrupt; that is, it is not the contents of *FPTR* that get stored into *INTERRUPT 0x23*. Rather, the function *(*fptr)()* gets called as part of Turbo C's *INTERRUPT 0x23* handling. The point is that, unlike the true interrupt handlers I will be examining later in this chapter, *(*fptr)()* should not be an interrupt type function.

Once installed, the *break handler* can perform any housekeeping chores necessary. Database applications may define *break handlers* to put various file entries away, paint programs may wish to UnDo the *current* command, editors might simply stop and await further input. Once finished with application specific tasks, the *break handler* has three choices: 1) it may exit the current program and return to DOS; 2) it may continue the user program; or 3) it may start execution at some other point in the user program.

*(*Fptr)()* returns to DOS by returning a 0 to the caller. Returning any other value will cause the Turbo C *break handler* to return the program to the point of interruption. But if you want to return the user to some earlier menu you will want to make use of the third option, to pass control to some other portion of the user program. To do this, you will need to use a C facility that I have yet to discuss, the *setjmp()* and *longjmp()* routines.

So far I have spoken little of the *GOTO* instruction in C, although I did note it back in Chapter 1. Although *GOTO* represents the best solution to some problems, I couldn't sleep at night thinking that had I encouraged its wholesale use. The *longjump()* is a somewhat different animal, however.

Simply said, *setjmp()* saves into a buffer the state of the computer at the point that it is called. *Setjmp()* then returns a 0 to the caller. *Longjmp()* is called to return to the state of the computer previously saved off in such a buffer. *Longjmp()* does not return to the caller at all. Instead, the program reappears from the previously called *setjmp()* routine. *Longjmp()* passes a value that is returned from *setjmp()* when it reappears. The program can use this value to determine from which *longjmp()* it has just come. This value cannot be 0, lest the program gets it confused with the 0 returned when *setjmp()* is first called. In practice it looks like Prg9_1.

```
/*Prg9_1 - control break Handler
   by Stephen R. Davis, 1987

  Use the Turbo C provided ctrlbrk() routine to establish
  our own control break handler.  We will put ourselves into
  an infinite loop.  Entering control break will enter us into
  infinite loop.  One more time and we exit.  This is an
  example of the longjmp as well as the installation of multiple
  control-break handlers.
*/

#include <stdio.h>
#include <dos.h>
#include <setjmp.h>

/*prototype definitions*/
int break1 (void);
int break2 (void);

/*global data definitions*/
jmp_buf save;

/*break1 - intercept the first control break*/
int break1 (void)
{
```

```
26[ 1]:      printf ("First break entered!\n");
27[ 1]:      longjmp (save, 1);
28[ 0]: }
29[ 0]:
30[ 0]: /*break2 - intercept the second control break*/
31[ 0]: int break2 (void)
32[ 0]: {
33[ 1]:      printf ("Second break entered!\n");
34[ 1]:      longjmp (save, 2);
35[ 0]: }
36[ 0]:
37[ 0]: /*Main - main program to exercise the break handler*/
38[ 0]: main ()
39[ 0]: {
40[ 1]:      int value;
41[ 1]:
42[ 1]:      value = setjmp (save);
43[ 1]:      switch (value) {
44[ 2]:           case 0:
45[ 2]:                   ctrlbrk (break1);
46[ 2]:                   printf ("Entering first loop\n");
47[ 2]:                   for (;;)
48[ 3]:                        printf ("  Infinite loop #1\n");
49[ 2]:           case 1:
50[ 2]:                   ctrlbrk (break2);
51[ 2]:                   printf ("Entering second loop\n");
52[ 2]:                   for (;;)
53[ 2]:                        printf ("    Infinite loop #2\n");
54[ 2]:           default:
55[ 2]:                   printf ("That's all folks\n");
56[ 1]:      }
57[ 0]: }
```

I have purposely kept this program very simple. Prg9_1 performs no useful function. Instead, it outputs the string *Infinite loop #1* in an infinite loop until the operator enters a *control break* (or *control C*). As soon as this happens, the program springs to its first control *break handler break1()*, where it outs the message *First break entered* and then jumps back to outputting the string *Infinite loop #2* in a likewise unceasing fashion. Entering control break again prints the message *Second break entered* and halts the program.

Let's examine each step of the program carefully. The state of the computer is saved by the call to *setjmp()* on line 42. The buffer used is named *SAVE* and is defined on line 21. The type *JMP_BUF* is defined in a *TYPEDEF* in the include file *SETJMP.H*. The value returned from *setjmp()* is immediately tested by the switch statement. When *setjmp()* is called it returns a 0.

CASE 0 installs the *break handler break1()* on line 45 and then dives into the first infinite loop on lines 47 and 48. When the operator enters a *control break*, Turbo C's *break handler* passes control to *break1(). Break1()* outs a message to assure the operator that the *break* was detected, and then performs a *longjmp()* to the state saved in the buffer *SAVE* passing it a 1. This returns you back to line 42, to the return from *setjmp()*, only this time with the value 1 and not 0, so that the program knows how it got there.

From this point you drop into *CASE 1*, where it first installs a new *break handler* and then begins outputting the second infinite series of strings. Entering a *control break* again sends you to this new *break handler*, which repeats the process with the value 2. *CASE 2* back in *main()* outs a terminating message and quits.

The first thing you are likely to notice is this *hopping about.* Although all of this is really under strict program control, it does not have the neat appearance of a normal C program. This is typical of interrupt handlers. Look beyond this and notice that this is really a very cleanly structured program.

Also notice that a single program can have more than one *break handler*, although only one may be active at any given time. This is very important. As a program moves from one menu to another, the types of housekeeping that the program may want to perform change. Of course, the *break handler* can examine the variables to determine where the user was when the break was entered. It is usually more convenient to devise separate *break handlers* for the different major subdivisions of the program.

Finally, notice that more than one state can be saved by calls to *setjmp()*. In this case, we defined only the one buffer *SAVE*. We could have defined several buffers, *SAVE1*, *SAVE2*, etc. Calling *longjmp()* and passing it any one of these buffers would return the program to the call to *setjmp()* that initialized that buffer. Although I can think of applications for this, I can also imagine a certain unwieldiness. With power comes responsibility.

Proper use of user defined *break handlers* requires that they be included in the initial design process. It is not generally possible to retrofit user defined *break handlers* onto an otherwise well designed program and end up with anything presentable. This is especially true for programs containing multiple *break handlers.*

Hardware Interrupts

Peripheral devices, such as modems, printers and disks, require periodic attention from the host computer to which they are tied. For example, a printer usually has a small buffer, typically enough to hold one line of text, but sometimes large enough for an entire page. A personal computer can ship over enough text to fill that buffer in just a few seconds, but then it must go do something else while the relatively slow printer catches up.

How does a computer know when a piece of hardware wants its attention? One answer is that the computer can ask. In the printer example, the computer first asks permission before sending each character. If the printer's buffer is full, it denies permission to the PC to ship any more data. The host PC might continue to ask in a loop until the printer's buffer is no longer full, at which point permission is granted to the PC to send characters until the buffer is again filled.

This technique is called polling and was exactly how DOS handled *breaks*, as you saw above. The problems are immediately obvious. First, most peripheral devices are excruciatingly slow compared to personal computers. Even a slow microprocessor is fast enough to service several external devices. My PC has had a modem, two printers, a floppy drive, and a hard disk all going simultaneously with plenty of processing to spare.

Unless the host computer is willing to stay riveted watching each line appear on the printer, it places the responsibility back on the user program to periodically return control to the operating system. Without going into the details of non-preemptive multitasking operating systems, this is too much responsibility to place on the user program. Besides, it seems an awful waste of computing power to spend 99 percent of the processor's time asking a slow device the same question over and over. A far better solution is to let the hardware ask for attention when it needs it. Modern microprocessors have a mechanism for this form of *yanking their sleeve* called the interrupt.

Peripheral devices have inputs to the host computer that they can use to signal an interrupt. When an interrupt arises, perhaps because your printer is trying to signal that its buffer is no longer full, the hardware in the computer communicates this fact to its microprocessor. The microprocessor interrupts its normal processing (hence the name interrupt). It first saves the location of the next machine instruction to be executed, much as if a *CALL* instruction had been performed. It then jumps to the address of the handler for that interrupt, which in this case might ship some more data over to the printer before returning back to the saved address to continue normal processing.

Interrupts in the Intel family of microprocessors are numbered from 0 to 255 *(0xff)*. In the PC the following interrupts and their meanings are defined:

Hardware Interrupts in the IBM PC and AT

Interrupt	Function
0	Divide by 0
1	Single step
2	Nonmaskable interrupt
3	break point
4	Overflow **
5	Bounds exceeded trap **
	Print screen
6	Illegal instruction trap **
7	Device (such as 80287) not available **
8	Hardware clock
9	Keyboard
A	EGA vertical retrace
B	Serial port (COM2)
C	" " (COM1)
D	Disk service
E	Diskette service
F	Parrallel port (LPT)

** not in 8088 and 8086 microprocessors

Some of the hardware interrupts are defined by the processor itself. Executing a divide instruction with a denominator of 0 (an illegal operation) always generates an interrupt 0. This function stem from the way Intel microprocessors are built. Other interrupts are generated external to the microprocessor and are assigned values by the way the PC's hardware is put together.

Hardware interrupts are handled much like the *soft* interrupts you used in Chapter 6 to invoke BIOS routines. Just as those soft interrupts, invoked through the *int86()* Turbo C library function, each hardware interrupt is assigned a 4 byte *FAR* address in low memory. These addresses point to the handler for that interrupt. The address of the handler for interrupt 0 is stored in locations 0 through 3, that for interrupt 1 in locations 4 through 7, etc. These addresses are known as interrupt vectors.

When an interrupt arises, the microprocessor waits until the completion of the current instruction. It then pushes the flag register onto the stack along with the *FAR* address of the next instruction. The effect is exactly as if the processor just decided to execute an *int86()* to the *BIOS* routine associated with that interrupt.

Once this handler has taken care of the problem, it returns back to the following machine instruction.

Interrupts can be *disabled* with the Turbo C *disable()* library routine. When disabled, the microprocessor will ignore external interrupt requests. Interrupts that arise during this time must wait until interrupts are subsequently *enabled* by calling the *enable()* library routine. Interrupts are always disabled within an interrupt routine itself unless specifically reenabled. This includes BIOS routines that have been explicitly invoked. There is one interrupt that cannot be disabled. This is called the NonMaskable Interrupt (NMI). The NMI in the PC is connected to the random access memory parity circuit.

Writing interrupt handlers is a tricky business. Interrupts should be *transparent* to the normally executing code. That is, the interrupt comes, gets serviced, and returns to the exact point where started without that program ever knowing that it got interrupted. During an interrupt, however, the microprocessor saves only the processor flags and the return address. It is up to the interrupt handler to save off any registers that it intends to use and restore them to their original, pristine condition before returning.

For example, suppose your PC was attempting to execute the following lines of C code:

```
j = 2;                              /*line 1*/
i = j * 5;                          /*line 2*/
```

Let's assume that to execute line 2 the program loads up the value of *J* into the *AX* register in preperation for the multiply, but before it can carry out the multiply instruction an interrupt comes. If the interrupt handler restores *AX* to 2 before returning, then all is well, but suppose that it is faulty and leaves the value of *AX* set to some other value. The multiplication will be flawed; the result will not be 10, but rather some other, undesired and unpredicted value. Interrupt handlers that do not properly restore the status of the machine lead to very unpredictable behavior. Such a handler will invariably lead the machine to collapse in total confusion, requiring a total reset to restore sanity.

This is why most programmers consider interrupt handlers to be well within the realm of assembly language programming. Normally, only assembly language provides control to the programmer to make sure that the contents of each register get safely saved off upon entry, and properly restored on exit. Turbo C does much of this work for you, however.

Turbo C defines a function type called *INTERRUPT*. It is used like other function classifications:

```
void interrupt proc (void);       /*declaring an interrupt
                                    function...*/
void interrupt *procptr (void);   /*...and a pointer to one*/
```

Turbo C adds instructions to the front of a function declared to be of type *INTERRUPT*, to store the microprocessor's registers onto the stack. When such a function is exited, Turbo C includes the instructions necessary to pop all of the registers back off of the stack, restoring them to their former glory. Upon exit, such functions pop all of the registers back off the stack and return with an IRET instruction. This is exactly what you need to write your own interrupt handlers!

Even though *INTERRUPT* type functions have a completely different interface, they can be called from normal Turbo C programs just like any function. They cannot be passed arguments (you will see to what purpose *INTERRUPT* type functions put arguments later in this chapter). There is not much purpose in making such a call, however, except as a debug aid. An *INTERRUPT* function whose address has been stored into an interrupt vector can also be invoked via the *int86()* call like a *BIOS* routine, as you will see.

Let's consider an example interrupt handler. I noted back in Chapter 7 that the PC has a hardware clock. This clock generates a hardware interrupt 18.2 times per second (interrupt *0x08)*. Once the PC has updated the time of day, it performs an interrupt *0x1c* to allow the user whatever processing desired. This interrupt is not normally used for anything so it will be ideal for experimentation.

Prg9_2a defines a handler for interrupt *0x1c*. This handler reads the current time, converts it into an ASCII string, and places this value in the upper right hand corner of the display. It also maintains a delta time (the time since the program began running) which it displays in the very next line. Of course, nothing "keeps" the clock in that position. As soon as the screen scrolls up, it scrolls right off of the top. But since the interrupt occurs 18 times per second, it won't stay gone for long. You may have already seen similar clock programs in the public domain.

Carefully examine this program, but before you do, start by just compiling and executing the program from the *IDE*. Try this both with and without *DEBUG* defined (*DEBUG* may be defined from the Environment selection off of the *Options* menu). It will be helpful when reading the program to see exactly what it does first.

```
/*Prg9_2a -- Display a clock on the screen
    by Stephen R. Davis, 1987

  As an example of an interrupt routine, inserted onto the timer
  tick interrupt.  On each clock tick, display an ASCII clock
  in the upper right hand corner of the clock.  Display the
  current time and the delta time since installed, both in
  24 hour format.

  If DEBUG is set, install routine in a harmless vector and
  invoke it from main().  This is to allow breakpoints to be
  set in the interrupt routine easily.  If DEBUG is
  either 0 or not defined, install normally (define via Options
  menu).

  (As always, this program may not be compatible with other
  TSR type programs.)
*/

#include <stdio.h>
#include <dos.h>
#include <stdlib.h>
#include <process.h>

/*first the prototyping definitions*/

void interrupt clock (void);
void display (int, int, int);
void out (char *, int, int);
void init (void);
int  restore (void);

/*define our data structures*/

union {
       long ltime;
       int stime [2];
      } p;
struct REGS regs;
int far *screen;
int prevtime, time, minute, hour;
char buffer [10];
void interrupt (*fn) ();

/*define the DEBUG relative information*/

#if DEBUG
      #define vect 0x48
      struct REGS reg2;
#else
      #define vect 0x1c
#endif

/*Clock - grab the interrupt and provide the function*/
void interrupt clock (void)
{
      /*get the time and convert it to minutes since midnite*/
      regs.h.ah = 0;
      int86 (0x1a, &regs, &regs);
      p.stime [0] = regs.x.dx;
      p.stime [1] = regs.x.cx;
      time = (int)(p.ltime / (long)1092);
```

```

     /*now display the current time in 24 hour format*/
     display (time, 0, 75);

     /*then display the delta*/
     if (prevtime == -1)
          prevtime = time;
     if ((time -= prevtime) < 0)
          time += (24 * 60);
     display (time, 1, 75);
}

/*Display - put a time on the screen in the position indicated.
            Remember we can't do any DOS calls here.*/
void display (number, y, x)
     int number, x, y;
{
     hour = number / 60;
     minute = _DX;
     sprintf (buffer, "%2.2u:%2.2u", hour, minute);
     buffer [5] = '\0';
     out (buffer, y, x);
}

/*Out - out a string onto the screen w/o using system call*/
void out (buffer, y, x)
     char *buffer;
     int y, x;
{
     int far *scrptr;

#if DEBUG
     /*print out the data to make sure it is correct*/
     printf ("%s", buffer);
#endif
     scrptr = screen + (y * 80 + x);
     while (*buffer)
          *scrptr++ = 0x1700 + *buffer++;
}

/*Main - exercise the above routine.  When DEBUG is set to 1,
         'vect' is directed to an otherwise unused vector (48).
         This allows us to easily debug the interrupt routine
         using our favorite debugger.  Once debugged, DEBUG is
         set to 0 and the vector is redirected to the TimerTick
         interrupt (1C).*/
main ()
{
     int i, j, k;

     init ();

     fn = getvect (vect);
     setvect (vect, clock);
     ctrlbrk (restore);

     /*loop around for at least 2 minutes so that you can see
       the clock increment to prove to yourself that it is
       working*/
     for (i = 0; i < 150; i++) {
         for (j = 0; j < 30000; j++)
              k = j * 5;
         printf ("  this is just dummy output  --"
                 "  watch the clock\n");
```

```
127[ 2]: #if DEBUG
128[ 2]:             /*invoke the interrupt so we can debug it*/
129[ 2]:             int86 (vect, &reg2, &reg2);
130[ 2]: #endif
131[ 1]:       };
132[ 1]:
133[ 1]:       /*restore the interrupt to its former value*/
134[ 1]:       setvect (vect, fn);
135[ 0]: }
136[ 0]:
137[ 0]: /*Init - set the screen address and clear the screen*/
138[ 0]: void init ()
139[ 0]: {
140[ 1]:      #define mono (int far *)0xb0000000 /*for mono displays...*/
141[ 1]:      #define cga  (int far *)0xb8000000 /*...for ega and cga*/
142[ 1]:      int mode;
143[ 1]:
144[ 1]:      prevtime = -1;
145[ 1]:
146[ 1]:      regs.h.ah = 0x0f;
147[ 1]:      int86 (0x10, &regs, &regs);
148[ 1]:      mode = regs.h.al;
149[ 1]:      if (regs.h.ah != 80)               /*fixed to 80 columns*/
150[ 1]:           abort ();
151[ 1]:
152[ 1]:      if (mode == 7)
153[ 1]:           screen = mono;
154[ 1]:      else
155[ 1]:           if (mode == 3 || mode == 2)
156[ 1]:                screen = cga;
157[ 1]:           else
158[ 1]:                abort ();
159[ 0]: }
160[ 0]:
161[ 0]: /*Restore - restore the old interrupt address in the event of a
162[ 0]:             control break*/
163[ 0]: int restore (void)
164[ 0]: {
165[ 1]:       /*restore the interrupt to its former value*/
166[ 1]:       setvect (vect, fn);
167[ 1]:
168[ 1]:       /*tell the operator what he has done*/
169[ 1]:       printf ("\nbreak!\n");
170[ 1]:
171[ 1]:       /*now exit the program back to DOS*/
172[ 1]:       return 0;
173[ 0]: }
```

As with all other C programs, execution begins with *main()*. The routine *init()* only gets called so the clock program can decide whether the display is of the monochrome or CGA variety. The call to *init()* can be removed if it is known that Prg9_2a will only be executed on a single type of display. The pointer *SCREEN* is initialized to MDA memory (mode 7) or CGA memory (mode 3). Line 116 installs the function, *clock()*, into interrupt *VECT*, which is either *0x1c*, if it is not in *DEBUG* mode, or a harmless *0x48* if it is. However,

Figure 9.1

```
this is just dummy output  --  watch the clock                          21:55
this is just dummy output  --  watch the clock                          00:01
this is just dummy output  --  watch the clock
this is just dummy output  --  watch the clock
this is just dummy output  --  watch the clock
this is just dummy output  --  watch the clock
this is just dummy output  --  watch the clock
this is just dummy output  --  watch the clock
this is just dummy output  --  watch the clock
this is just dummy output  --  watch the clock
this is just dummy output  --  watch the clock
this is just dummy output  --  watch the clock
this is just dummy output  --  watch the clock
this is just dummy output  --  watch the clock
this is just dummy output  --  watch the clock
this is just dummy output  --  watch the clock
this is just dummy output  --  watch the clock
this is just dummy output  --  watch the clock
this is just dummy output  --  watch the clock
this is just dummy output  --  watch the clock
this is just dummy output  --  watch the clock
this is just dummy output  --  watch the clock
this is just dummy output  --  watch the clock
this is just dummy output  --  watch the clock
```

Screen clock displayed in corner of display

before it can install itself in that slot it must first record what is already there. The contents of that vector are read on line 115 and stored into the variable FN, which is defined as a pointer to an interrupt function on line 43. Upon completion, main restores the contents of the interrupt (line 134). (The Turbo C library routines *getvect()* and *setvect()* are used to retrieve and store the contents of an interrupt vector.)

The actual program is another of those *do nothing* types. What the main program actually does is not terribly important. In this case, it periodically prints a line on the screen that directs your attention to the clock it is placing in the upper right-hand corner. This *do nothing main()* could be replaced by anything that you desire—it might be a word processor or a database application, or whatever else that might reasonably have a clock attached.

Notice, that already you must make use of a *break handler*. If the user gets impatient watching the same output appear over and over on the screen, he might be tempted to enter a *control break* to bring it to an early end. You must not allow the program to terminate without replacing the old interrupt address. If you do, the interrupt will point to a routine that is no longer loaded in memory.

Figure 9.2

```
C:\USER\C                                                        21:59
C>d:prg9_2a                                                      00:01
  this is just dummy output  --  watch the clock
21:5800:00  this is just dummy output  --  watch the clock
21:5800:00  this is just dummy output  --  watch the clock
21:5800:00  this is just dummy output  --  watch the clock
21:5800:00  this is just dummy output  --  watch the clock
21:5800:00  this is just dummy output  --  watch the clock
21:5800:00  this is just dummy output  --  watch the clock
21:5800:00  this is just dummy output  --  watch the clock
21:5800:00  this is just dummy output  --  watch the clock
21:5800:00  this is just dummy output  --  watch the clock
21:5900:01  this is just dummy output  --  watch the clock
21:5900:01  this is just dummy output  --  watch the clock
21:5900:01  this is just dummy output  --  watch the clock
21:5900:01  this is just dummy output  --  watch the clock
21:5900:01  this is just dummy output  --  watch the clock
21:5900:01  this is just dummy output  --  watch the clock
21:5900:01  this is just dummy output  --  watch the clock
21:5900:01  this is just dummy output  --  watch the clock
21:5900:01  this is just dummy output  --  watch the clock
21:5900:01  this is just dummy output  --  watch the clock
21:5900:01  this is just dummy output  --  watch the clock
21:5900:01  this is just dummy output  --  watch the clock
21:5900:01_
```

Prg9_2 in DEBUG mode

You could, of course, disable breaks by setting *BREAK=OFF*. This is not really a satisfactory answer. Users do not like being forced to wait for some long winded output in which they have long since lost interest. The *break* routine *restore()*, which you install at the beginning of *main()*, restores the interrupt to its former value even if the user breaks prematurely. (If you don't mind rebooting your machine, try commenting out the *break handler* and control break out of Prg9_2a. Your computer will crash as soon as another program overwrites the memory previously occupied by the program destroying the interrupt routine.)

Having installed *clock()* into the proper interrupt vector, each clock interrupt now automatically calls the routine. The actual program is reasonably straightforward, using many of the techniques you have already studied in this book. *BIOS* call *0x1a* reads the time in terms of number of clock ticks since midnight. This gets converted to minutes and seconds in 24-hour format and displayed on the screen at the *x* (column)-*y*(row) position indicated. The expression on line 98 converts this *x-y* location to screen address. This address is subsequently used for direct memory transfer.. The constant on line 100 sets the color of the background and foreground: *0x1700* provides for a blue background (*0x1000*) and a white foreground (*0x0700*). This can be changed to whatever is most pleasing. (Line 81 is nothing more than a bit of programming *slight of hand.* After performing the division of line 80, the 8086 processor leaves the residue in the *DX* register. Line 81 transfers this residue onto *MINUTE.* This has the same effect as the % operator without performing another division.)

For older CGA displays it may be necessary to add a check for retrace, just as we did with the direct screen output routines in Chapter 7. Failure to do so results in minor *tick marks* appearing randomly accross the screen with these older display cards.

Notice how this program uses the parameter *DEBUG.* If debug is defined from the *IDE*, the program includes extra statements that aid in the debugging process. This scaffolding was inserted in the program early on with the idea that it would be removed before publication. Debugging interrupt handlers is such a difficult task that I decided to leave it in to provide the reader a little more insight into the process.

Before attempting to make a function like *clock()* an interrupt routine, it should be completely tested. This can be done by just calling the function like any other. As mentioned earlier, *INTERRUPT* routines may be called from Turbo C. Calling the function in a conventional fashion allows the use of a normal debugger. New functions that can be easily perfected as simple routines may be quite difficult as interrupt routines. Since successful direct screen output is sometimes tricky, it is often convenient to add write statements such as the one in routine *out()* on line 96.

Once it is felt that the interrupt routine is working properly, the code may be added to *main()* to install it into an interrupt. Ideally, it should first be installed into an interrupt not otherwise in use. *Main()* can then use *int86()* to invoke the interrupt routine. While not as straightforward as calling directly, invoking an interrupt routine via *INT86()* is still much simpler than via a *real* interrupt. Make sure all registers are being restored properly by printing out the register structure before and after the call to *int86().* Normal debuggers will usually still work with this type of arrangement.

When there is little doubt that the interrupt routine is working properly, install it into the intended interrupt. If possible, do so in a small, *do nothing* program such as I have done. This reduces the number of variables that must be contended with. Most debuggers can't properly handle routines servicing interrupts that might be going off all around it. If a problem arises at this point it is usually necessary to back up one step to the harmless interrupt and investigate the problem. To simplify this transition *VECT* and the extra source code are conditionally defined depending on the value of *DEBUG*. It may be necessary to *move back and forth* several times before the routine functions properly.

Once this works, you are finally free to add this to the real application with all its complexity. This step is generally without peril—all of the problems should have been ironed out in previous steps. You may be tempted to short circuit this function and dump your interrupt routine into your application even before it has been properly checked out as a subroutine. This will not save you time, however, I assure you.

Terminate and Stay Resident Programs

Using the above techniques you can define interrupt handlers to add all sorts of capabilities to your programs. In the above example, adding a little clock on the screen can do a lot to liven up an existing application. Similarly, you could have built interrupt handlers for any sort of plug-in card that you might be building. This can be a powerful capability.

The clock was transient, however. As soon as the program terminated, it had to be careful to restore the timer interrupt vector to its old value. What if you wanted to create an interrupt handler that continued to function even after the main program had terminated and DOS had regained control?

Just as with C's handling of the heap via *malloc()* and *free()*, DOS maintains control of memory. When a program is executed, it is given control of all of the memory. It may restore some of this memory to the operating system via system calls. Whatever memory it still occupies is returned to DOS when it terminates via any of the normal mechanisms.

There is, however, a special system call known variously as *Keep Process* or *Terminate* and *Stay Resident* (system call *0x31*). (Use of the older interrupt *0x27* should be avoided.) When this system call is invoked, the caller is terminated, just like normal, but some of the memory occupied is not returned to the system. The amount that is reserved must be indicated by the caller.

You are no longer compelled to reinstall the old interrupt vector when you exit. You can simply tell DOS not to overwrite the memory being used by the interrupt handler. The clock stays up forever!

Figure 9.3

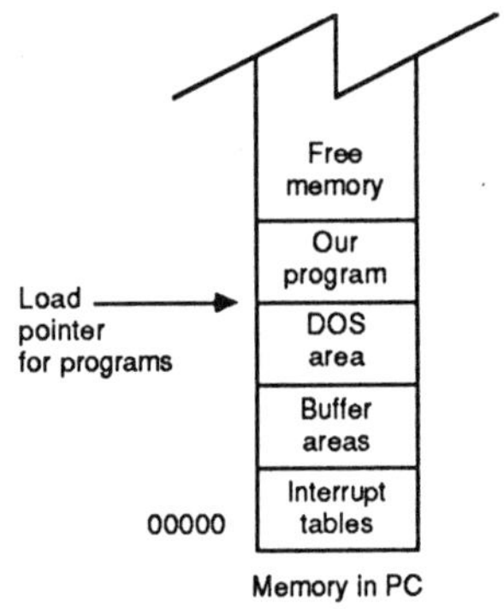

Before executing keep( )

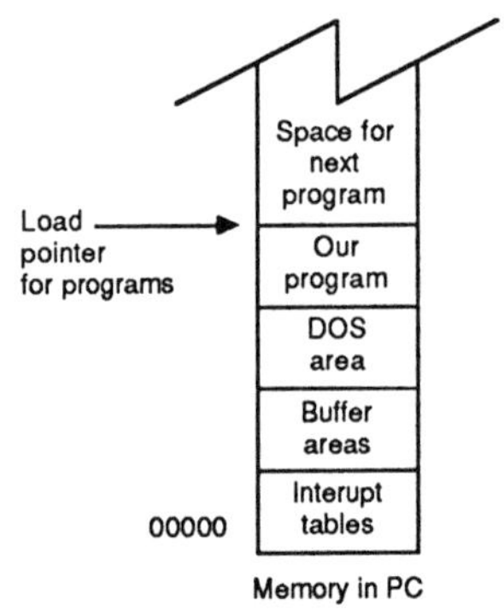

After executing keep( )

Performing this magic in Turbo C does involve a few concessions to reality, of course. You do not invoke system call *0x31* directly because Turbo C provides access via the library routine *keep()*. In addition to the return status, you must tell *keep()* how much memory the program needs to reserve for its own use. This is a difficult question to answer, one with which I struggled for a long time.

In assembly language, it's quite easy. The programmer has control of where everything is located so he knows exactly how much memory his program needs. Turbo C is not nearly so straightforward as the programmer does not have control of where everything is located. Still, you know that a program compiled under the TINY memory model cannot use more than 64k of memory. Therefore, the safest rule for TSR programs written under Turbo C is to compile the program under the TINY memory model and then instruct *keep()* to reserve 64k of memory for your program's use.

(In actual practice once you are absolutely sure that your program functions properly you can reduce the amount of memory reserved. Clever programmers will be tempted to examine the load map carefully for signs of the proper value. An almost as effective method is to simply determine empirically: keep reducing the amount of memory reserved for the program until it no longer executes properly. A third approach is to carefully zero out memory in the 64k window before loading the program. Load the program and then execute it for awhile. Now use a debugger to examine memory to determine how much memory appears to be used. In these example programs I have left the value at 64k. If you intend to get very serious about TSRs, you will probably want to invest in the source code to the Turbo C libraries so that you can control, or at least know, where data are being stored.)

An even more serious limitation involves DOS itself. DOS is non-reentrant. (Microsoft obviously did not use the good programming practices advocated in this book!) Actually, the primary reason this is so is that DOS uses its own stack, not relying on their being sufficient room on the caller's stack. But this means that DOS can easily get confused if your interrupt program attempts to make a system call.

Suppose that DOS is active when the interrupt arrives. Your program is immediately dispatched to service the request, leaving DOS stopped. Now if your program makes its own DOS call, the first thing DOS will do is grab its stack. Normally that's okay, but this time the stack is already in use by the DOS call that got interrupted. Your DOS request finishes without problem and then you return. But now the DOS program that got interrupted is completely confused. Somebody has come in and changed all of the values which it has been husbanding on the DOS stack. It's time to reboot.

This means you must be very careful about which Turbo C routines you decide to call. Not only can't you make a system call directly, you cannot call a Turbo C library routine that might make a system call. Besides, your program is no longer executing from the *Turbo C environment.* Values which Turbo C might initialize when your program first comes up, are going unmonitored. For the most part this all means that, except for some pretty simple functions, you are on your own when writing Terminate and Stay Resident programs.

Prg9_2b is the same clock program only converted now to continue supplying a clock on the screen after it terminates. In operation, Prg9_2b is virtually identical to its predecessor. The clock gets read, reformatted and placed in the upper right hand corner of the screen. For the most part the program is the same. *Main()* no longer waits around to put the old vector back. You do not need a *break handler* now since you will not actually be running, rather you'll just be servicing interrupts. The references to *DEBUG* have been removed. Finally, the call to *sprintf()* has been removed. Since you had better learn to depend on yourself from now on, a series of equations has taken its place. Notice that you are not forced to modify the call to *BIOS* routine *0x1a*. The *BIOS* is reentrant.

```
/*Prg9_2b -- Display a clock on the screen (Interrupt stealer)
     by Stephen R. Davis, 1987

   This program should be compiled under the TINY memory
   model, and may then be converted into .COM file using the command:

   EXE2BIN PRG9_2B.EXE PRG9_2B.COM

   It can also be executed as an .EXE file.  Do not execute from IDE!

   This version makes no effort to get along with other interrupt
   routines.
   (It may be necessary to run this program with the help of
    SSTACK.COM.  See text for details.)
*/

#include <stdio.h>
#include <dos.h>
#include <stdlib.h>
#include <process.h>

#ifndef __TINY__
      #error Should use TINY compilation model
#endif
#define vect 0x1c

/*first the prototyping definitions*/

void interrupt clock (void);
void display (int, int, int);
void out (char *, int, int);
void init (void);

/*define our data structures*/

union {
       long ltime;
       int stime [2];
      } p;
struct REGS regs;
int prevtime, time, minute, hour;
```

```
char buffer [6];
int far *screen;

char digits [] = {"0123456789"};

/*Clock - grab the interrupt and provide the function*/
void interrupt clock (void)
{
      /*get the current time using the BIOS call*/
      regs.h.ah = 0;
      int86 (0x1a, &regs, &regs);
      p.stime [0] = regs.x.dx;
      p.stime [1] = regs.x.cx;
      time = (int)(p.ltime / (long)1092);

      /*now display the current time in 24 hour format*/
      display (time, 0, 75);

      /*then display the delta*/
      if (prevtime == -1)
           prevtime = time;
      if ((time -= prevtime) < 0)
           time += (24 * 60);
      display (time, 1, 75);
}

/*Display - put a time on the screen in the position indicated.
             Remember we can't do any DOS calls here.*/
void display (number, y, x)
      int number, x, y;
{
      hour = number / 60;
      minute = _DX;

      /*stuff this into an ascii buffer for output*/
      buffer [0] = digits [hour / 10];
      buffer [1] = digits [hour % 10];
      buffer [2] = ':';
      buffer [3] = digits [minute / 10];
      buffer [4] = digits [minute % 10];
      buffer [5] = '\0';

      out (buffer, y, x);
}

/*Out - out a string onto the screen w/o using system call*/
void out (buffer, y, x)
      char *buffer;
      int y, x;
{
      int far *scrptr;

      scrptr = screen + (y * 80 + x);
      while (*buffer)
           *scrptr++ = 0x1700 + *buffer++;
}

/*Main - install the above routine.*/
main ()
{
      init ();
      setvect (vect, clock);
      printf ("Clock installed in interrupt %2x\n", vect);
      keep (0, 0x1000);
```

```
106[ 0]: }
107[ 0]:
108[ 0]: /*Init - set the screen address and clear the screen*/
109[ 0]: void init ()
110[ 0]: {
111[ 1]:     #define mono (int far *)0xb0000000 /*for mono displays...*/
112[ 1]:     #define cga  (int far *)0xb8000000 /*...for ega and cga*/
113[ 1]:     int mode;
114[ 1]:
115[ 1]:     prevtime = -1;
116[ 1]:
117[ 1]:     regs.h.ah = 0x0f;
118[ 1]:     int86 (0x10, &regs, &regs);
119[ 1]:     mode = regs.h.al;
120[ 1]:     if (regs.h.ah != 80)                 /*fixed to 80 columns*/
121[ 1]:          abort ();
122[ 1]:
123[ 1]:     if (mode == 7)
124[ 1]:          screen = mono;
125[ 1]:     else
126[ 1]:          if (mode == 3 || mode == 2)
127[ 1]:               screen = cga;
128[ 1]:          else
129[ 1]:               abort ();
130[ 0]: }
131[ 0]:
```

To insure that it does not exceed the 64k limit reserved for it, Prg9_2b should only be compiled and linked under the *TINY* memory model; the check on line 22 insures adherence to this rule. Unlike Prg9_2a, Prg9_2b must not be executed under the *IDE*. Since the *IDE* is located in memory between DOS and the executing program, memory cannot be properly reserved. Instead the user should leave the *IDE*. He may also convert the PRG9_2.*EXE* into a *.COM* file before executing by using the DOS utility *EXE2BIN* via the command:

```
exe2bin prg9_2b.exe prg9_2b.com
```

(Note: both this program and the next have a problem with overrunning the available stack space. Both seem to work fine with DOS 3.0 and earlier but fail with later versions of DOS. Although this problem will eventually be addressed in Prg9_2d, I do not want to introduce too much complexity at one time. The following assembler program should be executed before executing Prg9_2b or Prg9_2c to solve the stack problem until I can address it in C later in this chapter.)

```
        PAGE     66,132

; Program SSTACK - Set up larger stack for Interrupt Routine
;  by Stephen R. Davis, 1987
;
; Because of the extreme stack demands of Turbo C, it is necessary
; to set up a larger stack before entering interrupt routines written
; in Turbo C with some versions of DOS.  In particular, Programs 9_2b
; and c work fine with DOS 3.0 but require SSTACK with 3.1.  SSTACK
```

```
; should only be executed as a .COM program.
;

VECT    EQU     68H                     ;SET TO UNUSED INTERRUPT

CSEG    SEGMENT
        ASSUME CS:CSEG,DS:CSEG,SS:CSEG
        ORG      100H                   ;MAKE THIS INTO A .COM FILE

START:
        JMP     INSTALL

        ORG     200H
SAVESP  DW      0                       ;ALLOCATE PLACE TO STORE OLD SS:SP
SAVESS  DW      0
SFLAG   DW      0

INTRUPT:
        CMP     CS:SFLAG,0              ;IS FLAG CLEAR?
        JZ      NEWSTACK
        INT     68H
        IRET
NEWSTACK:
        MOV     CS:SFLAG,1
        MOV     CS:SAVESP,SP            ;SAVE CALLER'S STACK
        MOV     CS:SAVESS,SS
        MOV     SP,CS                   ;PUT IN OUR OWN
        MOV     SS,SP
        MOV     SP,200H

        INT     VECT                    ;NOW INVOKE CLOCK INTERRUPT

        MOV     SS,CS:SAVESS            ;NOW RESTORE CALLER'S STACK
        MOV     SP,CS:SAVESP
        MOV     CS:SFLAG,0
        IRET
ENDINT:

      MESSG   DB "Clock interrupt stack helper installed",0DH,0AH,"$"
      NOTUSMSG DB "Interrupt already in use -- try another",0DH,0AH,"$"
      USMSG   DD "Do not install SSTACK more than once",0DH,0AH,"$"

        ASSUME CS:CSEG,DS:CSEG,SS:CSEG
INSTALL:
        MOV     AX,3500H+VECT           ;CHECK THE TARGET VECTOR
        INT     21H
        OR      BX,BX                   ;IN USE?
        JNZ     ERR
                                        ;NO - GO AHEAD THEN
        MOV     AX,3508H                ;GET TIMER VECTOR
        INT     21H
        MOV     DX,BX                   ;INSTALL TIMER INTO 'VECT'
        MOV     AX,ES
        PUSH    DS
        MOV     DS,AX
        MOV     AX,2500H+VECT
        INT     21H
        POP     DS

        MOV     DX,OFFSET INTRUPT       ;INSTALL OURSELVES IN CLOCK INT
        MOV     AX,2508H
        INT     21H

        MOV     DX,OFFSET MESSG         ;SEND ALL'S WELL MESSAGE
```

```
        MOV     AH,09H
        INT     21H

        MOV     AX,3100H                ;KEEP PROCESS WITH 0 ERROR CODE
        MOV     DX,OFFSET ENDINT
        MOV     CL,4                    ;CONVERT BYTES TO PARAGRAPHS
        SHR     DX,CL
        INC     DX                      ;ACCOUNT FOR ROUND OFF
        INT     21H


ERR:
        MOV     AX,3508H                ;GET THE TIMER INTERRUPT
        INT     21H

        CMP     BX,OFFSET INTRUPT       ;IT IS US?
        MOV     DX,OFFSET NOTUSMSG      ;ASSUME IT ISN'T
        JNZ     NOTUS
        MOV     DX,OFFSET USMSG         ;IT IS US
NOTUS:
        MOV     AH,09H
        INT     21H

        MOV     AX,4CFFH                ;TERMINATE WITH FF ERROR CODE
        INT     21H

        CSEG    ENDS
        END      START
```

Interrupt Borrowing

So you can use the *keep()* library call to create interrupt handlers for devices outside of your own programs as long as you are willing to forgo the support of DOS and the Turbo C library. This is all very nice for interrupt handlers, but in reality the timer tick interrupt *0x1c* is not an interrupt handler. Instead, the hardware interrupt timer comes in on interrupt *0x08*. Once DOS has done all the processing it needs to, it executes an interrupt *0x1c*, much as you do with your own *int86()* calls.

Normally interrupt vector *0x1c* just points to an interrupt return—a sort of null program. This vector allows user programs to mark the passage of time just as DOS does. The way I have written this interrupt function, however, only one program can enjoy this capability at a time. In both Prg9_2a and Prg9_2b the program cavalierly removed whatever was there and placed itself into the vector to the exclusion of all others. If it continues this unfriendly behavior, the next installable is likely to do the same to it!

A program should make more effort to get along with its neighbors. How much better it would be if it could use the interrupt in an *invisible* way so that other routines that have already grafted themselves onto interrupt *0x1c* are not even aware of its presence. Is such a thing possible?

With only a very few changes, the antisocial Prg9_2b has been converted into the hospitable Prg9_2c.

```
/*Prg9_2c -- Display a clock on the screen (Interrupt borrower)
    by Stephen R. Davis, 1987

  This program should be compiled under the TINY memory
  model and may then converted into .COM file using the command:

  EXE2BIN PRG9_2C.EXE PRG9_2C.COM

  It can be executed as an .EXE file.  Do not execute from IDE!

  This version of the clock routine tries a little harder to
  get along with other timer interrupt routines by passing control
  along to them...it borrows the interrupt.
  (It may be necessary to use SSTACK.COM to execute this program.
   See text for details.)
*/

#include <stdio.h>
#include <dos.h>
#include <stdlib.h>
#include <process.h>

#ifndef __TINY__
      #error Should use TINY compilation model
#endif
#define vect 0x1c

/*first the prototyping definitions*/

void interrupt clock (void);
void display (int, int, int);
void out (char *, int, int);
void init (void);

/*define our data structures*/

union {
       long ltime;
       int stime [2];
      } p;
struct REGS regs;
void interrupt (*old)(void);
int prevtime, time, minute, hour;
char buffer [6];
int far *screen;

char digits [] = {"0123456789"};

/*Clock - grab the interrupt and provide the function*/
void interrupt clock (void)
{
      /*get the current time using the BIOS call*/
      regs.h.ah = 0;
      int86 (0x1a, &regs, &regs);
      p.stime [0] = regs.x.dx;
      p.stime [1] = regs.x.cx;
      time = (int)(p.ltime / (long)1092);

```

```
          /*now display the current time in 24 hour format*/
          display (time, 0, 75);

          /*then display the delta*/
          if (prevtime == -1)
               prevtime = time;
          if ((time -= prevtime) < 0)
               time += (24 * 60);
          display (time, 1, 75);

          /*pass control on to the next interrupt routine*/
          (*old)();
     }

     /*Display - put a time on the screen in the position indicated.
                 Remember we can't do any DOS calls here.*/
     void display (number, y, x)
          int number, x, y;
     {
          hour = number / 60;
          minute = _DX;

          /*stuff this into an ascii buffer for output*/
          buffer [0] = digits [hour / 10];
          buffer [1] = digits [hour % 10];
          buffer [2] = ':';
          buffer [3] = digits [minute / 10];
          buffer [4] = digits [minute % 10];
          buffer [5] = '\0';

          out (buffer, y, x);
     }

     /*Out - out a string onto the screen w/o using system call*/
     void out (buffer, y, x)
          char *buffer;
          int y, x;
     {
          int far *scrptr;

          scrptr = screen + (y * 80 + x);
          while (*buffer)
               *scrptr++ = 0x1700 + *buffer++;
     }

     /*Main - install the above routine.*/
     main ()
     {
          init ();
          old = getvect (vect);
          setvect (vect, clock);
          printf ("Clock intalled into vector %2x\n", vect);
          keep (0, 0x1000);
     }

     /*Init - set the screen address and clear the screen*/
     void init ()
     {
         #define mono (int far *)0xb0000000 /*for mono displays...*/
         #define cga  (int far *)0xb8000000 /*...for ega and cga*/
         int mode;

         prevtime = -1;

```

```
123[ 1]:        regs.h.ah = 0x0f;
124[ 1]:        int86 (0x10, &regs, &regs);
125[ 1]:        mode = regs.h.al;
126[ 1]:        if (regs.h.ah != 80)                /*fixed to 80 columns*/
127[ 1]:            abort ();
128[ 1]:
129[ 1]:        if (mode == 7)
130[ 1]:            screen = mono;
131[ 1]:        else
132[ 1]:            if (mode == 3 || mode == 2)
133[ 1]:                screen = cga;
134[ 1]:            else
135[ 1]:                abort ();
136[ 0]: }
137[ 0]:
```

Much as it did back in the first attempt, *main()* saves the address of interrupt *0x1c* into a local variable, in this case called *OLD*. It then continues to install its own function like normal. At the end of the interrupt function routine, however, it does not return directly. Instead it calls the routine whose address was previously stored in the vector it usurped (line 70). Effectively, it inserts itself between the old interrupt caller and interrupt routine in such a way that neither is aware of its existence. Note, *OLD* must be globally declared. Automatic variables, which are saved on the stack, do not retain their values from one interrupt to the next. *OLD* must also be declared void interrupt *(*OLD)()*. Otherwise Turbo C will not call it properly.

If another program were to come along and install itself in the chain, your program would be just as unaware as its victim was. In this way, chains of TSRs can be built on a single interrupt. This technique is known as *Interrupt Borrowing* and the programs are known as *Interrupt Borrowers* (as opposed to *Interrupt Stealers* like the first two interrupt handlers). This may not seem all that significant, but in fact it is very important.

As I have pointed out before, *BIOS* calls and even calls to DOS are also interrupts. If you can borrow a hardware interrupt then you can just as easily borrow a *BIOS* interrupt. For example, you could insert the address of your own routine in, interrupt *0x10*, the screen output *BIOS* routine. Every time a request for screen output came through interrupt *0x10*, it would come to you. Since you don't really want to go to all the trouble of emulating all of the different screen *BIOS* functions, you simply pass the request along to the *real BIOS* routine, who's address you have carefully saved off in your program somewhere else. Since the real *BIOS* routine is unchanged, the request gets serviced more or less the way it always did.

Figure 9.4

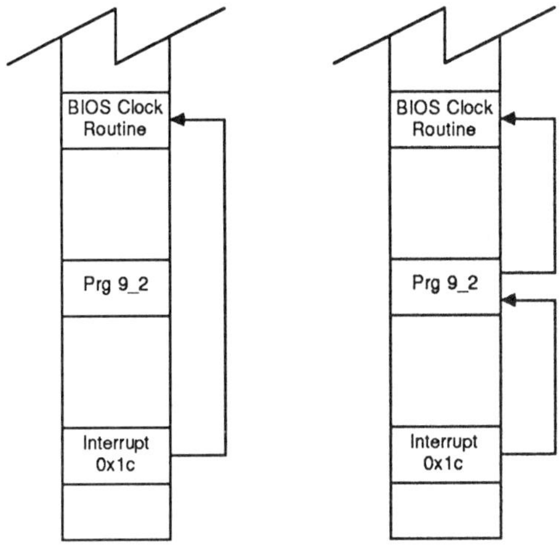

Before borrowing
clock interrupt

So if an interrupt borrower is invisible to both the caller and the called, then how is this any more than just an intellectual curiosity?

In the case of the hardware interrupt, the contents of the registers upon entry into the handler had little or no significance as they were completely unpredictable—a hardware interrupt can occur at any time. The contents of the registers during a *BIOS* interrupt do have significance, however, as this is how the calling program communicates with the *BIOS* routine. For example, suppose that the user program were trying to output a character to the screen using interrupt *0x10* . It would store the value *0x0e* into the *AH* register, the character into *AL*, and then make the call. An interrupt borrower can examine the contents of the registers and know what request is being made.

Still nothing to write home about, except that the borrower can just as easily change the values. Taking a simplistic example, suppose you decided that you didn't like lower case letters. Somehow they offend you (with all of the religious sects about, this may not be all that abstract an example). You could create an interrupt borrower that inserts itself between user programs and the interrupt 0x10 *BIOS* routine. Everytime a request comes through to output a character, your routine checks to make sure it is upper case. Lower case letters either get screened out (not a very good idea) or converted to the more acceptable upper case equivalent before output.

If you were to write and install such an interrupt borrower, you would end up with a computer that only knew how to output upper case letters. Programs using interrupt *0x10* still attempt to output lowercase letters. It's just that your interrupt borrower diligently converts them before passing them on to the real interrupt *0x10* for output. Of course, this does nothing to input. Letters are both upper and lower case internally—conversion is only on output. This is not such a wonderful program to write as the user can get quite confused when *A* no longer matches *A*, because one of them is actually lower case and the other upper. But, as they say, it's the thought that counts.

I noted earlier that a function of type *INTERRUPT* automatically saves the registers on the stack, but as they had no meaning then, I made no attempt to access them. In fact, Turbo C also allows such functions access to these variables. An *INTERRUPT* function may be declared as follows:

```
void interrupt normal (bp, di, si, ds, es, dx, cx, bx, ax)
     unsigned ax, bx, cx, dx, es, ds, si, di, bp;
{
}

void interrupt unusual (bp, di, si, ds, es, dx, cx, bx, ax,
                         ip, cs, flags)
     unsigned ax, bx, cx, dx, es, ds, si, di, bp, cs, ip, flags;
{
}
```

Accessing the argument *AX* within the interrupt routine accesses the value of the *AX* register when the interrupt occured. Changing its value, changes the value of the register upon return from the interrupt. This is the only case in Turbo C where changing the value of an argument in a function changes its value in the *caller*. It may seem that the declaration order of these arguments is backward, but really this is just a by-product of the order in which the registers are pushed before entering the function.

In the above example, *normal()* has been declared in the normal fashion. Access is granted to all of the registers except for *SS* and *SP*. It is also possible, should this prove necessary, to access the return address pushed on the stack via a declaration such as *unusual()* above. *CS:IP* represent the code segment and offset of the next instruction upon return from the interrupt, the return address. Normally, you would not want to change the return address, but you might be curious to examine it. You might, for example, want to know if you are interrupting DOS or not. You can tell where you came from by examining *CS:IP* off of the stack.

Figure 9.5

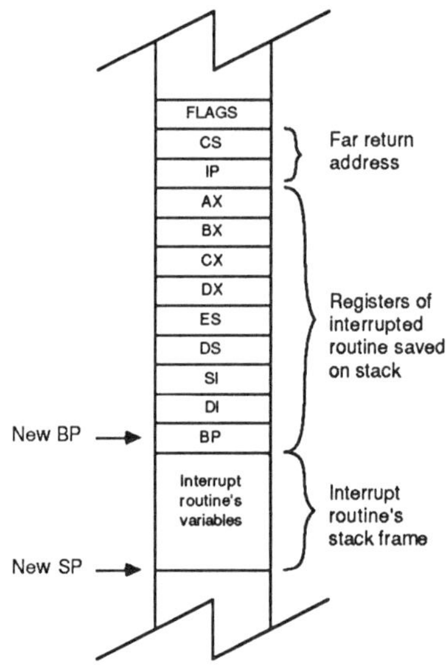

Stack structure of interrupt function

This provides the tool needed to implement the small letter filter discussed above. By examining the upper half of *AX*, you know what type of *BIOS* request is being made. If it is *0x0e*, then you can look at the lower half to know what the character is.

Let's use this principle to gain control of the clock program. Suppose we wanted to make the second line (the one with the delta) optional. In addition, let's add a reset for the delta time. The user might want to reset the delta counter at the beginning of each new task. At the end of the task, he or she can write down the amount of time spent, perhaps for IRS purposes, and then reset it for the next task.

Back in Prg9_2a, this would have been easy (everything was easier back then). Since the clock was a part of the executing program, this program had access to all of its variables. We would merely have invented some flags to control the clock's output and then defined a command for setting these flags. Of course, this would only have worked as long as the user remained within Prg9_2a.

Prg9_2c is not a part of the currently executing program. There is no direct connection between them, and it is not desirable for one to directly access the memory of the other. However, it is possible. The currently executing program could fetch the address of Prg9_2c from the vector to gain access to its memory. The program might know that a particular variable is some fixed offset from the beginning of the interrupt function. I mention this only to point out what a bad idea this is. Besides being very prone to error, this precludes another interrupt borrower getting in the chain after Prg9_2c.

A better approach would be to store the address of the flags into an otherwise unused interrupt. A control program could then come along later, fetch the address of the flags, and set them appropriately. This approach, while still not very structured, is much better than the one above. There are plenty of interrupts up in the higher areas that go, otherwise, completely unused. Many programs, including DOS itself, use this approach. If you do happen to be unlucky enough to encounter some other TSR trying to use the same interrupt, however, your program crashes. This is one reason why some TSRs cannot coexist in the same machine.

There is a better approach. Certain characters are very unusual during output. You could borrow interrupt *0x10* and watch for one or two of these very unusual characters. For example, you might toggle the second line whenever you saw the character ~ and reset it upon encountering ´. (While not a wise choice with Spanish or French, it works fine with English. In any case, with only slightly increased complication, you could use a whole string of unlikely characters to completely remove the possibility of accidentally resetting the clock.) Prg9_2d appears below, rewritten exactly along these lines.

```
/*Prg9_2d -- Display a clock on the screen w/ Keyboard Control
    by Stephen R. Davis, 1987

  This program should be compiled under the TINY memory
  mode and may then be converted into .COM file using the command:

  EXE2BIN PRG9_2D.EXE PRG9_2D.COM

  It can also be executed as an .EXE file.  Do not execute from IDE!

  This version adds the capability that the delta time can be
```

```
   hidden by entering '~' and cleared by entering '`'.  This is
   only intended as an example of a full TSR type program.
   (This version makes allowances for its own stack so that
    SSTACK should not be necessary.)
*/

#include <stdio.h>
#include <dos.h>
#include <stdlib.h>
#include <process.h>

#ifndef __TINY__
     #error Should use TINY compilation model
#endif

/*first the prototyping definitions*/

void interrupt clock (void);
void display (int, int, int);
void out (char *, int, int);
void interrupt screenout(unsigned, unsigned, unsigned, unsigned,
                         unsigned, unsigned, unsigned, unsigned,
                         unsigned);
void init (void);

/*define our data structures*/

union {
       long ltime;
       int stime [2];
      } p;
struct REGS regs;
void interrupt (*oldclock)(void);
void interrupt (*oldscreen)(void);
int prevtime, time, minute, hour, dflag, temp;
char buffer [6];

int far *screen;
char digits [] = {"0123456789"};

/*allocate space for our own stack area*/

int savess, savesp, sflag;
char stack [0x1000];

/*Clock - grab the interrupt and provide the function*/
void interrupt clock (void)
{
     /*put in our own stack*/
     if (!sflag) {
          savesp = _SP;
          savess = _SS;
          _CX = (int)&stack[sizeof(stack)];
          _SS = _DS;
          _SP = _CX;
     }
     sflag++;

     /*get the current time (long format) using the BIOS call
       1a.  Divide this down into number of minutes (short
       format).*/
     regs.h.ah = 0;
     int86 (0x1a, &regs, &regs);
     p.stime [0] = regs.x.dx;
```

```
     p.stime [1] = regs.x.cx;
     time = (int)(p.ltime / (long)1092);

     /*now display the current time in 24 hour format*/
     display (time, 0, 75);

     /*then display the delta*/
     if (prevtime == -1)
          prevtime = time;
     if ((time -= prevtime) < 0)
          time += (24 * 60);
     if (dflag)
          display (time, 1, 75);

     /*pass control on to the next interrupt routine*/
     (*oldclock)();

     /*now restore caller's stack*/
     if (!--sflag) {
          _SS = savess;
          _SP = savesp;
     }
}

/*Display - put a time on the screen in the position indicated.
            Remember we can't do any DOS calls here.*/
void display (number, y, x)
     int number, x, y;
{
     hour = number / 60;
     minute = _DX;

     /*stuff this into an ascii buffer for output*/
     buffer [0] = digits [hour / 10];
     buffer [1] = digits [hour % 10];
     buffer [2] = ':';
     buffer [3] = digits [minute / 10];
     buffer [4] = digits [minute % 10];
     buffer [5] = '\0';

     out (buffer, y, x);
}

/*Out - out a string onto the screen w/o using system call*/
void out (buffer, y, x)
     char *buffer;
     int y, x;
{
     int far *scrptr;

     scrptr = screen + (y * 80 + x);
     while (*buffer)
          *scrptr++ = 0x1700 + *buffer++;
}

/*Screenout - examine characters being output using BIOS
              int 0x10.  When a '`' is encountered, clear
              the duration clock; if a '~' is seen, toggle
              the delta display on and off.*/
void interrupt screenout (bp, di, si, ds, es,
                          dx, cx, bx, ax)
     unsigned ax, bx, cx, dx, si, di, bp, ds, es;
{
     /*check for our characters:*/
```

```
    if ((temp = (ax & 0xff00)) == 0x0900
                          || temp == 0x0e00) {
         if ((temp = (ax & 0x00ff)) == '`')
              prevtime = -1;
         if (temp == '~')
              dflag = !dflag;
    }

    /*pass control onto BIOS routine to get character*/
    _AX = ax;
    _BX = bx;
    _CX = cx;
    _DX = dx;
    (*oldscreen)();
    ax = _AX;
    bx = _BX;
    cx = _CX;
    dx = _DX;
}

/*Main - install the above routine.*/
main ()
{
    init ();                              /*set screen pointer*/
    oldclock  = getvect (0x1c);
    oldscreen = getvect (0x10);
    setvect (0x1c, clock);
    setvect (0x10, screenout);

    keep (0, 0x1000);
}

/*Init - set the screen address and clear the screen*/
void init ()
{
    #define mono (int far *)0xb0000000 /*for mono displays...*/
    #define cga  (int far *)0xb8000000 /*...for ega and cga*/
    int mode;

    prevtime = -1; dflag = 1;

    regs.h.ah = 0x0f;
    int86 (0x10, &regs, &regs);
    mode = regs.h.al;
    if (regs.h.ah != 80)                  /*fixed to 80 columns*/
         abort ();

    if (mode == 7)
         screen = mono;
    else
         if (mode == 3 || mode == 2)
              screen = cga;
         else
              abort ();
}
```

Prg9_2d is very similar to its forebears except for the addition of the interrupt function *screenout()*. If you examine *main()* you see that this routine gets installed into interrupt *0x10* at the same time that *clock()* gets stuffed into *0x1c*.

Screenout() watches interrupt *0x10 BIOS* calls. Those that have nothing to do with outputting a character (all but *0x09* and *0x0e*) are passed on without change. When a character is being output, the value of the character is checked for one of the special characters. When one is encountered, the corresponding action is taken. Notice that *screenout()* can manipulate the critical variables since it is in the same program as *clock()* (even though it borrows a different interrupt) and, therefore, has access to all of its data. (The critical variables are the previous time and *DFLAG*, which is used to control the display of the delta time.)

Notice how *screenout()* calls the interrupt routine on line 153. Arguments cannot be passed to a function declared to be of type *INTERRUPT* in the normal fashion. Even if they could, the *BIOS* routine was not written in Turbo C. It expects its arguments in the registers. Therefore, use the pseudovariables to load the registers on lines 149 through 152 and then store the returned values back into the registers on line 154 through 157. (A safer but lengthier approach would be to place the address stored in *OLDSCREEN* into an unused interrupt vector and then apply our trusty *int86()*.)

You should be very careful about using pseudovariables in this fashion. When you load a value into a register such as *_AX*, there is nothing to keep Turbo C from using the register itself and destroying its contents. To avoid this, such transfers should be kept very simple. Specifically, you should not transfer elements of arrays or structures into registers directly or values returned from functions. Instead, all such values should first be held in simple variables that can then be transferred to the pseudovariables as the very last step before making the call. The same applies in reverse for storing the registers after the call.

```
    _AX = arg1 [i];          /*won't work*/
    _BX = regs.arg2;

instead

    temp1 = arg1 [i];        /*much better*/
    temp2 = regs.arg2;
    _AX = temp1;
    _BX = temp2;
```

One other problem that Prg9_2d addresses is that of stack space. Prg9_2b and Prg9_2c had a problem with using too much stack under certain conditions. Under DOS 3.0 and earlier this did not seem to be a problem but this lead to a crash with DOS 3.1 and later. The program *SSTACK* was introduced to solve the problem, but that really wasn't satisfactory.

The problem is that Turbo C, like most high level languages, makes a lot of demands on stack space. This is particularly true if there are lots of subroutine calls with lots of arguments being passed about. Generally, the calling function has only allocated enough stack for its needs with a little extra thrown in. Hopefully, you will have enough room to save off the registers upon entry, but one of the first things you should do is set up your own, king-sized stack.

Prg9_2d demonstrates how this is done. Lines 62 and 63 first save off the old stack pointer. Lines 64 through 66 then direct the stack pointer at a large block of unused memory declared within the program. Since stacks grow downward in memory, we must start with the stack at the last word in this block instead of offset 0. The pseudovariable *_CX* is used to insure that *_SS* and *_SP* get set in succeeding machine instructions with *_SS* being stored first. The 8086 microprocessor requires this convention lest an interrupt come in the middle of initializing these values. (Interrupts are disabled for one instruction after the *SS* is loaded to allow *SP* to set up also.) The flag *SFLAG* insures that the program does not set the stack twice in a row in the unlikely event that it interrupts itself. Lines 95 and 96 restore the caller's stack before returning. (Prg9_3d does not require *SSTACK*.)

How does this program work? Try executing the following command program:

```
#include <stdio.h>
#include <dos.h>

struct REGS regs;

main ()
{
        regs.h.ah = 0x0e;
        regs.h.al = '~';        /*for delta toggle*/
      /*regs.h.al = '`';*/      /*for reset delta time*/
        regs.h.bl = 0x07;
        int86 (0x10, &regs, &regs);
}
```

Of course, you would add some *printf()* text to tell the user what is happening and you might even get fancy by allowing switches or a menu to indicate the user's preference, but the principle is the same. Notice that the ~ and ` do appear on the screen. Had it been desirable, you could just as easily have suppressed them from appearing by not making the call to *(*oldclock)()* for these characters.

But it isn't really necessary to go to all this trouble. DOS uses the BIOS routines to output to the screen. Once installed, Prg9_2 is, in fact, examining every character DOS outputs, waiting for either of its special chaacters. Simply entering ~ or ´ at the keyboard will cause DOS to echo the character via interrupt *0x10* and influence our program.

Commercial TSRs use the very same principles of operation I have presented here. If a program borrows both the input and output BIOS routines, it has control in both directions. It's pretty much like the Twilight Zone: it has control of the vertical and the horizontal. Such a program can modify the operation of the PC in almost every way conceivable.

Much as we defined special output characters to control the program, we also could have defined special input characters by borrowing interrupt *0x16*. When one of these characters appeared on our input doorstep, we might have opened a window on the screen, as done back in Chapter 7, and put any type of menu desired. These special input characters are known as *hot keys* and form the entry key into many TSR wonders. (In our example, ~ and ´ were *hot characters*.) The only thing to remember here is that you are pretty much on your own. Without being in the Turbo C environment, you should not make too much use of the Turbo C library.

DOS Calls from TSRs

Early on I made the flat statement that *Terminate* and *Stay Resident* programs should not make calls to the DOS operating system. This stemmed from the fact that DOS is built nonreentrantly. Under certain conditions you can make DOS calls without any problems, however.

In some cases you can logically deduce that DOS can not possibly be active. The most obvious case is if you have just defined a new interrupt that you intend to execute from user programs. Being of your own invention, it is not possible that DOS can execute such an interrupt, and you can make system calls with impunity. This does not apply to old *BIOS* interrupts that have simply been rerouted through new interrupt numbers. This only applies to truly new routines.

In addition, it turns out that DOS actually maintains two stacks: one for calls 0 through *0x0c* and another for calls *0x0d* and up. This means that these two sections of DOS are actually reentrant with respect to each other. Why this should be, I have no idea, but you can use this fact to your advantage. For example, the screen BIOS call can only be made from one of two places: either from user code or from the DOS calls below *0x0c*. Therefore, screen *BIOS* borrowers are free to make DOS calls above *0x0a*, which includes the disk handling calls. By the same token, handlers that borrow the disk handling interrupts are free to use the screen output DOS calls below *0x0c*.

Random interrupts, including the timer, can interrupt DOS at almost any time. If it becomes imperative to make DOS calls from routines that borrow these interrupts, then the programmer must install what is known as a *sentry*. In its simplest form, the programmer writes a second interrupt borrower, much as you did with Prg9_2d to watch interrupt *0x10*. This handler is quite simple. Inserted into the path of interrupt *0x21*, the DOS system call interrupt, it increments a flag whenever a DOS call is made and decrements the flag whenever it returns. All other interrupt routines can examine the flag. If it is greater than 0 then DOS is active and the program cannot safely make a DOS call; if it is 0, then there is no danger.

If an interrupt occurs and the handler cannot make a DOS call because the sentry indicates that DOS is active, it usually returns, waits for the next timer interrupt and tries again. If you have ever noticed that occasionally *SideKick* beeps at you when you try to enter, this is exactly what has happened. SideKick has determined that DOS is active, so it beeps the speaker and goes to sleep for a few clock ticks until it can return and try again. After three retries it gives up.

DOS sentries are generally fairly simple to write. There are only two problems. One is system call 0, the Terminate call. This DOS call requires the code segment of the calling program. By revectoring interrupt *0x21*, you will change the caller's code segment and confuse DOS and the call will not work. This is easily solved by substituting within the sentry the Terminate Process call, *0x4c*, for DOS call 0. This call has all of the capabilities and does not require the code segment of the caller.

The second problem is a little tougher. If you were to watch your sentry you would notice that you are almost constantly in DOS as long as you are sitting at a *COMMAND.COM* prompt. This means that while you are entering commands such as *CD*, *DIR*, etc. your interrupt handler will have little chance to sneak in. There are several ways out of this problem. Some involve holding the first key, or, sometimes, the entire command until the return is entered before returning control back to DOS.

Many programs rely instead on the undocumented DOS interrupt *0x28*. As long as *COMMAND.COM* is waiting for a command, it seems to continuously execute this interrupt. Its function is unclear, but this fact can be used to determine whether DOS is merely waiting for more input. If so, the interrupt program is free to execute system calls above *0x0c*. This trap may be used by itself or in conjunction with a sentry.

Interfacing Turbo C with Other Languages through Interrupts

You have already seen how you can write your own interrupt handlers. So far you have been writing handlers for interrupts that were already defined. By extension, you can just as easily define new interrupts and write programs for them. You might extend the *BIOS* routines by defining newer, more powerful routines. Having written and installed such handlers, you can invoke them from your user programs.

This is not all that exciting of a development. Programs written relying on these interrupts will require the interrupt handlers to be installed before they can properly execute. This being the case, you could just as easily have included the interrupt code within the user program itself. There is one case, however, where there is a decided advantage to having a separate interrupt handler.

The interface to the *BIOS* routines is very simple. Since it is common to want to call these routines from time to time, every langauge written for the PC includes a mechanism for loading up registers and executing an interrupt. This being the case, your Turbo C interrupt handler can be invoked from any other language, once installed in an unused interrupt using the same mechanism used to access the BIOS. While this technique is a bit clumsy, it does avoid all of the stack and library hassles inherent in attempting to link the objects from two different languages into the same executable file.

For example, consider Prg9_3 below. This program is written to define a new interrupt *0x48*, which beeps the speaker. It has two subfunctions. Passing it a 0 in *_AX* sets the frequency of the beep, but does not actually beep the speaker. Passing it a 1, beeps the speaker at the current frequency and for the duration indicated in register *_DX*. Time is measured in units of clock ticks.

```
/*Prg9_3 -- Define a new "BIOS" function for Turbo Pascal
    by Stephen R. Davis, 1987

  Using more or less the same approach as we took with the other
  interrupt programs, we can assign any function  we desire to
  a new interrupt.  This function defines a new BIOS routine for
  beeping the speaker -- included are 2 subfunctions, which we
  invoke exactly like the BIOS subfunctions.

  This function can be invoked from any computer language which
  can perform software interrupts.  This is one way of "linking"
```

```
12[ 0]:   Turbo C with other computer languages.
13[ 0]: */
14[ 0]:
15[ 0]: #include <stdio.h>
16[ 0]: #include <dos.h>
17[ 0]:
18[ 0]: #ifndef __TINY__
19[ 0]:      #error Should use TINY compilation model
20[ 0]: #endif
21[ 0]:
22[ 0]: /*first the prototyping definitions*/
23[ 0]:
24[ 0]: void interrupt beep (unsigned, unsigned, unsigned, unsigned,
25[ 0]:                      unsigned, unsigned, unsigned, unsigned,
26[ 0]:                      unsigned);
27[ 0]:
28[ 0]: /*define our data structures*/
29[ 0]:
30[ 0]: unsigned freq, duration, prev, pclock, i;
31[ 0]: #define clock ((volatile unsigned far *)0x0040006c)
32[ 0]:
33[ 0]: /*Beep - beep the speaker.  We define 2 subfunctions according
34[ 0]:          to the value in AX:
35[ 0]:          0 - set the frequency, DX - contains the loop count
36[ 0]:          1 - beep. Duration in clock ticks is in DX*/
37[ 0]: void interrupt beep (bp, di, si, ds, es,
38[ 0]:                      dx, cx, bx, ax)
39[ 0]:      unsigned ax, bx, cx, dx, si, di, bp, ds, es;
40[ 0]: {
41[ 1]:      enable ();                          /*re-enable interrupts*/
42[ 1]:      switch (ax) {
43[ 2]:           case 0:  /*set the frequency (in arbitrary units)*/
44[ 2]:                    freq = dx;
45[ 2]:                    break;
46[ 2]:           case 1: {/*beep the speaker for 'dx' clock ticks*/
47[ 3]:                         prev = inportb (0x61);
48[ 3]:                         duration = dx;
49[ 3]:                         while (duration--) {
50[ 4]:                              pclock = *clock;
51[ 4]:                              while (pclock == *clock) {
52[ 5]:                                   /*go ahead and beep a cycle*/
53[ 5]:                                   outportb (0x61, prev & 0xfc);
54[ 5]:                                   for (i = 0; i < freq; i++);
55[ 5]:                                   outportb (0x61, prev | 0x02);
56[ 5]:                                   for (i = 0; i < freq; i++);
57[ 4]:                              }
58[ 3]:                         }
59[ 3]:                         outportb (0x61, prev);
60[ 2]:                    }
61[ 1]:           }
62[ 0]: }
63[ 0]:
64[ 0]:
65[ 0]: /*Main - install the above routine.*/
66[ 0]: main ()
67[ 0]: {
68[ 1]:      setvect (0x48, beep);
69[ 1]:      keep (0, 0x1000);
70[ 0]: }
```

This program isn't too remarkable, given what you already know from the Prg9_2 series of interrupt handlers. The actual code to beep the speaker (lines

51–57) was taken more or less directly from the *Turbo C Reference*. The duration is determined by examining the lower word of the time of day stored in lower memory (*see* Chapter 7). Of course, Prg9_3 could have been made as complicated as desired. I could have invented a subfunction to play Beethoven's "Fifth Symphony". I could also have defined as many different subfunctions as necessary. Either way the principle is the same.

This interrupt routine must be invoked from a second program. In this case (to make a point) I have written the invoking function in Turbo Pascal. It is not without reason that I have chosen this language. Since Turbo Pascal does not generate a *.OBJ* file, nor go through a link step, it is not possible to combine Turbo Pascal with other languages in any other way. I could just as well have written the invoking program in Microsoft Fortran, Ryan- McFarland Cobol, Mark-Willian's C, or whatever. I can even invoke this routine from most interpretive languages.

```
{Prg9_3 - Invoke the Turbo C Interrupt Beep Routine
  by Stephen R. Davis, 1987

  Install the Turbo C beep routine first.  Then execute this
  program.  This shows that any language capable of executing
  interrupt routines can be interfaced with Turbo C.  This is
  similar to the interface to BIOS routines}

program Prg9_3;

type
     registers = record
                   case Integer of
                      1 : (ax, bx, cx, dx, bp, si,
                           di, ds, es, flags : Integer);
                      2 : (al, ah, bl, bh, cl, ch,
                           dl, dh : Byte);
                   end;

var
     freq, duration : Integer;
     regs : registers;

begin
     WriteLn ('This is a simple test of invoking a Turbo C');
     WriteLn ('interrupt routine from another language.');
     WriteLn;
     WriteLn ('Enter any frequency and duration desired.');
     WriteLn ('Turbo Pascal will beep using the Turbo C routine.');
     WriteLn ('For example: 20 10');
     WriteLn ('(units of freq are loop counts -- units of duration');
     WriteLn (' are clock ticks -- a duration of zero terminates)');
     WriteLn;

     repeat
          Write ('Enter freq and duration:');
          ReadLn (freq, duration);
          WriteLn;
          If duration >= 18*10 then  {reduce durations of...}
               duration := 18;       {...> 10 secs to 1 sec}
```

```
          regs.ax := 0;  {set the frequency}
          regs.dx := freq;
          intr ($48, regs);

          regs.ax := 1;  {now beep duration}
          regs.dx := duration;
          intr ($48, regs)

     until (duration = 0);
     WriteLn;
     WriteLn ('Thats all')
end.

end.
```

Whether you are familiar with Turbo Pascal or not, you will recognize the essential elements. A structure is defined to contain the *registers*. Values are stored into this structure, and the structure is passed to the interrupt, in this case using the statement *INTR ($48,REGS)*. The program first sets *AX* to 0 and performs the call to set the frequency. It then calls *INTR ($48)* again with *AX* = *1* to perform the actual beep for the indicated duration.

Conclusion

Interrupt handlers, both of the borrowing and stealing variety, are painfully difficult to write. Invariably, debugging such routines involves a certain amount of assembly language. In addition, a very thorough understanding of the 8086 family of microprocessors is required to get these programs working. In general, it is not a good idea to attempt such a project without some background in 8086 assembly language.

Even worse than writing them, these routines are notoriously difficult to debug. A good assembly level debugger is an absolute necessity. The assembly language output from *TCC -B* can be very helpful in this regard also. The biggest hinderance to debugging interrupt routines is that you can't just stop the computer. Once you have installed a routine into an interrupt, it is going to get executed every time that interrupt occurs, whether it works or not.

There are some debuggers especially designed for interrupt work. These debuggers *uninstall* interrupt handlers on every breakpoint. Even without one of these debuggers, it is still possible to write such handlers if you can demonstrate good self discipline.

First, you must always get all of your functions working properly as regularly *called* routines. All forms of input should be attempted. Print statements can be added to the routines to display intermediate values to make sure that all is going as expected. Normal source code debuggers can also be employed at this point.

Second, install the program into a harmless, unused interrupt. Write a small program which invokes this interrupt and execute it under the debugger. Using the debugger, you can inject test data and watch your program process it. Single step through the entire program at least once. Make sure that the registers and stack are properly restored upon return to the calling program. It is this step that most programmers skip and this is probably the most important of them all.

Finally, only now attempt to install your program into its intended interrupt. When problems arise, characterize them and then drop back to step two before fixing them. If your program intercepts more than one interrupt, move one interrupt at a time over to its intended location. If you move them all at once and your program dies, you have no idea which interrupt was the culprit.

Although difficult to write, interrupt handlers are very impressive in what they can do. In their day, Borland's *SideKick* and Rosesoft's *Prokey* were very popular items. These products would not have raised a single eyebrow had they been written as normal, stand-alone utilities. It was only the instant, pop-up action that made them so popular.

It is much to the credit of the inventors of Turbo C that so much support for such handlers is built into Turbo C. Hopefully, with these example programs as a shell from which to start, the reader will enjoy Turbo C all the more in this new arena of programming.

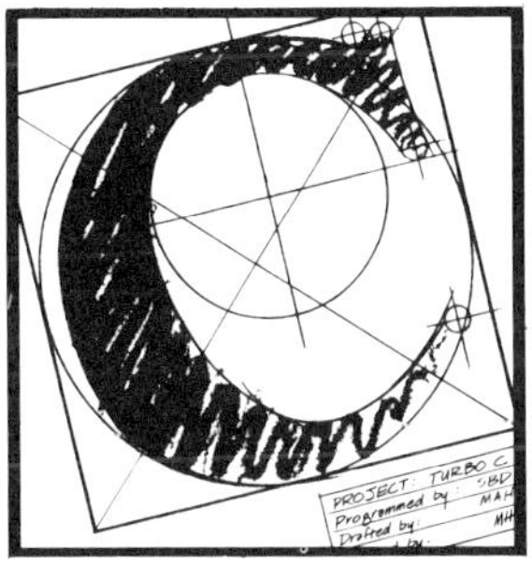

Conclusion

I have covered several topics germane to Turbo C on the IBM PC microcomputer. I have gone from basic pointers through linked lists and direct screen access, and from DOS calls all the way through to writing one's own terminate and stay resident popup utility in Turbo C. Although it is impossible to cover every concievable topic, I have tried to present a sufficient cross section to give any programmer a head start into the world of Turbo C on the PC. I would now like to leave you with a few parting thoughts.

Do not attempt to remember individual programs presented in this text, no matter how cute (or ugly) they might have been. I hope the reader comes away not with a few programs designed to solve particular problems, but with the beginnings of a toolkit of programming techniques that can be applied to all different types of problems. As they used to tell me as a young physics student, it is sufficient only that you remember the thought processes behind the programs—you can always recreate the programs.

If you intend to program in Turbo C, you must live Turbo C. Don't adopt the timid attitude of limiting yourself to some subset of the language, such as that which most resembles BASIC or some other language with which you are already familiar. By the same token, don't limit yourself to one set of programming techniques for solving problems. For better or worse you have decided to program in Turbo C. Immerse yourself in the language.

Adopt the C approach to programming. Analyze the problem carefully before starting. Build the scaffolding for the solution in your mind before you ever place the first brick at the keyboard. Build your program from the ground up. If you decide to define a new data structure, for example, write a single routine to create it, another to delete it and a third to access data out of it, if at all possible. Bundle together all the routines that directly access this data type into one module apart from routines designed to serve unrelated functions. Test these routines well before integrating them together with the rest of the system.

Make your routines as general as is reasonable—at the beginning of a project only one thing is certain: the requirements will change before you are finished. Making procedures restrictive invites the need to modify them long after they have been integrated with the rest of the system, and are difficult to retest.

When you have written and tested a nice, general purpose procedure, do not be afraid to document it and add it to your library. A mechanic doesn't start removing a screw by building a screw driver. Even if he did, he certainly wouldn't throw it away after the job was complete, only to build another one when he encounters a screw on the next job. Don't be afraid to add procedures to your library from other sources, such as books and magazines. Don't re-program solutions you already have just to prove you can. Keep a careful log book so you can remember what is in your library. Collect programming tools into an even more powerful programmer's workbench from which you can draw. The result is not only a better programmer, but one who has the freedom to enjoy solving new problems without constantly resolving the same old ones.

Borland's languages have gained quite a following in the programmer community, as has the C programming language. The combination should stay with us for quite some time.

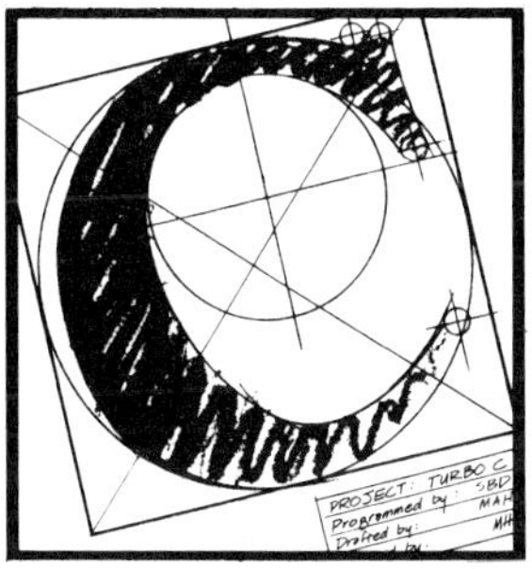

Appendix 1

DOS Function Calls

The following represents a truncated list of the MS- and PC-DOS operating system calls. All of these are accessed by loading the *AH* register with the indicated value and performing an interrupt *0x21*. This list does not explain in detail some of the more unusual function calls. Programmers intending to make direct use of these system calls should purchase a text describing the DOS calls in more detail, such as the MS-DOS *Programmer's Reference* from Microsoft Corporation. (Note that function calls after *0x58* are only available on DOS 3.0 and later.)

```
System              Description
 Call                 Input
                                          Output
00    Program Terminate
01    Keyboard Input
       AL = Character (WAITS AND ECHOS)
02    Display Output
       DL = Character
03    AUXiliary Input (ASYNCHRONOUS COMMUNICATIONS
                                ADAPTER)
                   AL returns Character (WAITS)
                   - unbuffered and non interrupt driven
                   - DOS bootup is 2,400 baud
                                no parity
                                one stop bit
                                8-bit word
04    AUXiliary Output (ASYNCHRONOUS COMMUNICATION
                                ADAPTER)
       DL = Character
05    Printer Output
       DL = Character
06    Console I/O DIRECT  (does not wait)
      If DL = FF
                   AL returns Character Read from Std. Input Device
                   Zero Flag returns 0 if SUCCESSFUL
                                   1 if character not ready
      If DL < FF
           Character In DL Output to Std. Output Device
      ***   No checks for Ctrl-Break or Ctrl-PrtSc
07    Console Input DIRECT (WAITS AND NO ECHO)
                   AL returns Character
      ***   No checks for Ctrl-Break or Ctrl-PrtSc
08    Console Input  ( WAITS AND NO ECHO )
                   AL returns Character
09    Output String (Output to Std. Output Device (display))
       DS:DX = Pointer To Start of String (string should end
               with 0x24 ($)
```

```
0A    Buffered Keyboard Input
       DS:DX = Pointer To Input Buffer
               (First byte specifies the buffer capacity)
               (Second byte is set to the number of Characters in buffer)
               (Characters are read UNTIL a carriage return is read)
0B    Check Standard Input Status
                   AL Returns FF if character available
                   AL Returns 00 otherwise
0C    Clear Keyboard Buffer and Invoke a Keyboard Function
       AL = Function to be Executed (Only 1,6,7,8,A allowed )
0D    Disk Reset
       Flushes all file buffers
0E    Select Disk Default
       DL = Drive number (0=A, 1=B)
                   AL Returns total number of drives
0F    Open File
       DS:DX Point to an unopened FCB
                   AL Returns 00 IF File found, else 0xff
10    Close File
       DS:DX Point to an unopened FCB
                   AL Returns 00 IF File found, else 0xff
11    Search for the First Entry
       DS:DX Point to an unopened FCB
                   AL Returns 00 IF File found, else 0xff
12    Search for the Next Entry
       DS:DX Point to an unopened FCB
                   AL Returns 00 IF File found, else 0xff
13    Delete File
       DS:DX Point to an unopened FCB
                   AL Returns 00 IF File found, else 0xff
14    Sequential Read
       DS:DX Point to an unopened FCB
                   AL Returns 00 if successful
                              01 if end-of-file
                              02 if DTA too small
                              03 if end-of-file, partial read
15    Sequential Write
       DS:DX Point to an unopened FCB
                   AL Returns 00 if successful
                              01 if end-of-file
                              02 if DTA too small
16    Create File
       DS:DX Point to an unopened FCB
                   AL Returns 00 IF empty slot found, else 0xff
17    Rename File
       DS:DX Point to an unopened FCB
                   AL Returns 00 IF File found, else 0xff
19    Current Disk
                   AL Returns default drive code (0=A,1=B,etc.)
1A    Set Disk Transfer Address
                   DS:DX = new address to be installed
1B    Get Default Drive Data (DEFAULT DRIVE)
                   AL - sectors per cluster
                   CX - bytes per sector
                   DX - clusters per drive
                   DS:BX - pointer to FAT ID
1C    Get Drive Data
       DL = drive (0 -> default, 1 -> A, etc)
                   AL - sectors per cluster
                   CX - bytes per sector
                   DX - clusters per drive
                   DS:BX - pointer to FAT ID
21    Random Read
       DS:DX Point to an unopened FCB
```

```
                AL Returns OO if successful
                           01 if end-of-file
                           02 if DTA too small
                           03 if end-of-file, partial read
22   Random Write
      DS:DX Point to an unopened FCB
                AL Returns OO if successful
                           01 if end-of-file
                           02 if DTA too small
23   File Size
      DS:DX Point to an unopened FCB
                AL Returns OO IF empty slot found, else 0xff
24   Set Relative Record Field
      DS:DX Point to an unopened FCB
25   Set Interrupt VECTOR
      AL    = Interupt Type (number)
      DS:DX = Address of New Routine
26   Create a New Program Segment (Use Function 4B)
27   Random BLOCK Read
      CX = number of blocks to read
      DS:DX Point to an unopened FCB
                AL Returns OO if successful
                           01 if end-of-file
                           02 if DTA too small
                           03 if end-of-file, partial read
                CX = number of blocks read
28   Random BLOCK Write
      CX = number of blocks to write
      DS:DX Point to an unopened FCB
                AL Returns OO if successful
                           01 if end-of-file
                           02 if DTA too small
                CX = number of blocks written
29   Parse Filename
      AL controls parsing
          bit 0 = 0 -> stop parsing if file seperator present
          bit 1 = 0 -> set drive number to 0 if no drive present
          bit 2 = 0 -> set filename to blanks if not present
          bit 3 = 0 -> set file extension to blanks if not present
      DS:SI point to string to parse
      ES:DI point to buffer for FCB
                AL 00 if no wildcards
                   01 wildcards found
                   FF error
                DS:SI point to first char after field
2A   Get DATE
                AL Returns DAY OF WEEK
                CX Returns YEAR
                DH Returns MONTH
                DL Returns DAY
2B   Set DATE
      CX:DX = DATE
                AL Returns FF if Unsuccessful
2C   Get TIME
                CH Returns HOURS
                CL Returns MINUTES
                DH Returns SECONDS
                DL Returns 1/100 SECONDS
2D   Set TIME
       CX:DX = TIME
                AL Returns FF if Unsuccessful
2E   Set/Reset VERIFY switch
      AL = 1 -> enable verify, 0 -> disable verify
2F   Get DTA
```

```
                  ES:BX point to DTA area
30   Get DOS Version Number
                  AL = major version
                  AH = minor version
                  BH = OEM serial number
                  BL:CX = serial number
31   Terminate Process and Remain Resident
      AL = return code
      DX = memory size [paragraphs]
33   CTRL-BREAK Check
      AL = 0 -> get check, 1 -> set check
      DL = 0 -> off, 1 -> on (if AL = 1)
                  DL = 0 -> off, 1 -> on (if AL = 0)
35   Get Vector
      AL = Interrupt Number
                  ES:BX Return Interrupt Vector  (CS:IP of routine)
36   Get Free Disk Space
      DL = drive (0 -> default, 1 -> A, etc)
                  AX = sectors per cluster (-1 on error)
                  BX = available clusters
                  CX = bytes per cluster
                  DX = clusters per drive
38   Return Country Dependent Information
39   MKDIR
      DS:DX point to pathname
                  CY = 1 -> error, AX contains error code
3A   RMDIR
      DS:DX point to pathname
                  CY = 1 -> error, AX contains error code
3B   CHDIR
      DS:DX point to pathname
                  CY = 1 -> error, AX contains error code
3C   CREATE a File Handle
      DS:DX point to pathname
                  AX contains file handle
                  CY = 1 -> error, AX contains error code
3D   OPEN a File
      AL contains access code
      DS:DX point to pathname
                  AX contains file handle
                  CY = 1 -> error, AX contains error code
3E   CLOSE a File Handle
      BX contains handle
      DS:DX point to pathname
                  CY = 1 -> error, AX contains error code
3F   Read From File or Device
      BX = file handle
      CX = bytes to read
      DS:DX points to buffer
                  AX = bytes read
                  CY = 1 -> error, AX contains error code
40   Write To a File or Device
      BX = file handle
      CX = bytes to write
      DS:DX points to buffer
                  AX = bytes written
                  CY = 1 -> error, AX contains error code
41   Delete a File From a Specified Directory
      DS:DX points to filename
                  CY = 1 -> error, AX contains error code
42   Move File Read/Write Pointer
      AL = method of moving
      BX = handle
      CX:DX = distance in bytes
```

```
                DX:AX new read/write pointer location
                CY = 1 -> error, AX contains error code
43   Change File Mode
      AL = 0 -> get attributes, 1 -> set attributes
      CX = attribues (if AL = 1)
      DS:DX point to filename
                CX = attribute (if AL = 0)
                CY = 1 -> error, AX contains error code
44   I/O Control for Devices
45   Duplicate a File Handle
      BX = file handle
                AX = new handle
                CY = 1 -> error, AX contains error code
46   Force a Duplicate of a Handle
      BX = handle
      CX = second handle
                CY = 1 -> error, AX contains error code
47   Get Current Directory
       DL = Drive Number
       DS:SI Point To a 64 BYTE area of user memory
                CY = 1 -> error, AX contains error code
48   Allocate Memory
      BX = number of paragraphs requested
                AX:0 returns pointing to allocated memory block
                CY = 1 -> error, AX contains error code
49   Free Allocated Memory
      ES segment of memory to be freed
                CY = 1 -> error, AX contains error code
4A   Set Block
      BX = paragraphs of memory
      ES:0 = address of memory area
                CY = 1 -> error, AX contains error code
4B   LOAD or EXECUTE a Program
     AL     = 0  Load/Execute Program
            = 3  Load Overlay
     DS:DX = point to ASCIIZ string containing drive,path,filename
     ES:BX = point to parameter block
                CY = 1 -> error, AX contains error code
4C   Terminate a Process    (EXIT)
      AL contains a binary return code
4D   Retrieve the Return Code of a SUB-PROCESS
                AX = return code
4E   Find First Matching File
      CX = attributes to match
      DS:DX point to pathname
                CY = 1 -> error, AX contains error code
4F   Find Next Matching File
                CY = 1 -> error, AX contains error code
54   Get VERIFY State
                AL Returns 00 if verify OFF
                01 if verify ON
56   Rename a File
      DS:DX point to old pathname
      ES:DI point to new pathname
                CY = 1 -> error, AX contains error code
57   Get/Set a File's DATE AND TIME
      AL = 0 -> get, 1 -> set
      BX = handle
      CX = time to set
      DX = date to set
                CX = time file last written
                DX = date file last written
                CY = 1 -> error, AX contains error code
58    Get/Set Allocation Strategy
```

```
        AL = 0 -> get, 1 -> set
        BX = 0 -> first fit, 1 -> best fit, 2 -> last fit
                   AX = (same as BX above)
                   CY = 1 -> error, AX contains error code
59      Get Extended Error
        BX = 0
                   AX = extended error code
                   BH = error class
                   BL = suggested action
                   CH = locus
5A      Create Temporary FIle
        CX = attribute
        DS:DX = pointer to pathname followed by 0 and 13 bytes
                of available memory
                   AX = handle
                   CY = 1 -> error, AX contains error code
5B      Create New File
        CX = attribute
        DX:DX = pointer to pathname
                   AX = handle
                   CY = 1 -> error, AX contains error code
5C      Lock/Unlock file subsection
        AL = 0 -> lock, 1 -> unlock
        BX = handle
        CX:DX = offset of region to be locked/unlocked
        SI:DI = length of region to be locked/unlocked
                   CY = 1 -> error, AX contains error code
5E      Get Machine Name
5F      Get Assign List Entry
62      Get PSP
                   BX:0 points to PSP of current program
```

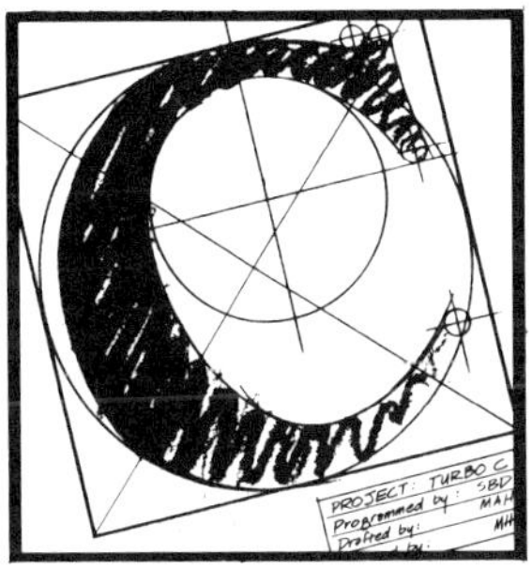

Appendix 2 The IBM PC's Interrupt Structure

The following list represents both the hardware and software interrupts of the PC, AT, and compatible machines. The software interrupts below *0x21* form the *Basic Input/Output Support* (BIOS) package. Those above *0x21* are actually part of the DOS operating system. This material is taken from the IBM PC *Technical Reference,* Microsoft's MS-DOS *Programmer's Reference,* and IBM's EGA manuals. These manuals are very helpful when undertaking detailed work with the BIOS interrupts. This is particularly true of the Enhanced Graphics Adapter—the EGA manual is a necessity to unravel its mysteries. (This and all other IBM technical manuals may be ordered from IBM's Technical Directory, Post Office Box 2009, Racine, WI 53404 [800/426-7282], part number 6280131; approximately $9.95, plus shipping.)

```
------------------   8088 Hardware Interrupts   ---------------------


NMI ---- Parity

====================== 8259 Controlled Interrupts ===========================

 0 ----- Timer                                          [  Int  8  ]
 1 ----- Keyboard                                       [  Int  9  ]
 2 ----- EGA Vertical Retrace                           [  Int  A  ]
 3 ----- Asysnchronous Communications (Alternate)       [  Int  B  ]
         SDLC          Communications
         BSC           Communications
         Cluster (primary)
 4 ----- Asysnchronous Communications (Primary)         [  Int  C  ]
         SDLC          Communications
         BSC           Communications
 5 ----- Fixed Disk                                     [  Int  D  ]
 6 ----- Diskette                                       [  Int  E  ]
 7 ----- Printer                                        [  Int  F  ]
         Cluster (Alternate)
```

```
------------------   8088  Software  Interrupts   ---------------------

---- INT 10   --------------- Video I/O -------------------------------------
     AH
 -10- 00  Set CRT Mode
            AL                    0=40 x 25 Black & white
                                  1= 40 x 25 Color
                                  2=80 x 25 Black & white
                                  3= 80 x 25 Color
                                  4=320 x 200 Medium resolution color
                                  5=320 x 200 Medium resolution black & white
                                  6=640 x 200 High resolution black & white
                                  7 = Monochrome
                                  ** B/W modes operate the same as color modes,
                                     but color burst is not enabled
 -10- 01  Set Cursor Type
            CH                    Start scan line (0-7 C/G, 0-14 Monochrome)
            CL                    End scan line (set start to 20H for no curs.)
                                  ** Hardware will always cause blink
                                  ** setting bit 5 or 6 will cause erratic
                                     results
                                                0    1   -  1/16 rate
                                                1    1   -  1/32 rate
 -10- 02  Set Cursor Position
            DH,DL                 Row, column (0,0 = Upper Left)
            BH                    Video page (Must be zero for Graphics modes)
 -10- 03  Read Cursor Position
            BH                    Video page (Must be zero for Graphics modes)
                      DH,DL       Row, column (0,0 = Home)
                      CH,CL       Cursor mode currently set
 -10- 04  Read Light Pen Position
                      AH          0=Light pen not trig, 1=valid info in regs:
                      BX          Pixel column (0-319 med-res,0-619 hi-res)
                      CH          Raster line
                      DH,DL       Row, column of character LP position
 -10- 05  Select Active Page     (valid only for alpha-text modes)
            AL                    New page (0-7 for 40x25,0-3 for 80x25)
 -10  06  Scroll Active Page Up
            AL                    Number of lines to scroll (0 if entire
                                  screen)
                                  { # of blank lines at bottom }
            BH                    Attribute to use in blanked lines
            CH,CL                 Row, column of upper left scroll corner
            DH,DL                 Row, column of lower right scroll corner
 -10- 07  Scroll Active Page Down
            AL                    Number of lines to scroll (0 if entire
                                  screen)
            BH                    Attribute to use in blanked lines
            CH,CL                 Row, column of upper left corner
            DH,DL                 Row, column of lower right corner
 -10- 08  Read Attribute / Character at current cursor position
            BH                    Video page  (valid only for alpha modes)
                      AL          Character read
                      AH          Attribute of char (alpha modes only)
 -10- 09  Write Attribute / Character at current cursor position
            AL                    Character to write
            BH                    Video page  (valid only for alpha modes)
            CX                    Count of characters to write (repeat count)
            BL                    Attribute of character (alpha)/color
                                  **     ( graphics )
                                  ** see int 1F if bit 7 of BL = 1
 -10- 0A  Write Character only at current cursor position
            AL                    Character to write
            BH                    Video page   (valid only for alpha modes)
            CX                    Count of characters to write (repeat count)
 -10- 0B  Set Color Palette   320 X 200 Graphics mode only
```

```
          BH                     Palette color ID being set ( 0-127 )
          BL                     Color value to be used with that color ID
-10- 0C  Write Dot
          AL                     Color value (If bit 7=1, value is XOR'ed in)
          DX,CX                  Row, column number
-10- 0D  Read Dot
          DX,CX                  Row, column number
                    AL           Returns Dot read
-10- 0E  Write Teletype to Active Page  ( 1.3 mS per Char )
          AL                     Character to write
          BL                     Foreground color in graphics mode
          BH                     Display page in Alpha mode
-10- 0F  Get Current Video State
                    AH           Returns Columns on screen
                    AL           Returns Mode currently set (see func. 0)
                    BH           Returns Current active display page
-10-10   Set Palette Registers (EGA only)
          AL = 0                 Set individual register
          BL                     Palette register to be set
          BH                     Value to set

          AL = 1                 Set overscan register
          BH                     Value

          AL = 2                 Set all palette registers and overscan
          ES:DX                  Points to 17 byte table

          AL = 3                 Toggle intensity/blinking bit
          BL                     0 -> enable intensity, else blinking
-10-11   Character Generator
          AL = (1)0              User alpha mode
          ES:BP                  Points to user table
          CX                     Count
          DX                     Character offset in table
          BL                     Block to load
          BH                     Number of bytes per character

          AL = (1)1              ROM Monochrome mode
          BL                     Block to load

          AL = (1)2              ROM 8x8 Double Dot mode
          BL                     Block to load

          AL = (1)3              Set Block Specifier
          BL                     Character gen specifier

          AL = 20                User graphics characters
          ES:BP                  Points to user table

          AL = 21                User graphics characters
          ES:BP                  Points to user table
          CX                     Bytes per character
          BL                     Row specifier

          AL = 22                ROM 8x14 mode
          BL                     Row specifier

          AL = 23                ROM 8x8 Double Dot mode
          BL                     Row specifier

          AL = 30                Information
-10-12   Alternate Select
          BL = 10                Return EGA information
                    BH           0 -> color mode, 1 - monochrome mode
```

```
                 BL        Memory available (0 - 64k, 1 -128k
                                              2 -192k, 2 -256k)
                 CH        Feature bits
                 CL        Switch setting

          BL = 20          Select alternate print screen routine
 -10-13  Write String
          ES:BP            Points to string to be written
          CX               Character count
          DX               Cursor position to begin string
          BH               Page number

          AL = 0
          BL               Attribute (string = char,char...)
                            cursor not updated
          AL = 1
          BL               Attribute (string = char,char...)
                            cursor updated
          AL = 2
                           String = char,att,char,att...
                            cursor not updated
          AL = 3
                           String = char,att,char,att...
                            cursor updated

---- INT 11     ------------- Equipment ----------------------------
         No input
                AX Returns Equipment attached : Bits set as follows
                                 A H                A L
                           0 0 X 0 0 0 0 X   0 0 0 0 0 0 X 0
                           ---   - -----     --- --- ---   -
                            1    2  3         4   5   6    7
                         1  Number of printers
                         2  Game I/O
                         3  Number of RS232 cards
                         4  Number of Drives if AL bit 0-1
                         5  Initial video mode
                                      00 - unused
                                      01 - 40 X 25 BW (color card)
                                      10 - 80 X 25 BW (color card)
                                      11 - 80 X 25 BW (mono)
                         6  System board RAM
                                      00 - 16K
                                      00 - 32K
                                      00 - 48K
                                      00 - 64K
                         7  IPL from diskette (disk drives avail.)


---- INT 12     ------------ Memory Size ---------------------------

                AX  Returns       Number of contiguous 1K blocks
                                ** read from switches on IBM's at POR
**


---- INT 13     ----------- Diskette I/O ---------------------------
      AH
 -13- 00  Reset Diskette System
          No input  No output  Hard resets all diskette drives, recal req'd
 -13- 01  Read Diskette Status
```

```
                 AL          Status byte : Bits set as follows
                             80         Attachment failed to respond
                             40         Seek operation failed
                             20         NEC controller failure
                             10         Bad CRC on diskette read
                             09         Attempt to DMA across a 64k bound
                             08         DMA overrun on operation
                             04         DMA overrun on operation
                             03         Write attempted on wrt prot disk
                             02         Address mark not found
                             01         Bad command passed to diskette I/O
 -13- 02  Read the desired sectors into memory
 -13- 03  Write the desired sectors from memory
 -13- 04  Verify the desired sectors
 -13- 05  Format the desired track
            DL                Drive number (0-3)
            DH                Head number  (0-1)
            CH                Track number (0-39) not checked
            CL                Sector number (1-8) not checked
            AL                Number of sectors (not used for format)
            ES:BX             Address of buffer (not required for verify)
                 AH           Status of operation (see above)
                 CY           1 if failed, 0 if ok


---- INT 14     --------- RS-232 I/O --------------------------------
     AH
 -14- 00  Initialize Communications Port
            DX                Interface card (0=COM1:, 1=COM2:)
            AL                Parameters to set up : Bits are as follows
                                    A L
                              0 0 0 0 0 0 0 0
                              ----- --- - ---
                                4    3  2  1
                           1  Word length (10=7 bit, 11=8 bit)
                           2  Stopbits (0=1, 1=2)
                           3  Parity (00=none, 01=odd 11=even)
                           4  Baud (000=110, 001=150, 010=300, 011=600,
                                 100=1200, 101=2400, 110=4800, 111-9600)
                 AH           Set as in status (call 3)
 -14- 01  Send Character to Communications Line
            DX                Interface card (0=COM1:, 1=COM2:)
            AL                Character to send
                 AH           Set as in status (call 3)
 -14- 02  Receive Character from Communications Line
            DX                Interface card (0=COM1:, 1=COM2:)
                 AL           Character
                 AH           0 if no error, set as status if nonzero
 -14- 03  Get Communications Status
            DX                Interface card (0=COM1:, 1=COM2:)
                 AH           Line status : Bits set as follows
                              F        Time out
                              E        Transmit shift reg empty
                              D        Transmit holding reg empty
                              C        Break detect
                              B        Framing error
                              A        Parity error
                              9        Overrun error
                              8        Data ready
                 AL           Modem status : Bits set as follows
                              7        Recieved line signal detect
                              6        Ring indicator
                              5        Data set ready
```

```
                          4       Clear to send
                          3       Delta recieved line signal detect
                          2       Trailing edge ring detector
                          1       Delta data set ready
                          0       Delta clear to send

---- INT 15     ----------- Cassette I/O ----------------------------
       AH
 -15-  00         Turn Cassette Motor On
 -15-  01         Turn Cassette Motor Off
 -15-  02         Read 1 or more blocks
 -15-  03         Write 1 or more blocks

---- INT 16     ----------- Keyboard I/O ----------------------------
     AH
 -16- 00  Read ASCII Next Character
                    AL        Character struck
                    AH        Scan code of key
 -16- 01  Check Typeahead Status
                    ZF        1 if no key available, 0 if key available
                    AL,AH     Character/Scan code if available. Keystroke
                              remains in buffer.
 -16- 02  Get Current Shift Status
                    AL        Shift flag status : Bits set as follows
                              80        Insert state
                              40        Caps lock state
                              20        Num lock state
                              10        Scroll lock state
                              08        Alt shift is depressed
                              04        Ctl shift is depressed
                              02        Left shift is depressed
                              01        Right shift is depressed

---- INT 17     ----------- Printer I/O ----------------------------
     AH
 -17- 00  Print Character
          DX                  Printer to be used (0,1,2)
          AL                  Character to print
                    AH        Status set as in call 2
 -17- 01  Initialize Printer Port
          DX                  Printer to be used (0,1,2)
                    AH        Status set as in call 2
 -17- 02  Get Printer Status
          DX                  Printer to be used (0,1,2)
                    AH        Printer status : Bits set as follows
                              80        Not busy (ready?)
                              40        Acknowledge
                              20        Out of paper
                              10        Selected
                              08        I/O error
                              01        Time out

---- INT 1A ---------- Time of Day -------------------------------
       AH
 -1A-   00    Read the current clock setting
                   CX  Returns High Portion of Count
                   DX  Returns Low Portion of Count
                   AL  0 if timer has not passed 24 hours since last read
```

```
 -1A-     01    Set the Current Clock
                       CX  High Count
                       DX  Low Count
                  *** counts occur at 1193180/65536 counts/sec ***
                      ( approx 18.2 per second ) issues Int 1C every count
 -1A-     02    Read AT cmos clock
                  carry set if not operating
                     ch returns hours
                     cl returns minutes
                     dh returns sec

---- INT  25  ----------  Absolute  Disk  Read  -------------------------
         AL   - Drive Number ( 0=A , 1=B )
         CX   - Number of Sectors to Read
         DX   - Beginning Logical Sector Number
      DS:BX   - Transfer Address
                    CARRY FLAG = 0 if Successful

---- INT  26  ----------  Absolute  Disk  Write  ------------------------
         AL   - Drive Number ( 0=A , 1=B )
         CX   - Number of Sectors to Read
         DX   - Beginning Logical Sector Number
      DS:BX   - Transfer Address
                    CARRY FLAG = 0 if Successful

---- INT  27    ----  Program  Terminate  but  Stay  Resident  -------------
         DX - last address in program
         (**bug** use last address + 100H to account for .com load )
```

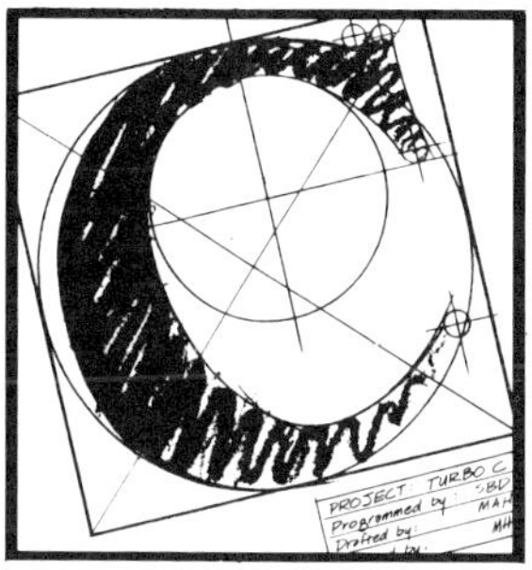

Appendix 3 Turbo C Library Routines

The following is a short listing of the functions of the Turbo C Library as listed in Borland's *Turbo C Reference Guide*. This list is intended only to minimize the number of references to the *Reference Guide* during the reading of this book and its programs.

Routine	Meaning	Include File(s)
void abort (void)	abort	stdlib.h process.h
int abs (int i)	absolute value	stdlib.h math.h
int absread (int drive, int nsects, int sectno, void *buffer)	read sector	dos.h
int abswrite (int drive, int nsects, int sectno, void *buffer)	write sector	dos.h
int access (char *filename, int amode)	return access	io.h
double acos (double x)	arccosine	math.h
int allocmem (unsigned size, unsigned *seg)	allocate DOS seg	dos.h
char *asctime (struct tm *tm)	time to ASCII	time.h
double asin (double x)	arcsine	math.h
void assert (int test)	abort if 0	assert.h
double atan (double x)	arctangent	math.h
double atan2 (double y, double x)	arctan (y/x)	math.h
int atexit (atexit_t func)	register exit fn	stdlib.h
double atof (char *numberptr)	string -> float	math.h stdlib.h
int atoi (char *numberptr)	string -> integer	stdlib.h

int atol (char *numberptr)	string -> long	stdlib.h
int bdos (int fnnum, unsigned dosdx, unsigned dosal);	perform DOS call	dos.h
int bdosptr (int fnnum, void *arg, unsigned dosal);	perform DOS call	dos.h
int bioscom (int cmd, char byte, int port)	comm BIOS call	bios.h
int biosdisk (int cmd, int drive, int head, int track, int sector, int numsectors, void *buffer)	disk BIOS call	bios.h
int biosequip (void)	equip BIOS call	bios.h
int bioskey (int cmd)	keyboard BIOS call	bios.h
int biosmemory (void)	memory BIOS call	bios.h
int biosprint (int cmd, int byte,	printer BIOS call	bios.h
long biostime (int cmd, long newtime) int port)	time of day BIOS call	bios.h
int brk (void *endds)	change data space	alloc.h
void *bsearch (void *key, void *base, int *nelem, int width, int (*fcmp)())	binary search	stdlib.h
double cabs (struct complex num)	absolute val	math.h
void *calloc (unsigned numelements, unsigned elementsize)	alloc heap mem	stdlib.h or alloc.h
double ceil (double x)	round up	math.h
char *cgets (char *string)	read string from mem	conio.h
int chdir (char *path)	change dir	dir.h
int _chmod (char *filename, int func, int attrib)	change file mode	io.h dos.h
int chmod (char *filename, int func, int attrib)	change file mode	io.h stat.h
unsigned _clear87 (void)	clear 8087 status	float.h
void clearerr (FILE *stream)	clear file error	stdio.h
int _close (int handle)	close file	io.h
int close (int handle)	close file	io.h
unsigned [long] coreleft (void)	enquire mem left	alloc.h
double cos (double x)	cosine	math.h
double cosh (double x)	hyper cosine	math.h

struct count *country (int countrycode, struct country *countrytype)	return country dependent info	dos.h
int cprintf (char *format...)	print to mem	conio.h
void cputs (char *string)	put string to mem	conio.h
int _creat (char *filename, int attribute)	create file	dos.h io.h
int creat (char *filename, int permission)	create file	stat.h io.h
int creatnew (char *filename, int attribute)	create new file	dos.h io.h
int creattemp (char *filename, int attribute)	create temp file	dos.h io.h
int cscanf (char *format...)	scan memory	conio.h
char *ctime (long *clock)	date/time -> string	time.h
void ctrlbrk (int (*fbrk)(void))	def Break handler	dos.h
double difftime (time_t time2, time_t time1)	calc delta time	time.h
void disable (void)	disable interrupts	dos.h
int dosexterr (struct DOSERR *eblkp)	set DOS error	dos.h
log dostounix (struct date *dateptr, struct time *timeptr)	DOS time -> Unix	dos.h
int dup (int handle)	duplicate file handle	io.h
int dup2 (int oldhandle, int newhandle)	duplicate file handle	io.h
char *ecvt (double value, int numdigits, int *decpt, int *sign)	float -> string	stdlib.h
void enable (void)	enable interrupts	dos.h
int eof (int *handle)	return EOF	io.h
int execl (char *fname, char *arg0, ...char *argn, NULL)	execute file	process.h
int execle (char *fname, char *arg0, ...char *argn, NULL, char *env [])	execute file	process.h
int execlp (char *fname, char *arg0, ...char *argn, NULL)	execute file (search path)	process.h
int execlpe (char *fname, char *arg0, ...char *argn, NULL, char *env [])	execute file (search path)	process.h
int execv (char *fname, char *argv [])	execute file	process.h
int execve (char *fname, char *argv [], char *env [])	execute file	process.h

int execvp (char *fname, char *argv [])	execute file (search path)	process.h
int execvpe (char *fname, char *argv[], char *env [])	execute file (search path)	process.h
void _exit (int status)	exit	process.h
void exit (int status)	exit	process.h
double exp (double x)	exponential	math.h
double fabs (double x)	absolute value	math.h
void far *faralloc (long nelems, long elemsize)	alloc heap far	alloc.h
void far *farrealloc (void far *block, unsigned long newsize)	realloc block	alloc.h
int fclose (FILE *stream)	close file	stdio.h
int fcloseall (void)	close all files	stdio.h
char *fcvt (double value, int ndigit, int *decpt, int *sign)	float -> string	stdlib.h
FILE *fdopen (int handle, char *type)	associate stream with handle	stdio.h
int feof (FILE *stream)	return EOF	stdio.h
int ferror (FILE *stream)	detect error	stdio.h
int fflush (FILE *stream)	flush stream	stdio.h
int fgetc (FILE *stream)	get character	stdio.h
int fgetchar (FILE *stream)	get character	stdio.h
char *fgets (FILE *stream)	get string	stdio.h
long filelength (int handle)	get file size	io.h
int fileno (FILE *stream)	get file handle	stdio.h
int findfirst (char *fname, struct ffblk *ffblk, int attribute)	find first	dir.h
int findnext (struct ffblk *ffblk)	find next	dir.h
double floor (double x)	round down	math.h
int flushall (void)	flush all streams	stdio.h
double fmod (double x, double y)	x modulo y	math.h
void fnmerge (char *path, char *disk, char *dir, char *filename, char *ext)	create filename	dir.h
void fnsplit (char *path, char *disk, char *dir, char *filename, char *ext)	parse filename	dir.h
FILE *fopen (char *filename,	open stream	stdio.h

char *type)		
unsigned FP_OFF (void far *ptr)	return offset	dos.h
unsigned FP_SEG (void far *ptr)	return segment	dos.h
void _fpreset (void)	reinit math package	float.h
int fprintf (FILE *stream, char *string...)	print to stream	stdio.h
int fputc (char char, FILE *stream)	put char	stdio.h
int fputs (char *string, FILE *stream)	put string	stdio.h
int fread (void *buffer, int size, int numelems, FILE *stream)	read stream	stdio.h
void free (void *ptr)	free alloc block	stdlib.h alloc.h
int freemem (unsigned seg)	free DOS block	dos.h
FILE *freopen (char *filename, char *type, FILE *stream)	open a stream	stdio.h
double frexp (double value, int *exponentptr)	split float	math.h
int fscanf (FILE *steam, char *string...)	scan file	stdio.h
int fseek (FILE *stream, long offset, int fromwhere)	pos file pointer	stdio.h
int fstat (char *handle, struct stat *buffer)	get open file info	stat.h
long ftell (FILE *stream)	ret file pointer	stdio.h
int fwrite (void *buffer, int size, int numelems, FILE *stream)	write stream	stdio.h
char *gcvt (double value, int numdigits, char *buffer)	float -> string	stdlib.h
void geninterrupt (int number)	generate interrupt	dos.h
int getc (FILE *stream)	get character	stdio.h
int getcbrk (void)	get Break setting	dos.h
int getch (void)	get character	conio.h
int getchar (void)	get character	stdio.h
int getche (void)	get character	conio.h
int getcurrdir (int drive, char *direc)	get directory	dir.h
char *getcwd (char *direc, int n)	get directory	dir.h
void getdate (struct date *block)	get DOS date	dos.h

void getdfree (int drive, struct dfree *block)	get free space	dos.h
int getdisk (void)	get curr disk	dir.h
char far *getdta (void)	get curr DTA	dos.h
char *getenv (char *envptr)	get from environment	stdlib.h
void getfat (int disk, struct fatinfo *block)	get disk FAT	dos.h
void getfatd (struct fatinfo *block)	get default FAT	dos.h
int getftime (int handle, struct ftime *block)	get file date/time	dos.h
char *getpass (char *prompt)	get password	conio.h
unsigned getpsp (void)	get current PSP	dos.h
char *gets (char *string)	get string	stdio.h
void gettime (struct time *block)	get time	dos.h
void interrupt (*getvect (int number))	get interrupt	dos.h
int getverify (void)	get verify state	dos.h
int getw (FILE *stream)	get integer	stdio.h
struct tm *gmtime (long *clock)	time -> GMT	time.h
int gsignal (int signal)	get signal	signal.h
void harderr (int (*fptr)(void))	set hardware error handler	dos.h
void hardresume (int code)	abort from error handler	dos.h
void hardretn (int errorcode)	return from error handler	dos.h
double hypot (double x, double y)	calc hypotenuse	math.
int inport (int port)	input from port	dos.h
int inportb (int port)	input from port	dos.h
int int86 (int number, union REGS *regs, union REGS *regs)	8086 interrupt	dos.h

int int86x (int number,
    union REGS *regs, union REGS *regs,
    struct SREGS *segregs)
	8086 interrupt	dos.h

int intdos (union REGS *regs, union REGS *regs)	DOS call	dos.h

int intdosx (union REGS *regs,
    union REGS *regs,
    struct SREGS *segregs)
	DOS call	dos.h

void intr (int number,	8086 interrupt	dos.h

struct REGPACK *regs)		
int ioctl (int handle, int cmd)	control I/O device	io.h
int isalpha (int chr)	check for alpha ctype	h,io.h
int isalnum (int chr)	check for alnum ctype	h,io.h
int isascii (int chr)	check for ASCII ctype	h,io.h
int isatty (int handle)	check for device type	io.h
int iscntrl (int chr)	check for control ctype	h,io.h
int isdigit (int chr)	check for number ctype	h,io.h
int isgraph (int chr)	check for printing ctype.	h,io.h
int islower (int chr)	check for lowercase ctype	h,io.h
int isprint (int chr)	check for printing ctype.	h,io.h
int ispunct (int chr)	check for punctuation ctype	h,io.h
int isspace (int chr)	check for space ctype.	h,io.h
int isupper (int chr)	check for uppercase ctype	h,io.h
int isxdigit (int chr)	check for hex number ctype	h,io.h
char *itoa (int value, char *string, int radix)	int -> string	stdlib.h
int kbhit (void)	check for key	conio.h
void keep (int status, int size)	exit and stay resident	dos.h
long labs (long n)	long absolute val	stdlib.h
double ldexp (double value, int exp)	value * 2** exp	math.h
void *lfind (void *key, void *base, int *number, int width, int (*fcmp)()))	linear search	stdlib.h
struct tm *localtime (long *clock)	local time	time.h
int lock (int handle, long offset, long length)	set file lock	io.h
double log (double x)	logarithm	math.h
double log10 (double x)	base 10 logarithm	math.h
void longjmp (jmp_buf *ptr, int val)	long jump	setjmp.h
void *lsearch (void *key, void *base, int number, int width, int (*fcmp)())	search and update	stdlib.h
long lseek (int handle, long offset, int key)	pos file pointer	io.h

char *ltoa (long value, char *buffer, int radix)	long -> string	stdlib.h
void *malloc (unsigned size)	alloc block from heap	stdlib.h alloc.h
int matherr (struct exception *e)	invoke math err	math.h
void *memccpy (void *dst, void *src, unsigned char ch, unsigned n)	copy block until 'ch' copied	string.h,mem.h
void *memchr (void *s, char ch, unsigned n)	search for 'ch'	string.h,mem.h
int memcmp (void *s1, void *s2, unsigned n)	compare strings	string.h,mem.h
int memicmp (void *s1, void *s2, unsigned n)	compare strings (case insensitive)	string.h,mem.h
void *memmove (void *dst, void *src, unsigned n)	copy block	string.h,mem.h
void *memcpy (void *dst, void *src, unsigned n)	copy block	string.h,mem.h
void *memset (void *ptr, char ch, unsigned n)	store block	string.h,mem.h
void far *MK_FP (unsigned seg, unsigned offset)	build far pointer	dos.h
int mkdir (char *pathname)	make a directory	dir.h
char *mktemp (char *template)	make a file name	dir.h
double modf (double value, double *expptr)	split float	math.h
void movedata (int srcseg, int srcoff, int dstseg, int dstoff, unsigned number)	copies bytes string.h	mem.h
void movmem (void *src, void *dst, unsigned number)	copies bytes	mem.h
int _open (char *fname, int access)	open a file	fcntl.h,io.h
int open (char *fname, int access, int permission)	open a file	io.h
void outport (int port, int word)	output to port	dos.h
void outportb (int port, char byte)	output to port	dos.h
char *parsfnm (char *cmdline, struct fcb *ptr, int option)	parse file name	dos.h
int peek (unsigned segment, unsigned offset)	examine word	dos.h
int peekb (unsigned segment, unsigned offset)	examine byte	dos.h

void perror (char *message)	quit w/ error	stdio.h
void poke (unsigned segment, unsigned offset, int value)	put word	dos.h
void pokeb (unsigned segment, unsigned offset, char value)	put byte	dos.h
double poly (double x, int n, double c[])	evaluate polynomial	math.h
double pow (double x, double y)	x ** y	math.h
double pow10 (int p)	10 ** p	math.h
printf (char *string...)	print string	stdio.h
int putc (int chr, FILE *stream)	put character	stdio.h
int putch (int chr)	put character	conio.h
int putchar (int chr)	put character	stdio.h
int putenv (char *string)	write to environment	stdlib.h
int puts (char *string)	put string	stdio.h
int putw (int w, FILE *stream)	put word	stdio.h
void qsort (void *base, int number, int width, int (*fcmp)())	quick sort	stdlib.h
int rand (void)	random number	stdlib.h
int randbrd (struct fcb *ptr, int recent)	random block read	dos.h
int randbwr (struct fcb *ptr, int recent)	random block write	dos.h
int read (int handle, void *buffer, int number)	read	io.h
void *realloc (void *ptr, unsigned newsize)	reallocate memory	stdlib.h alloc.h
int remove (char *filename)	remove fle	stdio.h
int rename (char *oldname, char *newname)	rename file	stdio.h
int rewind (FILE *stream)	repos read pointer	stdio.h
int rmdir (char *dirname)	remove dir	dir.h
	change space alloc	alloc.h
int scanf (char *format...)	scan input	stdio.h
char *searchpath (char *filename)	locate file in PATH	dir.h
void segread (struct REGS *table)	get segment registers	dos.h
int setblock (int seg, int newsize)	modify DOS alloc	dos.h

`void setbuf (FILE *stream, char *buffer)`	enable buffering	stdio.h
`int setcbrk (int value)`	set Break setting	dos.h
`void setdate (struct date *block)`	set date	dos.h
`int setdisk (int drive)`	set default disk	dir.h
`void setdta (char far *dta)`	set DTA	dos.h
`int setftime (int handle, struct ftime *ptr)`	touch file	io.h
`int setjmp (jmp_buf ptr)`	set longjmp addr	setjmp.h
`void setmem (void *ptr, int len, char value)`	put value in memory	mem.h
`int setmode (int handle, unsigned mode)`	set mode of file	io.h
`void settime (struct time *ptr)`	set time	dos.h
`int setvbuf (FILE *stream, char *buffer, int type, unsigned size)`	enable buffering	stdio.h
`void setvect (unsigned intnum, void interrupt (*fptr)())`	set int vector	dos.h
`void setverify (int value)`	set verify mode	dos.h
`double sin (double x)`	sine	math.h
`double sinh (double x)`	hyper sine	math.h
`unsigned sleep (unsigned seconds)`	delay	dos.h
`int spawnl (int mode, char *fname, char *arg0...*argn, NULL)`	spawn subprocess	process.h
`int spawnle (int mode, char *fname, char *arg0...*argn, NULL, char *env [])`	spawn subprocess	process.h
`int spawnlp (int mode, char *fname, char *arg0...*argn, NULL)`	spawn subprocess (search PATH)	process.h
`int spawnlpe (int mode, char *fname, char *arg0...*argn, NULL, char *env [])`	spawn subprocess (search PATH)	process.h
`int spawnv (int mode, char *fname, char *argv [])`	spawn subprocess	process.h
`int spawnve (int mode, char *fname, char *argv [], char *env [])`	spawn subprocess	process.h
`int spawnvp (int mode, char *fname, char *argv [])`	spawn subprocess (search PATH)	process.h
`int spawnvpe (int mode, char *fname, char *argv [], char *env [])`	spawn subprocess (search PATH)	process.h

Function	Description	Header
int sprintf (char *buffer, char *string...)	write to memory	stdio.h
double sqrt (double x)	square root	math.h
void srand (unsigned number)	seed random number generator	stdlib.h
int sscanf (char *buffer, char *string...)	scan memory	stdio.h
int (*ssignal (int sig, int (*action)())()	implement software signals	signal.h
int stat (char *fname, struct stat *ptr)	get file status	stat.h
unsigned _status87 (void)	get 8087 status	float.h
int stime (long *time)	set time	
char *stpcpy (char *dst, char *source)	copy one string to another	string.h
char *stpcat (char *dst, char *src)	concatenate string	string.h
char *strchr (char *str, char c)	look for a char	string.h
char *strcmp (char *s1, char *s2)	compare strings	string.h
char *strcpy (char *dst, char *src)	copy one string to another	string.h
char *strcspn (char *s1, char *s2)	search for absence	string.h
char *strdup (char *str)	make copy of string	string.h
char *strerror (char *msg)	build error message	string.h
int stricmp (char *s1, char *s2)	compare strings (ignore case)	string.h
unsigned strlen (char *str)	string length	string.h
char *strlwr (char *str)	upper to lowercase	string.h
char *strncat (char *dst, char *src, int maxlen)	concatenate	string.h
char *strnicmp (char *s1, char *s2 int maxlen)	compare strings (ignore case)	string.h
char *strnset (char *str, char ch, unsigned maxlen)	set string	string.h
char *strpbrk (char *s1, char *s2)	search for char from s2 in s1	string.h
char *strrchr (char *str, char c)	search for char	string.h
char *strrev (char *str)	reverse string	string.h
char *strset (char *str, char c)	set string	

Function	Description	Header
int strspn (char *s1, char *s2)	look for chars frm s2 in s1	string.h
char *strstr (char *s1, char *s2)	find s1 in s2	string.h
double strtod (char *str, char **eptr)	string -> double	string.h
long strtol (char *str, char **eptr)	string -> long	string.h
char *strtok (char *s1, char *s2)	search s1 for tokens	string.h
char *strupr (char *str)	lower to uppercase	string.h
void swab (char *src, char *dst, int number)	swap bytes	stdlib.h
int system (char *command)	execute DOS command	stdlib.h
double tan (double x)	tangent	math.h
double tanh (double x)	hyper tangent	math.h
long tell (int handle)	get location of file pointer	io.h
long time (long *tloc)	get time of day	time.h
int toascii (int c)	convert to ascii	ctype.h
int tolower (int c)	convert to lowercase	ctype.h
int toupper (int c)	convert to uppercase	ctype.h
int _tolower (int c)	convert to lowercase	ctype.h
int _toupper (int c)	convert to uppercase	ctype.h
void tzset (void)	Unix time compat	time.h
char *ultoa (unsigned long value, char *string, int radix)	u long -> string	stdlib.h
int ungetc (char c, FILE *stream)	return char	stdio.h
int ungetch (int c)	return char	conio.h
void unixtodos (long utime, struct date *ptr, struct time *ptr)	date/time to DOS format	dos.h
int unlink (char *filename)	remove file	dos.h
int unlock (int handle, long offset, long length)	unlock file	dos.h
void va_start (va_list param, lastfix)	start var args	stdarg.h
type va_arg (va_list param, type)	get next arg	stdarg.h
void va_end (va_list param)	finish var args	stdarg.h
int vfprintf (FILE *stream, char *string, va_list param)	print to stream	stdio.h stdarg.h

int vfscanf (FILE *stream, char *string, va_list param)	read frm stread	stdio.h stdarg.h
int vprintf (char *string, va_list param)	print	stdio.h
int vscanf (char *string, va_list param)	scan input	stdio.h
int vsprintf (char *buffer, char *string, va_list param)	print to memory	stdio.h
int vsscanf (char *buffer, char *string, va_list param)	scan from memory	stdio.h
int _write (int handle, void *buffer, int number)	write	io.h
int write (int handle, void *buffer, int number)	write	io.h

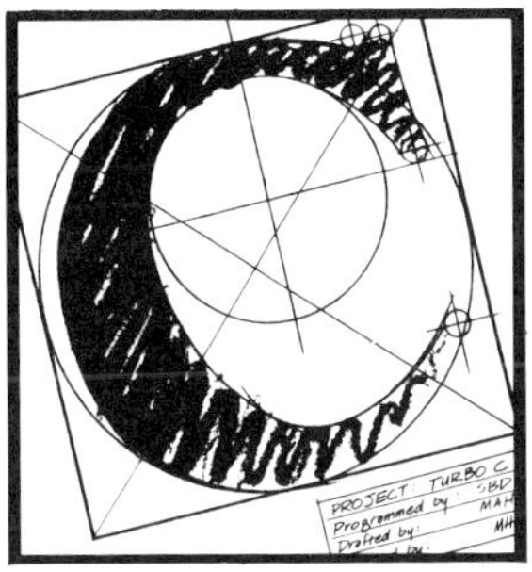

Appendix 4 Instruction Timings on the 8086 Family Microprocessors

Listed below are instruction timings for the 8088, 8086, and Real Mode 80286 using the Intel mnemonics. Use the numbers for the processor in your machine (8088 in the PC and it clones, 80286 the AT and its clones). All of the timings presented are rough timings for word accesses—use the 8086 timings for byte accesses on the 8088. Timings for the 80186 and 80188 are similar to the 8086 and 8088, resp., minus 8 clock ticks for memory accesses.

All measurements are in units of clock cycles. To convert this to actual time, divide by the computer's clock speed (4.77 MHz for the PC, 8.00 MHz for most *turbocharged* PC's, 6.00 or 8.00 MHz for the AT). Machines with wait state memory, such as the IBM AT, should derate their clocks by roughly 20 percent for each wait state.

These numbers can be used in conjunction with the assembly language listing output of the Turbo C compiler to calculate execution timings for Turbo C functions (see Chapter 8 for a discussion of the topic).

Instruction	8088	8086	80286
AAA	8	8	3
AAD	60	60	14
AAM	83	83	16
AAS	8	8	3
ADC			
REG,REG	3	3	2
REG,MEM	22	18	7
MEM,REG	32	24	7
REG,IMM	4	4	3
MEM,IMM	33	25	7
ADD			

```
   SEE ADC
AND
   SEE ADC
CALL
   NEAR                23        19         9
   FAR                 37        29        15
CBW                     2         2         2
CLC                     2         2         2
CLD                     2         2         2
CLI                     2         2         3
CMC                     2         2         2
CMP
   REG,REG              3         3         2
   REG,MEM             22        18         6
   REG,IMM              4         4         3
   MEM,IMM             22        18         6
CMPS              9+30/R    9+22/R     5+9/R
CWD                     5         5         2
DAA                     4         4         3
DAS                     4         4         3
DEC
   REG                  3         3         2
   MEM                 31        23         7
DIV
   REG                150       150        22
   MEM                170       170        25
IDIV
   REG                175       175        25
   MEM                190       190        28
IMUL
   REG                140       140        21
   MEM                160       160        24
IN                     13         9         5
INC
   SEE DEC
INT                    91        51        25
IRET                   56        32        19
J<CONDITIONAL>
   TAKE JMP            16        16         9
   DON'T TAKE JMP       4         4         3
JMP
   LABEL               15        15         9
   MEM - NEAR          26        26        13
   MEM - FAR           32        32        13
   REG                 11        11         9
LAHF                    4         4         2
LDS                    32        24         7
LEA                    10        10         3
LES                    32        24         7
LODS              9+17/R    9+13/R     5+4/R
LOOP<CND>
   TAKE JMP            18        18        10
   DON'T TAKE JMP       6         6         4
MOV
   REG,REG              2         2         2
   REG,ACC              2         2         2
   REG,MEM             20        16         5
   ACC,MEM             14        10         5
   REG,IMM              4         4         2
   MEM,IMM             22        18         3
MOVS              9+25/R    9+17/R     5+4/R
MUL
   REG                115       115        21
   MEM                145       140        24
```

NEG			
REG	3	3	2
MEM	32	24	2
NOP	3	3	2
NOT			
SEE NEG			
OR			
SEE ADC			
OUT	13	9	5
POP			
REG	12	8	5
MEM	33	25	5
POPF	12	8	5
PUSH			
REG	15	11	5
MEM	32	24	3
PUSHF	14	10	3
RCL			
REG,1	2	2	2
MEM,1	31	23	7
REG,CL	8+4/R	8+4/R	5+1/R
MEM,CL	36+4/R	28+4/R	8+1/R
RCR			
SEE RCL			
RET			
NEAR	20	16	13
FAR	34	26	17
ROL			
SEE RCL			
ROR			
SEE RCL			
SAHF	4	4	2
SAL			
SEE RCL			
SAR			
SEE RCL			
SBB			
SEE ADC			
SCAS	9+19/R	9+15/R	5+8/R
SHL			
SEE RCL			
SHR			
SEE RCL			
STC	2	2	2
STD	2	2	2
STI	2	2	2
STOS	9+14/R	9+10/R	4+3/R
SUB			
SEE ADC			
TEST			
SEE CMP			
XCHG			
REG,REG	4	4	3
REG,MEM	33	25	5
XLAT	15	11	5
XOR			
SEE ADC			

In the above table, */R* means per repetition. Thus, a *REP MOVS* requires 9 clock cycles to start and 17 clock cycles per transfer for an 8086. Times for the single instruction is similar to the *per repetition* times, so that a simple *MOVS* takes roughly 17 clock cycles on the 8086. We also assume an average address calculation time of 8 clock cycles on the 8086 and 8088.

The 8088 and 8086 timings were taken from *iAPX 86/88, 186/188 User's Manual—Programmer's Reference.* The 80286 timings were taken from *Microprocessor and Peripheral Handbook—Vol I.* Both are from Intel Literature Sales, Post Office Box 58130, Santa Clara, CA 95052 (800-548-4725).

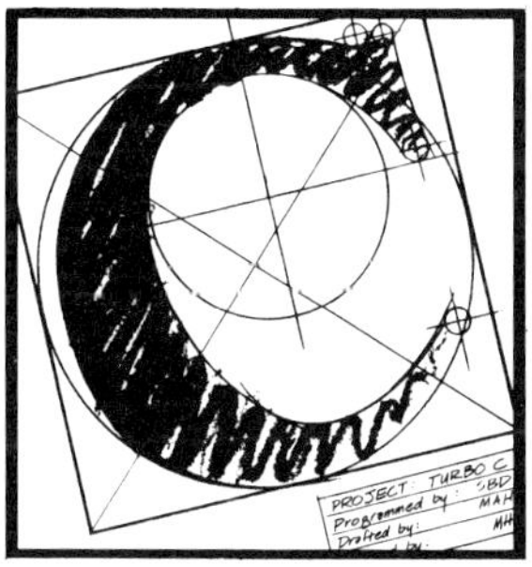

Appendix 5 The KOPY Program

The programs in this book are not presented as workable, everyday utilities with which to stock your DOS utilities directory, but as instructional examples. Some have been designed to demonstrate a programming technique, while others provide examples of particular calls to the Turbo C library, the BIOS, or DOS. Fully developing these programs into finished utilities would only obscure their purpose by adding a lot of unnecessary secondary code.

The principles necessary for this task have already been presented within the covers of this text; however, it may be educational to see just one of these developed into a complete utility. The most promising is Prg5_7, the global search and copy program. The principle it demonstrates is a particularly powerful one: that of searching for directories using a wild-card pattern, just as we might search for any other file. Polishing a program consists of two parts: 1) making sure the existing capabilities are free of bugs and 2) adding as many additional capabilities as is required to make the program user friendly and that can be tolerated by the existing program structure. (Starting with a sound structure, you might be surprised at how many features can be accommodated.)

As it sits, Prg5_7 has a few problems. First and foremost, it requires the user to end the target path with a \ . This is an understandable but unusual nomenclature. Second, if the target file exists, Prg5_7 generates an error message and continues on with the next file. The idea was to adopt the safest route, but this limits the program's usefulness considerably. The operator may reasonably want to overwrite the target. Third, the target directory is likely to be on a floppy disk. Floppy disks with their limited storage are prone to filling up. In the event that the target disk fills, Prg5_7 must be aborted to allow a new disk to be inserted. With the new disk in, however, we cannot restart Prg5_7 from where it left off. Finally, the keyboard input routine used does not listen for Control-Break. This makes aborting the program tricky at best.

If we are going to convert Prg5_7 into a complete utility, each of these problems will have to be addressed. As it turns out, this can be done with a minimum of fuss. The program KOPY presented below addresses all of these issues and more. Let's examine it closely. If the target path does not already end in a \ , then it is quite easy for the program to add one itself. From that point it can carry on like normal. Since this is a secondary function, apart from its main purpose, I decided to put this in a separate function, *addslash()*, which can be called immediately before the call to *copyall()*.

The second problem, that of existing files, must be handled in the *copy()* function itself. If the call to *creatnew()* to create the target file is unsuccessful, the most likely reason is that the file already exists. If so, we can attempt to overwrite it by using the call *open()* with the *O_TRUNC* option to truncate the target to zero. We do not want to try this without the operator's approval. The call to *getyval()* on line 206 assures us that we have the okay. (*Getyval()* returns a 1 if the user enters a *y* or a *Y* and a 0 otherwise.)

As is often the case, this feature introduces a new problem. What if the target directory is one of subdirectories in the search path. This would result in the possibility of the source and target files being the same file. Attempting such a copy will destroy the file. Prg5_7 handled the problem easily (if a little sloppily) by noting that the target file already existed. With overwrite we must explicitly check for the case. The call to *stricmp()* at the beginning of *copy()* does the trick. Be very careful to use *stricmp()*, the case insensitive compare, and not *strcmp()*. DOS does not care about case and we should not either. We would not want to allow *\UTIL\file.c* vs. *\UTIL\FILE.C* to slip through, for example.

The problem of a full floppy disk must also be solved in *copy()*. *Copy()* continues to write the target file until either the source file is exhausted, indicating a successful read, or the number of bytes written is less than the number of bytes we requested. This latter condition is most like generated by a full disk. I added lines 221 through 227 to handle this case.

KOPY first closes both files. In fact, it could have left the source file open, but it does not just in case of operator error. What if the source file were also located on the floppy disk? If the operator blindly followed our instruction and replaced the floppy disk with a new one, we would continue to read from a file that is no longer there. Chaos might ensue. No data would be lost, since the original file is still safe back on the disk the user removed, but we should avoid scaring him like that, if we can. By reopening the source file, we are checking to make sure that the source file is still where we think it is.

After closing both source and target files, the program deletes the portion of target file already written using *unlink()*. Finally, we prompt him to remove the *full* floppy and insert a new one. Once he has installed the new one, we loop back to the beginning of *copy()* and, more or less, start all over with the fresh disk. No attempt is made to pack the files optimally on the floppies.

Addressing the Control-Break issue is very simple. When Control-Break or Control-C are entered, *getch()* returns the value *0x03*. We need simply check for this. If we see this character, we can abort the program by calling *exit()*. This is exactly what the routine *getyval()* does on line 306. Since all input is via *getyval()*, this one check solves the problem universally.

This is what KOPY looked like when I took the next step in its development. At this point, I took a copy of KOPY and distributed it to a select few friends. Be careful not to introduce a program to the world too early. By allowing just a small group to see it, you can get others' opinions and, yet, still be able to recall the program when the inevitable bugs surface.

The first problem was obvious. Despite my instructions, the first user entered *KOPY C:*.DAT B:* thinking that this was going to copy all .DAT files on his hard disk to disk B (*C:*.DAT* is the proper path to search the entire hard disk). The program thought for awhile and then returned without generating any messages. Being unfamiliar with the program, he did not realize for some time that it had not copied anything. Problems like this are easily handled by defining a global variable such as *FOUND_ONE* on line 81. This flag is initially set to *FALSE*. If any files are found, indicating the user probably knows what he is doing, the program sets the flag to *TRUE*. If the program completes and *FOUND_ONE* is still *FALSE,* the program generates an error message. Since leaving off the initial \ , as in the above example, is the most common error, this instruction is included in the error message.

The universal comment I got from all users was one that had not even occurred to me: *how similar KOPY is with the DOS COPY command.* (Remember, at this point it was still called Prg5_7.) It was universally agreed to make KOPY a more powerful replacement for the DOS version (and, hence, the new name). But this was going to require a bit of rethinking. First, if no target is provided, COPY assumes the current directory. KOPY must do the same. This is quite easy as it turns out. If argv [2] is null, just use the path .\ instead (line 125–126). No matter where you are, "." is always the current directory.

This meant we needed another way of invoking the Find capability. The switch /F seemed simple enough. Therefore, *KOPY *.DAT* should mean copy all the

.DAT files to the current directory, while *KOPY /F *.DAT* meant simply find them all. All agreed, this was simple enough. Since we have already discussed the parsing of switches, I will only mention that the code to do so appears in lines 96 through 111 plus the global variable defined on line 81. (If you do not understand this section, review the technique presented in Chapter 3 as it is very flexible, understanding */A /B*, */A/B*, and */AB* equally well.)

If KOPY was really going to replace COPY, then the subdirectory search capability had be optional. If the user knew what directory his file was in, searching subdirectories was a waste of time. This was going to require another switch. There was some discussion as to whether the default should be *search subdirectories* or not. There are arguments both ways, but I left *search directories* as the default, perhaps because of how the program came to be in the first place. The */S* (*S* for single) switched KOPY into the *search single subdirectory* mode. If you preferr to reverse this decision, simply change the value of *INCLUDE_SUBDIRS* on line 82 and line 103.

One final capability arose from the way the program was used. Searching the entire disk for a particular type of file is most often useful when the hard disk is being backed up to floppy to gain more space. For example, entering *KOPY *.BAS B:* to get all of the old and unused BASIC programs onto floppy and off the harddisk. Having the option of deleting the source file after it has been copied gives KOPY the ability to do this very simply and in one command. */D* turns this option on. Of course, we only want to delete the file if the copy succeeds. The delete code (lines 236–238) was added to the function *copy()* so that it can only be executed if *copy()* did not return prematurely because of some error. Since we should never delete anything without permission, we again ask permission before each delete.

In order that delete might also work in find mode, the same three lines was also added to *find()* (lines 247–249). Therefore, *KOPY /D/F *.DAT* would remove all of the *.DAT* files from the current disk, one at a time, asking the operator's permission (the *only* way to implement such a powerful command). Allowing switches to be used in combination allows KOPY to be several commands in one.

All of my local *beta test sites* found this set of capabilities satisfactory. Once implemented, I passed out updated and corrected versions of KOPY to each. This is the version which appears below. Hopefully you will find it as useful as we did.

Let's review how KOPY came to be. We started with a simple program which was structurally well laid out. Adding capabilities to a haphazardly constructed program is asking for trouble. Copies were passed out to a small group with the understanding that this is a new and potentially buggy program. I solicited opinions for how the program could be improved.

Suggestions from beta testers should be seriously considered. In fact, more seriously considered that your own. Remember, you have been working with the program for quite a while. You know what its weak points are and how to avoid them. Others will approach it more honestly. Obvious weaknesses will strike them much more clearly then yourself. Do direct their suggestions along the lines of what can easily be done, given the existing program structure, however. Don't attempt too much. There are many features which I could have added to KOPY but didn't. Not only must the program support the capability easily, but the command structure must also. In my opinion, three switches is a lot for an operator to remember. For maximum effectiveness, all switches should be allowed in any combination. When either the program or the command format start appearing cluttered, its time to stop.

Try your hand at it. If you have read and followed the techniques presented here, you should be in position to join the ever growing army of Turbo C programmers successfully exploring their PCs.

```
/*Kopy - Copy or Find and optionally Delete files Everywhere
   by Stephen R. Davis, 1987
      214-454-2426

  Search all subdirectories for a particular file pattern.  All files
  found matching that pattern are copied to the target path.  Adding
  a "/d" deletes the source file after successfully copying.  A "/f"
  causes KOPY to search only, without copying.  The "/s" keeps KOPY
  in the current directory (like DOS COPY).
  E.g. KOPY C:\*.PAS B:     -> copy all Pascal files found on disk C:
                               (search all subdirectories) to B:
       KOPY /D \USER\*.PAS -> copy and delete all Pascal files found i
                               directory \USER and all of its subdirs
                               to the current directory
       KOPY /D/F \*.BAK    -> search for and delete all .BAK files on
                               current disk

  (Note: compiling with the label SWITCH defined in the
         Options/Compiler/Defines menu reverses the sense of
         the "/S" flag for those that prefer it the other way)
*/
char *banner = {
  "This program was developed for Borland's Turbo C (Ver 1.0) by \n"
  "Stephen R. Davis for the book:\n\n"
  "                              Turbo C:\n"
  "    The Art of Advanced Program Design, Optimization and Debugging\
  "                             M&T Books\n"
  "                         501 Galveston Drive\n"
  "                       Redwood City, CA 94063\n\n"
```

```
   "This program is released into the public domain without charge for\
   "the use and enjoyment of the public with the single provision that
   "banner remain intact.  Anyone wishing to learn more about getting t
   "most out of the IBM PC and its clones using Turbo C, can order a co
   "this book by calling:\n\n"
   "                        1-800-533-4372\n"
   "                    (in CA, 1-800-356-2002)\n"
   "                        8 am to 5 pm PST\n\n"};

#include <stdio.h>
#include <dir.h>
#include <io.h>
#include <dos.h>
#include <process.h>
#include <fcntl.h>
#include <conio.h>
#include <ctype.h>
#include <string.h>

#define TRUE 1
#define FALSE 0

/*define error message*/
char *errmsg = {
   "This program copies all files from the source path and all\n"
   "of its subdirectories which match the source pattern to the\n"
   "target path.  If no target path is given, the current directory\n"
   "is assumed.  Adding a /D switch in front of the first argument\n"
   "deletes the source file after successfully copying and after\n"
   "prompting operator.  Adding a /F simply finds without copying.\n"
   "The switch /S keeps KOPY in the specified directory and \n"
   "suppresses subdirectory search (like DOS COPY).\n\n"
   "For example:\n\n"
   "KOPY /D C:\\*.DAT               copy and delete all .DAT files from\n
   "                               all of the directories on disk C to\n"
   "                               the current directory.\n\n"
   "KOPY /S \\USER\\*.DAT B:\\COPY  copy all the .DAT files from \\USER
   "                               to directory COPY on drive B.\n\n"
   "KOPY /F/D \\*.BAK               find and delete all *.BAK files on\n"
   "                               current disk\n\n"
   "If the target disk fills you will be prompted to insert a new one.\
   };

/*prototyping definitions*/
void main (unsigned, char **);
void copyall (char *, char *, char *);
void copy (char *, char *);
void find (char *);
void append (char *, char *, char *);
void addslash (char *);
void arg_error (void);
int getyval (char *);

/*define global flags*/

char found_one = FALSE, delete = FALSE, find_only = FALSE;

char include_subdirs =
#ifdef SWITCH
     FALSE;  /*default subdirectory search to off*/
#else
     TRUE;   /*    "          "        "     " on*/
#endif

```

```
/*Main - parse user input and start the ball rolling*/
void main (argc, argv)
     unsigned argc;
     char *argv [];
{
     char sourcedisk [MAXDRIVE], sourcedir [MAXDIR];
     char sourcefile [MAXFILE], sourceext [MAXEXT];
     char fromdir [MAXPATH], pattern [MAXFILE+MAXEXT];
     char *secondarg, *switchptr, *srcfile;

     /*first check for switches -- ignore case and extra '/'s*/

     while (*(switchptr = argv [1]) == '/') {
          while (*++switchptr) {
               switch (tolower (*switchptr)) {
                    case 'd': delete = TRUE;
                              break;
                    case 'f': find_only = TRUE;
                              break;
                    case 's': include_subdirs = !include_subdirs;
               }
          }

          /*now skip over this argument*/
          argc--;
          argv [1] = argv [0];
          argv++;
     }

     /*check the argument count*/
     if (argc == 1 || argc > 3)
          arg_error ();

     /*parse argument 1 into its two halves
      (if no source path given, assume "*.*") */
     fnsplit (argv [1], sourcedisk, sourcedir, sourcefile, sourceext);
     if (!*(srcfile = sourcefile))
          srcfile = "*.*";

     /*now reconstruct the two halves*/
     fnmerge (fromdir, sourcedisk, sourcedir,          0,          0);
     fnmerge (pattern,          0,          0,    srcfile, sourceext);

     /*if no second argument, assume the current directory*/
     if (!(secondarg = argv [2]))
          secondarg = ".\\";
     addslash (secondarg);

     /*now just copy/find them everywhere*/
     copyall (fromdir, pattern, secondarg);
     if (!found_one) {
          printf ("No files found");
          if (include_subdirs && (sourcedir [0] != '\\'))
               printf (" (use %s\\%s%s to search entire disk)\n",
                         sourcedisk, sourcefile, sourceext);
          printf ("\n");
     }

     /*exit normally*/
     exit (0);
}

/*Copyall - copy/find all files matching a given pattern from the
            current directory and all subdirectories*/
```

```
void copyall (fromdir, pattern, todir)
     char *fromdir, *pattern, *todir;
{
     char spath [MAXPATH], tpath [MAXPATH];
     struct ffblk block;

     /*first copy/find all files patching the pattern*/
     append (spath, fromdir, pattern);
     if (!findfirst (spath, &block, 0))
          do {
               append (spath, fromdir, block.ff_name);
               append (tpath,   todir, block.ff_name);
               if (!find_only)
                    copy (spath, tpath);
               else
                    find (spath);
          } while (!findnext (&block));

     /*now check all subdirectories, if desired*/
     if (include_subdirs) {
          append (spath, fromdir, "*");
          if (!findfirst (spath, &block, FA_DIREC))
               do {

                    /*only pay attention to directories*/
                    if (block.ff_attrib & FA_DIREC)

                         /*ignore directories '.' and '..'*/
                         if (block.ff_name [0] != '.') {

                              /*now tack on name of directory + '\'*/
                              append (spath, fromdir, block.ff_name);
                              addslash (spath);

                              /*and copy its contents too*/
                              copyall (spath, pattern, todir);
                         }
               } while (!findnext (&block));
     }
}

/*Copy - given two patterns, copy the source to the destination file*/
#define NSECT 64
void copy (from, to)
     char *from, *to;
{
     int fhandle, thandle, number;
     char buffer [NSECT*512], failure;

     /*don't copy a file to itself*/
     if (!stricmp (to, from))
          return;
     found_one = TRUE;

     do {
          /*open the source for reading binary*/
          _fmode = O_BINARY;
          if ((fhandle = open (from, O_RDONLY)) == -1) {
               perror ("\nError opening source file");
               return;
          }

          /*now open the destination*/
          printf ("\nCopying %s -> %s", from, to);
```

```
          if ((thandle = creatnew (to, 0)) == -1) {
               if (!getyval ("  overwrite target?")) {
                    close (fhandle);
                    return;
               }
               if ((thandle = open (to, O_RDWR, O_TRUNC)) == -1) {
                    perror ("\nError opening target file");
                    return;
               }
          }

          /*now perform the copy*/
          failure = FALSE;
          while (number = read (fhandle, buffer, NSECT*512))
               if (number != _write (thandle, buffer, number)) {
                    /*disk full, close source and delete target*/
                    close (fhandle);
                    close (thandle);
                    unlink (to);
                    getyval ("\nDisk full - "
                             "insert new disk and hit any key");
                    failure = TRUE;
                    break;
               }
     } while (failure);
     printf (" copied ");

     close (fhandle);
     close (thandle);

     /*delete source, if requested*/
     if (delete)
          if (getyval (" delete source?"))
               unlink (from);
}

/*Find - in case of find, ask user permission to delete file if
         "/d" switch and whether we should continue if subdirectory
         search enabled*/
void find (fname)
     char *fname;
{
     found_one = TRUE;
     printf ("\nFound %s", fname);
     if (delete) {
          if (getyval (" -- delete?"))
               unlink (fname);
     } else
          if (include_subdirs)
               if (!getyval ("  -- continue?"))
                    exit (0);
}

/*Append - concatenate two strings together*/
void append (to, from1, from2)
     char *to, *from1, *from2;
{
     /*copy the first string*/
     while (*from1)
          *to++ = *from1++;

     /*now the second*/
     while (*from2)
          *to++ = *from2++;
```

```

     /*and then tack on a terminator*/
     *to = '\0';
}

/*Addslash - add a slash onto a directory name which doesn't
               already end in '\' or ':'*/
void addslash (dirptr)
     char *dirptr;
{
     /*skip to next to last character in path*/
     while (*dirptr)
          dirptr++;
     dirptr--;

     /*now check last character*/
     if (*dirptr != '\\' && *dirptr != ':') {
          *++dirptr = '\\';
          *++dirptr = '\0';
     }
}

/*Arg_error - print error message and then abort*/
void arg_error (void)
{
     printf (errmsg);
     if (!include_subdirs)
          printf ("(Note: This version has the meaning of the "
                  "/S switch inverted.)\n");
     getyval ("\nEnter any key to continue");
     printf ("\n\n\n\n\n\n\n%s", banner);
     exit (1);
}

/*Getyval - out a string and then await a response.
              Exit program if Break (Control-C).  Return a 1
              if entered 'y', else 0*/
int getyval (msg)
     char *msg;
{
     char entered;

     printf (msg);
     if ((entered = getch ()) == 0x03) exit (1);
     return (tolower (entered) == 'y');
}
```

Bibliography

The following books contributed to the development of this book:

Turbo C User's Guide and *Turbo C Reference Guide*
Borland International
4585 Scotts Valley Drive
Scotts Valley, CA 95066

Microsoft MS-DOS Operating System—Programmer's Reference
Microsoft Corporation
10700 Northrup Way
Bellevue, WA 98004

The C Programming Language
Brian Kernighan and Dennis Ritchie
Prentice-Hall, Inc
Englewood Cliffs, NJ 07632

IBM Technical Reference
IBM Technical Directory
Post Office Box 2009
Racine, WI 53404

IBM Enhance Graphics Adapter
IBM Technical Directory
Post Office Box 2009
Racine, WI 53404

Draft Proposed American National Standard for Information Systems—Programming Language C
Doc No. X3J11/86-157
available from:
Computer and Business Equipment Manufacturers' Association
311 First Street, NW
Suit 500
Washington, DC 20001

C Programmer's Library
Jack Purdum, Timothy Leslie, Alan Stegemoller
Que Corporation
7999 Knue Rd, Suit 202
Indianapolis, IN 46250

The following column is very useful for the intermediate to advanced C programmer. Taken collectively, this column represents a wealth of C knowledge:

Let's C Now
Rex Jaeschke
DEC Professional Magazine
Post Office Box 503
Spring House, PA 19477

Index

More Software Tools from M&T Books

C Tools

C Chest and Other C Treasures
Item #40-2 $24.95 (book)
Item #49-6 $39.95 (book/disk)
This comprehensive anthology contains the popular "C Chest" columns from *Dr. Dobb's Journal of Software Tools*, along with the lively philosophical and practical discussions they inspired, in addition to other information-packed articles by C experts. The software in the book is also available on disk with full source code. MS-DOS format.

Turbo C: The Art of Advanced Program Design, Optimization, and Debugging
Item #38-0 $24.95 (book)
Item #45-3 $39.95 (book/disk)
Overflowing with example programs, this book fully describes the techniques necessary to skillfully program, optimize, and debug in Turbo C. All programs are also available on disk with full source code. MS-DOS format.

Dr. Dobb's Toolbook of C
Item #89303-615-3 $29.95
From *Dr. Dobb's* and Brady Communications, this book contains a comprehensive library of valuable C code. *Dr. Dobb's* most popular articles on C are updated and reprinted here, along with new C programming tools. Also included is a complete C compiler, an assembler, text processing programs, and more!

The Small-C Handbook
Item #81-X $17.95
The Small-C Handbook with MS/PC-DOS Addendum
Item #76-3 $22.95
Also from *DDJ* and Brady Communications, the handbook is a valuable companion to the Small-C compiler, described below. The book explains the language and the compiler, and contains entire source listings of the compiler and its library of arithmetic and logical routines.

Small-C Compiler
Item #01-1 $19.95
Like a home study course in compiler design, the *Small-C Compiler* and *The Small-C Handbook* provide all you need to learn how compilers are contructed, as well as teaching the C language at its most fundamental level. Full source code is included on disk in both CP/M and MS/PC-DOS versions.

Small Tools: Programs for Text Processing
Item #78-X $29.95
This package of text-processing programs written in Small-C is designed to perform specific, modular functions on text files. Source code only is included. Small Tools is available in both CP/M and MS/PC-DOS versions and includes complete documentation.

Small-Mac: An Assembler for Small-C
Item #77-1 $29.95
Small-Mac is a macro assembler designed to stress simplicity, portability, adaptability, and educational value. Small-Mac is available for CP/M systems only and includes source code on disk with complete documentation.

Small-Windows: A Library of Windowing Functions for the C Language
Item #35-X $29.95
Small-Windows is a complete windowing library for C. The package includes video functions, menu functions, window functions, and more. The package is available for MS-DOS systems for the following compilers: Microsoft C Version 4.0, Small-C, and Lattice C. Documentation and full C source code is included.

UNIX-Like Tools for MS-DOS

On Command: Writing a Unix-Like Shell for MS-DOS

Item #29-1 $39.95

Learn how to write shells applicable to MS-DOS, as well as to most other programming environments. This book and disk include a full description of a Unix-like shell, complete C source code, a thorough discussion of low-level DOS interfacing, and significant examples of C programming at the system level. All source code is included on disk.

/util: A Unix-Like Utility package for MS-DOS

Item #12-7 $29.95

This collection of utilities is intended to be accessed through SH but can be used separately. It contains programs and subroutines that, when coupled with SH, create a fully functional Unix-like environment. The package includes a disk with full C source code and documentation in a Unix-style manual.

NR: An Implementation of the Unix NROFF Word Processor

Item #33-X $29.95

NR is a text formatter that is written in C and compatible with Unix's NROFF. *NR* comes configured for any Diablo-compatible printer, as well as Hewlett Packard's ThinkJet and LaserJet. Both the ready-to-use program and full source code are included. For PC compatibles.

MS-DOS Tools

Program Interfacing to MS-DOS

Item #34-8 $29.95

Program Interfacing to MS-DOS will orient any experienced programmer to the MS-DOS environment. The package includes a ten-part manual with sample program files and a detailed description of how to build device drivers, along with the device driver for a memory disk and a character device driver on disk with macro assembly source code.

Taming MS-DOS

Item #24-0 $19.95 (book)

Item #59-3 $34.95 (book/disk)

Taming MS-DOS takes you beyond the basics, picking up where your DOS manual leaves off. You'll learn how to create a memory-resident clock, how to rename subdirectories and change file attributes, how to create configurable AUTOEXEC.BAT files, and how to customize CONFIG.SYS and use ANSI.SYS to change the appearance of DOS. You'll also find extensive batch file coverage with example routines that use redirection operators, filters, and pipes and ready-to-use assembly-language programs that enhance DOS. Full source code is included on disk.

Tele Operating System

Tele Operating System Toolkit

This task-scheduling algorithm drives the Tele Operating System and is composed of several components. When integrated, they form an independent operating system for any 8086-based machine. Tele has also been designed for compatibility with MS-DOS, UNIX, and the MOSI standard.

SK: THE SYSTEM KERNEL

Item #30-5 $49.95

The System Kernel contains an initialization module, general-purpose utility functions, and a real-time task management system. The kernel provides MS-DOS applications with multitasking capabilities. The System Kernel is required by all other components. All source code is included on disk in MS-DOS format.

DS: WINDOW DISPLAY

Item #32-1 $39.95

This component contains BIOS level drivers for a memory-mapped display, window management support and communication coordination between the operator and tasks in a multitasking environment. All source code is included on disk in MS-DOS format.

FS: THE FILE SYSTEM

Item #65-8 $39.95

The File System supports MS-DOS disk file structures and serial communication channels. All source code is included on disk in MS-DOS format.

XS: THE INDEX SYSTEM
Item #66-6 $39.95
The Index System implements a tree-structured free-form database. All source code is included on disk in MS-DOS format.

Z80 Assembly Language

Dr. Dobb's Z80 Toolbook
Item #07-0 $25.00 (book)
Item #55-0 $40.00 (book/disk)
This book contains everything users need to write their own Z80 assembly-language programs, including a method of designing programs and coding them in assembly language and a complete, integrated toolkit of subroutines. All the software in the book is available on disk in the following formats: 8" SS/SD, Apple, Osborne, or Kaypro.

Forth

Dr. Dobb's Toolbook of Forth
Item #10-0 $22.95 (book)
Item #57-7 $39.95 (book/disk)
This comprehensive collection of useful Forth programs and tutorials contains expanded versions of *DDJ*'s best Forth articles and other material, including practical code and in-depth discussions of advanced Forth topics. The screens in the book are also available on disk as ASCII files in the following formats: MS/PC-DOS, Apple II, Macintosh, or CP/M: Osborne, 8" SS/SD.

Dr. Dobb's Toolbook of Forth, Volume II
Item #41-0 $29.95 (book)
Item #51-8 $45.95 (book/disk)
This complete anthology of Forth programming techniques and developments picks up where the Toolbook of Forth, First Edition left off. Included are the best articles on Forth from *Dr. Dobb's Journal of Software Tools,* along with the latest material from other Forth experts. The screens in the book are available on disk as ASCII files in the following formats: MS-DOS, Apple II, Macintosh, and CP/M: Osborne, or 8" SS/SD.

68000 Programming

Dr. Dobb's Toolbook of 68000 Programming

Item #13-216649-6 $29.95 (book)

Item #75-5 $49.95 (book/disk)

From *DDJ* and Brady Communications, this collection of practical programming tips and tools for the 68000 family contains the best 68000 articles reprinted from *DDJ* along with much new material. The book contains many useful applications and examples. The software in the book is also available on disk in the following formats: MS/PC-DOS, Macintosh, CP/M 8", Osborne, Amiga, and Atari 520ST.

68000 Cross Assembler

Item #71-2 $25.00

This manual and disk contain an executable version of the 68000 Cross Assembler discussed in *Dr. Dobb's Toolbook of 68000 Programming,* complete with source code and documentation. The Cross-Assembler requires CP/M 2.2 with 64K or MS-DOS with 128K. The disk is available in the following formats: MS-DOS, 8" SS/SD, and Osborne.

Turbo Pascal Tools

The Turbo Pascal Toolbook

Item #25-9 $25.95 (book)

Item #61-5 $45.95 (book/disk)

This book contains routines and sample programs to make your programming easier and more powerful. You'll find an extensive library of low-level routines; external sorting and searching tools; window management; artificial intelligence techniques; mathematical expression parsers, including two routines that convert mathematical expressions into RPN tokens; and a smart statistical regression model finder. More than 800K of source code is available on disk for MS-DOS systems.

80286, 80386 Programming

Dr. Dobb's Toolbook of 80286, 80386 Programming
Item #42-9 $24.95 (book)
Item #53-4 $39.95 (book/disk)
This toolbook is a comprehensive discussion on the powerful 80X86 family of microprocessors. The editors of *Dr. Dobb's Journal of Software Tools* have gathered their best articles, updated and expanded them, and added new material to create this valuable resource for all 80X86 programmers. All programs are available on disk with full soruce code.

The New BASICs

The New BASICs: Programming Techniques and Library Development
Item #37-2 $24.95 (book)
Item #43-7 $39.95 (book/disk)
This book will orient the advanced programmer to the syntax and programming features of The New BASICs, including Turbo BASIC 1.0, QuickBASIC 3.0, and True BASIC 2.0. You'll learn the details of implementing subroutines, functions, and libraries to permit more structured coding. Programs and subroutines are available on disk with full source code. MS-DOS format.

Public-Domain Software

Public-Domain Software: Untapped Resources for the Business User
Item #39-9 $19.95 (book)
Item #47-X $34.95 (book/disk)
Organized into a comprehensive reference, this book introduces the novice and guides the experienced user to a source of often overlooked software—public domain and Shareware. This book will tell you where it is, how to get it, what to look for, and why it's for you. The sample programs and some of the software reviewed is available on disk in MS-DOS format. Includes $15 worth of free access time on CompuServe!